DATE DUE

2-20-05			
	DISCARDED		

Demco, Inc. 38-293

Healthcare Human Resource Management

Walter J. Flynn
University of Minnesota

Robert L. Mathis
University of Nebraska at Omaha

John H. Jackson
University of Wyoming

Patrick J. Langan
University of Minnesota

THOMSON
™
SOUTH-WESTERN

Australia · Canada · Mexico · Singapore · Spain · United Kingdom · United States

THOMSON
━━━★━━━ ™
SOUTH-WESTERN

Healthcare Human Resource Management
Walter J. Flynn, Robert L. Mathis, John H. Jackson, and Patrick J. Langan

VP/Editor-in-Chief: Mike Roche
Executive Editor: John Szilagyi
Senior Acquisitions Editor: Charles McCormick
Developmental Editor: Mardell Toomey
Senior Production Editor: Deanna Quinn

Media Technology Editor: Vicky True
Media Developmental Editor: Josh Fendley
Media Production Editor: Kelly Reid
Manufacturing Coordinator: Diane Lohman

Marketing Manager: Larry Qualls
Design Project Manager: Stacy Jenkins Shirley
Cover and Internal Designer: Jennifer Lambert, Jen2Design, Cincinnati, OH
Compositor: Shepherd, Inc.
Printer: Phoenix Color

Library of Congress Control Number: 2002117395

ISBN: 0-324-17576-0

Brief Contents

Contents

CHAPTER 7

CHAPTER 12   *Healthcare Compensation Practices* 264

Preface

WHY A BOOK ON HEALTHCARE HUMAN RESOURCE MANAGEMENT

As the authors of this textbook, we have long recognized the unique aspects of healthcare HRM and the need for a textbook specifically focused on this area. Collectively, we have experience in Healthcare HRM as practitioners, consultants and professors. Here we provide both the HRM student and practitioner a comprehensive, focused source of information on this important body of knowledge and specialized field of practice.

PRIMARY AUDIENCES FOR THIS BOOK

There are several audiences that will find this book to be a useful resource. Some include college and university students and faculty members, various HR practitioners in healthcare organizations, and healthcare professionals and managers in numerous fields where the HR management issues affect organizational and individual performance

COLLEGE/UNIVERSITY STUDENTS AND FACULTY MEMBERS

Given the ever-changing nature of the healthcare industry, there is an on-going need for current, topical information on healthcare HR management. The importance of human relations skills and HR management knowledge for application in the healthcare industry has grown in the past decade due to significant recruitment and retention issues for healthcare workers. Graduates of healthcare related administration/management degree programs must have a solid knowledge base of HRM topics to be successful in their careers.

The types of courses that are well suited for this text include:

▶ Undergraduate courses in HR management for healthcare administration majors.
▶ Undergraduate courses in human resources for management with an emphasis on the healthcare industry.
▶ Graduate courses in human resources for Healthcare Administration programs.

- ► College curriculums for management tracks for degrees in:
  - ► Nursing
  - ► Respiratory Care
  - ► Radiology Technicians
  - ► Allied Health
  - ► Public Health
  - ► Health Promotion
- ► Distance learning programs related to the above.

HEALTHCARE HR PROFESSIONALS AND HEALTHCARE MANAGEMENT PRACTITIONERS

HR management issues will continue to be a major focus for all individuals with management responsibilities in healthcare organizations. Both the academic and practical experience the authors have means that the book strikes a balance between the theoretical and the practical aspects of healthcare HR. This balance makes the textbook not only useful for college/university students and faculty members, but equally useful for healthcare managers, supervisors, and professionals with significant HR responsibilities. Even highly experienced healthcare HR management professionals will find the presentation of both theory and actual healthcare organizational HR practices insightful and informative.

ORGANIZATION OF THIS BOOK

The textbook includes fourteen chapters covering the major healthcare HR management topic areas. Each chapter discusses a particular HR management topic, which can be used in instruction as a stand-alone presentation, or in conjunction with the other chapters. Regardless of the means used, this book provides a comprehensive source of information on healthcare HR management theory and practice.

Chapter 1 discusses the nature and challenges of healthcare HR management through an overview of the current and future states of the healthcare industry. The chapter also describes the various types of organizations that make up the healthcare industry, including physician practices, hospitals, and dental clinics.

Chapter 2 presents a unique review of the HR competencies that are important for healthcare HR professionals. The chapter discusses healthcare organizational structures and the placement of HR departments within the organizational structure, and HR budgets and staffing. The Joint Commission on Accreditation of Healthcare Organizations (JCAHO) is also presented, detailing the key quality standards that impact healthcare HR management.

Chapter 3 describes the importance of strategic HR management. The chapter discusses the process and relevance of effective HR planning against the backdrop of the important HR management issues that confront healthcare organizations, including staffing and retention.

Chapter 4 discusses the legal issues affecting the healthcare workplace, with particular focus being placed on Equal Employment Opportunity regulations and issues. Chapter 5 reviews the importance of job design and analysis as it affects all aspects of HR management in healthcare organizations.

Chapter 6 presents a comprehensive discussion of the critical topics for healthcare organizations of recruitment and selection. The chapter includes a discussion on strategic recruiting and an overview of various other recruitment methods that are proving successful in the healthcare industry.

Chapter 7 explores employee retention, presenting many of the acknowledged "best practices" that are achieving retention results in healthcare organizations. Given both the current state and the anticipated future critical shortage of healthcare workers, employee retention is one of the most important responsibilities that healthcare HR professionals and healthcare managers have.

Chapter 8 provides a comprehensive discussion on training and development in healthcare organizations. The JCAHO standards dealing with orientation and training also are highlighted in the chapter, as they relate to the verification and development of healthcare worker competencies.

Chapter 9 focuses on the topic of performance management. This chapter includes a review of both the theoretical and practical aspects of establishing performance criteria and developing and conducting performance appraisals for healthcare workers.

Chapters 10 and 11 deal with the interrelated healthcare HR management topics of employee and labor relations. Chapter 10 focuses on a variety of concerns that affect managing healthcare workers. Chapter 11 deals specifically with the complexities of managing healthcare workers that are covered under collective bargaining agreements.

Chapters 12 and 13 present healthcare compensation, benefits and variable pay practices. Chapter 12 details the various compensation programs and processes, including executive pay plans, utilized in healthcare organizations. Chapter 13 discusses the benefits and variable pay programs that make-up the total compensation provided to healthcare workers.

Chapter 14, describes health, safety, and security issues in healthcare organizations and how they affect HR management. The health, safety, and security concerns present in healthcare environments are emphasized as part of healthcare HR management.

TEXTBOOK FEATURES

To enhance the readability and healthcare focus, there are a number of features in the book, including:

Examples Specific to the Healthcare Focus

The healthcare environment is the focus of each HRM topic covered. "Best Practice" examples appear throughout, enriching the discussion of current theory.

Healthcare HR Insights

Each chapter begins with a "Healthcare HR Insight," which are actual examples of programs, solutions, and/or initiatives undertaken by various healthcare organizations relevant to the topic covered in the chapter. Special attention has been given by the authors to ensure that healthcare institutions of different types are represented in the Healthcare HR Insights.

Joint Commission on Accreditation of Healthcare Organizations (JCAHO)

JCAHO is a quality review organization that accredits healthcare organizations relative to a set of quality standards. These standards include such areas as patient care, governance, life safety code, etc. More recently JCAHO has added a comprehensive set of standards pertaining to human resources, these additional (new) standards have required significantly more preparation and practitioner knowledge in order to successfully demonstrate competency. Due to the influence of JCAHO on healthcare HR management, Chapter Two presents a detailed review of the various JCAHO standards that directly pertain to HR. In addition, many of the chapters contain a "JCAHO Feature" that specifically links JCAHO standards to HR management topics in each chapter.

Study Aides

Figures, including illustrations, process maps, charts, and tables, are used throughout the chapters to assist readers in examining the topics discussed.

Glossary: Key Vocabulary and Concepts

Key vocabulary and concepts are contained in the glossary. For ease of reference they also appear in bold print in the text to alert readers that each definition is included in the glossary.

Chapter Ending Cases

At the end of each chapter case studies are offered to allow readers to analyze a case scenario that is relevant to the chapter content. The cases describe actual situations that have been experienced by healthcare organizations, but the names have been disguised. The problems and issues to be analyzed are framed by discussion questions at the end of the case.

SUPPLEMENTAL MATERIALS

In order to facilitate and enhance the use of the book by faculty members and instructors, an Instructor's Manual, Test Bank, PowerPoint, and Web site are available:

Instructor's Manual content includes:
▶ Chapter Outlines;
▶ Overhead transparency masters derived from key textbook figures;
▶ Teaching suggestions;
▶ Chapter Ending Cases include a discussion guide, analysis of the questions and recommended solutions.

Test Bank content includes:
▶ Multiple-choice
▶ True-false
▶ Short essay questions

All questions include answers with reference to pages in the text.

PowerPoint content includes:
▶ Slides for each chapter that are suited for academic or training purposes
▶ Interest in the form of graphics and art that will add excitement to
▶ Lectures or presentations
▶ Complete coverage of all key terms and contents

The above ancillary products—the *Instructor's Manual, Test Bank* and *PowerPoint* are conveniently packaged together on an Instructor's CD-ROM, ISBN, 0-324-20122-2.

Web Site

The Web site for the book, *http://flynn.swlearning.com,* contains a variety of additional reference materials, including graphics, HR management policies, and forms.

ACKNOWLEDGEMENTS

There are a number of individuals that assisted the authors in the development of this book that we would like to acknowledge. One who deserves special recognition is Kathy Flynn, who spent many long hours transcribing draft after draft of the manuscript during development. Her work truly contributed to the quality of the book.

Some of the leading healthcare professionals whose ideas and assistance were invaluable include Lori Southwood, SPHR; Kris Carlton; Pam Lindemoen; Deb Waggoner; Donna Klinkner; Candace Fenske; Carol Klotz; Milly Prachar; Nancy Good; Randee Lyons; Brock Nelson; Julie Schmidt; Laura T. Young; Patrick Drescich; Roger Mazour and Ron Lilek.

Additionally, the reviewers were so important to the creation of a quality text:

James. W Begun
University of Minnesota

Russ Crockett
Director, Human Resources,
Shriners Hospital for Children,
Salt Lake City, Utah

Kathryn Dansky
The Pennsylvania State University

Andra Gumbus
Sacred Heart University

Kristina L. Guo
Florida International University

Cindy Harrison
American Society for Healthcare
Human Resources Administration
Vice-President/Human Resources,
Chelsea Community Hospital

Brandon Melton
President, American Society
for Healthcare Human Resources
Administration; Sr. Vice President,
Human Resources Lifespan Corporation

Deborah Ruthenbeck,
Manager of Internal
Communications & Recognition
Florida Society for Healthcare
Human Resource Administration President,
Orlando Regional Healthcare

Tony Sinay
Des Moines University

Wayne Sorensen
Southwest Texas State University

The authors thank Charles McCormick, Jr., Senior Acquisitions Editor, and Mardell Toomey, Developmental Editor, for their guidance and support. We also appreciate the support of our Senior Production Editor, Deanna Quinn.

About the Authors

Walter J. Flynn, SPHR

Mr. Flynn was born in Kentucky and is currently a partner in the human resources consulting firm of Langan and Flynn, LLC, based in St. Paul, Minnesota. His firm specializes in working with hospitals, extended care facilities and physician practices.

Mr. Flynn's education includes an M.B.A. from Xavier University, Cincinnati, Ohio, a B.S. from Northern Kentucky University, and advanced work in Quality Management, Diversity Awareness, and Executive Practices. In addition, he has attained the Senior Professional Human Resources (SPHR) designation from the Society for Human Resources Management (SHRM).

His career positions include: Vice President, Human Resources for Cincinnati's Children Hospital; Personnel Director for the Central Trust Co. and Managing Consultant for R. J. Kemen and Associates. In addition he holds faculty appointments at The Carlson School of Management, University of Minnesota and Kennedy-Wester University and has held faculty appointments at the University of Cincinnati, Northern Kentucky University and Thomas More College.

Dr. Robert L. Mathis

Dr. Robert Mathis is Professor of Management at the University of Nebraska at Omaha (UNO). At UNO he has received the University's "Excellence in Teaching" award.

Born and raised in Texas, he received a BBA and MBA from Texas Tech University and doctorate from the University of Colorado where his doctoral dissertation was on the job satisfaction of nurses. Dr. Mathis has co-authored several books and has published numerous articles covering a variety of topics over the last 25 years. On the professional level, Dr. Mathis has held numerous national offices in the Society for Human Resource Management and in other professional organizations, including the Academy of Management. He also has served as President of the Human Resource Certification Institute (HRCI) and is certified as a Senior Professional in Human Resources (SPHR) by HRCI.

He has had extensive consulting experiences with both large and small organizations in a variety of areas. Firms assisted have been in healthcare, telecommunications, telemarketing, financial, manufacturing, retail, and utility industries. He has extensive specialized consulting experience in establishing or revising compensation plans for small and medium-sized firms. Internationally, Dr. Mathis has consulting and training experience with organizations in Australia, Lithuania, Taiwan, Germany, Romania, and Moldova.

Dr. John H. Jackson

Dr. John H. Jackson was born in Alaska and is currently Professor of Management at the University of Wyoming. After he received his BBA and MBA from Texas Tech University, he worked in the telecommunications industry in human resources management for several years. After leaving that company, he completed his doctoral studies at the University of Colorado and received his Ph.D. in Management and Organization.

During his academic career Dr. Jackson has authored four other college texts and over 50 articles and papers, including ones appearing in *Academy of Management Review, Journal of Management, Human Resources Management,* and *Human Resources Planning.* Also, he has consulted widely with a variety of organizations. During the past several years Dr. Jackson has served as an expert witness in a number of HR-related cases.

At the University of Wyoming he served two terms as Department Head in the Department of Management and Marketing. Dr. Jackson has received teaching awards at Wyoming and was one of the early developers and instructors on two-way interactive education via television in the state. In addition, he designed one of the first classes in the nation on *Business Environment and Natural Resources.* In addition to teaching, Dr. Jackson is president of Silverwood Ranches, Inc., a small ranch in the Wyoming mountains.

Patrick J. Langan

Mr. Langan was born in Minnesota and is currently a partner in the human resources consulting firm of Langan and Flynn, LLC based in St. Paul, Minnesota. His firm specializes in human resources consulting for the healthcare industry.

Mr. Langan's education includes an M.B.A. from The College of St. Thomas, St. Paul, Minnesota and a B.A. in Healthcare Administration from Southwest State University in Marshall, Minnesota. He has also completed advanced work in Quality Management, Diversity Awareness and Labor Relations. In addition he is a professor of Healthcare Management at the Carlson School of Business, University of Minnesota, where he has received the Teaching Excellence Award.

Mr. Langan's executive human resources positions include: Vice President of Human Resources Children's Hospitals and Clinics, Minneapolis/St. Paul, Minnesota, and Vice President of Human Resources and Ancillary Services, St. Francis Regional Medical Center, Shakopee, Minnesota.

Healthcare Human Resource Management

CHAPTER 1

The Nature and Challenges of Healthcare HR Management

Learning Objectives

After you read this chapter, you should be able to:

▶ Identify the types of healthcare organizations.

▶ Describe the current and future states of the healthcare industry.

▶ List and briefly describe human resource management activities.

▶ Explain the unique aspects of managing human resources in healthcare organizations.

▶ Discuss several of the human resource challenges in healthcare.

Healthcare HR Insights

The challenge to human resource professionals in every industry is to add value in what they do by truly supporting the strategic initiatives of the firm, and to move beyond focusing on cost control and administrative activities.[1] Healthcare organizations have traditionally looked to their HR staff members to perform the work of payroll, benefit administration, records management, and regulatory compliance. But because healthcare organizations have changed—driven by new technology, consumers demanding better care and lower costs, and increasing competition—the expectations for HR has also changed. Healthcare organizations today need their HR departments to function as strategic business partners. In fact, HR departments in healthcare organizations of all sizes and types must be both proficient at the administrative work and provide support for the strategic initiatives of the organization.

The human resource department of Cincinnati's Children's Hospital, a 350-bed Pediatric Medical Center, accepted the strategic challenge by radically redesigning its structure around a customer service model of human resource service delivery. The key change was to assign an HR generalist to a group of operating departments or a single division. For example, the HR generalists are responsible for coordinating the delivery of *all* HR activities to "their" operating departments. Supporting the HR generalists are HR specialists, who function as content experts in compensation, benefits, information systems, employee relations, compliance, and other areas.

The department managers report higher levels of satisfaction with HR because now they have a consistent individual in human resources to go to, and that contact understands their business and needs. Overall, this design has contributed to the hospital's ability to recruit and retain employees, through the increased effectiveness and support to department managers provided by HR.

Used with permission of Children's Hospital Medical Center, Cincinnati, Ohio.

At the beginning of this and all other chapters a "Healthcare HR Insight" will describe an HR initiative, program or management scenario that a healthcare organization has faced. These HR insights depict how effective management of human resources can have a meaningful impact on healthcare organizations.

Human resource (HR) Management in healthcare organizations refers to the strategies, tactics, plans, and programs that healthcare organizations utilize to accomplish the work of the organization through its employees. Key initiatives and tasks of HR include the following:

▶ *Workforce Planning*—Providing the necessary plans and programs to meet the staffing needs of the organization
▶ *Staffing and Selection*—Recruiting and selecting qualified and competent employees for the organization

▶ *Compensation and Benefits*—Strategizing, designing, and managing the compensation and benefit programs for the organization

▶ *Employee and Labor Relations*—Providing the programs, policies, and support to the organization that result in effective and productive relationships between the employees and the organization

▶ *Government Compliance*—Managing the programs, policies, and documentation of the HR activities to meet the various government regulations and regulatory agencies requirements that affect the healthcare workplace

▶ *Training and Development*—Assessing organizational training and development needs and providing meaningful and effective training, design, and delivery to meet those needs

▶ *Health Safety and Security*—Assuring that the healthcare workplace is healthy, safe, and secure and that managers and employees are aware of their responsibilities to protect themselves and others from workplace hazards and risks

NATURE OF HEALTHCARE ORGANIZATIONS

The healthcare industry as depicted in Figure 1-1 is a diverse group of organizations providing medical care, residential care, and various forms of therapies and health services. Notice that physician offices and clinics comprise the largest group of establishments.

FIGURE 1-1 Types of Healthcare Facilities

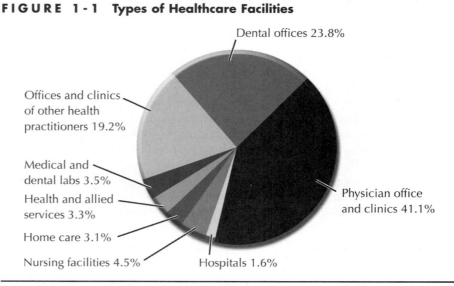

Dental offices 23.8%

Offices and clinics of other health practitioners 19.2%

Medical and dental labs 3.5%

Health and allied services 3.3%

Home care 3.1%

Nursing facilities 4.5%

Hospitals 1.6%

Physician office and clinics 41.1%

Source: U.S. Department of Labor, Bureau of Labor Statistics

TYPES OF HEALTHCARE ORGANIZATIONS

Healthcare organizations can be divided into several categories. Some of these—such as hospitals—employ hundreds of people in large buildings. Others—such as home care—involve few employees, and the "facility" is wherever the patient is. In between are many organizations that make up the healthcare spectrum.

▶ *Physician Offices and Clinics*—Physicians and surgeons practice individually or in groups of practitioners who have the same or different specialties. Group practice has become the recent trend, including clinics, freestanding emergency care centers, and ambulatory surgical centers. In some areas, physicians and surgeons are increasingly working as salaried employees of group medical practices, clinics, or integrated healthcare systems.

▶ *Hospitals*—Hospitals provide complete healthcare, ranging from diagnostic services to surgery and continuous nursing care. Hospitals can be small, freestanding rural facilities, or they can be part of a vast, multifacility, geographically dispersed, integrated system. Some hospitals specialize in treatment of the mentally ill, cancer patients, or children, while others are full-service providers.

▶ *Nursing and Personal-Care Facilities*—Nursing facilities provide inpatient nursing, rehabilitation, and health-related personal care to those who need continuous healthcare, but do not require hospital services. Other facilities, such as nursing and convalescent homes, help patients who need less assistance but also need special rehabilitation services.

▶ *Home Care*—Skilled nursing or medical care is sometimes provided in the home, under a physician's supervision. Home healthcare services are provided mainly to the elderly.

▶ *Health and Allied Services*—Among the diverse establishments in this group are kidney dialysis centers, drug treatment clinics and rehabilitation centers, blood banks, and providers of childbirth preparation classes.

▶ *Medical and Dental Laboratories*—Such laboratories provide analytic and diagnostic services to the medical profession or directly to patients following a physician's prescription. Workers may analyze blood, take X-rays, or perform other clinical tests. In dental laboratories, workers make dentures, artificial teeth, and orthodontic appliances.

▶ *Offices and Clinics of Other Health Practitioners*—This segment includes offices of chiropractors, ophthalmologists, optometrists, and podiatrists, as well as occupational and physical therapists, psychologists, audiologists, speech-language pathologists, dietitians, and other miscellaneous health practitioners. This segment also includes alternative-medicine practitioners, such as acupuncturists, homeopaths, hypnotherapists, and naturopaths.

▶ *Dentist's Offices and Clinics*—Almost one out of every four healthcare establishments is a dentist's office. Most employ only a few workers who provide general or specialized dental care, including dental surgery and pediatric orthodontic.

Healthcare in whatever form or type of facility requires a significant number of employees in order to deliver care. The healthcare industry can be characterized as a labor-intensive industry with wide diversity in position types requiring a broad cross-section of skill sets, professional training, and academic preparation. Many healthcare positions require four-year college degrees.

Employment in Healthcare

The healthcare industry accounts for more than 11 million jobs in the United States. According to the Bureau of Labor Statistics, twenty of the fastest-growing positions in the United States, are healthcare related. Figure 1-2 shows the composition of healthcare employment by type of organization. Hospitals account for less than 2% of all health service facilities, yet they employ nearly 40% of all healthcare workers.[2]

The Spectrum of Healthcare Jobs

The delivery of healthcare requires workers in a variety of job categories and different levels of educational preparations. Apart from the myriad of medical and clinical positions present in healthcare delivery there are also significant requirements for workers with skills in the following fields:

▶ Management and administration
▶ Physical plant operations
▶ Safety and security

▶ Information technology
▶ Food and nutritional services

FIGURE 1-2 Employment in Healthcare

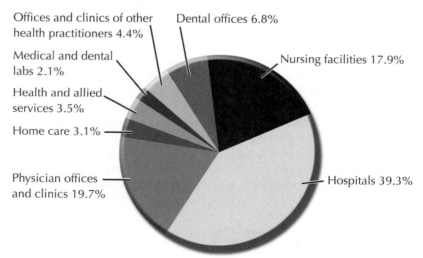

Offices and clinics of other health practitioners 4.4%
Dental offices 6.8%
Medical and dental labs 2.1%
Nursing facilities 17.9%
Health and allied services 3.5%
Home care 3.1%
Physician offices and clinics 19.7%
Hospitals 39.3%

Source: U.S. Department of Labor: Bureau of Labor Statistics

The scope of jobs in healthcare depicted in Figure 1-3 on page 8 shows a healthcare position hierarchy. It also depicts two other relationships: the levels and the number of positions required in each job category.

Types of Jobs   It is useful to understand the various levels of positions to appreciate the distribution of power and responsibility within healthcare organizations. Large health systems are especially hierarchial with significant numbers and levels of jobs, while clinics and physician groups have very flat hierarchies with few levels. Purposely not depicted on this illustration are physicians, who by definition would fall in the clinical professional category. However, depending on the nature and size of a healthcare organization, physicians could also be associated with any level of management or supervision.

Number of Positions   The graphical depiction of a pyramid is a model for considering the labor requirements of the various levels in a healthcare organization. At the top of the pyramid is executive management, which would represent the fewest number of individuals required across the industry. At the base of the pyramid are service workers, who would represent the category of workers having the largest numbers of individuals.

THE CHANGING NATURE OF HEALTHCARE

Understanding the current condition of healthcare and considering future trends in the industry are important to the discussion of healthcare's HR challenges. Reasonably easy access to care, effectiveness of treatment, and continuous advancement in technology make the U.S. healthcare system one of the best in the world. However, the healthcare system is confronted with serious issues. In a recent study, (a strategic assessment of the healthcare environment in the United States), the following characteristics were noted:

▶ *Financial Crunch*—The industry is confronting eroding earnings and limited access to capital for investment in new buildings and equipment.
▶ *Rise of Consumerism*—Many consumers in today's healthcare system describe their experiences as confusing, inconvenient, or worse. Also, consumers demand personalized service and convenient patient contacts or they may choose other healthcare providers.
▶ *Labor and Talent Shortages*—Healthcare organizations are coping with a "skill set shortage" that is characterized by growing job dissatisfaction. They are having difficulty attracting and retaining qualified staff, managing careers, and improving compensation and benefits for employees.
▶ *Scientific Advancement*—Healthcare organizations have limited capital to buy and promote new technology. Yet there is significant pressure to move new technology into the mainstream of care delivery.
▶ *Assessing and Applying Information*—Healthcare institutions and consumers have significant issues with accessing needed, useful data.[3]

FIGURE 1-3 Healthcare Position Hierarchy

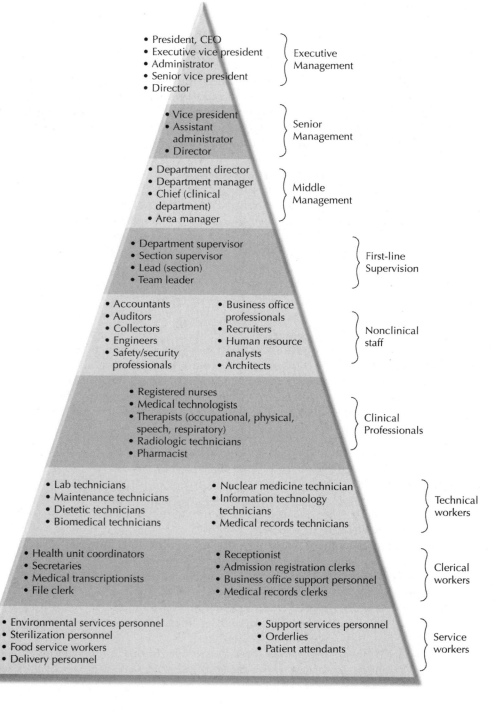

- President, CEO
- Executive vice president
- Administrator
- Senior vice president
- Director

} Executive Management

- Vice president
- Assistant administrator
- Director

} Senior Management

- Department director
- Department manager
- Chief (clinical department)
- Area manager

} Middle Management

- Department supervisor
- Section supervisor
- Lead (section)
- Team leader

} First-line Supervision

- Accountants
- Auditors
- Collectors
- Engineers
- Safety/security professionals
- Business office professionals
- Recruiters
- Human resource analysts
- Architects

} Nonclinical staff

- Registered nurses
- Medical technologists
- Therapists (occupational, physical, speech, respiratory)
- Radiologic technicians
- Pharmacist

} Clinical Professionals

- Lab technicians
- Maintenance technicians
- Dietetic technicians
- Biomedical technicians
- Nuclear medicine technician
- Information technology technicians
- Medical records technicians

} Technical workers

- Health unit coordinators
- Secretaries
- Medical transcriptionists
- File clerk
- Receptionist
- Admission registration clerks
- Business office support personnel
- Medical records clerks

} Clerical workers

- Environmental services personnel
- Sterilization personnel
- Food service workers
- Delivery personnel
- Support services personnel
- Orderlies
- Patient attendants

} Service workers

Facing Changes in Healthcare

Healthcare and change have been synonymous since the late 1960s with the passage of Medicare legislation and the continued rise in healthcare costs. Federal and state governmental involvement in healthcare, coupled with ever-increasing costs, has been a primary impetus behind the changes in healthcare in recent years. Managed care and the growth of government regulation, including the Balanced Budget Act of 1997 (discussed in the next section), have driven the changes. Also, there have been continuing pressures to reduce the cost of delivering healthcare in all forms.

No part of the healthcare delivery system has been left untouched by these influences. Consolidation continues for acute-care hospitals and systems as their profit margins fall. Medicare reimbursements for skilled nursing facilities, home health agencies and rehabilitation hospitals have declined, resulting in difficult financial times for these organizations. As many as 25% of all Medicare-certified homehealth care agencies have closed since the passage of the Balanced Budget Act in 1997.[4]

Here are some predictions about the future of the healthcare industry based on a wide variety of information. The primary predictions are as follows:

▶ *The "Wired" Healthcare Consumer*—Internet-informed consumers will be well armed with the latest information on medical advances and new pharmaceuticals, which will increase patients' demands for the latest drugs and treatments.

▶ *Technology Advances*—Genetic therapies, electronic medical records, telemedicine, Web marketing, and the reemergence of centers of excellence will be spurred along by Internet-based information. These advances will significantly affect access to care and information. This access will broaden the base of care delivery, not bound by geography, but influenced by awareness of new or better providers of care.

▶ *Cost and Clinical Performance*—Hospitals will continue to struggle financially. As many as 500 hospitals will close by 2005. Efforts to improve clinical performance will be emphasized to reduce medical errors and to provide differentiation for those hospitals that demonstrate capability in this area.

▶ *Managed Care*—Existing managed-care plans will face more aggressive providers, and health systems will push for more attractive contracts and higher reimbursements.

▶ *How Healthcare Is Delivered and Funded*—Many changes are predicted, including the following:
  ▸ Health system reform focusing first on uninsured children and then on uninsured adults
  ▸ Relief from the Balanced Budget Act of 1997, so that reimbursements can be increased.
  ▸ Regulation of pharmaceutical prices
  ▸ Growing role for states in health reform, to allow states more control in managing healthcare costs.

▶ *Workforce Availability*—Labor shortages will continue. The aging population in the U.S. will require more healthcare at the same time more older workers depart from the (healthcare) workforce. Union organizing will continue with some success. Hospitals will continue to outsource services, even beyond the typical areas such as food services and facilities management. More providers will offer incentives to employees to reward quality improvement and customer service.[5]

Balanced Budget Act of 1997

In 1997 the average hospital profit margin was 6.1%, in 1999 the margin fell to 3.2%; one year later (2000) it stood at 2.6%. The Medicare program, which is the largest public payer of healthcare services, spent $231.1 billion on healthcare for the 38.4 million individuals it covers in 1998. Of the total expenditure, $128.5 billion was spent on hospital care and $13.8 billion on home healthcare.

The dollars spent in the U.S. on hospital care and home health have continued to increase. Congress passed the Balanced Budget Act (BBA) in 1997, which was designed to significantly reduce Medicare spending by 2002. In fact, the BBA has worked beyond expectations. The Congressional Budget Office is projecting that Medicare spending will be $191.5 billion less than what was anticipated when BBA was enacted.

With the growth of integrated systems that include hospitals, long-term care, rehabilitation, and home health and ambulatory care, the magnitude of BBA is even greater. Many of the provisions of the BBA were designed to dramatically reduce Medicare payments to post–acute-care providers by nearly $30 billion over a five-year period.

Another significant change the BBA imposed on hospitals is the expanded Medicare definition of a hospital transfer. The BBA expanded the definition so that acute care hospitals that discharge Medicare beneficiaries classified in one of ten specified diagnosis-related groups (DRGs) are now paid primarily based on length of stay and no longer automatically receive the full DRG rate. Patients in these ten DRGs tend to have a disproportionate use of post–acute-care services. The financial impact of the transfer payment policy on hospitals was $3 billion between 1998 and 2002.[6]

Hospitals and health systems have taken aggressive steps to reduce their costs including the following:

▶ Outsourcing many nonclinical support services such as housekeeping, food services, and groundskeeping
▶ Improving clinical efficiencies by adopting treatment protocols and standards of practice
▶ Redesigning work processes for more efficient use of staff resources
▶ Requiring the use of generic drugs and limit the use of brand-name drugs

Over the last fifteen years, with the exception of a brief period in the mid-1990s, hospital expenses have grown at an annual rate of 6% or greater. Hospitals and other providers will be hard-pressed to absorb additional cost cutting because of other cost pressures, including:

► Costs of new information technology
► Costs of new medical technology
► Rising pharmaceutical costs

At one end of the spectrum is the challenge of recruiting and retaining the key providers of patient care. At the other end of the spectrum is the need to manage human resources with declining financial resources. Because labor costs account for more than 50 percent of the expenses in most healthcare organizational expenses, any rise in labor expense will have enormous impact. With the current staffing crisis in healthcare, the industry has become very aggressive. For instance market-based salary administration programs are targeting employees in critical care jobs. This strategy to attract and retain workers has clearly had an impact on the continued decline in profit margins. In response to the full effect of BBA and other financial pressures, hospitals are closing services, laying off less critical staff, and cutting or freezing employee wages.

JOINT COMMISSION ON ACCREDITATION OF HEALTHCARE ORGANIZATIONS

Every industry possesses unique characteristics that affect the management of human resources. This is especially true in the healthcare industry. One of the most unique characteristics of the healthcare industry is the effect of errors of healthcare workers that could result in death or injury to patients, clients, or residents. This characteristic requires healthcare employers to have the highest of standards in assuring staff competence, safe practice, ethical treatment, and confidentiality.

The Joint Commission on Accreditation of Healthcare Organizations (JCAHO) is a quality accreditation organization whose members subscribe to a standard-based review process. Compliance with quality standards as demonstrated through onsite reviews by JCAHO, is critical to ensure that the consumers of healthcare are receiving consistent levels of safe, quality care.

JCAHO has standards for eleven hospital functions or performance areas. These performance areas are grouped by patient-focused and organization-focused functions as illustrated in Figure 1-4. Additional areas surveyed are referred to as structures such as governance, management, medical staff, and nursing. JACHO expects healthcare providers to use a collaborative and multidisciplinary approach to improve performance, pursue quality initiatives, and develop staff competencies. The multidisciplinary approach is evident because standards for all the functions are reviewed. Many human resource standards are linked to the standards for other departmental and division functions. As an example, staff education is shared among HR and other departments.

FIGURE 1-4 JCAHO Hospital Functions/Performance Areas

Patient Focused

- Patient rights and organization ethics
- Assessment of patients
- Care of patients
- Education
- Continuum of care

Organization

- Improving organization performance
- Leadership
- Management of the environment of care
- Management of human resources
- Management of information
- Surveillance, prevention and infection control

Within each of the organizational function areas, a number of standards deal with the responsibilities of HR management:

▶ Human resource planning
▶ Staff training and education
▶ Specialized training
▶ Assessment of staff competency

Each one of these responsibilities has standards associated with it that include policy, practice, and documentation of compliance requirements. The JCAHO feature describes the JCAHO standards that impact HR activities in healthcare organizations.

THE JOINT COMMISSION ON ACCREDITATION OF HEALTHCARE ORGANIZATIONS

Standards That Impact HR

HR departments in healthcare organizations that are surveyed by JCAHO are responsible for the HR standards, however there are standards in other functional areas that have a significant HR focus these include:

▶ Leadership (LD)
▶ Environment of care (EC)
▶ Information management (IM)

JCAHO Standard	*Responsibility*
HR, LD	Staff competency
HR, LD, IM, EC	Education and training needs
HR, LD	Staffing plans and levels

THE HR FUNCTION IN HEALTHCARE

The human resource management function in healthcare organizations is slowly moving to become an equal contributor to other organizational areas. Over the last two decades, this trend has evolved for two main reasons: one, out of necessity to provide HR services more efficiently and effectively, and second, the need for human resource training, skills, understanding, and competency. HR professionals in human resource management in healthcare are more and more viewed as strategic partners with their operations, finance, and administration colleagues.

Necessity to Provide Service

The HR management functions of recruitment and selection, training and development, performance management, compensation, and employee relations were typically managed (and some cases, still are) in healthcare organizations by managers who have not had sufficient training in these areas. HR departments were focused on the administrative aspects of payroll, benefits administration, and recordkeeping. As the challenges and complexities of healthcare HR management have grown, healthcare managers have recognized that they require more strategic support from their HR departments.

HR Professionals

The development and performance expectations for healthcare HR professionals has been raised. Dedicated, competent professionals who could successfully perform in any healthcare management or administrative role are choosing the HR field for their careers. The executive suites and boardrooms of hospitals, health systems, long-term care facilities, and other healthcare providers are now familiar environments for HR professionals.

HR MANAGEMENT ACTIVITIES

The central focus for HR management is to contribute to organizational success. As Figure 1-5 depicts, HR management usually is composed of several groups of interlinked activities. However, the performance of these HR activities is done in the context of a specific organization, which is represented by the inner rings in Figure 1-5. A brief description of the major HR activities follows

▶ *HR Planning and Analysis*—Through *HR planning,* managers attempt to anticipate forces that will influence the future supply of and demand for employees. Having a *human resource information system (HRIS)* to provide accurate and timely information for HR planning is crucial.
▶ *EEO Compliance*—Compliance with equal employment opportunity (EEO) laws and regulations affects all other HR activities. For instance, strategic

FIGURE 1-5 HR Management Activities

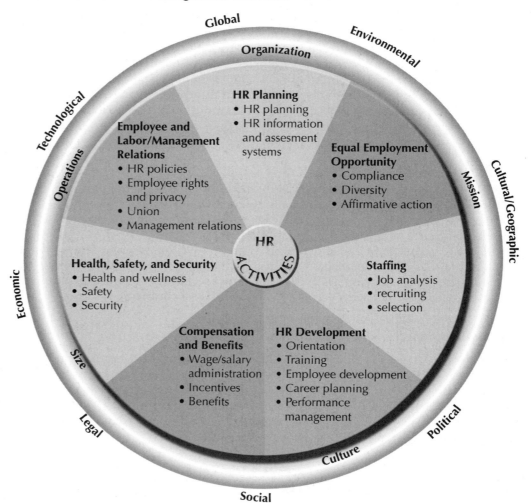

HR plans must ensure availability of a *diversity* of individuals to meet *affirmative action* requirements. In addition, when recruiting, selecting, and training individuals, all managers must be aware of EEO requirements, including accommodations of individuals with disabilities.

▶ *Staffing*—The aim of staffing is to provide an adequate supply of qualified individuals to fill the jobs in an organization. By studying what workers do, *job analysis* provides the foundation for the staffing function. From this analysis, *job descriptions* and *job specifications* can be prepared and used to *recruit* applicants for job openings. The *selection process* is then concerned with choosing the most qualified individuals to fill jobs in the organization.

▶ *HR Development*—Beginning with the *orientation* of new employees, HR training and development also includes *job-skill training*. As jobs evolve and change, ongoing *re-training* is necessary to accommodate technological changes. Encouraging *development* of all employees, including supervisors and managers, is necessary to prepare organizations for future challenges. *Career planning* identifies paths and activities for individual employees as they develop within the organization. Assessing how employees perform their jobs and make improvements is the focus of *performance management.*

▶ *Compensation and Benefits*—Compensation rewards people for performing organizational work through *pay, incentives,* and *benefits.* Employers must develop and refine their basic *wage* and *salary* systems. Also, *incentive programs* such as gainsharing are growing in usage. Additionally, the rapid increase in the costs of benefits, especially healthcare benefits, will continue to be a major issue.

▶ *Health, Safety, and Security*—The physical and mental health, safety and security of employees are vital concerns. The traditional concern for *safety* has focused on eliminating accidents and injuries at work. Additional concerns are *health* issues arising from hazardous work with certain chemicals and newer technologies. Also, workplace *security* has grown in importance, in response to the increasing number of acts of workplace violence.

▶ *Employee and Labor–Management Relations*—The relationship between managers and their employees must be handled effectively if both the employees and the organization are to prosper together. Whether or not a *union* represents the employees, *employee rights* must be addressed. It is important to develop, communicate, and update *HR policies and procedures and rules* so that managers and employees alike know what is expected.

ROLES OF HR MANAGEMENT

As Figure 1-6 depicts, HR management may play three roles in organizations. The traditional administrative and operational roles of HR management have broadened to include more strategic elements. It should be emphasized that as HR roles shift to the right of Figure 1-6, the previous roles still must be met and the additional ones performed. Also, the continuum shows that as it becomes more strategic, the primary focus of HR considers longer time horizons and the broader impact of HR decisions.

The administrative role of HR management is heavily oriented to processing and keeping employee records. Maintaining employee files and HR-related data bases, processing employee benefits claims, answering questions about tuition and sick-leave policies, and compiling and submitting required state and federal

FIGURE 1-6 HR Management Roles

	ADMINISTRATIVE	OPERATIONAL	STRATEGIC
Focus	Administrative processing and record keeping	Operational support	Organization-wide, global
Timing	Short term (less than 1 year)	Intermediate term (1–2 years)	Longer term (2–5 years)
Typical Activities	▶ Administering employee benefits ▶ Conducting new employee orientations ▶ Interpreting HR policies and procedures ▶ Preparing equal employment reports	▶ Managing compensation programs ▶ Recruiting and selecting for current openings ▶ Conducting safety training ▶ Resolving employee complaints	▶ Assessing workforce trends and issues ▶ Engaging in community workforce development planning ▶ Assisting in organizational restructuring and downsizing ▶ Advising on mergers or acquisitions ▶ Planning compensation strategies

government reports are all examples of the administrative nature of HR management. These activities must be performed efficiently and promptly.

One of the most important shifts in the emphasis of HR management in the past few years has been the recognition of HR as a strategic business contributor. Based on the research and writings of a number of HR scholars, including David Ulrich of the University of Michigan, HR as a *strategic business partner* has been stressed.[7] This emphasis involves HR in several areas:

▶ Strategic planning participation
▶ Decision making on mergers, acquisitions, and downsizing
▶ Redesigning organizations and work processes
▶ Ensuring financial accountability for HR results
▶ Planning for attracting and retaining sufficient numbers of qualified employees
▶ Developing the capabilities of all individuals in the organization
▶ Identifying and rewarding individual, team, and organizational performance

A complete understanding of strategic sources of competitive advantages through the management of human resources must include analyses of the internal strengths and weaknesses of the people in an organization. HR management strengths must include working with operating executives and managers to revise the organization and its components. Ulrich likens this need to that of being an organizational architect. He suggests that HR managers should function much as architects do when redesigning buildings. In this role, HR professionals prepare new ways to align the organization and its work with the strategic thrust of each segment of the organization.

HR CHALLENGES IN HEALTHCARE

The current state of healthcare and predictions about the industry require healthcare organizational leaders that can manage while facing financial constraints, increasing economic pressure, an aging population, the consumer revolution, and rapidly advancing technology.[8] HR leadership is especially critical, because many of the current realities and future eventualities in healthcare are human-resource focused.

The list of challenges is both daunting and exciting. HR professionals have the opportunity to make contributions to their organizations and their industry by working with their executive and management colleagues and providing solutions for the difficult issues and problems the industry faces. Some of the most prominent challenges include recruitment and retention of sufficiently qualified staff, and managing changes in HR likely to occur due to the pressures facing healthcare organizations of all types.

Recruitment and Retention

Today's staffing woes are likely to continue or even worsen for a number of key healthcare positions. For instance, as nurses retire and fewer young people opt for the profession, the growing number of aging baby boomers is putting more demands on healthcare resources. Recently, more than 126,000 RN positions were unfilled nationally.[9]

The recruitment and staffing issues are clearly not exclusive to nursing; all healthcare professions have been affected. In a study covering a recent two-year period of more than 700 hospitals, vacancy rates of 21% for pharmacists, 18% for radiological technologists, and 12% for laboratory technologists were indicated.[10] The percentage of college freshman who plan to major in health services has continued to fall, from 20.5% of high school graduates who said they planned a career in health services, compared to 17.9% just four years later.[11]

The American Hospital Association's American Society for Healthcare Human Resources Administration (ASHHRA), in its study of the developing shortage of healthcare workers, noted that in the last twenty years, healthcare has moved from a favored to a less-favored employment sector. This insight reflects five observations as listed below:

1. In a manufacturing economy, healthcare was high-tech; but in an information economy, young people see healthcare as low-tech.
2. In the 1960s and 1970s, healthcare was safe, secure, and prestigious employment, but in today's labor market, healthcare is seen as chaotic and unstable.
3. In a traditional society, healthcare was one of only a few employment options for women; today healthcare industry is only one of many of their career choices.

4. In a long-stay hospital system, staff had strong, supportive relationships with patients, but in a short-stay hospital system, staff is focused on disease protocols, regulatory compliance, and documentation. The result is that the staff have less connection with patients.

5. In a mass-production society where production schedules controlled work hours, people saw the 24/7 demands of hospitals as less attractive, but acceptable; but in an information society where people schedule work to their own convenience, workers see the 24/7 demands of hospitals as unacceptable. The intensity of the 24/7 schedule is heightened by the presence of short-stay, high-activity patients who place continuous demands on hospital staff for care and support.[12]

Managing Change

The healthcare industry is changing rapidly; every aspect of the care delivery continuum has been impacted. Managing organizational change remains one of the most important challenges facing healthcare HR professionals today.[13]

The current and future state of the industry discussed earlier in this chapter highlighted organizational consolidation, declining margins affected by lower reimbursements, technology advances, consumers demanding improvement in clinical performance, and other environmental and market forces. These changes have had a significant effect on the management of human resources in healthcare organizations. Key issues include:

▶ *Doing More with Less*—In response to declining margins, healthcare organizations have undertaken a seemingly endless stream of budget cutting initiatives.

▶ *Compliance with Quality Standards*—With the increasing pressure on the healthcare delivery system to improve clinical performance, performing to quality standards is a critical challenge. As detailed in this chapter, meeting the Joint Commission for the Accreditation of Healthcare Organizations (JCAHO) quality standards requires healthcare organizations to continually improve their delivery of services.

▶ *Implementing Diversity Planning and Culturally Competent Care*—Healthcare providers, both institutional and individual, must ensure that each person, regardless of race, ethnicity, gender, age and ability to pay their medical bills receive medical care in a competent, sincere, and equal manner. Unfortunately, this ideal scenario does not take into account the lack of diversity among care providers and the lack of culturally competent policies in health care delivery settings.[14]

▶ *Preparing Healthcare Workers for New Technologies*—New technologies are leading to significant advances in the delivery and quality of services. These advances are also contributing to productivity gains and more cost-effective care. Key initiatives include new drugs, new imaging (X-ray) technologies, genetic mapping and testing, and the transfer of medical information from paper to computer.[15] As these advances are implemented, all healthcare workers—whether physician or lab aide—must receive orientation and training to effectively and safely operate with new technologies. The skill sets of future healthcare workers must include not only clinical and administrative capabilities, but also computer knowledge and related capabilities to facilitate their use of ever-improving healthcare technology.

▶ *Balancing Professional and Personal Lives*—Many of today's workers are experiencing significant difficulty in juggling work and family responsibilities. In work environments that demand 24 hours a day, 7 days a week coverage, this is especially true. Healthcare workers are continually confronted with work and schedule demands that conflict with family responsibilities.

There are no simple answers to this issue. The patients, residents, and clients of healthcare providers require care outside what is considered a "normal" work day of 8:00 A.M. to 5:00 P.M. Creative work and family programs, integrated employee benefit systems, and flexible scheduling programs will continue to be implemented across the healthcare industry.

▶ *Succession Planning*—At a time when qualified healthcare executives and managers are needed the most, the healthcare industry is experiencing a shortage of skilled leaders. Chief financial officers (CFO) chief information officers, (CIO) and medical executives are all in high demand, but chief executive officers (CEO) continue to be the most difficult positions to fill. Witt/Kiefer, a leading search firm that specializes in healthcare executive recruitment, reports recruitment for key healthcare executive positions takes longer now than just a few years ago.

With external recruitment taking significantly longer and costing more both in terms of lost productivity and increases in search time and related costs, healthcare organizations are turning to internal sources for promotion. Recruiters and some industry leaders acknowledge that healthcare organizations need to make a greater investment in professional development internally. There is a perception that mentoring and internal development have been underemphasized as healthcare organizations have grappled with financial and operational issues.[16]

Using the succession planning and internal development models that have been successful for many organizations outside of the healthcare industry is key. It is critical to identify high-performing management talent early in their careers and then guide them through planned, job experiences among different service areas.

Facing the Future

All of these changes and challenges facing healthcare organizations require that HR management issues be considered. The management of human resources will determine, to a large extent, how successfully healthcare organizations will survive, change, and grow.

CASE

	Bed Size	Employees	Unions	Mission
Hospital A	100	1,100	4	General pediatrics
Hospital B	180	2,000	5	Specialty care

For more than a half-century, two acute-care pediatric specialty hospitals existed within ten miles of each other in a large metropolitan area. Over several years, competition intensified for patients, physicians, and staff. The competition resulted in duplication of services and increased costs, one of which was higher wages and benefits needed in order for each hospital to compete for skilled healthcare workers. Acknowledging the financial issues of the two organizations, the two Boards of Trustees initiated merger discussions. The characteristics of the two hospitals are shown in the box above.

The two Boards prepared a "Rationale for Merger" document that indicated that a merger could result in several benefits as follows:

▶ More efficient utilization of healthcare resources through

  ▶ A single workforce, with coordinated services, requiring less duplication in positions

  ▶ A single operating budget, reducing the need for two management structures

▶ A reduction or elimination in operational redundancy and program duplication

▶ Proactive leadership to gain community support and to increase the ability of the combined organization to negotiate favorable reimbursement contracts

Another area the Boards had to consider was the structural impact of the merger, including:

▶ Consolidation of two Boards to one, two management staffs to one, and ways to consolidate union contracts

▶ Combination of pay and benefits programs

▶ The merger of two different organizational cultures with all of the "politics" and personal anxieties common in mergers.

This was an important decision for the two organizations. The impact on the community, patients, and employees would be far-reaching and compelling. Much of the planning had HR dimensions.

Questions

1. Describe the leadership role of human resources in a successful merger of these two organizations.
2. What are the key human resource challenges and opportunities to a merger of this magnitude?

END NOTES

1. Edward E. Lawler III and Susan A. Mohrman, "Beyond the Vision: What Makes HR Effective?" *Human Resource Planning* (December 2000), 10.
2. U.S. Department of Labor, Bureau of Labor Statistics, 2002.
3. "VHA, Deloitte & Touch Offer Strategies for Hospitals and Healthcare Systems," *Health Care Strategic Management* (June 2001), 4–5.
4. Mike Schraeder, "Health Care," *Business Horizons* (September/ October 2001), 2–3.
5. Adapted from Russel C. Coile, Jr., "Futurescan 2001: A Millennium Forecast of Healthcare Trends 2001–2005," Healthcare Administration Press, 2001.
6. "A Comprehensive Review of Hospital Finances in the Aftermath of the Balanced Budget Act of 1997." *http//www.HCIA.com.*
7. David Ulrich, *Human Resource Champions* (Boston: Harvard Business School Press, 1997).
8. "Forecasting the Health Care Future," *Marketing Health Services* (Fall 2001), 16–22.
9. "Staffing Watch?" *Hospitals and Health Networks* (December 2000), 20.
10. "Staffing Watch?" *Hospitals and Health Networks* (July 2001), 28.
11. "Staffing Watch?" *Hospitals and Health Networks* (October 2001), 30.
12. "Workforce Supply for Hospitals and Health Systems," *Trustee* (June 2001), 1–4.
13. Betty R. Anson, "Taking Charge of Change in a Volatile Healthcare Marketplace," *Human Resource Planning* (June 2001), 1–4.
14. Everard O. Ruthledge and Nathaniel Wesley, Jr., "The Struggle for Equality in Healthcare Continues," *Journal of Healthcare Management* (September/ October 2001), 313–326.
15. Julie Rovner, "Health and Health Care 2010: The Forecast, the Challenge," Special supplement to *ADVANCES* (2000), 1 (Robert Wood Johnson Foundation).
16. Mary Chris Jaklevic, "Wanted: A Few Good Leaders," *Modern Healthcare* (October 2, 2000), 38.

CHAPTER 2

Healthcare HR Competencies, Structures, and Quality Standards

Learning Objectives

After you have read this chapter, you should be able to:

▶ Define the competencies required for healthcare HR professionals.

▶ Describe the importance of attaining HR management credentials.

▶ Explain the relationship between the type of healthcare organization and the level of senior HR position.

▶ Discuss how the healthcare industry compares to other industries on HR staffing and expenditures.

▶ Explain the importance of HR programs to the delivery of safe, competent healthcare.

Healthcare HR Insights

In the employment classifieds of a major newspaper of a large Midwestern city the following ad appeared:

Director of Human Resources

The Medical Group has an immediate need for a Director of Human Resources. The Director is responsible for all aspects of the Group's human resources program.

Qualified candidates will possess a B.S. in Human Resource Management or the equivalent, 5+ years of management-level HR experience, preferably in a healthcare environment, and strong communication and organizational skills.

The Medical Group offers a comprehensive compensation package, a professional work environment and an opportunity to contribute to the success of the organization.

As recently as five years ago, few medical groups would have recognized the need or even considered the importance of staffing a director-level HR position. However, as HR issues and challenges have increased for healthcare organizations, healthcare HR leadership positions are becoming more and more commonplace. Healthcare organizations of all types and sizes now have HR professionals providing HR strategic and operational leadership.[1]

As highlighted in the previous chapter, at the forefront of the healthcare industry's challenges are HR management issues. In order to meet these challenges, healthcare organizations must have competent HR leaders; effective HR structures and programs; and an understanding of the relationship between the delivery of quality care and effective HR policies and practices.[2] This chapter will provide an overview of these areas and establish the framework for managing the HR activities discussed throughout the book.

HEALTHCARE HR MANAGEMENT COMPETENCIES

There is an old joke that "Personnel" Managers are ex-athletes who couldn't sell life insurance. More specifically for healthcare HR managers, the characterization was that administrators were reassigned to HR because they liked people or just prior to their retirement so they couldn't get the organization into any trouble. Unfortunately, these painful characterizations were occasionally self-fulfilling, and were based on some degree of truth. However, the era of utilizing ill-prepared or ineffective individuals in healthcare HR positions is over. Today's healthcare HR professional must possess key competencies, complimented with the appropriate educational and professional preparation.

Competence is more than a list of skills; it encompasses how healthcare HR professionals define their work. How HR professionals define and understand their job affects how they operate. The healthcare HR professionals of today must view their work in a broader, more strategic sense than in the past. Organizational HR needs are too great to only focus on the operational responsibilities of the job.

Healthcare HR professionals cannot work in isolation or function without significant involvement with their key stakeholders, including the employees, managers, and senior management. Competent healthcare HR professionals can and do contribute to the success of healthcare organizations through effective HR programs and practices.

Key Competencies

The American Society for Healthcare Human Resources Administration developed "Key Middle Management Competencies" that also provide a set of model competencies for HR professionals.[3] These competencies are depicted in Figure 2-1.

FIGURE 2-1   Model Competencies for HR Professionals

- Analytical thinker
- Committed to service
- Possesses personal integrity

- Results-oriented
- Agent for change
- Resource manager

Effective HR Leader

- Skilled communicator
- Team builder
- Use collaborative approach
- Developer of talent

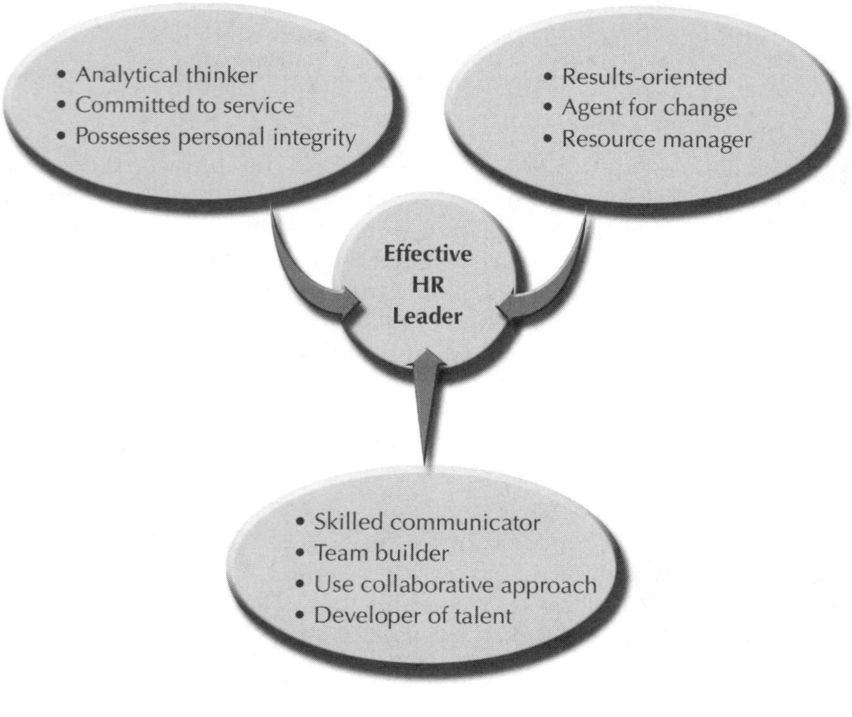

Emotional Intelligence as a Core Competency

Emotional intelligence is another critical set of HR management skills equally relevant to the successful contribution of HR to the organization. **Emotional intelligence** is defined as proficiencies in intrapersonal and interpersonal skills in the areas of self-awareness, self-regulation, self-motivation, social awareness, and social skills. For HR management in the healthcare environment, a strong case can be made for the importance of high emotional intelligence.[4]

A common theme in the skill sets and competencies of effective healthcare HR professionals are strong intra- and interpersonal communications. The nature of healthcare requires that HR professionals be effective communicators in one-to-one interviews, small group discussions and meetings, and when presenting to large groups. Being socially aware of how to treat people with respect and dignity and communicate effectively with them is also a critical emotional intelligence competency.

HR professionals typically have a great deal of organizational power due to the nature of their responsibilities. They regularly make decisions that can affect others' lives, careers, and financial well-being. Self-regulation as a part of emotional intelligence is important to ensure that HR professionals make appropriate decisions that are consistent with effective management of people as well as with HR policy and practice.

Strategic HR Thinking

Another important competency for healthcare HR professionals to contribute to organizational success is thinking and working strategically. HR professionals who go beyond the operational and administrative roles to contribute strategically are able to do the following:

▶ Identify the neglected employee issues and develop solid knowledge for organizational leaders to use in the strategic planning processes.
▶ Contribute to the success of the organization by applying HR theory and knowledge to affect organizational results.
▶ Create long-range (ten years out) agendas that are not just focusing on the present.
▶ Identify, promote, and reward organizational change and problem solving.[5]

HR Management Credentials

One of the characteristics of a professional field is having a means to certify the knowledge and competence of members of the profession. The most well-known certification program for HR generalists is administered by the Human Resource Certification Institute (HRCI), which is affiliated with the Society for Human Resource Management (SHRM). Figure 2-2 describes the credential levels and the criteria that must be met to achieve either the Professional in Human Resources (PHR) or Senior Professional in Human Resources (SPHR) designations. Studying

FIGURE 2-2 **Human Resource Certification Institute—Certification Levels**

Designation ⟹ **Professional in Human Resources (PHR)**

Criteria:

▸ 2 to 4 years of exempt-level HR work experience
▸ HR experience has focused on HR program implementation with a tactical and logistical orientation

Designation ⟹ **Senior Professional in Human Resources (SPHR)**

Criteria:

▸ 6 to 8 years of exempt-level HR work experience
▸ Experience includes ultimate accountability in an HR department

and preparing for the PHR or SPHR exams is an excellent opportunity to increase the HR knowledge base of an HR professional.

Credentials carry importance for healthcare professionals because they are an indication of an individual's drive, initiative, and ambition—all qualities that acknowledge an individual's desire to succeed. But professional credentials must be viewed in the larger context of the individual's education, skill set, and record of career achievements. Credentials are not a measure of performance, but can serve as documented proof that the holder has an established record of the specific learning of a body of knowledge.[6] As accounting professionals pursue CPAs to attest to their knowledge of accounting theory and law, HR professionals should consider pursuing certification through HRCI to similarly document their HR knowledge.

THE HR FUNCTION IN HEALTHCARE ORGANIZATIONS

There is significant variability in the characteristics of healthcare organizations across the industry. The size and type of care provided (e.g., acute, ambulatory, long-term care) all influence the structure of the organization and the level and type of HR function that exists in the various healthcare sites and locations.

Figure 2-3 depicts the relationships between type of organization, human resource structure, and the typical titles of the senior-level human resource position. As this figure illustrates, the size and type of organization have the most significant impact on the structure and the level that the senior human resource position enjoys within the organization.

FIGURE 2-3   Organizational Characteristics of HR in Healthcare

TYPE OF ORGANIZATION	TITLE(S) OF SENIOR-LEVEL POSITIONS
Health system	Senior vice-president Corporate vice-president
Health system hospital	Vice-president Director, assistant administrator, human resources
Integrated long-term care facility	Senior vice-president Corporate vice-president
Hospital (freestanding)	Vice-president Director, assistant administrator, human resources
Clinic, ambulatory care center (hospital/system based)	Clinic manager Manager, human resources
Clinic, ambulatory care center (freestanding)	Director, human resources Manager, human resources
Physician practice	Practice manager Practice administrator HR assistant

In large health systems, hospitals, medical centers, or nursing home systems, the senior HR leader typically carries the title of Vice-President. In smaller healthcare organizations with less formal or flatter structures, Manager or Director titles are prevalent. In the very small environments, HR duties are frequently one of the duties of the practice's administrator, supported by administrative assistants or payroll employees.

HR DEPARTMENTS AND HEALTHCARE ORGANIZATION CHARTS

Consistent with the wide variety of titles and levels of responsibilities corresponding to the differences in the sizes and types of healthcare organizations, the actual organizational placement of healthcare HR departments varies widely.

Figure 2-4 depicts the organizational chart of Pender Community Hospital in Pender, Nebraska. Pender Community Hospital is a small, rural hospital providing full-service healthcare from one location. The senior HR leader reports to the Hospital's Controller and, as depicted, is also responsible for patient accounting. Although the HR manager does not report to the administrator, the manager frequently advises the administrator directly. Additional organizational charts are depicted on the book's Web site at *http://flynn.swlearning.com.*

FIGURE 2-4 **Organizational Chart of Pender Community Hospital, Pender, Nebra**

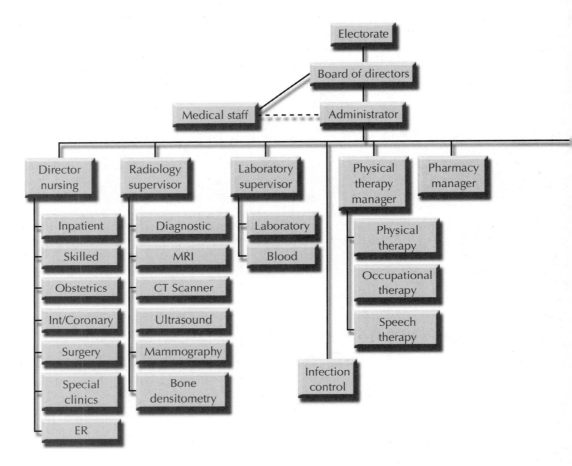

MEASURING HEALTHCARE HR MANAGEMENT

Statistical comparisons are useful to understand the broad context of the overall healthcare industry's commitment to HR. Two useful ways to measure HR are to look at staffing rates and budget expenditures, relative to other industries.

Staffing Ratios

HR activities, budgets, and staffing are regularly surveyed by the Bureau of National Affairs (BNA). BNA has surveyed and reported on human resource staffing levels over the past several years. Figure 2-5 depicts the BNA com-

FIGURE 2-4   Organizational Chart of Pender Community Hospital, Pender, Nebraska (continued)

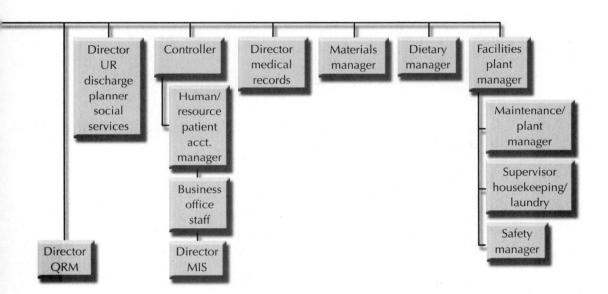

parison of the healthcare HR staffing ratios compared to other industries. Notice, for all industries, the median ratio of HR department staff to total headcount is 1.0 human resources staff member for every 100 employees in an organization.

Budgets

HR department expenditures have consistently grown over the last decade across all industries.[7] The amount of human resource expenditures per employee offers another important insight as to the organizational commitment to the human resource function.

Taken at face value, these statistics might suggest a lesser commitment across the board by healthcare organizations compared to non-healthcare

FIGURE 2-5 HR Staffing and Budgets Across Industries

MEDIAN HR STAFF PER 100 EMPLOYEES

INDUSTRY	RATIO
Communications and Information (High)	1.7
All Industries	1.0
Healthcare	0.7
Wholesale and Retail Trade (Low)	0.6

MEDIAN HR EXPENDITURES PER EMPLOYEE

INDUSTRY	EXPENDITURES
Finance, Insurance and Real Estate (High)	$1,709.00
All Industries	$813.00
Healthcare	$636.00
Wholesale and Retail Trade (Low)	$259.00

FIGURE 2-6 HR Metrics Categories

Function Measures
These measure the efficiency and effectiveness of the HR function, such as cost-per-hire data.

Operational Measures
These measure productivity and profitability relating to management and HR activities, including data relating to revenue per employee.

Strategic Measures
These are future oriented and part of the organizational planning. Data such as employee satisfaction or required versus current employee skill sets are strategic measures.

organizations. However, as noted earlier in the chapter, the healthcare industry varies both in size of organizations and how health care is provided. Similarly, this variety makes it difficult to capture absolute statistics on who in a healthcare organization is performing HR duties. As an example, in a small rural nursing home the HR function might be the responsibility of an assistant administrator who "wears many hats," including HR. That individual would most likely not be recorded in a BNA survey as an HR staff member, nor would that person's salary be accounted for as an HR expenditure.

HR METRICS

Measurement of human resources, or HR metrics, falls into three broad categories, as depicted in Figure 2-6.[8] As healthcare HR departments take steps to

FIGURE 2-7   HR Ratios and Measures for Assessment

HR FUNCTION   USEFUL RATIOS

- Selection

$$\frac{\text{Long-term vacancies}}{\text{Total jobs}}$$

$$\frac{\text{Vacancies filled internally}}{\text{Total vacancies}}$$

$$\frac{\text{Time to fill vacancy}}{\text{Total vacancies}}$$

$$\frac{\text{Offers accepted}}{\text{Offers extended}}$$

- Training

$$\frac{\text{Number of days training}}{\text{Number of employees}}$$

$$\frac{\text{Total training budget}}{\text{Total budget}}$$

- Compensation

$$\frac{\text{Total compensation costs}}{\text{Total revenue}}$$

$$\frac{\text{Benefits cost}}{\text{Payroll expenses}}$$

- Employee relations

$$\frac{\text{Resignations per year}}{\text{Total employees}}$$

$$\frac{\text{Absences}}{\text{Days worked per month}}$$

- Overall HR

$$\frac{\text{Part-time employees}}{\text{Total employees}}$$

$$\frac{\text{HR employees}}{\text{Total employees}}$$

demonstrate their organizational importance, providing a quantitative measure of their productivity is important.[9]

Within these categories, there are many useful and practical ratios and measures for assessment that provide important insights as to the effectiveness of the organizational HR program. However, it is important to choose those ratios that are relevant to the organization and measure those items that will aid the organization in improving HR results. Figure 2-7 details a series of HR ratios and measures that are typically used by healthcare organizations.

It is important to note that the types of ratios and measures depicted in Figure 2-7 are useful only when used in comparison to other data. *Comparison methodology* includes both internal and external data.

Internal data can be compared in several ways:

▶ By time: monthly, quarterly, or annually
▶ By department compared to other departments or the total organization
▶ By position (i.e. Dental Assistants, RNs, pharmacists, etc.)

External data can be compared across groups:

▶ By industry (total healthcare)
▶ By an industry segment (nursing homes, community hospitals, clinics)
▶ By a position group (professionals, managers, etc.)

The key to the effective use of HR metrics is to consistently conduct measurements and then take action based on the data. As an example, understanding the amount of time it regularly takes to fill an open position (vacancy) might suggest that there are selection process issues or compensation or benefit issues that should be addressed. Many healthcare organizations carefully study this particular ratio over time to monitor the success of their recruitment efforts and develop new initiatives if the ratio suggests a concerning trend.

A final consideration in establishing the framework for effectively managing the healthcare HR function is understanding the linkage between quality patient care delivery and HR programs.

The Delivery of Quality Care and HR Management

The process of ensuring consumers of healthcare in the United States that a particular provider of care is competent and safe takes many forms. It includes governmental oversight through the Medicare reimbursement program; local, county, and state health departments oversight; independent agencies who supply quality review information on health insurance plans and their preferred providers; and quality review organizations that perform comprehensive standard-based assessments of their subscribing members.[10]

Competitive Position   Healthcare organizations are experiencing significant change in response to ever-increasing costs, technology advances, and recruitment and retention issues. To ensure a competitive position in this climate, healthcare organizations must have a competent workforce.

Providing high-quality healthcare and achieving a competitive position in their respective marketplaces are clearly linked for healthcare providers. Business and industry groups have required health plans to disclose quality standards information on providers, evaluate the effectiveness of providers' care in certain disease categories, and to otherwise communicate how healthcare providers are providing quality care.[11] The pressure from healthcare plans on the providers to disclose outcomes information, consumer satisfaction information, and other monitors of safe patient care is having a significant impact on the healthcare industry at every level of delivery—from sole practitioner physicians to multistate integrated healthcare systems.

The dominant quality review organization in the United States is the Joint Commission on Accreditation of Healthcare Organizations (JCAHO). In this section a review of each of the JCAHO quality standards that have HR programming dimensions and how healthcare organizations meet those standards is presented.

JCAHO Process

The JCAHO surveys healthcare organizations in each of eleven administrative and clinical functions. Under each of these functions are a series of standards that must be defined and operationalized by the healthcare organizations that subscribe to JCAHO. The standards are action statements that provide specific expectations for quality achievement on a detailed basis within each function.

A team of JCAHO reviewers surveys healthcare organizations every three years to determine their accomplishment on the various standards for all of the functions. An organization that attains a satisfactory survey receives accreditation from the JCAHO. Accreditation carries with it an indication that, within the functions surveyed, the organization is substantially meeting the standards. Oftentimes, surveyed organizations will achieve overall accreditation, but will be given recommendations in certain areas to undertake improvement. These recommendations are referred to as *Type 1s.* The receipt of a Type 1 requires the organization to develop remediation plans to correct the issue. The organization is encouraged to pay close attention to Type 1 issues, because excessive Type 1s can affect the accreditation status, and JCAHO survey data are critically reviewed by insurance companies, business and industry, healthcare watchdog groups, and the individual consumers of healthcare.

Methodology of Review   The JCAHO surveyors attempt to be as comprehensive in their review of the organization's attainment of quality as possible. The JCAHO surveyors consider a variety of data points as evidence of quality and performance to determine the organization's accomplishment on a particular standard. Examples of evidence of performance for HR standards include the following:

▶ Interviews with staff members, departmental directors, and senior managers
▶ Performance evaluations or competency assessment processes
▶ Employee personnel records and job descriptions
▶ Organizational and departmental policies and procedures
▶ Staff development plans and education records
▶ Committee reports and meeting minutes
▶ Description of licensure, certificates, and credential verifications

Due to the importance JCAHO has placed on the HR standards, HR professionals typically play key roles in the preparation for a JCAHO survey and the actual on-site review.

F I G U R E   2 - 8   Healthcare Leadership Responsibilities and HR Standards

JCAHO AND MANAGEMENT OF HUMAN RESOURCES

The JCAHO's statement on HR management notes that the broad goals of the HR function are to identify and provide the right number of competent staff to meet the needs of the patients, clients, or residents served by the healthcare provider. As depicted in Figure 2-8, healthcare leaders are responsible for the following broad processes to fulfill this goal:

▶ *Planning*—This defines the qualifications, competencies, and staffing necessary to fulfill the provider's mission.
▶ *Providing Competent Staff*—The staff includes both employees of the organization and those contracted to provide service or care. Applicants' credentials must be assessed and confirmed prior to employment or service delivery.
▶ *Assessing, Maintaining, and Improving Staff Competence*—This includes ongoing periodic competence assessment and performance evaluation of staff to ensure the continuing ability of staff to perform.
▶ *Promoting Self-Development and Learning*—Leaders encourage self-development and continued learning.

FIGURE 2-9   Key Human Resource Standards

DESCRIPTION OF HUMAN RESOURCE STANDARD
Staff qualifications and performance expectations are defined.
An adequate number of staff is provided with appropriate qualifications.
Clinical and service screening indicators are used in combination with HR indicators to assess staffing effectiveness.
The relationship between patient outcomes and human resources screening indicators, such as use of overtime or staff vacancy rates, should be evaluated to determine staffing effectiveness.
Staff competence is assessed, maintained, and improved on a continuous basis.
Staff development needs are evaluated to determine and plan continuing staff education.
A work environment is created that helps staff members determine their development needs and then helps them acquire new knowledge and skills.
An orientation process is used to provide job training and information and assess the ability of the staff to fulfill initial job responsibilities.
Nonclinical staff receive orientation regarding their responsibilities relating to patient care.
Ongoing education and training is provided to maintain and improve staff competence.
Data on competence patterns and trends are assessed to identify and respond to the learning needs of the staff.
Performance evaluation, performance improvement reports, staff surveys, and needs assessment data are analyzed to assess staff competence and training needs. Data are reported to the governing body (Board) on an annual basis and are responded to by training and education.
Performance expectations are established on the individual staff member's job description and assessed.
A system is in place to periodically assess the competence of staff members. Assessment includes an evaluation of the staff members' ability to address the ages of the patients they serve.
Staff members who request not to participate in any aspect of providing patient care on the grounds of conflicting cultural values or religious beliefs are addressed.

JCAHO HR Standards—Description and Intent

HR standards are not the exclusive domain of HR professionals in healthcare organization. The JCAHO evaluates the extent to which these standards are met through a multidisciplinary approach. Figure 2-9 describes the key HR standards. These standards serve as a valuable set of guiding principles for HR policies and practices for healthcare organizations that are reviewed by JCAHO. As can be seen from these standards, healthcare HR professionals play a key role in ensuring the delivery of safe, competent healthcare by developing programming to meet these standards and documenting performance against the standards.

In addition to the impact of the HR standards on the HR function, there are other categories that also have an impact, including *leadership* (LD) and *environment of care* functions (EC). These standards, described in Figure 2-10, as with the HR standards, should be met through a multidisciplinary approach.

Throughout the book, JCAHO standards and how they impact on the HR function in healthcare organizations will be discussed. For those healthcare

FIGURE 2-10   Key Leadership Standards

DESCRIPTION OF LEADERSHIP STANDARD
Staff involved in caring for patients under legal or correctional restrictions should be appropriately oriented and educated. Issues surrounding restraint, restriction, or rights, and providing continuing care, should be planned for and facilitated.
Patient care services, including education, are based on the identified needs of the patients and consistent with the organization mission.
A budgeting process is part of the organization's plan for providing care that meets patient care needs.
The budget is responsive to staffing and educational needs of the organization. Consideration is given to performance improvement activities, including risk management and utilization management.
Programs are in place for the recruitment, retention, development, and continuing education of staff members.
Delivering quality patient care is directly linked to the organization's ability to recruit, retain, and develop a competent staff. Organizational leadership must appropriately plan and develop programming to ensure appropriate levels of staff, especially considering the: ▶ organization's mission;   ▶ case mix of its patients; and   ▶ patient care expectations.
Department heads and directors must determine the qualifications and competence of caregivers who are not licensed independent practitioners
Healthcare provision often includes a variety of staff, including those individuals who are employees of the organization, contracted individuals, and those who utilize the facility to provide care to their patients. All staff must have their qualifications and competence assessed to ensure the quality of patient care delivery.
Department heads and directors must provide orientation, in-service training and continuing education.
Staff must be trained in basic approaches to and methods of both performance improvement and patient safety improvement.
Performance improvement (PI) is a key requirement of JCAHO standards. Consistent with the various stages of the quality movement in healthcare, JCAHO has adopted an aggressive posture on the importance of continuously improving the various processes and methods of providing care. Further, this is not the exclusive purview of the organization's leaders or HR, rather *all* staff should be trained on the basic approaches to PI and should be aware of the various PI efforts being undertaken by the organization.
The hospital establishes and manages a physical environment that is designed to eliminate hazards and reduce the risk of staff injuries.
The hospital plans for worker safety.
Worker safety is a key hospital activity. It includes safety planning and developing a process for reporting and investigating occupational inquiries and exposures.
Safety and security orientation and training are regularly conducted. Staff understands their roles in maintaining a safe, secure environment.[12]

organizations that do not subscribe to JCAHO, these standards can still provide a useful template for how quality standards apply to the HR function within their environment.

THE ROLE OF HR

The HR professional in today's healthcare organization has a significant role in the quality of patient, resident, or client care. The challenges that confront healthcare organizations require HR professionals who are competent and skilled in dealing effectively with employees, supervisors, managers, and executives. How HR positions are staffed, who they report to, and the budgets available to them are extremely important. Finally, HR professionals play a vital role in providing safe, competent care as guided by the various quality standards of JCAHO.

CASE

St. Michael's Hospice Care, a not-for-profit hospice program with 250 employees, had never staffed a full-time Human Resource Manager position. In its twenty-year history, it had grown from less than a dozen initial employees to its current size. As growth occurred St. Michael's added various HR programs in response to competitive pressures, but not necessarily with any real strategic planning or direction.

Recruitment, retention, and competing cost issues continually challenged the success of the hospice program. The Administrator was constantly juggling her responsibilities and priorities between administration, finance, HR, and community relations. After a particularly heated Board of Trustees meeting where the program's HR issues were the main agenda

items, she decided to staff an HR manager position. Her decision was based on a variety of reasons, with the primary one being her desire to have an experienced HR colleague who could assist her with this critical area of responsibility. She knew she would need Board approval to staff the position, but she was confident she could make a strong argument to do so.

Questions

1. What would be some key points the Administrator could make for creating an HR manager position at St. Michael's Hospice Care Program?
2. Briefly detail the kinds of activities an HR manager should address, given what was described about St. Michaels.

END NOTES

1. Adapted from "In Our Hands, How Hospital Leaders Can Build A Thriving Workforce," *AHA Commission on Workforce for Hospitals and Health Systems* (April 2002), and "Competing For Talent, Recovering America's Hospital Workforce," *Health Care Advisory Board* (Fall 2001), and "Classified Ad: Director of Human Resources," *St. Paul Pioneer Press* (July 14, 2002).

2. Gail L. Warden and John R. Griffith, "Ensuring Management Excellence in the Healthcare System," *Journal of Healthcare Management* (July/August 2001), 228–237.

3. Adapted from "Key Middle Management Competencies Advice from the American Society for Healthcare Resources Administration," *AHA Commission on Workforce for Hospitals and Health Systems* (April 2002), 34–35.

4. Brenda Freshman and Louis Rubino, "Emotional Intelligence: A Core Competency for Health Care Administrators," *The Health Care Manager* (June 2002), 1–9.

5. Jorgen Sandberg, "Understanding Competence at Work," *Harvard Business Review* (March 2001), 24–28.

6. Carson F. Dye, "Credentials and Their Impact on Career Advancement," *Healthcare Financial Management* (June 2000), 80.

7. Bureau of National Affairs, 2001 Survey of Human Resources Activities, Budgets and Staffs.

8. Malcolm Macpherson, "Performance Measurement in Not-for-Profit and Public-Sector Organizations," *Measuring Business Excellence* (2001), 13–17.

9. Lance Richards, "HR Metrics Measured," *globalhr* (December/January 2002), 22–25.

10. Kristen Hallom, "HHS: Quality Care Key for Nursing Homes," *Modern Healthcare* (March 20, 2000), 8.

11. Lauren M. Walker, "The Quality Thing," *Business and Health* (2001), 44–47.

12. Adapted from "2002 Hospital Accreditation Standards," *Joint Commission on Accreditation of Healthcare Organizations* (2002).

CHAPTER 3

Strategic HR Management

Learning Objectives

After you have read this chapter you should be able to:

▶ Describe why a strategic view of HR is important.

▶ Discuss HR as an organizational core competency.

▶ Explain how HR planning contributes to the attainment of organizational strategies and objectives.

▶ Define HR planning in healthcare organizations.

▶ Identify three HR management challenges found in healthcare organizations.

Healthcare HR Insights

The importance of conducting an assessment of the labor market for hard-to-fill healthcare positions is critical. Patient care and service delivery can be severely impacted if an adequate supply of qualified employees is not continually available in key clinical positions. A major health system in Minnesota annually develops a "Recruitment/Workforce Development Business Plan" for its hard-to-fill positions as part of its overall HR planning. In a recruitment plan, the health system identified radiology technicians as a critical position for recruitment and retention planning initiatives. Detailed below is its workforce assessment for radiology technicians.

Radiology Workforce Overview

During the past two decades, healthcare employment has outpaced workforce growth in Minnesota. The recruitment and retention of talent is the number-one priority for both large and small healthcare organizations today, and will continue to be so for the next twenty years. Proactive workforce strategies are essential for healthcare providers to stay competitive in a tight labor market.

The shortage of radiology technicians is critical. The numbers are small and the demand is great, especially in small towns, where without a rad tech a service or clinic cannot function and must close. Overall, on a statewide level, these positions take the longest to fill. Another problem is that enrollment in radiological technician training programs is not increasing to meet the extraordinary demand. Also, the majority of these training programs are affiliated with healthcare organizations that hire graduates directly. Fewer people are in current classes when compared to other disciplines such as nursing. It is critical for the system to be involved in radiology workforce development initiatives and to strengthen creative partnerships with training programs not affiliated elsewhere.

Radiology workforce initiatives in the past twelve months have included the following:

▶ **Develop Pipeline Partnership for Radiology Technologists Positions**
The system is partnering with local colleges to develop a new radiology pipeline to fill current radiology technologist vacancies. This includes providing clinical rotations and radiology technologist scholarships.
▶ **Ultrasound Technician Scholarship**
The system is partnering with a local college to co-sponsor an Ultrasound Technician Scholarship at one of our community hospitals.

Proposed Radiology Technician Workforce Initiatives

Considering the current and projected demands for healthcare workers, the system must continue to strengthen the activities implemented previously, and continue to attract individuals into healthcare occupations and the system's workforce. The following additional initiatives are planned:

▶ **System-Level Recruitment**
With the creation of a system-level recruiting team, the health system recognizes the importance of having someone knowledgeable about the radiological job market. A dedicated radiology recruitier, will allow better coordination of recruitment efforts across the spectrum of sourcing activities (i.e., job fairs, ads, relationships with schools and training programs.)

▶ **Mammography Certification Program**
Because all mammography certification programs are currently out of state, the system will work with a local college to review the potential to offer a mammography certification program.

▶ **Healthcare Education–Industry Partnership Collaboration**
The system will work with the Minnesota State Colleges and Universities Healthcare Education–Industry Partnership to review the feasibility of implementing a radiology curriculum for a limited scope program (possibly a one-year program).

Used with permission, Fairview Health System, Minneapolis, Minnesota.

In Chapter 1, the strategic role of HR management in healthcare was introduced. A crucial strategic link is HR planning and the workforce and environmental issues that impact the HR planning process. HR management can and should play an integral role in the strategic management of an organization. Effective HR management has the potential to create a competitive advantage for an organization.

STRATEGIC HR MANAGEMENT

Many factors determine whether or not a healthcare organization will be successful. Effectiveness, efficiency, and the ability to adapt to changes in the market and many other issues are involved. Adept management will decide where the organization needs to go, how to get there, and then regularly evaluate to see if they are on track. Strategic objectives, the external environment, internal business processes, and defining how effectiveness will be measured and defined should all be addressed in the strategic management process.

HR management is (or should be) involved with all these points. For example, how can effective HR help improve the organizational productivity in a nursing home or independent practice? How can it enhance innovativeness in a medical center? This kind of thinking is indicative of strategic thinking.[1]

Strategic HR management uses employees to help an organization gain or keep a competitive advantage against its competitors. This advantage may occur through the HR department's formal contributions to organization-wide planning efforts, or by simply being knowledgeable about issues facing the organization and being prepared to make HR-related suggestions.

The development of specific business strategies must be based on the areas of strength that an organization has. Referred to as *core competencies,* these strengths are the foundation for creating a competitive advantage for an organization. A **core competency** is a unique capability in the organization that creates high value and differentiates the organization from its competition. In many organizations, HR is—or should be—a core competency.

Human Resources as a Core Competency

Certainly, many organizations have voiced the idea that their human resources differentiate them from their competitors. Organizations as widely diverse as The Mayo Clinic, The Cleveland Clinic, and Sloan-Kettering have focused on human resources as having special strategic value for their organizations.

The people in an organization become a core competency through the HR activities of attracting and retaining employees with unique professional and technical capabilities, investing in training and development of those employees, and compensating them in ways that retain and keep them competitive with their counterparts in other organizations. For example, smaller, community hospitals have attracted patient referrals because they emphasize a more personal, caring attitude rather than the impersonal approach characteristic of large medical centers. They emphasize their staff members as an advantage. Figure 3-1 shows some possible areas where human resources might become part of a core competency.

People can be the basis for an organization's core competency when they have special capabilities to make decisions and to be innovative in ways that

FIGURE 3 - 1   Possible Human Resource Areas for Core Competencies

competitors cannot easily imitate.[2] Thus, successful organizations select, train, and retain good employees. An employee group without those special abilities would *not* be a good basis for competitive advantage.

Organizational Culture

The shared values and beliefs of a workforce constitute its **organizational culture.** Managers must consider the culture of the organization because otherwise excellent strategies can be negated by a culture that is incompatible with the strategies.[3] As an example, if a clinic describes itself as being innovative and meeting the continuing technology education needs of its employees but the employees prefer a traditional, predictable work environment, the culture may be incompatible with the clinic's strategy.

In addition, the culture of the organization, as viewed by the people in it, affects attraction and retention of competent employees. Numerous examples can be given of key technical, professional, and administrative employees leaving organizations because of cultures that seem to devalue people and create barriers to the use of individual capabilities.[4]

THE HR STRATEGIC PLANNING PROCESS

Strategic planning must include planning for the people necessary to carry out the organizational strategic plan. **HR strategic planning** is the process of analyzing and identifying the need for and availability of human resources in order to accomplish the organizational objectives.[5]

The steps in the HR planning process are shown in Figure 3-2. Notice that the HR planning process begins with considering the organizational *objectives and strategies.* Then both *external* and *internal assessments* of HR needs and supply sources must be done and *forecasts* must be developed. Key to assessing internal HR is having information accessible through a human resource information system (HRIS). Once the assessments are complete, mismatches between *HR supply* and *HR demand* must be identified. HR strategies and plans to address the imbalance, both short and long term, must be developed.

HR strategies are the means used to aid the organization in managing the supply and demand for employees. These strategies provide overall direction for how HR activities will be developed and managed. Finally, specific *HR plans* are developed to provide more specific direction for the management of HR activities.

Scanning the External Environment

At the heart of strategic planning is the knowledge gained from scanning the external environment for changes. **Environmental scanning** is the process of studying the environment of the organization to pinpoint opportunities and threats. Scanning especially affects HR planning because each organization

FIGURE 3-2   HR Strategic Planning Process

must draw from the same labor market that supplies to all other employers. Indeed, one measure of organizational effectiveness is the ability of an organization to compete for a sufficient supply of human resources with the appropriate capabilities.

Many factors can influence the supply of labor available to an employer. Some of the more significant environmental factors include workforce composition and work patterns, geographic competitive concerns, economic conditions, and government influences.

Workforce Composition and Work Patterns   Changes in the composition of the workforce, combined with varied work patterns, have created workplaces and organizations that are very different from those of a decade ago. The traditional work schedule, in which employees work full time, eight hours a day, five days a week at the employer's place of operations, is in transition. Organizations have been experimenting with many different possibilities for change: the four-day, forty-hour week; the four-day, thirty-two-hour week; the three-day week; and flexible scheduling.

Many employers have adopted some flexibility in work schedules and locations. The healthcare industry has been especially aggressive in adopting approaches to flexibility in staffing as part of its recruitment and retention efforts. Changes of this nature must be considered in HR planning. Also, a growing number of healthcare employers are allowing workers to use different working arrangements. Some employees work partly at home and partly at an office, and share office space with other *office nomads*. As an example, many hospitals, clinics, and physician practices have all or part of their medical transcription work performed by employees who work out of their homes. *Telecommuting* is the process of going to work via electronic computing and telecommunications equipment.

Other employees have *virtual offices,* which means that their offices are wherever they are, whenever they are there. An office could be an unused treatment room, a conference room, or even their car. The shift to such arrangements means that work is done anywhere, anytime, and that people are judged more on results than on "putting in time." Greater trust, less direct supervision, and more self-scheduling are all job characteristics of those with virtual offices and other less-traditional arrangements.

Geographic and Competitive Concerns   Employers must consider the following geographic and competitive concerns in making HR plans:

▶ Population growth/decline in the area
▶ Other employers in the area
▶ Employee resistance to geographic relocation
▶ Direct competitors in the area
▶ Impact of international competition on the area

Economic Conditions   The general business cycle of recessions and booms also affects HR planning. Such factors as interest rates, inflation, and economic growth help determine the availability of workers and figure into organizational plans and objectives. Decisions on wages, overtime, and hiring or laying off workers all hinge on economic conditions.

Government Influences   A major element that affects labor supply is the government. Today, healthcare managers are confronted with an expanding and often bewildering array of government rules as regulation of HR activities has steadily increased. Government regulations have especially affected the healthcare industry in such areas as patient safety, medical records confidentiality, and funding. As a result, HR planning must be done by individuals who understand the legal requirements of various government regulations.

Internal Assessment of Organizational Workforce

Analyzing the jobs that will need to be done and the skills of people currently available to do them is the next part of HR planning. The needs of the organization must be compared against the labor supply available. The starting point for evaluating internal strengths and weaknesses is an audit of the jobs currently being done in the organization.

In the rapidly changing healthcare environment, the audit of jobs is especially important. As an example, the shift from inpatient to ambulatory care has had a significant impact on how care is provided and what jobs are necessary to provide that care. Healthcare providers, whether acute care hospitals, nursing homes, or physician practices, have had to continually re-assess their jobs. The following questions are addressed during the internal assessment:

▶ What jobs now exist?
▶ How many individuals are performing each job?
▶ What are the reporting relationships of jobs?
▶ How essential is each job?
▶ What jobs will be needed to implement the organizational strategy?
▶ What are the characteristics of anticipated jobs?

Organizational Capabilities Inventory   As those doing HR planning gain an understanding of current jobs and the new jobs that will be necessary to carry out organizational plans, they can prepare an "inventory" of current employees and their capabilities. The basic source of data on employees is the HR records in the organization. By using different databases, HR planners can identify the employees' capabilities, knowledge, and skills. Then these inventories could be used to determine long-range needs for recruiting, selection, and HR development.[6]

Human Resource Information Systems   Computers have simplified the task of analyzing vast amounts of data, and they can be invaluable aids in HR management, from payroll processing to record retention. With computer hardware, software, and databases, organizations can keep records and information better, as well as retrieve data more easily. A **Human Resource Information System (HRIS)** is an integrated system designed to provide information used in HR decision making. An HRIS has many uses in an organization. The most basic is the automation of payroll and benefit activities. With an HRIS, employees' time records are entered into the system, and the appropriate deductions and other individual adjustments are reflected in the final paychecks. As a result of HRIS development and implementation in many organizations, several payroll functions are being transferred from accounting departments to HR departments. Another common use of HRIS is EEO/affirmative action tracking.

HRIS and the Internet   The dramatic increase in the use of the Internet is raising possibilities and concerns for HR professionals, particularly when establishing an HRIS. Use of Web-based information systems has allowed the firms' HR units in healthcare organizations to become more administratively efficient and to be able to deal with more strategic and longer-term HR planning issues.[7]

Ensuring Security and Privacy   Two other issues of concern are *security* and *privacy*. Controls must be built into the system to restrict indiscriminate access to

HRIS data on employees. For instance, health insurance claims might identify someone who has undergone psychiatric counseling or treatment for alcoholism, and access to such information must be limited. Likewise, performance appraisal ratings on employees must be guarded.

Forecasting

The information gathered from external environmental scanning and assessment of internal strengths and weaknesses is used to predict or forecast HR supply and demand in light of organizational objectives and strategies. **Forecasting** uses information from the past and present to identify expected future conditions. Of course, projections for the future are subject to error. Changes in the conditions on which the projections are based might even completely invalidate them, which is the chance forecasters take. Usually, though, experienced people are able to forecast with enough accuracy to benefit organizational long-range planning.

Approaches to forecasting HR range from a manager's best guess to a rigorous and complex computer simulation of the labor force. As depicted in Figure 3-3, simple assumptions might be sufficient in certain instances, but complex models might be necessary for others. It is beyond the scope of this text to discuss in detail the numerous methods of forecasting available.

FIGURE 3-3 Forecasting Methods

JUDGMENTAL METHODS

- **Estimates** can be either top-down or bottom-up, but essentially people who are in a position to know are asked, "How many people will you need next year?"

- **Rules of thumb** rely on general guidelines applied to a specific situation within the organization. For example, a guideline of 1 HR employee per 150 employees aids in forecasting the number of HR employees needed in a healthcare organization. However, it is important to adapt the guidelines to recognize widely varying departmental needs.

- **The Delphi technique** uses input from a group of experts. The experts' opinions are sought using separate questionnaires on what forecasted situations will be. These expert opinions are then combined and returned to the experts for a second anonymous opinion. The process continues through several rounds until the experts essentially agree on a judgment. For example, this approach was used to forecast effects of technology on HR management and staffing needs.

- **The nominal group technique,** unlike the Delphi technique, requires experts to meet face to face. Their ideals are usually generated independently at first, discussed as a group, and then compiled as a report.

STATISTICAL METHODS

- **Statistical regression analysis** makes a statistical comparison of past relationships among various factors. For example, a statistical relationship between nursery unit census and the number of nurses needed to provide care may be useful in forecasting the number of nurses that will be needed if the number of beds on the unit are decreased.

HR forecasting should be done over three planning periods: *short range,* *intermediate,* and *long range.* The most commonly used planning period is short range, usually a period of six months to one year. This level of planning is routine in many organizations because very few assumptions about the future are necessary for such short-range plans. The main emphasis in HR forecasting to date has been on forecasting organizational need for HR, or HR demand. The demand for employees can be calculated on an organizationwide basis or calculated based on the needs of individual units in the organization.

Demand versus Supply of Human Resources   Forecasting HR can be done using two frameworks. One approach considers specific openings that are likely to occur and uses that information as the basis for planning. The openings (or demands) are created when employees leave positions because of promotions, transfers, or terminations. The analysis always begins with the top positions in the organization, because from those there can be no promotions to a higher level.

Once the need for human resources has been forecasted, then their availability or supply must be identified. Forecasting the availability of human resources considers both external and internal supplies. The external supply of potential employees available to the organization must be estimated. Here are some of the factors that may be considered:

▶ Net migration into and out of the area
▶ Individuals entering and leaving the workforce
▶ Individuals graduating from schools and colleges
▶ Economic forecasts for the next few years
▶ Technological developments and shifts

Figure 3-4 depicts the important organizational relationships that must be considered in the development of a healthcare HR strategic plan. Consistent with the contention that healthcare HR strategic planning is critical, the HR plan is derived in direct support to the organization's strategic plan, and enjoys equal status to the other functional area including patient care, finance, and marketing. Ultimately, it is truly about supporting and fulfilling the *care mission* of the organization.[8]

Successful HR Planning

There are several critical success factors to HR planning in healthcare organizations. The human resource plan should be strategically aligned, purposeful and measurable, and carefully stated. Each of these areas is discussed next.

Strategic Alignment   The HR plan must be aligned with organizational strategies and objectives. This requires HR staff and executives to be fully knowledgeable and involved in the broader strategic management of the organization to ensure that the HR plan is meeting the organizational objectives. As an example, many large surgical specialty practices have found that owning and operating same-day surgery facilities is an excellent source of revenue, especially with declining reimbursements payments. The strategic decision by

FIGURE 3-4 **HR Planning and Internal Organizational Relationships**

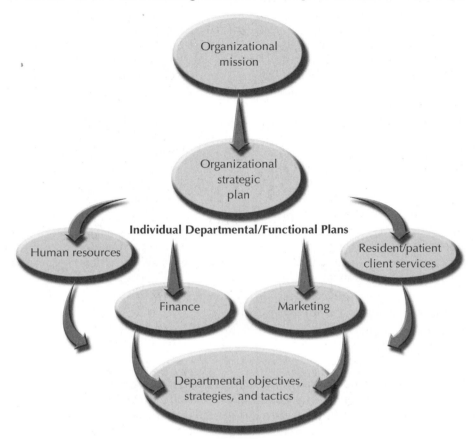

the surgeons to operate a same-day surgery center must be supported by an HR plan that would include the staffing, compensation, and employee relations of surgical nurses and technicians for the facility. The success and viability of the surgery center would, in large part, be dependent on the successful implementation of the HR plan.

Purposeful and Measurable The HR plan must be developed so that there is no ambiguity about its purpose and what it is to accomplish. In implementing and sustaining the elements of an HR plan, it is important that it is developed in such a way that progress can be tracked.

Utilizing the same-day surgery clinic example, the HR plan component for staffing the facility should include trigger points relating to patient volumes. As the facility increases the number of surgeries performed, the employment, orientation, and training of new staff must be appropriately identified and sequenced to ensure that staffing levels correspond to the growth in the patient care delivery needs of the facility.

Clearly Stated   The HR plan should be written and updated annually. HR leaders should be responsible for presenting the plan to the top executives and/or the Board or other appropriate organizational entities. Periodic updates regarding the plan's progress should also be provided. As with the other organizational plans for such areas as finance, facility management, or information technology, the HR plan should be well documented and thoroughly discussed by the Board or the ownership of the organization. In the surgery center example, the implementation of the staffing component of the HR plan would carry significant costs that should be acknowledged and agreed to by the Board.

INPUTS TO THE HEALTHCARE HR STRATEGIC PLAN

A strategic plan cannot be created in a vacuum. Figure 3-5 depicts the inputs to the healthcare HR strategic plan: For the HR plan to be useful, it must take into

FIGURE 3-5   Inputs to the Healthcare HR Strategic Plan

account a number of important internal and external organizational inputs. A look at each of these areas in Figure 3-5 follows:

▶ *Organizational Mission*—The purest definition of *mission* is answering the question, "Why does the organization exist?" Healthcare organizations rarely struggle with this question; in fact, one of the true strengths of healthcare providers is the clarity of their care delivery mission. Two examples of healthcare organizational mission statements follow:

   ▶ *Orthopedic Specialty Practice*—It is the mission of Metro Orthopedics to provide the highest quality of orthopedic surgical care.

   ▶ *Nursing Home*—The mission of Spring Valley Nursing Facility is to be respectful and compassionate in all aspects of our care for our residents. We will be mindful of their special needs and the importance of communicating with their loved ones.

▶ *Organizational Objectives and Strategies*—In many instances, organizational objectives and strategies include significant HR considerations, especially regarding workforce planning, compensation, and executive and management staffing. The HR plan should cover the regular and routine HR aspects of supporting organizational functioning such as staffing and employee relations. It should also include new initiatives or objectives of the organization, such as the implementation of new service lines, acquisitions, or mergers.

▶ *Environmental Assessment*—As detailed earlier in the chapter, evaluating the environment is extremely important to the management of human resources. The HR plan must fully and comprehensively consider external environmental issues and opportunities.

▶ *Organizational Resources and Capabilities*—The HR plan must take into effect the volume or productivity requirements of the organization. For instance, for hospitals, measurement of patient census, patient days, admissions, and average length of stay are critical data points to be used in developing staffing plans in order to match resources with organizational capabilities.

▶ *Financial Realities*—Financial decisions, including budgetary allocations and capital expenditures, affect every aspect of HR management. The HR plan must be financially responsible and realistic, while maintaining consistent levels of support for such HR activities as staffing, compensation, and benefit administration. Financial resources needed for new human resource initiatives also must be considered.

▶ *Plans of Other Functional Areas*—Effective HR planning should be both supportive and compatible with the planning of all the other functional areas within the organization, such as patient care, surgery, or finance. The actual development of the HR plan should be in line with the development of the plans for the other areas.

HEALTHCARE TRENDS AND HR PLANNING

HR's leadership role in healthcare is especially important due to the current state and future trends of the industry. Many of the most compelling issues and concerns in healthcare are, in fact, HR issues. Acknowledging this fact, the American Hospital Association (AHA) Strategic Planning Policy Committee identified seven major strategic HR implications and issues for hospitals and other healthcare providers:

1. *Healthcare is fundamentally about people caring for people.* It depends on appropriate numbers of motivated and well-trained caregivers and support personnel. Although electronic and automated systems might change the nature of some work, they will not replace hands-on care.
2. *Women have greater options.* Given employment preference changes and greater career opportunities for women, it is unlikely that the favorable employment environment of the 1960s and 1970s will return for hospitals.
3. *Healthcare leaders must view their human resources as a strategic asset.* This asset is different from, but as important as, adequate revenue, capital acquisition, and market share.
4. *Preferred work arrangements in healthcare organizations require a broader perspective on employee relations to build loyalty and create a sense of stability.* Some providers have expanded the use of agency and temporary staff to create more staffing flexibility. Without a more stable employer relationship, these employees have loyalty to their profession rather than to the organization. At the same time, regular staff, full-time and part-time, find the work environment increasingly hectic and uncertain. Some are looking to unions and collective bargaining as a means of increasing their sense of stability.
5. *Education needs of healthcare workers are a critical issue.* Educational systems need providers to help them identify what skills and capabilities are most in demand in the labor market.
6. *New technologies should allow staff to focus on the care giving and support functions of their positions.* This capability is essential for providers to attract, develop, and retain employees.
7. *The workforce will only expand if hospitals can recruit staff from the general economy.* The workforce shortage can only be corrected if a concerted effort is made to make healthcare careers seem more attractive than other employment options.[9]

Therefore, HR strategic planning for healthcare providers of all sizes and types is critical. As noted in the JCAHO feature on the next page the careful crafting and implementation of a well-reasoned, dynamic, and responsive plan is vital to the survival of a healthcare organization. Failure to have an HR plan results in a reactive approach to managing human resources, which is likely to affect the HR activities of recruitment and retention; training and development; employee labor relations; and other critical areas of HR management.[10]

HEALTHCARE HR MANAGEMENT CHALLENGES

The environment faced by HR management is a challenging one because changes are occurring rapidly across a wide range of issues. A study by the Hudson Institute, titled *Workforce 2020,* has highlighted some of the more important workforce issues that are identified in the following sections.[11]

Workforce Availability and Quality

Workforce availability and quality issues are not unique to the healthcare industry. In many parts of the United States, significant workforce shortages exist due to an inadequate supply of workers with the skills needed to perform the jobs being added. A few years ago, news reports have regularly described tight labor markets, with unemployment rates in some locales below 3%. During more recent times, the unemployment rates have increased; however, the shortage of healthcare workers continues. Also, industries and companies continually report shortages of qualified, experienced workers. Today, *contingent workers* (temporary workers, independent contractors, leased employees, and part-timers) represent

THE JOINT COMMISSION ON ACCREDITATION OF HEALTHCARE ORGANIZATIONS

Staffing Plan Development

As detailed in Chapters 1 and 2, the major quality review organization for hospitals, nursing facilities, laboratories, and outpatient care facilities associated with hospitals is the Joint Commission for the Accreditation of Healthcare Organizations (JCAHO) which includes HR planning in its review process. The major thrust of those standards include the following:

The *staffing plans* should
▶ Meet patient care needs for each unit or area
▶ Include staff qualifications—skills, knowledge, licensure, education, and certification
▶ Plan to manage gaps between planned and actual staffing levels at anytime

Development and implementation of a *competency system* should
▶ Ensure the recruitment, employment and maintenance of a well qualified and competent staff
▶ Include ongoing competency assessment
▶ Design programs to meet staff learning and development needs

more than 20% of the workforce. Many employers operate with a core group of regular employees with critical skills, and then expand and contract the workforce through the use of contingent workers. This practice requires determining staffing needs and deciding in advance which employees and positions should form the core group and which should be more flexible.

Economic and Technological Change

Several economic changes have altered employment and occupational patterns in the United States. A major change is the shift of jobs from manufacturing and agriculture to service industries and telecommunications. This shift has meant that some organizations have had to reduce the number of employees, while others have had to attract and retain employees with different capabilities than previously were needed. This is especially true for healthcare. As noted in Chapter 1, more than 11 million individuals are employed within healthcare, and the addition of new jobs in healthcare is predicted to continue. Figure 3-6 depicts this trend.

Occupational Shifts

Projections of the growth and decline in jobs illustrate the economic and employment shifts currently occurring. It is interesting to note that most of the fastest-growing occupations (percentage wise) are related to information technology or healthcare. The increase in technology jobs is due to the rapid increase in the use of information technology, such as databases, system design and analysis, and desktop publishing. Also, as depicted in Figure 3-6 healthcare

F I G U R E   3 - 6   Projected Growth in Key Healthcare Occupations, 2000 to 2010

MANAGEMENT OCCUPATIONS	2000	PROJECTED 2010
Medical and Health Services Managers	167,000	225,000
PROFESSIONAL OCCUPATIONS		
Medical Records and Health Information Technicians	118,000	182,000
Social Workers	110,000	151,000
Physical Therapists	109,000	149,000
SERVICE OCCUPATIONS		
Home Health Aides	261,000	416,000
Dental Assistants	237,000	327,000
Home Care Aides	160,000	267,000
OFFICE AND ADMINISTRATIVE SUPPORT		
Receptionists and Information Clerks	288,000	365,000
Medical Secretaries	280,000	336,000
Billing and Posting Clerks	166,000	214,000

Source: U.S. Department of Labor Bureau of Labor Statistics.

jobs are also growing—primarily due to the aging of the U.S. population and workforce, a factor discussed later.

Lost manufacturing jobs in the United States are increasingly being replaced with jobs in information technology, financial services, healthcare, and retail services. It is estimated that manufacturing jobs will represent only 12 to 15% of all U.S. jobs by 2010. In summary, the U.S. economy is becoming a service economy, and that shift is expected to continue. More than 80% of U.S. jobs are in service industries, and most new jobs will also be in services.

Diversity

Diversity is seen in demographic differences in the workforce. The shifting makeup of the U.S. population accounts for today's increased workforce diversity. Many organizations are hiring employees from a more diverse pool of potential workers. Organizations have been seeing the effects of changing demographic trends for several years. A more detailed look at some of the key changes follows, as noted by the U.S. Department of Labor:[12]

▶ Total workforce growth will be slower between 2000 and 2006 than in previous decades.
▶ Only one-third of the entrants to the workforce between 2000 and 2005 will be white males.
▶ Women will constitute a greater proportion of the labor force than in the past, and 63% of all U.S. women will be in the workforce by 2005.
▶ Minority racial and ethnic groups will account for a growing percentage of the overall labor force. Immigrants will expand this growth.
▶ The average age of the U.S. population will increase, and more workers who retire from full-time jobs will work part time.
▶ As a result of these and other shifts, employers in a variety of industries will face shortages of qualified workers.

Women in the Workforce The influx of women into the workforce has major social and economic consequences. Implications for HR management of more women working include the following:

▶ Greater flexibility in work patterns and schedules to accommodate women with family responsibilities, part-time work interests, or other pressures[13]
▶ More variety in benefits programs and HR policies, including child-care assistance and parental leave programs
▶ Greater employer awareness of gender-related legal issues such as sexual harassment and sex discrimination

Aging of the Workforce Most of the developed countries—including Australia, Japan, most European countries, and the United States—are experiencing an aging of their populations. Implications of the aging of the U.S. workforce include the following:

▶ Retirement will change in character as organizations and older workers choose phased retirements, early retirement buyouts, and part-time work.

▶ Service industries, including the healthcare industry, are actively recruiting senior workers for many jobs.[14]

▶ Retirement benefits will increase in importance, particularly pension and healthcare coverage for retirees.

Individuals with Disabilities in the Workforce   With the passage of the Americans with Disabilities Act (ADA) in 1990, employers were reminded of their responsibilities for employing individuals with disabilities. At least 43 million Americans with disabilities are covered by the ADA. Implications of greater employment of individuals with disabilities include the following:

▶ Employers must define more precisely what are the essential tasks in jobs and what knowledge, skills, and abilities are needed to perform each job.

▶ Accommodating individuals with disabilities will become more common as employers provide more flexible work schedules, altering facilities, and purchasing special equipment.

▶ Employment-related health and medical examination requirements must be revised to avoid discriminating against individuals with disabilities.

Individuals with Differing Sexual Orientations in the Workforce   A growing number of employers are facing legislative efforts to protect individuals with differing sexual orientations from employment discrimination, though at present only a few cities and states have passed such laws. Implications of these issues include the following:

▶ The potential for workplace conflicts is heightened as people with different lifestyles and sexual orientations work together. Training to reduce such workplace conflicts will be necessary.

▶ Generally, managers must recognize that they should not attempt to "control" off-the-job behavior of employees unless it has a direct, negative effect on the organization.

Balancing Work and Family   For many workers in the United States, including healthcare workers, balancing the demands of family and work is a significant challenge. Although this balancing has always been a concern, the growth in the number of working women and dual-career couples has resulted in greater tensions for many workers. To respond to these concerns, many employers are facing pressures to provide "family-friendly" policies and benefits. The assistance given by employer's ranges from maintaining references on childcare providers to establishing on-site childcare and eldercare facilities. Also, according to the Family and Medical Leave Act, employers with at least fifty workers must provide up to twelve weeks of unpaid parental/family leave.

Organizational Restructuring

Many healthcare organizations have restructured in the past few years in response to lower revenues and heightened cost pressures. As part of the organizational changes, many organizations have "rightsized" by: (1) eliminating layers of managers; (2) closing facilities; (3) merging with other organizations; or (4) outplacing workers. A common transformation has been to flatten organizations by removing several layers of management and to improve productivity, quality, and service while also reducing costs. As a result, jobs are redesigned and people affected. One of the challenges that HR management faces with organizational restructuring is dealing with the human consequences of such changes.[15] One of the major reasons why healthcare organizations engage in restructuring is to increase productivity.

Organizational Productivity in Healthcare

The more productive a healthcare organization is, the better its ability to provide care at lower cost. Better productivity does not necessarily mean more care is provided; perhaps fewer people (or less money or time) were used to provide the same amount of care. A useful way to measure the productivity of a workforce is the total cost of people per unit of output. In its most basic sense, **productivity** is a measure of the quantity and quality of work done, considering the cost of the resources it took to do the work. It is also useful to view productivity as a ratio between organizational input and output. There are many useful measures of productivity for healthcare organizations, such as the following:

▶ *Hospitals*—Cost per adjusted patient day
▶ *Clinics*—Cost per clinic hour
▶ *Surgical Centers*—Cost per surgery hour
▶ *Nursing Homes*—Cost per resident day

The difficulty for most healthcare organizations is to define a consistent unit of output for which costs can be measured. These measures also must be set so that they can to be tracked and compared over a period of time.

Productivity at the organizational level ultimately affects profitability and competitiveness in a for-profit organization and total costs in a not-for-profit organization. Decisions made about the value of an organization often are based on its productivity.

Perhaps the resources used for productivity in organizations most closely scrutinized are human resources. Many of the activities undertaken in an HR system deal with individual or organizational productivity. Appraisal systems, training, selection, job design, and compensation are HR activities concerned directly with productivity.

The healthcare industry has made significant efforts to improve organizational productivity. Many productivity improvement efforts have focused on the workforce. The early stages included downsizing, reengineering jobs, increasing computer usage, and working employees harder. These approaches have done as much good as possible in some firms. Some ideas for the next step in productivity improvement include the following:

▶ Outsourcing
▶ Making workers more efficient with capital equipment
▶ Replacing workers with equipment and technology
▶ Helping workers work better
▶ Redesigning the work

The pursuit of productivity in healthcare is a continual process. Healthcare industry leaders are very aware of their responsibility to provide safe, competent care at the lowest cost possible to healthcare consensus. New, innovative initiatives are continually brought forward to achieve these important objectives. At the center of many of these initiatives are HR plans and programs.

CASE

Loganville Community Hospital (LCH) is a twenty-six-bed hospital located in a rural area of East Central Nebraska. It is seventy-five miles away from the closest large city and serves a region of Nebraska with a population base of approximately 14,000 people.

LCH employs 200 employees, 40 of which are in nursing positions; including 14 R.N.s and 26 L.P.N.s.

LCH's Board of Trustees is made up of various community and business leaders who are concerned about the hospital's future. As a community hospital, its operating and capital budget is supported through a small tax levy. Due to excellent fiscal control and planning, the financial condition of the hospital far exceeded its peer group. However, the Board commissioned a study of its workforce and was alarmed by the following findings:

▶ By the year 2010, 66% of the current nursing employees will be at retirement age.

▶ The primary source of nursing candidates has been from individuals with nursing training that live within a thirty-mile radius of Loganville. Of the current nursing employees, 80% are originally from Loganville (attended Loganville High School) and went away to college for nursing training and returned to the area to pursue their careers. However, most recent graduates of Loganville High School are not entering nursing school as often, and are not returning to Loganville as others before them did.

▶ No current workforce replacement plan is in place to deal with the nursing employee attrition expected over the next decade.

Questions

1. Define the role of HR in dealing with this critical workforce planning issue.
2. Apply the HR planning process in addressing this issue.

END NOTES

1. Luis Gomez-Mejia "Moving Forward," *HR News* (Spring 2000), 1–2.

2. Michael A. Hitt, et al., "Direct and Moderating Effects of Human Capital on Strategy and Performance in Professional Services Firms," *Academy of Management Journal,* 44 (2001), 13.

3. Caroline J. Fisher, "Like It or Not . . . Culture Matters," *Employment Relations Today* (Summer 2000), 43–51.

4. Daniel M. Cable, et al., "The Source and Accuracy of Job Applicants' Beliefs About Organizational Culture," *Academy of Management Journal,* 43 (2000), 1076–1086.

5. Mary Cheddie, "How to Become a Strategic Partner," *HR Focus* (August 2001), 1, 13+.

6. Patricia M. Buhler, "Managing in the New Millennium," *Supervision* (October 2001), 13.

7. Bill Roberts, "Native or Enabled: What's the Difference?" *HR Magazine* (August 2001), 101–109.

8. David Brown, "HR's Role in Business Strategy: Still a Lot of Work to be Done," *Canadian HR Reporter* (November 5, 2001), 20+.

9. "Workforce Supply for Hospitals and Health Systems," *Trustee* (June 2001), 1–4.

10. Ellen G. Lanser, "Lessons form the Business Side of Healthcare," *Healthcare Executive* (September/October 2000), 14–19.

11. Richard W. Judy and Carol D'Amico, *Workforce 2020: Work and Workers in the 21st Century* (Indianapolis, IN: Hudsen Institute, 1997).

12. U.S. Department of Labor, Bureau of Labor Statistics, 2001.

13. D'Vera Cohn, "Percentage of New Mothers in Workplace Fell Last Year," *The Washington Post* (October 18, 2001), A. 2.

14. Sharon D. Laduke, "Shades of Grey," *Nursing Management* (April 2001), 42.

15. Jeffrey A. Schmidt, "The Correct Spelling of M & A Begins with HR," *HR Magazine* (June 2001), 102–108.

CHAPTER 4

Legal Issues Affecting the Healthcare Workplace

Learning Objectives

After you have read this chapter, you should be able to:

▶ Describe the major laws affecting the healthcare workplace.

▶ Define what are lawful and unlawful pre-employment inquiries.

▶ Discuss the components of an Affirmative Action Plan (AAP).

▶ Identify the important elements of a sexual harassment prevention program.

▶ Describe the steps in responding to an EEO complaint.

▶ Compare and contrast legal responsibilities and ethics.

Healthcare HR Insights

A major hospital maintains a large security force. The security personnel are employees of the hospital. The most important role of the security employees is to maintain a safe and secure environment for the patients, visitors, and employees of the hospital.

One of the key functions of the security employees is fire safety, both from a preventative perspective and in the event of an emergency as a first responder. The security department managers determined that significant similarities existed in terms of physical capability requirements for their security officers and the local city fire personnel. Consequently, the hospital adopted the physical requirement standards for new hire assessment that were utilized by the city fire department. These standards included rigorous weight lifting and carrying requirements.

Applicants for open positions in the security department were required to pass a series of physical ability tests (PATs) designed to assess their ability to perform certain duties in the event of a fire rescue situation. The most difficult of these tests was the requirement to lift and carry a 160-pound manikin 100 feet. This test was designed to simulate a rescue of an unconscious adult from an unsafe situation. Based on an applicant's ability to successfully complete this test within a reasonable time period, he/she would be considered for employment with the hospital in a security officer position.

A female applicant, with extensive security experience including military police training, applied for a security position with the hospital. The initial assessment of her credentials, including an evaluative interview, indicated that she was qualified for the position pending her performance on the PATs. She successfully completed every test except the fire rescue simulation. She was unable to lift and carry the manikin; consequently, she was formally notified that she could not be employed by the hospital in the position of security officer because she did not pass all aspects of the PATs.

The applicant subsequently filed a charge against the hospital with the Equal Employment Opportunity Commission (EEOC) alleging discrimination on the basis of sex and disability. In her charge she alleged that the PAT was designed to eliminate female applicants from qualifying for the security officer position. Further, due to a back injury she had sustained in the Army, which left her with a chronic back condition, she had protection under the Americans with Disability Act (ADA) as a disabled individual. She was contending that the fire rescue requirement of the security officer position was not an essential function of the job.

In response to EEOC investigative inquiries, the hospital's HR department, in conjunction with the legal department, countered the charges, denying discrimination on the basis of sex or disability. They also defended the use of the PAT as job-related, including the requirements of all hospital security officers to be able to rescue unconscious victims in fire situations.

The EEOC evaluated the hospital's arguments, including an assessment of the security department statistics on the number of male and female applicants and employees. The statistical assessment indicated that since the PAT was implemented, no females had been employed by the hospital in the capacity of a security officer.

The EEOC ruled in favor of the female applicant ordering the hospital to employ her and provide her with back pay. Further, they instructed the hospital to discontinue the use of the fire rescue simulation test or to adjust the test to eliminate any disparate treatment or impact. The hospital agreed to employ the female applicant and pay her back pay and suspend the use of the fire rescue simulation pending further study.

Ensuring that all employment-related decisions are fair and consistent with equal employment opportunity law is an important responsibility of healthcare HR professionals. Applicants must be adequately assessed for job-related skills, knowledge, and ability to comply with EEO requirements. HR professionals in healthcare organizations must design effective processes for evaluating the job-related competency of applicants and protect their employment rights.

The major thrust of employment law is equal opportunity for all individuals in the crucial area of employment rights. The Civil Rights Act of 1964, which contained Title VII—Equal Employment Opportunity, was the first modern-day legislation designed to deal with employment discrimination in this country. At the time of its passage, Congress had found a pattern of exclusion, discrimination, segregation, and inferior treatment of minorities and women in many employment areas.

Ensuring equal opportunity and fair treatment in the healthcare workplace is the responsibility of every healthcare leader who makes employment-related decisions. Clearly HR professionals in healthcare organizations shoulder a significant portion of the responsibility due to their role in the organization. Consequently, HR practitioners must be extremely knowledgeable about the laws that impact the workplace to provide leadership, compliance oversight, and consultation to the managers and staff.

EQUAL EMPLOYMENT OPPORTUNITY AND AFFIRMATIVE ACTION

Equal employment opportunity (EEO) Equal employment opportunity (EEO) is a broad concept holding that individuals should have equal treatment in all employment-related actions. Individuals who are covered under equal employment laws are protected from illegal discrimination, which occurs when individuals having a common characteristic are discriminated against based on that characteristic. Various laws have been passed to protect individuals who share certain characteristics, such as race, age, or gender. Those having the designated characteristics are referred to as members of a **protected class.** The following bases for protection have been identified by various federal laws:

▶ Race, ethnic origin, color (African Americans, Hispanic Americans, Native Americans, Asian Americans)
▶ Gender (women, including those who are pregnant)
▶ Age (individuals over age 40)
▶ Individuals with disabilities (physical or mental)
▶ Military experience (Vietnam-era veterans)
▶ Religion (special beliefs and practices)

Affirmative Action

To remedy areas in which it appears that individuals in protected classes have not had equal employment opportunities, some employers have developed affirmative action policies. Affirmative action occurs when employers identify problem areas, set goals, and take positive steps to guarantee equal employment opportunities for people in a protected class. Affirmative action focuses on hiring, training, and promoting protected-class members where they are *underrepresented* in an organization in relation to their availability in the labor markets from which recruiting occurs. Sometimes employers have instituted affirmative action voluntarily, but many times employers have been required to do so because they are government contractors with more than fifty employees and more than $50,000 in government contracts annually.

Reverse Discrimination

When equal employment opportunity regulations are discussed, probably the most volatile issue concerns the view that affirmative action leads to *quotas, preferential selection,* and *reverse discrimination.* At the heart of the conflict is the employer's role in selecting, training, and promoting protected-class members when they are underrepresented in various jobs in an organization. Those who are not members of any protected class have claimed that there is discrimination in reverse.

This reverse discrimination may exist when a person is denied an opportunity because of preferences given to a member of a protected class who may be less qualified. Specifically, some critics charge that white males are at a disadvantage today, even though they traditionally have held many of the better jobs. Affirmative action as a concept is under attack by some courts and employers, as well as by some males and nonminorities. Whether that trend continues will depend on future changes in the makeup of the U.S. Supreme Court and the results of presidential and congressional elections.

FIGURE 4-1 **Major Federal Equal Employment Opportunity Laws and Regulations**

ACT	YEAR	PROVISIONS
Equal Pay Act	1963	Requires equal pay for men and women performing substantially the same work
Title VII, Civil Rights Act of 1964	1964	Prohibits discrimination in employment on basis of race, color, religion, sex, or national origin
Executive Orders 11246 and 11375	1965 1967	Require federal contractors and subcontractors to eliminate employment discrimination and prior discrimination through affirmative action
Age Discrimination in Employment Act (as amended in 1978 and 1986)	1967	Prohibits discrimination against persons over age 40 and restricts mandatory retirement requirements, except where age is a bona fide occupational qualification
Executive Order 11478	1969	Prohibits discrimination in the U.S. Postal Service and in the various government agencies on the basis of race, color, religion, sex, national origin, handicap, or age
Vocational Rehabilitation Act Rehabilitation Act of 1974	1973 1974	Prohibit employers with federal contracts over $2,500 from discriminating against individuals with disabilities
Vietnam-Era Veterans Readjustment Act	1974	Prohibits discrimination against Vietnam-era veterans by federal contractors and the U.S. government and requires affirmative action
Pregnancy Discrimination Act	1978	Prohibits discrimination against women affected by pregnancy, childbirth, or related medical conditions; requires that they be treated as all other employees for employment-related purposes, including benefits
Immigration Reform and Control Act	1986 1990 1996	Establishes penalties for employers who knowingly hire illegal aliens; prohibits employment discrimination on the basis of national origin or citizenship
Americans with Disabilities Act	1990	Requires employer accommodation of individuals with disabilities
Older Workers Benefit Protection Act of 1990	1990	Prohibits age-based discrimination in early retirement and other benefits plans
Civil Rights Act of 1991	1991	Overturns several past Supreme Court decisions and changes damage claims provisions
Congressional Accountability Act	1995	Extends EEO and Civil Rights Act Provisions to U.S. congressional staff

Major Employment Laws

Numerous federal, state, and local laws address equal employment opportunity concerns. Figure 4-1 presents an overview of the major laws, regulations, and concepts. They are discussed in more detail in the remainder of this chapter.

Civil Rights Act of 1964, Title VII

Although the first civil rights act was passed in 1866, it was not until the passage of the Civil Rights Act of 1964 that the keystone of antidiscrimination legislation was put into place. The Civil Rights Act of 1964 was passed in part to bring about equality in all employment-related decisions. As is often the case, the law contains ambiguous provisions giving considerable leeway to agencies that enforce the law. The Equal Employment Opportunity Commission (EEOC) was established to enforce the provisions of Title VII, the portion of the act that deals with employment. This section discusses key aspects of the Civil Rights Act; other sections will deal with specific provisions of the act in more detail.

EEOC Compliance

Employers must comply with EEOC regulations and guidelines. To do so, management should have an EEO policy statement and maintain all required EEO-related records. This policy should be widely disseminated throughout the organization. All employers with fifteen or more employees are required to keep certain records that can be requested by the EEOC. The basic report that must be filed with the EEOC is the annual report form EEO-1.

Pre-Employment versus After-Hire Inquiries   Figure 4-2 lists pre-employment inquiries and identifies whether they may or may not be discriminatory. The following list further identifies circumstances that permit or prohibit certain pre-employment inquiries:

▶ Employers acting under bona fide Affirmative Action Programs or acting under orders of Equal Employment law enforcement agencies of federal, state or local governments may make some of the prohibited inquiries to the extent that the inquiries are required by such programs or orders.

▶ Employers having federal defense contracts are exempt to the extent that certain inquiries are required by federal law for security purposes.

▶ Any inquiry is prohibited that, although not specifically listed above, elicits information that is not job related and that may be used to discriminate on the basis of race, color, religion, sex, national origin, disability, or ancestry in violation of law.

Once an employer tells an applicant he or she is hired (the "point of hire"), inquiries that were prohibited earlier may be made. After hiring, medical examination forms, group insurance cards, and other enrollment cards containing inquiries related directly or indirectly to sex, age, or other bases may be requested. Photographs or evidence of race, religion, or national origin also may be requested after hire for legal and compliance purposes, but not before. Such data should be maintained in a separate personnel records system in order to avoid their use in making appraisal, discipline, termination, or promotion decisions.

FIGURE 4-2 Lawful and Unlawful Pre-Employment Inquiries

INQUIRIES BEFORE HIRING	LAWFUL	UNLAWFUL
1. Name	Name	Inquiry into any title, which indicates race, color, religion, sex, national origin, handicap or ancestry
2. Address	Inquiry into place and length of current address	Inquiry into foreign address that would indicate national origin
3. Age	▲ Requiring proof of age in form of work permit issued by school authorities ▲ Requiring proof of age by birth certificate or otherwise after hiring	Requiring birth certificate or baptismal record before hiring
4. Birthplace or National Origin		▲ Any inquiry into place of birth ▲ Any inquiry into place of birth of parents, grandparents, or spouse
5. Race or Color		Any inquiry that would indicate race or color
6. Sex		Any inquiry that would indicate sex
7. Religion–Creed		▲ Any inquiry that would indicate or identify religious denomination or custom ▲ Telling applicant of any religious identity or preference of the employer ▲ Requesting religious leaders' recommendation/reference
8. Physical Limitations (requirements)	Inquiries necessary to determine applicant's ability to substantially perform job related functions and to determine accommodations, if any	▲ Disease diagnosis ▲ Receipt of worker's compensation
9. Citizenship	▲ Whether a U.S. Citizen ▲ Whether applicant can legally work in the United States	▲ If native-born or naturalized ▲ Whether parents or spouse are native-born or naturalized ▲ Proof of citizenship before offer
10. Photographs		Requiring photographs before hiring
11. Arrests and Convictions	Inquiries into conviction of specific crimes related to the job for which the applicant applied	▲ Any inquiry which would reveal arrests without convictions ▲ Convictions unrelated to the job responsibilities

INQUIRIES BEFORE HIRING	LAWFUL	UNLAWFUL
12. Education	▸ Inquiry into nature and extent of academic, professional, or vocational training ▸ Inquiry into language skills such as reading and writing of foreign languages, if job related	▸ Any inquiry asking specifically the nationality or racial or religious affiliation of a school ▸ Inquiry as to what mother tongue is or how foreign language ability was acquired
13. Relatives	Names of relatives already employed by employer	Any inquiry about a relative that would be unlawful if made about the applicant
14. Organizations	Inquiry into organization memberships and offices held, excluding any organization, the name or character of which indicates the race, color, religion, sex, national origin, handicap or ancestry of its members	Inquiry into *all* clubs and organizations where membership is held
15. Military Service	▸ Inquiry into service in U.S. Armed Forces when such service is a qualification for the job ▸ Requiring military discharge certificate after being hired	▸ Inquiry into military service in armed service of any country but United States ▸ Requesting military service records ▸ Type of discharge
16. Work Schedule	Inquiry into willingness to work required work schedule	Any inquiry into willingness to work any particular religious holiday
17. Other Qualifications	Any question required to reveal qualifications for the job applied for	Any non-job related inquiry which may reveal information permitting unlawful discrimination
18. References	General, personal, and work references not relating to race, color, religion, sex, national origin, handicap or ancestry	Request references specifically from any persons who might reflect race, color, religion, sex, national origin, handicap, or ancestry of applicant

Bona Fide Occupational Qualification (BFOQ)   Title VII of the 1964 Civil Rights Act specifically states that employers may discriminate on the basis of sex, religion, or national origin if the characteristic can be justified as a "bona fide occupational qualification reasonably necessary to the normal operation of the particular business or enterprise."[1] Thus, a **bona fide occupational qualification (BFOQ)** is a legitimate reason why an employer can exclude persons on otherwise illegal bases of consideration.

What constitutes a BFOQ has been subject to different interpretations in various courts across the country. In a Pennsylvania case, a social services agency exempted women from evening duty in a high-crime area. The agency said its policy was implemented to protect female program administrators as a BFOQ after several women quit rather than work the evening shift. However, a male employee who was terminated for complaining about having to work the night shift sued the agency. The court ruled that the agency had not proved that sex was a reasonably necessary BFOQ, and found for the male employee. In other instances, legal uses of BFOQs have been found for hiring female caregivers in sensitive positions dealing with female patients.

Disparate Treatment and Disparate Impact   It would seem that the motives or intentions of the employer might enter into the determination of whether discrimination has occurred. However it is the outcome of the employer's actions, not the intent, that will be considered by the regulatory agencies or courts when deciding if illegal discrimination has occurred. Two concepts used to activate this principle are *disparate treatment* and *disparate impact.*

Disparate treatment occurs when protected-class members are treated differently from others. For example, if female applicants must take a special skills test not given to male applicants, then disparate treatment may be occurring. If disparate treatment has occurred, the courts generally have said that intentional discrimination exists.

Disparate impact occurs when there is substantial underrepresentation of protected-class members as a result of employment decisions that work to their disadvantage. The landmark case that established the importance of disparate impact as a legal foundation of EEO law is *Griggs v. Duke Power* (1971).[2] The decision of the U.S. Supreme Court established two major points:

1. It is not enough to show a lack of discriminatory intent if the employment tool results in a disparate impact that discriminates against one group more than another or continues a past pattern of discrimination.
2. The employer has the burden of proving that an employment requirement is directly job-related as a "business necessity." Consequently, the intelligence test and high school diploma requirements of Duke Power were ruled not to be related to the job.

Therefore, employers covered by Title VII must be able to document through numerical calculations and statistical analyses that disparate treatment and disparate impact have not occurred.

Burden of Proof   Another legal issue that arises when discrimination is alleged is the determination of which party has the *burden of proof*. At issue is what individuals who are filing suit against employers must prove in order to establish that illegal discrimination has occurred. Building on an earlier case *(McDonnell Douglas v. Green)*, the U.S. Supreme Court in *Reeves v. Sanderson Plumbing Products* ruled that circumstantial evidence could shift the burden of proof to the employer.[3]

Based on the evolution of court decisions, current laws and regulations state that the plaintiff charging discrimination: (1) must be a *protected-class member* and (2) must prove that *disparate impact* or *disparate treatment* existed. Once a court rules that a *prima facie* (preliminary) case has been made, the burden of proof shifts to the employer. The employer then must show that the bases for making employment-related decisions were specifically job related and consistent with considerations of business necessity.

Retaliation   Employers are prohibited by EEO laws from retaliating against individuals who file discrimination charges. Retaliation occurs when employers take punitive actions against individuals who exercise their legal rights. For example, an organization was ruled to have engaged in retaliation when an employee who filed a discrimination complaint had work hours reduced, resulting in a loss of pay, and no other employees' work hours were reduced.[4]

Civil Rights Act of 1991

The Civil Rights Act of 1991 requires employers to show that an employment practice is *job-related for the position* and is consistent with *business necessity*. The act clarifies that the plaintiffs bringing the discrimination charges must identify the particular employer practice being challenged and must show only that protected-class status played *some factor*. For employers, this means that an individual's race, color, religion, sex, or national origin *must play no factor* in their employment practices.

Compensatory/Punitive Damages and Jury Trials   The major impact of the 1991 act is that it allows victims of discrimination on the basis of sex, religion, or disability to receive both *compensatory* and *punitive damages* in cases of intentional discrimination. Compensatory damages typically include payments for emotional pain and suffering, loss of enjoyment of life, mental anguish, or inconvenience. However, limits were set on the amount of compensatory and punitive damages. Additionally, the 1991 act allows jury trials to determine the liability for and the amount of compensatory and punitive damages, subject to the caps just mentioned instead of decisions in these cases being made by judges.

AFFIRMATIVE ACTION REGULATIONS

Throughout the last thirty years, employers with federal contracts and other government entities have had to address additional areas of potential discrimination. Several acts and regulations have been issued that apply specifically to government contractors. These acts and regulations specify a minimum number of employees and size of government contracts. The requirements primarily come from federal Executive Orders 11246, 11375, and 11478. Many states have similar requirements for firms with state government contracts.

Executive Orders 11246, 11375, and 11478

Numerous Executive Orders have been issued that require employers holding federal government contracts not to discriminate on the basis of race, color, religion, national origin, or sex. An **Executive Order** is issued by the President of the United States to provide direction to government departments on a specific area. The Office of Federal Contract Compliance Programs (OFCCP) in the U.S. Department of Labor has responsibility for enforcing nondiscrimination in government contracts.[5]

Affirmative Action Plans (AAPs)

Under federal, state, and local regulations, many government contractors are required to compile affirmative action plans (AAPs) to report on the composition of their workforces. An Affirmative Action Plan is a formal document that an employer compiles annually for submission to enforcement agencies. Generally, contractors with at least 50 employees and $50,000 in government contracts annually must submit these plans.

Courts have noted that any employer that is not a government contractor may have a *voluntary* AAP, although the employer *must* have such a plan if it wishes to be a government contractor. Where an employer that is not a government contractor has a required AAP, a court has ordered the employer to have an AAP as a result of past discriminatory practices and violations of laws.

The contents of an AAP and the policies flowing from it must be available for review by managers and supervisors within the organization. Plans vary in length; some are long and require extensive staff time to prepare. Figure 4-3 depicts the phases in the development of an AAP.[6]

Internal Background Review   In the internal background review the EEO and AAP *policy statements* are presented, including the employer's commitment to equal employment and affirmative action. Then the *workforce analysis* is done by detailing the makeup of the workforce as seen on an organization chart and by depicting departmental groupings, job titles and pay levels, and the lines of progression. This analysis details the status of employees by gender, race, and other bases. The final part of the internal background review is to prepare a *job group analysis*. Unlike the workforce analysis, in which data are classified by organizational unit, the job group analysis looks at similar jobs throughout the organization, regardless of department. For instance, EEO

FIGURE 4-3 **Components of an Affirmative Action Plan (AAP)**

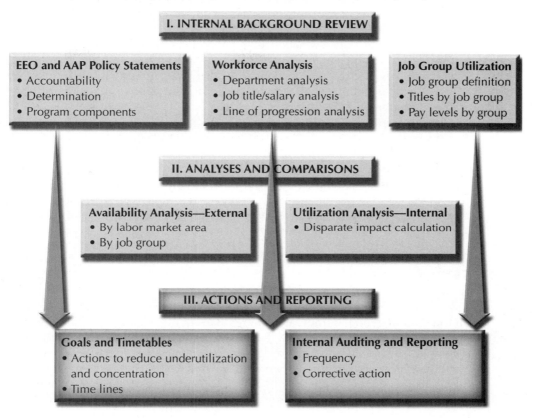

I. INTERNAL BACKGROUND REVIEW

EEO and AAP Policy Statements
- Accountability
- Determination
- Program components

Workforce Analysis
- Department analysis
- Job title/salary analysis
- Line of progression analysis

Job Group Utilization
- Job group definition
- Titles by job group
- Pay levels by group

II. ANALYSES AND COMPARISONS

Availability Analysis—External
- By labor market area
- By job group

Utilization Analysis—Internal
- Disparate impact calculation

III. ACTIONS AND REPORTING

Goals and Timetables
- Actions to reduce underutilization and concentration
- Time lines

Internal Auditing and Reporting
- Frequency
- Corrective action

demographic data on incumbents in all nursing jobs will be reported, regardless of departments. For instance, a hospital may have eight levels of nurses in twelve different units.

Analyses and Comparisons   As part of the second phase, two different types of analyses and comparisons are done. The first one is an **availability analysis**, which identifies the number of protected-class members available to work in the appropriate labor markets in given jobs. This analysis can be developed with data from a state labor department, the U.S. Census Bureau and other sources. Another major section of an AAP is the **utilization analysis**, which identifies the number of protected-class members employed and the types of jobs they hold in an organization.[7]

One of the difficulties in conducting the analyses is how to report and count individuals who are multiracial/ethnic. Under long-standing regulations, a multiracial person such as Tiger Woods would be reported in two or more categories. The enforcement agencies have recognized such concerns and are expected to develop new reporting categories and guidelines within the next two years.

Once all of the data have been analyzed and compared, then *underutilization* statistics must be calculated by comparing the workforce analyses with the utilization analysis. It is useful to think of this stage as comparing to see if the internal workforce is a representative sampling of the available external labor force from which employees are hired.

Actions and Reporting   Using the underutilization data, *goals and timetables* for reducing the underutilization of protected-class individuals must then be identified. Actions that will be taken to recruit, hire, promote, and train more protected-class individuals are described. Also, the AAP must be updated and reviewed each year to reflect changes in the utilization and the availability of protected-class members. If an audit of an AAP is done by the OFCCP, the employer must be prepared to provide additional details and documentation.

SEXUAL HARASSMENT AND GENDER DISCRIMINATION

Title VII of the Civil Rights Act of 1964 prohibits discrimination in employment on the basis of gender. Other laws and regulations are aimed at eliminating such discrimination in specific areas. Healthcare employers are consistently challenged to provide a workplace free from sexual harassment. The very nature of healthcare delivery and the occupational need to discuss the body and body functions lends itself to discussions among providers that minimally could blur the lines of appropriate speech and conduct to actually creating a hostile environment. This section begins with a discussion of sexual harassment and then discusses other forms of gender-based discrimination.

Sexual Harassment

Sexual harassment is a form of sex discrimination that violates Title VII of the Civil Rights Act of 1964. The EEOC has issued guidelines designed to curtail sexual harassment. The two types of sexual harassment are defined as follows:

1. *Quid pro quo* harassment occurs when an employer or supervisor links specific employment outcomes to the individuals' granting sexual favors.
2. *Hostile environment* harassment occurs when the harassment has the effect of unreasonably interfering with work performance or psychological well-being or when intimidating or offensive working conditions are created.

Unwelcome sexual advances, requests for sexual favors, and other verbal or physical conduct of a sexual nature constitutes sexual harassment when submission to or rejection of this conduct explicitly affects an individual's employment, unreasonably interferes with an individual's work performance, or creates an intimidating, hostile or offensive work environment.

Sexual harassment can occur in a variety of circumstances, including but not limited to the following:

▶ The victim as well as the harasser may be a woman or a man. The victim does not have to be of the opposite sex.
▶ The harasser can be the victim's supervisor, an agent of the employer, a supervisor in another area, a co-worker, or a nonemployee. (See Figure 4-4.)
▶ The victim does not have to be the person harassed but could be anyone affected by the offensive conduct.
▶ Unlawful sexual harassment may occur without economic injury to or discharge of the victim.
▶ The harasser's conduct must be unwelcome.

It is helpful for the victim to directly inform the harasser that the conduct is unwelcome and must stop. The victim should use any employer complaint mechanism or grievance system available.

Linking any condition of employment—including pay raises, promotions, assignments of work and work hours, performance appraisals, meetings, disciplinary actions, and many others—to the granting of sexual favors can be the basis for a charge of *quid pro quo* ("something for something") harassment. Certainly, harassment by supervisors and managers who expect sexual favors as a

---

FIGURE 4-4   Potential Sexual Harassers

condition for a raise or promotion is inappropriate behavior in a work environment. This view has been supported in a wide variety of cases.

The second type of sexual harassment involves the creation of a *hostile work environment*. In *Harris v. Forklift Systems, Inc.*, the U.S. Supreme Court ruled that in determining if a hostile environment exists, the following factors should be considered.[8]

▶ Whether the conduct was physically threatening or humiliating, rather than just offensive
▶ Whether the conduct interfered unreasonably with an employee's work performance
▶ Whether the conduct affected the employee's psychological well-being

Employers should ensure **reasonable care** in their HR policies and practices by doing the following:

▶ Establishing a sexual harassment policy
▶ Communicating the policy regularly
▶ Training all employees, especially supervisors and managers, on avoiding sexual harassment
▶ Investigating and taking action when complaints are voiced

Prompt action by the employer to investigate sexual harassment complaints and then to punish the identified harassers aid an employer's defense. If harassment situations are taken seriously by employers, the ultimate outcomes are more likely to be favorable for them.

According to the U.S. Equal Employment Opportunity Commission, when investigating allegations of sexual harassment, EEOC looks at the whole record, the circumstances, such as the nature of the sexual advances and the context in which the alleged incidents occurred. A determination on the allegations is made from the facts on a case-by-case basis.

Prevention is the best tool to eliminate sexual harassment in the workplace. The first action an employer should take is to have a clearly stated policy on sex harrassment prevention. A sample policy can be found on the book's Web site: *http://flynn.swlearning.com*. Employers are encouraged to take steps necessary to prevent sexual harassment from occurring. They should clearly communicate to employees that sexual harassment will not be tolerated. They can do so by establishing an effective complaint or grievance process and by taking immediate and appropriate action when an employee complains.

Pregnancy Discrimination

The Pregnancy Discrimination Act (PDA) of 1978 requires that any employer with fifteen or more employees treat maternity leave the same as other personal or medical leaves. Closely related to the PDA is the Family and Medical Leave Act (FMLA) of 1993, which requires that individuals be given up to twelve weeks of family leave without pay and also requires that those taking family leave be allowed to return to jobs. The FMLA applies to both men and women.

In court cases it generally has been ruled that the PDA requires employers to treat pregnant employees the same as nonpregnant employees with similar abilities or inabilities. Therefore, an employer was ruled to have acted properly when terminating a pregnant employee for excessive absenteeism due to pregnancy-related illnesses because the employee was not treated differently than any other employees with absenteeism problems.[9] However, in another case, a dental employee who was fired five days after she told her manager that she was pregnant was awarded $18,460 by a court decision that ruled her employer violated the PDA.[10]

Two other areas somewhat related to pregnancy and motherhood also have been subjects of legal and regulatory action. The U.S. Equal Employment Commission has ruled that denial of health insurance coverage for prescription contraceptives under employer-provided health plans violates the PDA. A result of this ruling is that employers who have changed their health insurance plans to offer contraceptive coverage may face increases in benefit costs.[11]

A number of states have passed laws that guarantee breast-feeding rights at work for new mothers. Although attempts have been made to enact such legislation at the federal level, that legislation has not yet been enacted.

Equal Pay and Pay Equity

The Equal Pay Act of 1963 requires employers to pay similar wage rates for similar work without regard to gender. A *common core of tasks* must be similar, but tasks performed only intermittently or infrequently do not make jobs different enough to justify significantly different wages.[12] Differences in pay may be allowed because of:

▶ Differences in seniority
▶ Differences in performance
▶ Differences in quality and/or quantity of production
▶ Factors other than sex, such as skill, effort, and working conditions

For example, a university was found to have violated the Equal Pay Act by paying a female professor a starting salary lower than salaries paid to male professors with similar responsibilities. In fact, the court found that the woman professor taught larger classes and had more total students than some of the male faculty members.[13]

Another pay-related concept is *pay equity,* which is that the pay for jobs requiring comparable levels of knowledge, skill, and ability should be similar, even if actual duties differ significantly. This concept has also been identified as *comparable worth* in some cases. But except where state laws require pay equity for public-sector employees, U.S. federal courts generally have ruled that the existence of pay differences between jobs held by women and jobs held by men is not sufficient to prove that illegal discrimination has occurred.

A major reason for the development of the pay equity idea is the continuing gap between the earnings of women and men. For instance, in 1980, the average annual pay of full-time women was 60% that of full-time men workers. By 2001, the reported rate of 72% showed some progress.[14] More in-depth data and research studies have shown that when education and experience differences of men and women are considered, women earn about 90% of what men in comparable positions earn.[15]

The Glass Ceiling

For years, women's groups have alleged that women encounter a glass ceiling in the workplace. The **glass ceiling** refers to discriminatory practices that have prevented women and other protected-class members from advancing to executive-level jobs.

A related problem is that women have tended to advance to senior management in a limited number of functional areas, such as human resources and corporate communications. Because jobs in these "supporting" areas tend to pay less than jobs in sales, marketing, operations, or finance, the overall impact is to reduce women's career progression and income. Limits that keep women from progressing only in certain fields often have been referred to as *glass walls* or *glass elevators*. Some firms have established formal mentoring programs in order to break down glass walls.

AGE DISCRIMINATION

The Age Discrimination in Employment Act (ADEA) of 1967, amended in 1978 and 1986, makes it illegal for an employer to discriminate in compensation, terms, conditions, or privileges of employment because of an individual's age. The later amendments first raised the minimum mandatory retirement age of 70 and then eliminated it completely. The ADEA applies to all individuals over age 40 working for employers with twenty or more workers. However, the act does not apply if age is a job-related occupational qualification.

The Older Workers Benefit Protection Act (OWBPA) of 1990 was passed to amend the ADEA to ensure that equal treatment for older workers occurs in early retirement or severance situations. Many early retirement and downsizing efforts by employers target older workers by hoping to entice them to choose early retirement buyouts and enhanced severance packages. In exchange, employers often require the workers to sign waivers indicating that by accepting the retirement incentives, the workers waive their rights to sue the employers for age discrimination. The OWBPA provides regulations on the use of these waivers.

AMERICANS WITH DISABILITIES ACT (ADA)

The passage of the Americans with Disabilities Act (ADA) in 1990 represented an expansion in the scope of impact of laws and regulations on discrimination against individuals with disabilities. The ADA contains the following requirements dealing with employment.

▶ Discrimination is prohibited against individuals with disabilities who can perform the essential job functions, a standard that is somewhat vague.

▶ A covered employer must have reasonable accommodation for people with disabilities so that they can function as employees, unless undue hardship would be placed on the employer.

▶ Pre-employment medical examinations are prohibited, except after a conditional employment offer is made.

As defined by the ADA, a disabled person is someone who has a physical or mental impairment that substantially limits that person in some major life activities, who has a record of such impairment, or who is regarded as having such impairment. A growing area of concern under the ADA is individuals with mental disabilities. Generally, employers have prevailed when charges of discrimination against a person with a mental disability have been brought against them. A mental illness is often more difficult to diagnose than a physical disability. In an attempt to add clarification, the EEOC has released explanatory guidelines, but the situations are still confusing:

▶ *Essential Job Functions*—The ADA requires that the essential job functions be identified in written job descriptions that indicate the amount of time spent performing various functions and their criticality. Most employers have interpreted this provision to mean that they should develop and maintain current and comprehensive job descriptions for all jobs.

▶ *Reasonable Accommodation*—A reasonable accommodation is a modification or adjustment to a job or work environment that enables a qualified individual with a disability to have equal employment opportunity. Employers are required to provide reasonable accommodation for individuals with disabilities to ensure that legal discrimination does not occur.

▶ *Undue Hardship*—Reasonable accommodation is restricted to actions that do not place an undue hardship on an employer. An action places undue hardship on an employer if it imposes significant difficulty or expense. The ADA offers only general guidelines on when an accommodation becomes unreasonable and places undue hardship on an employer.

OTHER BASES OF DISCRIMINATION

There are several other bases of discrimination that various laws have identified as illegal. This expansion continues to be a concern to employers.

Immigration Reform and Control Act (IRCA)

To deal with problems arising from the continued flow of immigrants to the United States, the Immigration Reform and Control Act (IRCA) was passed in 1986 and has been revised in later years. The IRCA makes it illegal for an employer to discriminate in recruiting, hiring, or terminating based on an individual's national origin or citizenship. Recent revisions to the IRCA changed some of the restrictions on the entry of immigrants to work in U.S. organizations, particularly those organizations with high-technology and other "scarce skills" areas. Employers are required to examine identification documents for new employees, who also must sign verification forms about their eligibility to work legally in the United States.

Religious Discrimination

Title VII of the Civil Rights Act identifies discrimination on the basis of religion as illegal. However, religious schools and institutions can use religion as a bona fide occupational qualification (BFOQ) for employment practices on a limited scale.

Sexual Orientation

Some states and cities have passed laws prohibiting discrimination based on sexual orientation or lifestyle. Even the issue of benefits coverage for "domestic partners," whether heterosexual or homosexual, has been the subject of state and city legislation.

Veterans' Employment Rights

The employment rights of military veterans and reservists have been addressed by the passage of the Vietnam-Era Veterans Readjustment Act. The act requires that affirmative action in hiring and advancing Vietnam-era veterans be undertaken by federal contractors and subcontractors with contracts of $10,000 or more.

Military Employment Rights

Under the Uniformed Services Employment and Re-employment Rights Act of 1994, employees are required to notify their employers of military service obligations. Employees serving in the military must be provided leaves of absence and have reemployment rights for up to five years. Other provisions protect the right to benefits of employees called to military duty.

ENFORCEMENT AGENCIES

Government agencies at several levels have powers to investigate illegal discriminatory practices. At the state and local levels, various commissions have enforcement authority. At the federal level, the two most prominent agencies are the Equal Employment Opportunity Commission (EEOC) and the Office of Federal Contract Compliance Programs (OFCCP).

Federal and state agencies with EEO enforcement authority frequently must coordinate investigations of illegal discriminatory practices between each other when charges are filed with both agencies by the same complainant.

Equal Employment Opportunity Commission (EEOC)

The EEOC is responsible for enforcing the employment-related provisions of the act. The agency initiates investigations, responds to complaints, and develops guidelines to enforce various laws. The EEOC has enforcement authority for charges brought under a number of federal laws, including the responsibility to investigate equal pay violations, age discrimination, and discrimination based on disability. As Figure 4-5 shows, the greatest number of equal employment charges are based on race or national origin and sex discrimination. That pattern has been constant for the past decade.

Office of Federal Contract Compliance (OFCCP)

The OFCCP, part of the Department of Labor, was established to ensure that federal contractors and subcontractors have nondiscriminatory practices. The major thrust of the OFCCP in healthcare organizations is to require that covered employers have affirmative action plans to counter prior discriminatory practices.

Many large healthcare providers, especially teaching and research hospitals who receive substantial Medicare reimbursement or National Institute of Health (NIH) grants, are periodically surveyed by OFCCP to determine their ongoing compliance with the Executive Orders.

FIGURE 4-5   Equal Employment Charges by Type

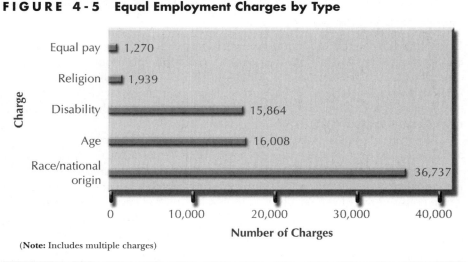

(**Note:** Includes multiple charges)

Source: Equal Employment Opportunity Commission, 2001.

State and Local Enforcement Agencies

In addition to federal laws and Executive Orders, many states and municipalities have passed laws prohibiting discrimination on a variety of bases and state and local enforcement bodies have been established. Often, these laws are modeled after federal laws; however, state and local laws sometimes provide greater remedies, require different actions, or prohibit discrimination in areas beyond those addressed by federal law.

UNIFORM GUIDELINES ON EMPLOYEE SELECTION PROCEDURES

The Uniform Guidelines on Employee Selection Procedures were developed by the EEOC, the U.S. Department of Labor's OFCCP, the U.S. Department of Justice, and the Office of Personnel Management. The guidelines provide a framework used to determine whether employers are adhering to federal laws on discrimination. The guidelines apply to most employment-related decisions, not just to the initial hiring process. The major means of compliance identified by the guidelines are: (1) no disparate impact and (2) job-related validation.

"No-Disparate-Impact" Approach

Under the guidelines, disparate impact is determined by the four-fifths rule. If the selection rate for any protected group is less than 80% (four-fifths) of the selection rate for the majority group or less than 80% of the group's representation in the relevant labor market, discrimination exists. Thus, the guidelines have attempted to define discrimination in statistical terms.

Job-Related Validation Approach

Under the job-related validation approach, virtually every factor used to make employment-related decisions—recruiting, selection, promotion, termination, discipline, and performance appraisal—must be shown to be specifically job related. *Validity* is simply the extent to which a test actually measures what it says it measures. An employment test that is valid must measure the person's ability to perform the job for which he or she is being hired.

The ideal condition for employment-related tests is to be both valid and reliable. *Reliability* refers to the consistency with which a test measures an item. For a test to be reliable, an individual's score should be about the same every time the individual takes the test (allowing for the effects of practice). Unless a test measures a trait consistently (or reliably), it is of little value in predicting job performance.

The 1978 Uniform Selection Guidelines recognize three types of validation:

▶ Content validity
▶ Criterion-related validity (concurrent and predictive)
▶ Construct validity

Content validity is a logical, nonstatistical method used to identify the knowledge, skills, and abilities (KSAs) and other characteristics necessary to perform a job. A test has content validity if it reflects an actual sample of the work done on the job in question.

There are two approaches to **criterion-related validity.** When an employer measures *concurrent* validity, a test is given to current employees and the scores are correlated with their job performance. A high correlation suggests that the test can differentiate between the better-performing employees and those with poor performance records. To measure *predictive* validity, test results of applicants are compared with their subsequent job performance. However, predictive validity requires: (1) a fairly large number of people (usually at least thirty) and (2) a time gap between the test and the performance (usually one year). As a result, predictive validity is not practical in many situations. Because of these and other problems, other types of validity often are used.

Construct validity shows a relationship between an abstract characteristic inferred from research and job performance. These are called *constructs*. Examples of psychological constructs are motivation and learning.

ELEMENTS OF EEO COMPLIANCE

Healthcare employers must comply with a variety of EEO regulations and guidelines. To do so, management should have an EEO policy statement and maintain all required EEO-related records.

EEO Policy Statement

It is critical that all healthcare employers have a written EEO policy statement. This policy should be widely communicated by posting it on bulletin boards, printing it in employee handbooks, reproducing it in organizational newsletters, and reinforcing it in training programs. The contents of the policy should clearly state the organizational commitment to equal employment, and incorporate the listing of the appropriate protected classes.

EEO Records

All employers with fifteen or more employees are required to keep certain records that can be requested by the Equal Employment Opportunity Commission, the Office of Federal Contract Compliance Programs (OFCCP), or other state and local enforcement agencies. Under various laws, employers also are required to post an "officially approved notice" in a prominent place where employees can see it. This notice states that the employer is an equal opportunity employer and does not discriminate.

EEO Records Retention   All employment records must be maintained as required by the EEOC. Required records include application forms and records concerning hiring, promotion, demotion, transfer, layoff, termination, rates of pay or other terms of compensation, and selection for training and apprenticeship. Even application forms or test papers completed by unsuccessful applicants may be requested. The length of time documents must be kept varies, but generally *three years is recommended as a minimum*. Complete records are necessary to enable an employer to respond should a charge of discrimination be made.

Annual Reporting Form   The basic report that must be filed with the EEOC is the annual report form EEO–1. The following employers must file this report:

▶ All employers with 100 or more employees, except state and local governments
▶ Subsidiaries of other companies where total employees equal 100
▶ Federal contractors with at least 50 employees and contracts of $50,000 or more
▶ Financial institutions with at least 50 employees in which government funds are held or saving bonds are issued

The annual report must be filed by March 31 for the preceding year. The form requires employment data by job category, classified according to various protected classes.

Applicant Flow Data   Under EEO laws and regulations, employers may be required to show that they do not discriminate in the recruiting and selection of members of protected classes. Because collection of racial data on application blanks and other premployment records is not permitted, the EEOC allows employers to use a "visual" survey or a separate *applicant flow form* that is not used in the selection process. This form is filled out voluntarily by the *applicant,* and the data must be maintained separately from other selection-related materials. These analyses may be useful in showing whether an employer has underutilized a protected class because of an inadequate applicant flow of protected class members, in spite of special efforts to recruit them. Also, these data are reported as part of affirmative action plans that are filed with the OFCCP.

EEOC Investigation Process

When a discrimination complaint is received by the EEOC or similar agency, it must be processed. To handle a growing number of complaints, the EEOC has instituted a system that categorizes complaints into three categories: *priority, needing further investigation,* and *immediate dismissal.* If the EEOC decides to pursue a complaint, it uses the process outlined here. In certain cases where a complaint is filed with both the EEOC and the State Civil Rights Agency, the EEOC may request the state agency to investigate first. However, regardless of the state agency's findings, the EEOC may continue its involvement in the investigation.

Compliance Investigative Stages   In a typical situation, an EEO complaint goes through several stages before the compliance process is completed. First, the charges are filed by an individual, a group of individuals, or their representative. A charge must be filed within 180 days of when the alleged discriminatory action occurred. Then the EEOC staff reviews the specifics of the charges to determine if it has *jurisdiction,* which means that the agency is authorized to investigate that type of charge. If jurisdiction exists, a notice of the charge must be served on the employer within ten days after the filing; the employer is asked to respond. Following the charge notification, the EEOC's major effort turns to investigating the complaint.

During the investigation, the EEOC may interview the complainants, other employees, company managers, and supervisors. Also, it can request additional records and documents from the employer. Assuming that sufficient cause is found that alleged discrimination occurred, the next stage involves mediation efforts by the agency and the employer. **Mediation** is a dispute process in which a trained mediator assists the parties in reaching a negotiated settlement. The EEOC has found that use of mediation has reduced its backlog of EEO complaints and has resulted in faster resolution of complaints. More than 90% of employers using mediation said they would use it in future cases.[16]

If the employer agrees that discrimination has occurred and accepts the proposed settlement, then the employer posts a notice of relief within the company and takes the agreed-on actions. If the employer objects to the charge and rejects conciliation, the EEOC can file suit or issue a **right-to-sue letter** to the complainant. The letter notifies the complainant that he or she has 90 days in which to file a personal suit in federal court.

In the court litigation stage, a legal trial takes place in the appropriate state or federal court. At that point, both sides retain lawyers and rely on the court to render a decision. The Civil Rights Act of 1991 provides for *jury trials* in most EEO cases. If either party disagrees with the court ruling, either can file appeals with a higher court. The U.S. Supreme Court becomes the ultimate adjudication body.

Employer Responses to EEO Complaints

The general steps in responding effectively to an EEO complaint are outlined in Figure 4-6 and discussed next. Employers who vigorously investigate their employees' discrimination complaints before they are taken to outside agencies can control many problems and expenses associated with EEO complaints. An internal employee complaint system and prompt, thorough responses to problem situations are essential tools in reducing EEO charges and in remedying illegal discriminatory actions.

Review Claim and Employee's Personnel File   By reviewing the claim, the HR staff can determine the validity of the complaint and begin to develop a response. Also, the personnel files on the employees involved should be reviewed to determine the nature and adequacy of internal documentation. For many employers, contacting outside legal counsel at this point also may be advisable.

Take No Retaliatory Action It is crucial that no retaliatory actions, even snide remarks, be used against individuals filing EEO complaints. The HR staff also should notify relevant managers and supervisors of the complaint, instructing them to refrain from any retaliatory actions, such as changing job assignments or work schedules unnecessarily. However, appropriate disciplinary action that is work-related still can be administered.

F I G U R E   4 - 6   Stages in Responding to EEO Complaints

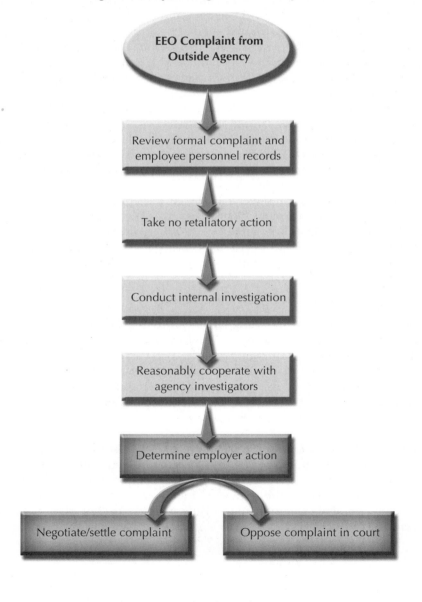

Conduct Internal Investigation A thorough internal investigation of the facts and circumstances of the claim should be conducted. Some firms use outside legal counsel to conduct these investigations in order to obtain a more objective view. Once the investigative data have been obtained, then a decision about the strength or weakness of the employer's case should be determined.

Reasonably Cooperate with Agency Investigators If the case is weak, possible settlement discussions may begin with the enforcement agency representatives. However, if the employer believes that a strong case exists, then the employer likely will draft a response stating the relevant facts and reasons why the employer does not believe the complaint is valid.

Determine Whether to Negotiate, Settle, or Oppose Complaint Once the agency investigation has been completed, the employer will be notified of the results. Also, the remedies proposed by the agency investigators will be identified. At that point, the HR staff, outside legal counsel, and senior managers often meet to decide whether to settle the complaint, negotiate different terms of the settlement, or to oppose the charges and begin court proceedings.

ETHICS, LAW, AND HR HEALTHCARE MANAGEMENT

As the issues faced by healthcare HR professionals have increased in number and complexity, so have the pressures and challenges of acting ethically. Ethical issues pose fundamental questions about fairness, justice, truthfulness, and social responsibility. Concerns have been raised about the ethical standards used by managers and employees, including those in healthcare organizations.

For HR professionals, there are ethical ways in which they should act relative to a given HR issue. However, determining ethical actions is not always easy. Just complying with the laws does not guarantee ethical behavior. Business ethicists argue that laws and ethics intersect, as depicted in Figure 4-7, but are not the same.

Dealing with discrimination in the healthcare workplace is clearly not just a legal issue. Healthcare employers can make legally correct decisions relative to employment promotion, pay increases, or other employment actions and yet violate ethical standards.

F I G U R E 4 - 7 Relationship between Ethics and Laws

Although many large medical centers and university-based health organizations that receive federal funding must have an AAP and commit to pursuing affirmative action in attracting and recruiting qualified minority applicants, it is difficult to determine true compliance with that requirement. Organizations can merely go through the motions of affirmative action and focus on the documentation aspects of an AAP to prepare for OFCCP audits, or they can truly be very aggressive in efforts that produce results, whereby the numbers of protected group members are significantly increased.

Ethical arguments against discrimination generally fall into three categories:

1. *Utilitarian* arguments suggest that discrimination leads to an inefficient use of human resources.
2. *Rights* arguments claim that discrimination violates basic human rights.
3. *Justice* arguments state that discrimination results in an unjust distribution of society's benefits and burdens.

Laws and regulations cannot cover every situation that HR professionals will face. Instead, healthcare HR professionals must also be guided by values and personal behavior codes of conduct that represent fairness and equal treatment.

CASE

Cloverdale Family Practice Center (CFPC) is a twenty-five-physician multispecialty clinic operating in four locations. In addition to the twenty-five physicians on staff, CFPC employees seventy individuals in clinical, administrative, and clerical support roles.

CFPC has an excellent reputation for providing quality care. The clinics' large patient base, combined with its ability to provide competent care, has resulted in financial stability and the ability to invest in state-of-the-art equipment and facilities. The management of CFPC includes a physician CEO (elected to a five-year term by the board of directors), a practice administrator, and five department heads for the areas of clinic operations, labs, radiology, finance, and the business office.

Six months ago, CFPC was involved in a sexual harassment lawsuit in which a former employee as the plaintiff prevailed and the jury awarded the plaintiff $500,000 in compensatory, punitive damages and legal fees. The facts of the case included some disturbing issues about the work environment at CFPC. As disclosed during trial testimony, the plaintiff and her witnesses described an environment at CFPC where young, attractive females were continually subjected to sexual innuendos, suggestive comments, and jokes of a sexual nature by three of the CFPC physicians. Both current and past female employees of CFPC described behavior on the part of the defendants (three physicians) that was characterized as creating a hostile environment due to sexual harassment.

The attorneys for CFPC argued that the female plaintiff and others willingly participated in the sexual "banter" and had failed to advise the defendants that their behavior was making them uncomfortable or that they felt the physicians were creating a hostile environment. However, testimony from numerous terminated female employees indicated that they had disclosed their concerns to

CFPC's administrative management, who did not take any action to stop the alleged harassment.

The trial and the verdict, although not front-page news, did receive some media coverage, and clearly all of CFPC's physicians and employees were well aware of the proceedings. Many of them were deposed and/or interviewed by the plaintiff's or CFPC's attorneys. The trial and the verdict took a significant toll on the work attitudes of the physicians and employees and tarnished CFPC's otherwise unblemished reputation.

Questions

1. Describe the role of HR management in preventing sexual harassment.
2. Develop a plan for CFPC, going forward, to eliminate sex harassment issues.

END NOTES

1. Civil Rights Act of 1964, Title VII, Sec. 703a.
2. *Griggs vs. Duke Power Co.,* 401 U.S. 424 (1971).
3. *Reeves v. Sanderson Plumbing Products, Inc.,* 530 U.S. 99-536, June 12, 2000.
4. *O'Neal v. Ferguson Construction Co.,* 10th Ct. U.S. 99-2037, January 24, 2001.
5. For details, see *http://www.dol.gov/ofccp*.
6. In depicting the components of AAPs, the authors acknowledge the assistance of Raymond B. Weinberg, SPHR, CCP, and Kathleen Shotkoski, SPHR, of Omaha, Nebraska.
7. Reginald E. Jones and Dara L. Dehaven, "OFFCP's Revised 60-2 Regulations," *Legal Report* (January/February 2001), 1–4.
8. *Harris v. Forklift Systems, Inc.,* 114 S. Ct. 367 (1993).
9. *Arimindo V. Padlocker, Inc.,* 11th Cir, 99-4144, April 20, 2000.
10. "Additional Pregnancy Bias Rulings," *Fair Employment Practices* (March 9, 2000), 78.
11. "EEOC Ruling on Contraceptives May Be Costly for Employers," *HR Executive* (February 2001), 10)
12. "Comparing Apples and Apples, Plaintiffs Must Cut To The Core," *Bulletin to Management* (January 11, 2001), 14.
13. *Ryduchowski v. Port Authority of NY and NY,* 20 Cir, 99-7397, February 8, 2000; and *EEOC v. Eastern Michigan University,* E.D. Michigan, 98-71806, September 3, 1999.
14. U.S. Census Bureau, 2001.
15. Howard J. Well, "The Gender Wage Gap and Wage Discrimination: Illusion or Reality?" *The Regional Economist* (October 2000), Available at *http://www.stls.org/publications*.
16. "Mediation, Small Business Initiative Cited in FY2000 Report," *Fair Labor Practices* (February 1, 2001), 16.

CHAPTER 5

Job Design and Analysis

Learning Objectives

After you have read this chapter, you should be able to:

▶ Explain the relationship between productivity and job design.

▶ Describe the importance of job analysis.

▶ Discuss the typical uses of job analysis.

▶ List the common methods of job analysis.

▶ Identify the stages of the job analysis process.

▶ Define the elements of job descriptions and job specifications.

▶ Explain the relationship of JCAHO standards to job descriptions.

Healthcare HR Insights

St. Francis Hospital, located in the New York Metropolitan area, undertook a major organizational and cultural change effort through job redesign to create a new Patient-care Model in response to increasing financial pressures in a changing environment. The model that was developed emphasized a decentralization of nursing staff and a team-based approach to patient care. RN's became the team leaders on the subunits within the larger unit with responsibility for all aspects of day-to-day patient care. Nurse Extenders and Comfort Care Providers assisted the RNs in delivering patient care.

St. Francis Hospital's HR professionals, in collaboration with patient-care management, provided leadership in creating this new model. The new model was designed after considering the patient populations and the dynamics of the workforce and the marketplace. To implement this model, significant work was required to change from the current traditional approach that was hierarchical and centralized. The goals of the new model focused on job design that would cause greater responsiveness in caring for patients.

Three months following the first unit's conversion to the new model the patients' feedback was overwhelming positive. In addition, staff satisfaction surveys indicated that employees were satisfied with the new concept of nursing and the team-oriented approach to care-giving.[1]

HR professionals can provide job-design assistance that can have a significant impact on the effectiveness of a department or even an organization. It is critical to understand departmental objectives and work processes and evaluate the skills and abilities necessary to perform the various jobs that contribute to meeting those objectives and facilitating the work.

Both employees and jobs in healthcare organizations change over time. An understanding of what is occurring in jobs in healthcare organizations is developed through job analysis and the development of job descriptions and job specifications. In addition, the information that comes from job analysis is the foundation for recruiting, selection, compensation, and many other HR activities.

Because healthcare organizations are changing and jobs vary in different organizations, managers and employees alike are finding that designing and analyzing jobs requires greater attention than in the past. Understanding the work done in the organization must be based on facts and data, not just personal perceptions of managers, supervisors, and employees.

ACCOMPLISHING STRATEGIC OBJECTIVES THROUGH JOB DESIGN

It has become evident that analyzing what employees actually do in their jobs is vital to accomplishing the strategic objectives of healthcare organizations. Job design is a critical process, as is depicted in Figure 5-1.

FIGURE 5-1 **Organizational Objectives Accomplished Through Job Design**

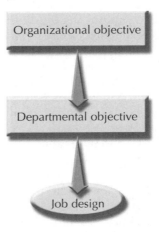

As organizational objectives are planned and implemented, individual departments or functional areas are required to establish objectives that contribute to the accomplishment of the broader organizational objectives.[2] These departmental objectives directly affect job design because job design ultimately outlines the duties and responsibilities that are required to accomplish the departmental objectives.

Productivity and Job Design

Job design refers to organizing tasks, duties, and responsibilities into a productive unit of work. It involves job content and the effect of jobs on employees. Identifying the components of a given job is an integral part of job design.

Job design can influence *performance* in many jobs, especially those where employee motivation can make a substantial difference. In healthcare organizations, job design can play an important role in the retention of key clinical employees. As an example, hospitals have adopted clinical ladder programs that encourage and reward nurses that remain in "bed-side" nursing positions.[3] These programs include significant focus on job design that includes expanding the autonomy of the nurse in managing the nursing care of their patients. Lower costs through reduced turnover and absenteeism may also result from good job design. Job design can also affect *job satisfaction*. Because people are more satisfied with certain job configurations than with others, it is important to be able to identify what constitutes a "good" job. Jobs designed to take advantage of important job characteristics are more likely to be positively received by employees. Such characteristics help distinguish between "good" and "bad" jobs. Many approaches to enhancing productivity and quality reflect efforts to expand some of the basic job characteristics.[4]

Person Job Fit   The person/job fit is a simple but important concept that involves matching characteristics of people with characteristics of jobs. Obviously, if a person does not fit a job, either the person can be changed or replaced, or the job can be altered. In the past, it was much more common to make the "round" person fit the "square" job. However, successfully "reshaping" people is not easy to do.[5] By redesigning jobs, the person/job fit can be improved more easily. Jobs may be designed properly when they are first established or "reengineered" later.

Because of the effects of job design on performance, employee satisfaction, health, and many other factors, many organizations are changing or have already changed the design of some jobs.[6] One movement that has affected the design and characteristics of jobs and work is **re-engineering,** which is rethinking and redesigning work to improve cost, service, and speed. The re-engineering process may include such techniques as creating work teams, training employees in multiple skills so they can do multiple jobs, pushing decision making as far down the organizational hierarchy as possible, and reorganizing operations and offices to simplify and speed work.

Work Analysis

Work analysis studies the workflow, activities, context, and output of a job. This analysis can be conducted on a department, clinical or administrative process, or individual level. At one level, the management engineering approach of time and motion studies is useful in work analysis. At another level, what is done in one department can be looked at in relation to work activities performed elsewhere in the organization. Analyzing work activities and processes requires looking at what capabilities individuals need, as well as what they do. That certainly would be true in office support jobs, such as the secretarial job, are examined.

NATURE OF JOB ANALYSIS

The most basic building block of HR management, **job analysis,** is a systematic way to gather and analyze information about the content and human requirements of jobs and the context in which jobs are performed. Job analysis usually involves collecting information on the characteristics of a job that differentiate it from other jobs. Information that can be helpful in making the distinction includes the following:

▶ Work activities and behaviors
▶ Equipment used
▶ Interactions with others
▶ Working conditions

▶ Performance standards
▶ Supervision given and received
▶ Financial and budgeting impact
▶ Knowledge, skills, and abilities needed

Although the terms *job* and *position* are often used interchangeably, there is a slight difference in emphasis. A **job** is a grouping of common tasks, duties, and responsibilities. A **position** is a job performed by one person. Thus, if there are two people operating sterilization equipment, there are two positions (one for each person) but just one job (sterilization technician).

Task-Based Job Analysis

Analyzing jobs based on what is done on the job focuses on the tasks, duties, and responsibilities performed in a job. A **task** is a distinct, identifiable work activity composed of motions, whereas a **duty** is a larger work segment composed of several tasks that are performed by an individual. Because both tasks and duties describe activities, it is not always easy or necessary to distinguish between the two. For example, if one of the employment supervisor's duties is to interview applicants, one task associated with that duty would be asking questions. The **job responsibilities** are obligations to perform certain tasks and duties.

THE IMPORTANCE OF JOB ANALYSIS IN HEALTHCARE ORGANIZATIONS

The Competency Approach to Healthcare Job Analysis

The **competency approach** to job analysis focuses on the competencies that individuals need in order to perform jobs, rather than focusing on the tasks, duties, and responsibilities that compose a job. Instead of thinking of individuals having jobs that are relatively stable and that can be written up into typical job descriptions, it may be more relevant to focus on the competencies used.[7] **Competencies** are basic characteristics that can be linked to enhanced performance by individuals or teams. The groupings of competencies may include:

▶ Skill
▶ Knowledge
▶ Ability
▶ Training
▶ Education
▶ Licensure, certification and/or registration

The competency approach also attempts to identify the hidden factors that are often critical to superior performance. For instance, many supervisors talk about employees' attitudes, but they have difficulty identifying what they mean by *attitude*. The competency approach uses some methodologies to help supervisors identify examples of what they mean by appropriate attitude and how those factors affect performance. Examples of common competencies often include the following:

▶ Team orientation
▶ Technical expertise
▶ Leadership
▶ Adaptability

In many healthcare positions, the competency approach encourages employees to develop competencies that may be used in different work situations, rather than being boxed into a single job. As detailed in the JCAHO Feature, the JCAHO recognizes the importance of job design and analysis in the development of staffing plans and organizational competence systems. Development of employees focuses on enhancing their competencies, rather than preparing them for moving to specific jobs. In this way, they can develop capabilities useful in their jobs as changes occur.

THE JOINT COMMISSION ON ACCREDITATION OF HEALTHCARE ORGANIZATIONS

Joint Commission Standards and Job Analysis

Healthcare organizations that comply with the JCAHO standards and review process must establish staffing plans and a competency system. Both staffing plans and a competency system require significant attention to job design and analysis.

The **HR** and **leadership standards** relating to HR planning require the leaders of healthcare organizations to analyze their staffing needs and provide the appropriate types and sufficient number of staff to meet care needs. The HR and leadership standards relating to the establishment of a competency system expect the leaders of an organization to develop and maintain a system that ensures the following:

▶ Recruitment, employment, and retention of competent healthcare workers
▶ On-going assessment of staff competency
▶ Ability of the organization to maintain and increase staff knowledge in performance of their jobs

The foundation for these HR and leadership standards is job design and analysis. Job analysis—discovering how people's jobs are being done—is a critical element in meeting JCAHO standards. The standards require the assessment and maintenance of staff competence, which is done by defining job qualifications, competencies, and performance expectations.

Continuum of HR Activities and Healthcare Competencies

There is a series of HR activities designed to provide a competent work force. These activities can be viewed as a continuum that starts with pre-employment activities and continues throughout an individual's employment in the organization. Job design and analysis is the critical first component of the continuum. Every activity on the continuum is dependent on accurate and consistent job design and analysis.[8] This is illustrated in Figure 5-2.

FIGURE 5-2 Healthcare Competency Approach

USES OF JOB ANALYSIS

Healthcare HR managers use job analysis as the foundation for a number of other HR activities. For instance, job analysis provides an objective basis for hiring, evaluating, training, accommodating and supervising persons with disabilities, as well as improving the efficiency of the organization. It is a logical process to determine the following:

▶ *Purpose*—The reason for the job
▶ *Essential Functions*—The job duties that are critical or fundamental to the performance of the job
▶ *Job Setting*—The work station and conditions where the essential functions are performed
▶ *Job Qualifications*—The minimal skills an individual must possess to perform the essential functions.

The process of analyzing jobs in organizations requires planning of several factors. As Figure 5-3 (on the next page) indicates, some of the considerations are how it is to be done, who provides data, and who conducts the analysis and uses the data so that job descriptions and job specifications can be prepared and reviewed. Once those decisions are made, then several results are linked to a wide range of HR activities. The most fundamental use of job analysis is to provide the information necessary to develop job descriptions and specifications.

In most cases, the job description and job specifications are combined into one document that contains several different sections. A brief overview of each follows next; a more detailed discussion appears later in the chapter.

A **job description** is a document that indicates the tasks, duties, and responsibilities of a job. It identifies what is done, why it is done, where it is done, and—briefly—how it is done.

Performance standards should flow directly from a job description, telling what the job accomplishes and how performance is measured in key areas of the job description. If employees know what is expected and how performance is to be measured, they have a much better chance of performing satisfactorily.

While the job description describes activities to be done in the job, the **job specifications** list the knowledge, skills, and abilities (KSAs) an individual needs to perform a job satisfactorily. KSAs include education, experience, work skill requirements, personal abilities, and mental and physical requirements. It is important to note that accurate job specifications identify what KSAs a person needs to do the job, not necessarily what qualifications the current employee possesses.

Job Families, Departments, and Organization Charts

Once all jobs in the organization have been identified, it is often helpful for communicating with employees to group the jobs into job families and display them on an organization chart. There are various ways of identifying and grouping job families. A **job family** is a grouping of jobs with similar characteristics. In identifying job families, significant emphasis is placed on measuring the similarity of jobs. A **department** depicts a distinct grouping of organizational responsibilities.

FIGURE 5-3   Decisions in the Job Analysis Process

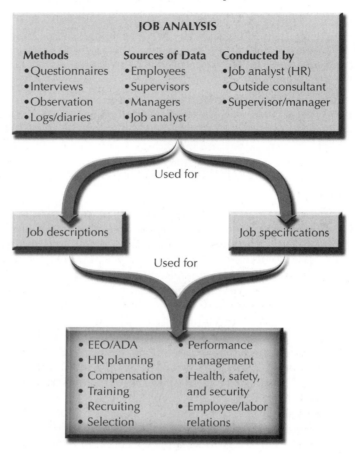

Healthcare organizations have various departmental structures; an example of a traditional structure would group organizational responsibilities as depicted in Figure 5-4.

An **organization chart** depicts the relationships among jobs in an organization. Organization charts have traditionally been hierarchical and showed the reporting relationships for authority and responsibilities. In most organizations, these charts can help clarify who reports to whom.

Job Analysis and HR Activities

The completion of job descriptions and job specifications, based on job analysis, is at the heart of many other HR activities, as Figure 5-5 indicates. But even if legal requirements did not force employers to do job analysis, effective HR management would demand it.

FIGURE 5-4   Hospital Organizational Chart

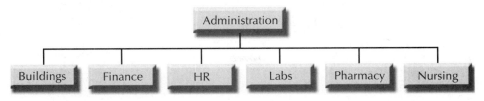

FIGURE 5-5   Job Analysis and Other HR Activities

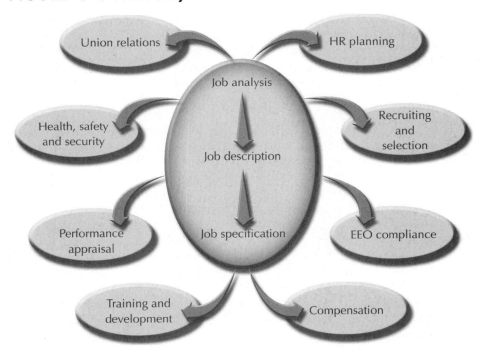

HR Planning   HR planning requires auditing of current jobs. Current job descriptions provide the basic details necessary for this internal assessment, including such items as the jobs available, current number of jobs and positions, and reporting relationships of the jobs. By identifying the functions currently being performed and calculating the time being spent to perform them, managers and HR specialists can redesign jobs to eliminate unnecessary tasks and combine responsibilities where desirable.

Recruiting and Selection   Equal employment opportunity guidelines clearly require a sound and comprehensive job analysis to validate recruiting and selection criteria. Without a systematic investigation of a job, an employer may be using requirements that are not specifically job related. Organizations use job analysis to identify job specifications necessary for obtaining qualified employees for anticipated job openings, whether recruited internally or externally.

EEO Compliance Many aspects of EEO compliance require accurate and verifiable job analysis information. Job analysis is critical in determining the essential functions of a job, and deciding what the necessary qualifications are for a job. This information is crucial for use in the selection process in a non-discriminatory manner.

Compensation Job analysis information is vital when determining compensation. As part of identifying appropriate compensation, job analysis information is used to determine job content for *internal* comparisons of responsibilities and *external* comparisons with the compensation paid by competing employers. Information from job analysis can be used to give more weight, and therefore more pay, to jobs with more difficult tasks, duties, and responsibilities.

Training and Development By defining which activities make up a job, the analysis helps the supervisor explain that job to new employees. Information from job descriptions and job specifications can also help in career planning by showing employees what is expected in jobs that they may choose in the future. Job specification information can point out areas in which employees might need to develop in order to further their careers.

Performance Appraisal With performance standards to compare what an employee is supposed to be doing with what the person actually has done, a supervisor can determine the employee's performance level. The **performance appraisal** process should then tie to the job description and performance standards.[9] Developing clear, realistic performance standards can also reduce communication problems in performance appraisal feedback among managers, supervisors, and employees.

Safety and Health Job analysis information is useful in identifying possible job hazards and working conditions associated with jobs. From the information gathered, managers and HR specialists can work together to identify the health and safety equipment needed, specify work methods, and train workers.

Union Relations Where workers are represented by a labor union, job analysis is used in several ways. First, job analysis information may be needed to determine whether the job should be covered by the union agreements. Second, it is common in unionized environments for job descriptions to be very specific about what tasks are and are not covered in a job. Finally, well-written and specific job descriptions can reduce the number of grievances filed by workers.

JOB ANALYSIS AND LEGAL ISSUES

Permeating the discussion of equal employment laws, regulations, and court cases in preceding chapters is the concept that legal compliance must focus on the jobs that individuals perform. The 1978 Uniform Selection Guidelines make it clear that HR requirements must be tied to specific job-related factors if employers are to defend their actions as a business necessity.

The Americans with Disabilities Act (ADA)

The Americans with Disabilities Act (ADA) has increased the emphasis on job analysis, job descriptions, and job specifications. HR managers in healthcare organizations must identify job activities and then document the steps taken to identify job responsibilities.[10] One result of the ADA is increased emphasis by employers on conducting job analysis, as well as developing and maintaining current and accurate job descriptions.

Healthcare organizations must identify how physical aspects of jobs are determined. Given that many service workers and technical/professional employees in healthcare perform significant physical work, the job analysis process must accurately define essential functions for two reasons: First, the job analysis process must appropriately define the physical requirements to ensure safe performance of the job duties for both the employee doing the job and the patients they care for. Second, the physical requirements of the essential functions must be accurately determined to facilitate nondiscriminatory hiring decisions.

In determining **essential functions**—the fundamental job duties of the employment position that an individual with a disability holds or desires must be evaluated. A useful approach is to answer the following questions:

1. What three or four activities actually constitute the job? Is each necessary? For example a secretary types, files, answers the phone, takes dictation.
2. What is the relationship among the tasks? Is there a special sequence that the tasks must follow?
3. Do the tasks necessitate sitting, standing, crawling, walking, climbing, running, stooping, kneeling, lifting, carrying, digging, writing, operating, pushing, pulling, fingering, talking, listening, interpreting, analyzing, seeing, coordinating, or other physical activities?
4. How many other employees are available to perform the job function? Can that function be done by any other employees?
5. How much time is spent on the job performing each particular function? Are the tasks performed less frequently as important as those done more frequently?
6. Would removing a function fundamentally alter the job?
7. What happens if a task is not completed on time?

Having identified the essential job functions through a job analysis, an employer must be prepared to make reasonable accommodations. Again, the core job duties and KSAs must be considered. Figure 5-6 highlights these considerations.

FIGURE 5-6 **Determining Essential Functions**

CONSIDERATIONS	ESSENTIAL FUNCTIONS	NONESSENTIAL FUNCTIONS
Percentage of time spent	▶ Significant time spent: often 20% of time or more	▶ Generally less than 10% of time
Frequency	▶ Performed regularly: daily, weekly, monthly	▶ Performed infrequently or when substituting in part of another job
Importance	▶ Task has consequences to other parts of job or other jobs	▶ Task is unrelated to job and has little consequence if not performed

Wage/Hours Regulations and the Fair Labor Standards Act

Typically, a job analysis identifies the percentage of time spent on each duty in a job. This information helps determine whether someone should be classified as exempt or nonexempt under the wage/hour laws. As will be noted in Chapter 12, the Federal Fair Labor Standards Act (FLSA) and most state wage/hours laws indicate that the percentage of time employees spend on manual, routine, or clerical duties affects whether they must be paid overtime for hours worked in excess of forty hours per week.

To be exempt from overtime, the employees must be classified duties as *executive, administrative, professional,* or *outside sales* employees. Primary has been interpreted to mean occurring at least 50% of the time. Additionally, the exemption regulations state that no more than 20% of the time can be spent on manual, routine, or clerical duties.

Meeting wage and hour regulations has been an especially difficult task for healthcare organizations. For instance, many different professional category clinical positions, such as RNs and pharmacists, in healthcare organizations could meet the wage and hour tests for exemption from the act; yet a significant number of these organizations treat employees in these positions as non-exempt. This usually occurs because of the variability in hours that the RNs or pharmacists are required to work and the need to pay them overtime as an inducement to work beyond their regular shift, rather than a legal requirement to do so. Meeting the requirements of the Fair Labor Standards Act (FLSA) by appropriately designating whether the analyzed job is exempt under the act or nonexempt is extremely important. Misclassification could result in significant back pay awards to misclassified employees.

BEHAVIORAL ASPECTS OF JOB ANALYSIS

A detailed examination of jobs, while necessary, can be a demanding and threatening experience for both managers and employees, in part because job analysis can identify the difference between what is currently being performed in a job and what *should* be done.

Employees and managers also tend to inflate the importance and significance of their jobs.[11] Because job analysis information is used for compensation purposes, both managers and employees hope that "puffing up" their jobs will result in higher pay levels. Some employees may fear that an analysis of their jobs will put a "straitjacket" on them, limiting their creativity and flexibility by formalizing their duties. However, it does not necessarily follow that analyzing a job will limit job scope or depth. Having a well-written and well-communicated job description can assist healthcare employees by clarifying what their roles are and what is expected of them. Perhaps the most effective way to handle anxieties is to involve the employees in the revision process. Many healthcare organizations use job analysis techniques that include the employees whose jobs are being analyzed in the job analysis process. These techniques are described in the next section.

JOB ANALYSIS METHODS

Job analysis information can be gathered in a variety of ways. Common methods are observation, interviews, questionnaires, and specialized methods of analysis. Combinations of these approaches frequently are used, depending on the situation and the organization. Each of these methods is discussed in some detail next.

Observation

When the observation method is used, a manager, job analyst, or industrial engineer observes the individual performing the job and takes notes to describe the tasks and duties performed. Observation may be continuous or based on intermittent sampling. Use of the observation method is limited because many jobs do not have complete and easily observed job duties or complete job cycles. Thus, observation may be more useful for repetitive jobs and in conjunction with other methods.

Interviews

The interview method of gathering information requires that a manager or HR specialist visit each job site and talk with the employees performing each job. A standardized interview form is used most often to record the information. Frequently, both the employee and the employee's supervisor must be interviewed to obtain a complete understanding of the job. The interview method can be quite time-consuming, especially if the interviewer talks with two or three employees doing each job. Professional and managerial jobs often are more complicated to analyze and usually require longer interviews. For these reasons, combining the interview with one of the other methods is suggested.

Questionnaires

Job analysis questionnaires are a widely used method of gathering data on jobs. Survey instruments are developed and given to employees and managers to complete. The major advantage of the questionnaire method is that information on a large number of jobs can be collected inexpensively in a relatively short period of time. However, the questionnaire method assumes that employees can accurately analyze and communicate information about their jobs. Employees may vary in their perceptions of the jobs, and even in their ability to read and understand the questionnaire. For these reasons, the questionnaire method is usually combined with interviews and observations to clarify and verify the questionnaire information.

Computerized Job Analysis

As computer technology has expanded, researchers have developed computerized job analysis systems. An important feature of computerized job analysis sources is the specificity of data that can be gathered. All of this specific data is compiled into a job analysis database. A computerized job analysis system often can reduce the time and effort involved in writing job descriptions. These systems have banks of job duty statements that relate to each of the tasks and scope statements of the questionnaires.

THE JOB ANALYSIS PROCESS

The process of job analysis must be conducted in a logical manner, following appropriate management and professional psychometric practices. Therefore, a multistage process usually is followed, regardless of the job analysis methods used. The stages for a typical job analysis are outlined here, but they may vary with the methods used and the number of jobs included. Figure 5-7 illustrates the basic stages of the process.

Planning

It is crucial that the job analysis process be planned before gathering data from managers and employees. Probably the most important consideration is to identify the objectives of the job analysis. Maybe it is just to update job descriptions. Or, it may include as an outcome revising the compensation programs in the organization. Another objective could be to redesign the jobs in a department or division of the organization. Also, the objective could be to change the structure in parts of the organization to align it better with new organizational strategies.

Preparation and Communication

Preparation consists of identifying the jobs under review. Another task in the identification phase is to review existing documentation. Existing job descriptions, organization charts, previous job analysis information, and other industry related resources all may be useful to review. A crucial step is to communicate and explain the process to managers, affected employees, and other concerned

F I G U R E   5 - 7   Stages in the Job Analysis Process

I. Planning the Job Analysis
   A. Identify objectives of job analysis
   B. Obtain top management support

II. Preparing for Job Analysis
   A. Identify jobs and methodology
   B. Review existing job documentation
   C. Communicate process to managers/employees

III. Conducting the Job Analysis
   A. Gather job analysis data
   B. Review and compile data

IV. Developing Job Descriptions and Job Specifications
   A. Draft job descriptions and specifications
   B. Review drafts with managers and employees
   C. Identify recommendations
   D. Finalize job descriptions and recommendations

V. Maintaining and Updating Job Descriptions and Job Specifications
   A. Update job descriptions and specifications as organization changes
   B. Periodically review all jobs

people, such as union stewards. Explanations should address the natural concerns and anxieties people have when someone puts their jobs under close scrutiny, and anticipate issues likely to arise.

Conducting the Job Analysis

With the preparation completed, the job analysis can be conducted. The methods selected will determine the timeline for the project. Sufficient time should be allotted for obtaining the information from employees and managers. Once details from job analysis have been compiled, they should be sorted by job family and organizational unit. This step allows for comparison of details from similar jobs throughout the organization. The data also should be reviewed for completeness, and follow-up may be needed in the form of additional interviews or questions to be answered by managers and employees.

Developing and Maintaining Job Descriptions, Job Specifications, and Performance Standards

The output from analysis of a job is used to develop a job description and job specifications and performance standards. Together, they summarize job analysis information into a readable format and provide the basis for legally defensible job-related actions. They also serve individual employees by providing documentation by management that identifies their jobs.

In most cases, the job description and job specifications are combined into one document that contains several different sections. A job description identifies the tasks, duties, and responsibilities in a job. It describes what is done, why it is done, where it is done, and briefly, how it is done. It should identify areas where clarification is needed.

Generally, organizations have found that having managers and employees write job descriptions is not recommended. HR can write them, and when they are finished, they can be distributed by the HR department to managers, supervisors, and employees. It is important that each supervisor or manager review the completed description with individual employees so that there is understanding and agreement on the content that will be linked to performance appraisals, as well as to all other HR activities.

Once job descriptions and specifications have been completed and reviewed by all appropriate individuals, a system must be developed for keeping them current. Otherwise, the entire process, beginning with job analysis, may have to be repeated in several years.

JOB DESCRIPTION COMPONENTS

The Americans with Disabilities Act (ADA) focused attention on the importance of well-written job descriptions. Legal compliance requires that they accurately represent the actual jobs. Job titles should be descriptive of job functions performed. There is a real art to writing job descriptions that are sufficiently clear without being overly detailed. It is important to use precise action verbs that accurately describe the employee's tasks, duties, and responsibilities.

Overviews of the most common components are presented next.

Identification

The first part of the job description is the identification section, in which the job title, reporting department, relationships, location, and FLSA status analysis may be given. Usually, it is advisable to note other information that is useful in tracking jobs and employees through a human resource information system.

General Summary

The second part is the general summary, which is a concise statement of the general responsibilities and components that make the job different from others. One HR specialist has characterized the general summary statement as follows: "In thirty words or less, describe the essence of the job."

Essential Functions and Duties

The third part of the typical job description lists the essential functions and duties. It contains clear, precise statements on the major tasks, duties, and responsibilities performed. Writing this section is the most time-consuming aspect of preparing job descriptions. As depicted in Figure 5-8, the general format for an essential function statement is: (1) *action verb*, (2) *to what applied*, (3) *what/how, how often*.

The language of the ADA has stressed the importance of arranging job duties so that the most essential (in criticality and amount of time spent) be

---

FIGURE 5-8 Use of Action Verbs in Job Descriptions

When writing a job description, it is important to use action verbs to describe the tasks and to have duties grouped together that have a logical flow. The following guide could be used when preparing the "specific duties" area of the job description:

- ▶ Begin with the action verb
- ▶ State what does it apply to
- ▶ State how the information is obtained
- ▶ State how, why and how often is it done

Example:

action verb	what it applies to	how the information is obtained	how, why and how often
pulls	patient charts	from clinics and practitioners	delivers and retrieves patient charts from clinics and practitioners

FIGURE 5-9 Sample Job Description

Title: Medical Records Clerk	Pay Grade: Non-Exempt, Hourly
Department: Medical Records	Date Approved: 10/10/2002
Supervisor: Medical Records Supervisor	

Job Summary: Maintain patients' medical records. Provides complete coverage of front office.

Job Accountabilities:

* E/M/NA	%Time	
E	30%	Maintains confidentiality of medical records. Controls access to file room. Ensures that records are signed out and returned.
E	30%	Pulls patient charts. Delivers and retrieves patient charts from clinics and practitioners.
E	20%	Files information such as progress notes, laboratory reports, X-ray results, and correspondence into patient charts.
E	5%	Creates new charts with appropriate labels and dividers.
E	5%	Releases patient information to requesting parties following established confidentiality procedures. Answers patient inquiries for laboratory results.
M	5%	Makes copies of dictated reports and forwards as indicated.
M	3%	Batches patient information into the computer and retrieves patient demographic data.
M	1%	Answers telephones and greets patients. Schedules patient appointments.
M	1%	Monitors laboratory result reports with laboratory order forms.
		Performs other related duties as assigned or requested. The organization reserves the right to add or change duties at any time.

* Select E (ESSENTIAL), M (MARGINAL) or NA (NON-APPLICABLE) to denote importance of each job function to position.

listed first and the supportive or marginal ones listed later. Within that framework, specific functional duties should be grouped and arranged in some logical pattern. If a job requires an accounting supervisor to prepare several reports, among other functions, statements relating to the preparation of reports should be grouped together. The *miscellaneous clause* typically listed last is included to assure some managerial flexibility. A typical job description, such as the one depicted in Figure 5-9, contains several major parts.

FIGURE 5-9   Sample Job Description (continued)

Job Specifications

Skills: Administrative

Understand and apply policies and procedures.	Prioritize different projects.
Assemble and organize numerical data.	Read handwritten text.
Answer telephones.	

Education and Experience

Minimum education: Less than high school	Preferred education: High school or equivalent
Preferred experience: 6–12 months	Preferred field-of-expertise: Medical Records

Physical Requirements

Physical Requirements	Rarely 0–12%	Occasionally 12–33%	Frequently 34–60%	Regularly 67–100%
Seeing—Reading reports, filing				X
Hearing—Communicate with co-workers				X
Standing/walking			X	
Climbing/stooping/kneeling			X	
Lifting/pulling/pushing			X	
Fingering/grasping/feeling— Write, type, and use telephone			X	

Skills: Computer Software ____X____	Scanning Equipment ____X____	
Fax ____X____		

The above statements are intended to describe the general nature and level of work being performed. They are not intended to be construed as an exhaustive list of all responsibilities, duties, and skills required of personnel so classified and do not create an employment contract.

SIGNATURES

Employee: _____ Date: _____

Supervisor: _____ Date: _____

Job Specifications

The next portion of the job description gives the qualifications needed to perform the job satisfactorily. The job specifications typically are stated as: (1) knowledge, skills, and abilities, (2) education and experience, and (3) physical requirements and/or working conditions. The components of the job specifications

FIGURE 5-10 **Sample Job Duty Statements and Performance Standards**

Job Title: Central Sterile Manager
Supervisor: Director of Surgical Operations

DUTY	PERFORMANCE STANDARDS
Develop, review, evaluate, and ensure the implementation of a central sterilization process for the surgery department.	▶ Monitor and forecast workload of department and recommend staffing levels to director to meet workload requirements. ▶ Prepare annual budget for department. ▶ Ensure appropriate review and evaluation of hospital procedures and sterilization equipment as they pertain to infection control.
Identify sterilization problems and outcomes, and document and recommend corrective actions.	▶ Follow all related departmental policies, procedures, guidelines, and standards in carrying out technical functions. ▶ Perform routine and specialized environmental checks per departmental guidelines. ▶ Ensure new equipment meets standards of sterilization and infection control.

provide information necessary to determine what accommodations might and might not be possible under Americans with Disabilities Act regulations.

Job specifications can be developed from a variety of information sources. Obviously, the job analysis process provides the primary starting point. But any KSA included must be based on what is really needed to perform a job. Furthermore, the job specifications listed should reflect what is necessary for satisfactory job performance, not what the ideal candidate would have. In light of the ADA, it is crucial that the physical and mental dimensions of each job be clearly identified. If lifting, stooping, standing, walking, climbing, or crawling is required, it should be noted. Also, weights to be lifted should be specified, along with specific visual and hearing requirements of jobs.

Performance Standards

Performance standards can flow directly from the job description and indicate what the job accomplishes and how performance is measured in key areas of the job description. The reason for including the performance standards is clear. If employees know what is expected and how performance is to be measured, they have a much better chance of performing satisfactorily. Figure 5-10 shows job description duty statements and some performance standards used for a Central Sterile Manager in a hospital.

Unfortunately, performance standards often are omitted from job descriptions. Even if performance standards have been identified and matched to job descriptions, they may not be communicated to employees if the job descriptions are not provided to employees, but used only as tools by the HR department and managers. Such an approach limits the value of job descriptions.

Disclaimer and Approvals

The final section on many job descriptions contains approval signatures by appropriate managers and a legal disclaimer. This disclaimer allows employers to change employees' job duties or request employees to perform duties not listed, so that the job description is not viewed as a "contract" between the employer and the employee.

CASE

Saint Regis Medical Center had acquired three physician practices in its service area to broaden its ability to provide primary care. Based on extensive studies, the Center was confident that it could reduce the costs of operations at these practices by consolidating and centralizing business activities. These business activities include accounting and finance; billing; purchasing and materials management; and facilities maintenance. Additionally, the Center would be able to spread the general costs of administration over the three facilities.

After nearly six months of operating these three new acquisitions, Saint Regis's financial analysis found very poor budgetary results had occurred. All three practices were over budget by more than 10%, and projections were for even larger shortfalls. The most significant budgetary issue was labor costs.

In further analyzing the problem, the main issue appeared to be the staffing mix of MDs, RNs and assistive (non-licensed) personnel. When the practices were acquired, the staffing mix was a simple combination of M.D.s and non-licensed medical assistants. When Saint Regis took over the practices, it changed the staffing mix to include RNs. This was consistent with the staffing model in the other clinics Saint Regis currently owned and operated. The budgetary problem was directly related to the increased expense of the RNs wages.

Saint Regis decided to evaluate the care delivery processes and the skill sets necessary at these clinics to determine if the staffing mix could be changed. The HR department was requested to undertake a job analysis, consider alternative job designs, and make recommendations.

Questions

1. Outline the steps that should be taken to evaluate the work at the practices to determine the appropriate staffing mix.
2. What methods of job analysis would be most effective for this assignment?

END NOTES

1. Betty R. Anson, Taking Charge of Change in a Volatile Healthcare Marketplace, *Human Resource Planning* (2000), 21–33.
2. Shari Caudron, "How HR Drives Profits," *Workforce* (December 2001), 26.
3. Deborah L. Ressler, "Experienced RNs Remain at Patients' Bedside," September 12, 2000. *http//www.vitalsigns.com*
4. A. E. M. Van Vianen, "Person-Organization Fit: The Match Between Newcomers' and Recruiters'

Preferences for Organizational Cultures," *Personal Psychology,* 53 (2000), 113–149.

5. Institute for Job and Occupational Analysis. Organization Dedicated to Research and Application of Job Analysis and Occupational Analysis Technologies and Methods. *http://www.ijoa.org.*

6. Eric Raimy, "Back to the Table," *Human Resource Executive* (March 2001), 1.

7. David Fine, "Establishing Competencies for Healthcare Managers," *Healthcare Executive,* (March/April 2002), 66–67.

8. *Comprehensive Accreditation Manual for Hospitals: The Official Handbook,* CAMH Refresher Course (January 2002), HR Section—1 to 32.

9. Kathy Gagne, "Using Performance Management to Support an Organization's Strategic Business Plan," *Employment Relations Today* (Winter 2002), 53.

10. Don Caruth and Gail Handlogten, "Avoiding HR Lawsuits," *Credit Union Executive* (November–December 2001), 25.

11. Tammy Joyner, "Staff, Let's Play the Name Game," *Omaha World Herald* (July 1, 2001).

CHAPTER 6

Healthcare Recruitment and Selection

Learning Objectives

After you have read this chapter, you should be able to:

▶ Specify the decisions necessary as part of a strategic approach to recruitment.

▶ Describe the methods utilized for both internal and external recruitment.

▶ Discuss the criteria used to evaluate the effectiveness of organizational recruitment efforts.

▶ Compare and contrast job performance, selection criteria, and predictors.

▶ Identify the legal requirements of the selection process and outline that process.

▶ Explain the importance of conducting pre-employment background investigations.

Healthcare HR Insights

Information systems and Internet-based technologies are radically changing the way healthcare HR departments are performing the HR functions of recruitment and selection. As an example, Charleston Area Medical Center Health System in West Virginia has developed a system of posting its jobs online and receiving employment applications online. A process that once took thirteen days has been reduced to three days, and further time improvements are anticipated.

Wentworth–Douglass Hospital in Dover, New Hampshire, also posts jobs on the Internet and on its intranet site, thereby reaching both external and internal candidates online. It further digitized the selection process through the use of scanning technology. The HR staff scans paper resumes and applications, allowing department heads the opportunity to view candidate information online.

Carson City Hospital in Carson City, Michigan, has made a significant commitment to online recruitment. Applications for employment are taken almost exclusively online. The hospital's Web page allows job seekers to apply online. Current staff members use a separate system to learn of job openings and apply for transfers online.

Baylor Health Care System in Dallas, Texas, has made a significant move away from traditional recruitment methods of paper-driven and newspaper-driven recruitment modes to an electronic mode. All of its job postings are on the company's Web site, and it uses intranet-based employment services such as *Monster.com* to develop external applicant flow.[1]

All of these examples depict the effectiveness of utilizing information systems and Internet-based technologies in the recruitment of healthcare workers. It also suggests that these approaches to recruitment will continue to be utilized and improved as the healthcare labor market becomes more competitive.

There are number of demographic changes that are and will continue to affect the need for skilled, competent healthcare workers. To further underscore the point, consider the following:

> In the United States, someone turns 50 every eight seconds and will continue to do so for the next decade. The aging baby boomers, nearly 80 million strong, total nearly one-third of the U.S. population. As baby boomers age, their need for health care will grow. By 2020 those individuals that will be 65 or older will require, on average, six times more healthcare dollars per capita than they do today.[2]

A further illustration is contained in an *American Hospital News.com* survey of healthcare CEOs regarding industry issues and concerns, labor and staffing was cited as the CEOs' number-one concern, with financial and compliance issues rounding out the top three.[3] Effective recruitment and selection is critical in healthcare organizations in order to tap appropriate labor markets.

RECRUITING AND LABOR MARKETS

There actually is not one but several **labor markets** that are the external sources from which healthcare employers attract employees. There are many ways to identify labor markets, including by geographical area, type of skill, and educational level. Some specific labor market segments might include managerial, clerical, professional and technical, and service and support. Classified differently, some markets are local, others regional, and others national. There are international labor markets as well. To understand the labor markets in which recruiting takes place, one must consider three different concepts: *labor force population, applicant population,* and *applicant pool.*

The **labor force population** includes all individuals who are available for selection if all possible recruitment strategies are used. This vast array of possible applicants may be reached in very different ways.

The **applicant population** is a subset of the labor force population that is available for selection using a particular recruiting approach. At least four recruiting decisions affect the nature of the applicant population:

▶ *Recruiting Method*—Advertising media chosen
▶ *Recruiting Message*—What is said about the job and how it is said
▶ *Applicant Qualifications Required*—Education level and amount of experience necessary
▶ *Administrative Procedures*—Time of year recruiting is done, follow-ups with applicants, and use of previous applicant files

The **applicant pool** consists of all people who are actually evaluated for selection. The applicant pool at this step will depend on the reputation of the organization as a place to work, the screening done in the organization, and the information available to the applicant population. Assuming a suitable candidate is present, the final selection is made from the applicant pool.

The supply and demand of workers in the labor force population has a substantial impact on the staffing strategies of organizations. Internal labor markets also influence recruiting because many healthcare employers choose to promote from within whenever possible, and hire externally only when internal applicants are unavailable or when internal movement recreates entry-level openings. A discussion of these and other strategic decisions to be made in recruiting follows.

PLANNING AND STRATEGIC DECISIONS REGARDING RECRUITING

The decisions that are made about recruiting help dictate not only the types and numbers of applicants, but also how difficult or successful recruiting efforts may be. Figure 6-1 shows an overview of these recruiting decisions. **Recruiting** involves identifying where to recruit, whom to recruit, and what the job require-

FIGURE 6-1 **Recruiting Decisions**

ments will be. Another key consideration is deciding to what extent internal and/or external searches are to be made.

Internal versus External Recruiting

Both advantages and disadvantages are associated with promoting from within the organization (internal recruitment) and hiring from outside the organization (external recruitment) to fill openings. Most organizations combine the use of internal and external methods. Historically, hospitals have followed a policy of promotion from within. However, operating in rapidly changing environments and competitive conditions, healthcare organizations are placing a heavier emphasis on external sources in addition to their internal sources. Figure 6-2 lists the various recruiting methods, both internal and external, that healthcare organizations utilize. It also notes which method is the most effective for each type of worker.

Flexible Staffing

Decisions as to who should be recruited hinge on whether to seek traditional full-time employees or use more flexible approaches. Healthcare organizations are finding a need to turn to creative staffing approaches to attract and retain workers. Part-time workers are the most traditional flexible staffing approach in healthcare, with about one out of four RNs working in part-time positions.[4]

Healthcare employers that use **temporary employees** can hire their own temporary staff or use agencies supplying temporary workers on a rate-per-day or per-week basis. The use of temporary workers might make sense for healthcare organizations if their work is subject to fluctuations or as an opportunity to evaluate an employee before placing them on the regular payroll. HR departments in many large healthcare organizations have developed internal temporary staffing departments to reduce the handling costs of external temporary agency use for temporary employees.

Some healthcare organizations employ **independent contractors** to perform specific services on a contract basis, such as information technology workers when hospitals were preparing for Y2K. However, those contractors must be independent, as determined by the U.S. Internal Revenue Service and the U.S. Department of Labor. (See Chapter 12 for details.)

Float Pools

Nursing departments typically use RN **resource pools**, where RNs are specifically hired to be available to "float" to various units when census or acuity needs are higher than core staffing needs can meet.[5] Resource pools (or *float pools*) are an especially good way to allow a new nurse the opportunity to work in a variety of settings before deciding which unit, department or even type of nursing is the most desirable. However, due to the ever-increasing specialization within nursing, such as oncology or cardiac care, float nurses cannot be expected to safely work in all areas of a hospital or treatment center.

Employee Leasing

In physician practices and clinics, **employee leasing** is a concept that has grown rapidly in recent years. The employee leasing process is simple: An employer signs an agreement with an employee leasing company, after which the existing staff is hired by the leasing firm and leased back to the company. For a fee, the practice or clinic "leases" its employees from the leasing company, which then writes the paychecks, pays the taxes, prepares and implements HR policies, and keeps all the required records.

FIGURE 6-2 Choosing a Healthcare Recruiting Method

	SERVICE WORKER	OFFICE/CLERICAL	PROFESSIONAL/TECHNICAL	EXECUTIVE/MANAGERIAL
1. Promotion from within	*	*	*	*
2. Job posting and bidding	*	*	*	
3. Contacts and employee referrals	*	*	*	
4. Executive search firm			—	—
5. Internet recruiting sites		*	*	*
6. Media advertisements	*	*	*	*
7. Public employment agency	*	*	—	
8. Private employment agency	*	*	*	*
9. Schools and colleges		*	*	*
10. Clinical rotations, and internships		*	*	
11. Fellowships			*	*
12. Volunteers		*	*	*
13. Professional associations			*	
14. Fellow				
15. Military service	—	—	*	—
16. Former employees		*	*	—
17. Special events	*	*	*	—
18. Temporary help		*	*	

Key: *A good recruiting method
—A possible recruiting method
Source: Developed by Walter J. Flynn, SPHR. May not be used without permission.

119

INTERNAL RECRUITING

Internal recruiting means focusing on current employees and others with previous contact with an employing organization. Friends of current employees, former employees, and previous applicants may be sources. Promotions, demotions, and transfers also can provide additional people for an organizational unit, if not for the entire organization. Among the ways in which internal recruiting sources have an advantage over external sources is that they allow management to observe the candidate for promotion (or transfer) over a period of time and to evaluate that person's potential and specific job performance. Also, an organization that promotes its own employees to fill job openings may give those employees added motivation to do a good job.

Job Posting and Bidding

The major means for recruiting employees for other jobs within healthcare organizations is through **job posting and bidding,** whereby the employer provides notices of job openings and employees respond by applying for specific openings. The organization can notify employees of job vacancies by posting notices in cafeterias, break rooms, and on the organizational Web site.

Internal Recruiting Database

Computerized internal talent banks, or applicant tracking systems, can be used to furnish a listing of the KSAs available for organizations. Employers that must deal with a large number of applications and job openings have found it beneficial to use such software as part of a human resource information system. With the growth of e-mail and intranets, more healthcare organizations are using this approach to internally post the positions.

Job posting and bidding systems can be ineffective if handled improperly. Jobs generally are posted before any external recruiting is done. The organization must allow a reasonable period of time for current employees to check on available jobs before it considers external applicants. A sample of a hospital job posting policy is available at: *http://flynn.swlearning.com.*

Promotion and Transfer

Many healthcare organizations choose to fill vacancies through promotions or transfers from within whenever possible. Although most often successful, promotions from within have some drawbacks as well. The person's performance on one job might not be a good predictor of performance on another, because different skills may be required on the new job. Also, if an organization does not have a diverse workforce, promotions may not be an effective way to speed up the movement of protected-class individuals through the organization.

Current Employee Referrals

One of the most reliable sources of people to fill vacancies is composed of friends and/or family members of current employees. Employees can acquaint potential applicants with the advantages of a job with the company, furnish letters of introduction, and encourage them to apply. These are external applicants recruited using an internal information source. Some employers pay employees incentives for referring individuals with specialized skills that are difficult to recruit through normal means. As an example, in a large midwestern orthopedic and occupational health clinic, employees are encouraged to refer qualified applicants for open positions with the enticement of a $1,000 bonus. If a clinic employee refers a candidate who is hired and successfully completes six months of employment, the referring employee receives half of the bonus, and when the new employee completes a full year of employment, the referring employee receives the balance of the bonus.

Former employees and former applicants are also good internal sources for recruitment. In both cases, there is a timesaving advantage, because something is already known about the potential employee.

EXTERNAL RECRUITING

If internal sources do not produce enough acceptable candidates for jobs, many external sources are available. These sources include schools, colleges and universities, media sources, trade and competitive sources, employment agencies, executive search firms, and the Internet.

Schools, Colleges, and Universities

High schools or vocational/technical schools may be a good source of new employees for many organizations. A successful recruiting program with these institutions is the result of careful analysis and continual contact with individual schools. There are a number of positions within healthcare organizations where a high school degree or GED is an appropriate educational requirement; these jobs include a wide variety of service worker, clerical, and clinical support positions.

At the college or university level, the recruitment of graduating students is a large-scale operation for many healthcare organizations. Most colleges and universities maintain placement offices in which employers and applicants can meet.

Media Sources

Media sources such as newspapers, magazines, television, radio, and billboards are widely used. Whatever medium is used, it should be tied to the relevant labor market and provide sufficient information on the company and the job.

When using recruitment advertisements in the media, employers should ask five key questions:

1. What is the ad suppose to accomplish?
2. How should the message be presented?
3. Who are the people we want to reach?
4. Where should it be placed?
5. What should the advertising message convey?

Professional Associations

Many healthcare professional societies and associations publish newsletters or magazines containing job ads. Such publications may be a good source of applicants for specialized professionals. In addition many professional associations maintain recruitment links on their Web sites, such as the site for the Society for Human Resources Management (*http://www.shrm.org*).

Employment Agencies

Every state in the United States has its own state-sponsored employment agency. These agencies operate branch offices in many cities throughout the state and do not charge fees to applicants or employers. Private employment agencies are also found in most cities. For a fee collected from either the employee or the employer (usually the employer), these agencies do some preliminary screening for an organization and put the organization in touch with applicants.

Executive Search Firms

Some employment agencies focus their efforts on executive, managerial, and professional positions. These executive search firms are split into two groups: (1) contingency firms that charge a fee only after a candidate has been hired by a client company, and (2) retainer firms that charge a client a set fee whether or not the contracted search is successful. Both types of firms are widely used by healthcare organizations to staff specialized clinical, management, and executive positions.

INTERNET RECRUITING

Healthcare organizations first started using computers as a recruiting tool by advertising jobs on a *bulletin board service* from which prospective applicants would contact the employer. Then some organizations began to take e-mail applications. Today, the Internet has become a primary means for many healthcare employers to search for job candidates and applicants to look for jobs. The explosive growth in the Internet is a key reason. Estimates are that there are more than 160 million Internet users in the United States and 1.2 billion worldwide. In the United States, it is estimated that 74% of those with Internet access, aged 18 years or older, annually use the Internet as part of job searching.[7] Internet users tap the Internet to search for jobs almost as frequently as reading newspaper classified ads. Also, resumes are submitted or posted on the Internet by many of these Internet users.

HR professionals and recruiters are using the Internet regularly, also. When HR recruiters were asked what sources generate more new hires, 77% of those responding indicated Internet job postings produced more new hires, compared with 17.5% citing newspaper ads.[8] Various surveys found that 80% to 90% of employers use the Internet for recruiting. Estimates are that there are more than 100,000 recruiting Web sites on which to post jobs and review resumes of various types that employers and job candidates can access. But the explosive growth of Internet recruiting also means that HR professionals can be overwhelmed by the breadth and scope of Internet recruiting.

E-Recruiting Methods

There are several different methods used for Internet recruiting. The most commons ones are job boards, professional/career Web sites, and employer Web sites.

Job Boards   Numerous **job boards** exist on which employers can post jobs or search for candidates. Common ones are *http://www.monster.com* and *http://www.hotjobs.com*. Another one in wide use, that operates in colloboration with the American Society for Healthcare Human Resources Administration (ASHHRA) is *http://www.CareerBuilder.com*.

Although job boards provide access to lots of candidates, many individuals accessing the sites are *job browsers* who are not serious about changing jobs, but are checking out compensation levels and what job availability exists in their areas of interest. One estimate is that about one-third of all visitors to the job boards are just browsing, not seriously considering changing employment.[9] Despite these concerns, HR recruiters find the general job boards useful for generating applicant responses. Also, a recruiter for a firm can pretend to be an applicant in order to check out what other employers are looking for in similar job candidates and competitor compensation information in order to maintain recruiting competitiveness.[10]

Professional/Career Web Sites   Many professional associations have employment sections on their Web sites. As illustration, for HR jobs see *http://www.shrm.org* or *http://www.astd.org*. Also, a number of private corporations have set up specialized health career Web sites in order to focus on such areas as nurse anestheticists, physician assistants, or other areas. Using these more targeted Web sites limits somewhat the recruiters' search time and efforts. Also, posting jobs on such Web sites is likely to target applicants specifically interested in the job field and may reduce the number of less-qualified applicants who actually apply.

Employer Web Sites   While job boards and other job sites are very popular, many recruiters have found employer Web sites to be effective and efficient when recruiting candidates.[11] Numerous employers have included employment and career information as part of their organizational Web sites. On many of these sites, job seekers are encouraged to e-mail resumes or complete online applications.

Effective Online Job Postings

The rapid growth of the Internet for recruiting has changed the way many organizations find applicants. Instead of using newspaper ads as a primary source for recruiting, online job posting is an integral part of most recruiting efforts. However, developing effective online job announcements is not simply putting a newspaper ad into an electronic form. Some of the suggestions for preparing effective online job posting follow:

▶ *Make the Posting Appealing*—It must grab people's interest, so use some graphics, company logo, and other simple artwork to make the posting stand out.

▶ *Make it Readable*—Use easy-to-read language, including avoidance of too many abbreviations and jargon not easily recognizable by applicants. Also, do not use all capital or bolded letters, as it looks too dense.

▶ *Recognize that Shorter is Better*—Too many employers start online ads with fifty- to sixty-word paragraphs on the company and general descriptive words that are overused, such as *challenging, progressive,* and so on.

▶ *Start with Clear Job Title and Overview*—The job title and the brief description of the job responsibilities determine if anything else is read. These items are like the headline and first paragraph of a news article. If they are not interesting, the rest of the details do not get read.

▶ *Describe the Employer Concisely*—A brief description of the employer, especially the division and location of the job, should provide information and create interest in the organization.

▶ *State Necessary Qualifications Clearly*—Care should be taken that the level of qualifications are reflected accurately, so that exceptional candidates see that the qualifications are not too low, thus discouraging them from applying. Alternatively, "puffing up" qualifications may eliminate candidates who see the job as above their capabilities.

▶ *Provide Salary and Benefits Information*—A job posting should provide a salary range and emphasize competitive benefits, especially by noting any special benefits available. However, care should be taken to avoid a "laundry-list" look to the benefits.

▶ *Indicate How to Apply*—It is important to build in automatic links to e-mail or to an employment application so that an applicant can *click to apply*. As back up, fax number and mailing address information should be provided, along with a contact name or code number. Generally, it is recommended that phone numbers only be included if the employer wishes to field telephone inquiries, which may be too numerous in some cases but desirable in others.

It is important that the recruiting and employment portions of the employer Web sites be seen as part of the firm's marketing efforts. Therefore, the employment sections of organizational Web sites must be shaped to market jobs and careers effectively.[12] Also, the Web site should market the employer by providing information on the organization, organizational growth potential, and organizational operations, so that potential applicants can learn general information about the employer. Unfortunately, many employers' Web sites do not incorporate career and employment information effectively.

Advantages of Internet Recruiting

There are a number of advantages that employers have found using Internet recruiting. A primary one is that many employers have experienced *cost-savings* using Internet recruiting compared to other sources such as newspaper advertising, employment agencies and search firms, and other external sources. Some employers have experienced savings from several hundred dollars per hire to as high as $4,000 to $6,000 for senior professional and management jobs.[13]

Internet recruiting also can save considerable time. Applicants can respond quickly to job postings by sending e-mails, rather than using *snail mail*. Recruiters can respond to qualified candidates more quickly and establish times for interviews or request additional candidate information.

An *expanded pool of applicants* can be generated using Internet recruiting. Depending on the Internet sources used, jobs can be exposed to a large number of candidates. One side benefit of the Internet is that jobs literally are posted globally, so potential applicants in other geographic areas and countries can view job openings posted on the Web.

Disadvantages of Internet Recruiting

The positives associated with Internet recruiting also come with some disadvantages. By getting broader exposure, employers also may get *more unqualified applicants*. A survey of HR recruiters found that one-third of them said Internet recruiting has created additional work for HR staff members.[14] More resumes must be reviewed, more e-mails dealt with, and specialized applicant tracking software may be needed to handle the increase in applicants caused in many Internet recruiting efforts.

As previously noted, many individuals who access job sites are browsers who may submit resumes just to see what happens, but who are not seriously looking for new jobs. Another issue with Internet recruiting is that applicants may have *limited Internet access*. This is especially true of individuals from lower socioeconomic groups and certain racial/ethnic minority groups. Data from a U.S. Department of Labor study found that there is a *digital divide*, whereby fewer Hispanic and African-American job seekers have Internet access at home, or even at all.[15] Consequently, employers might not be getting as diverse a recruitment pool as might be desired through the Internet recruiting. Despite these disadvantages, it is likely that Internet recruiting will continue to grow in usage. Employers and job seekers alike are seeing e-recruiting as a major part of external recruiting.

OTHER SOURCES FOR HEALTHCARE RECRUITMENT

Thanks in part to the unique aspects of the educational preparation for most clinical degrees and some administrative degrees, many healthcare employers have a ready-made source of applicant flow. Clinical rotations, preceptorships, and internships are part of the education and clinical development for such fields as nursing, pharmacy, medical technology and other therapies. Fellowships are a part of the education development for Healthcare Administration degrees. The individuals in these educational areas pursue their "clinicals" in hospitals, clinics, nursing homes, and other healthcare provider environments, so they are easily accessed to discuss current or future openings and career opportunities.

Clinical Rotations

In all clinical-preparation degree programs, a clinical rotation is required to facilitate the students' learning in the "hands-on" aspect of their professions. These rotations are typically hosted by clinics, hospitals, nursing homes, or other care provision facilities. Many organizations that host clinical rotations take full advantage of the opportunity to recruit the students while they are on site.[16]

Preceptorships and Internships

Similar to clinical rotations, preceptorships and internships are part of the educational experience but usually occur at the later stages or end of a health professional's training. Many healthcare organizations have incorporated the preceptorships and internships into their normal recruitment cycle—in some instances, exclusively relying on the individuals who complete their preceptorships or internships at their facilities to fill open positions.

Fellowships

Many undergraduate and graduate degree programs in Healthcare Administration, Public Health, and Health Planning include post-graduation fellowship programs. These fellowships place the new graduates in high-level support positions to administrators, CEOs, or other healthcare executives. The *"fellows,"* as they are called, receive on-the-job training typically by doing special projects or studies, such as preparing for a JCAHO site visit. Some of the fellowships result in opportunities for the fellows to move into middle-management positions at the completion of the experience.

Summer Employment, Shadowing, and Volunteer Pools

Many healthcare employers have relied on college students for summer replacement work. These summer replacements may be an excellent recruitment source once they graduate. In order to encourage health careers, healthcare employers have established *shadowing programs.* These programs simply provide an individual who is considering a healthcare occupation or educational program the opportunity to accompany a healthcare professional during a workday. The shadowing experience allows the potential employee or student to gain a unique, up-close glimpse of the healthcare environment and position responsibilities.

Volunteer pools have also been used to attract applicants. Hospitals and extended care facilities have historically availed themselves of volunteers who perform a wide array of hospitality, reception, delivery, or related services. Many healthcare facilities have well-developed programs with hundreds of volunteers that augment their paid staff. In addition to providing labor cost savings, the volunteers are an excellent source of applicants for positions.

RECRUITING EVALUATION

Evaluating the success of recruiting efforts is important. General areas for evaluating recruiting include the following:

▶ *Quantity of Applicants*—Because the goal of a good recruiting program is to generate a large pool of applicants from which to choose, quantity must be sufficient to provide a choice and fill job vacancies.
▶ *EEO Goals Met*—The recruiting program is the key activity used to meet goals for hiring protected-class individuals. This is especially relevant when a company is engaged in affirmative action to meet such goals.
▶ *Quality of Applicants*—There is the issue of whether the qualifications of the applicant pool are sufficient to fill the job openings, whereby the applicants meet job specifications and perform the jobs.
▶ *Cost per Applicant Hired*—Cost varies, depending on the position being filled, but knowing how much it costs to fill an empty position puts turnover and salary levels in perspective.
▶ *Time Required to Fill Openings*—The length of time it takes to fill openings is another means of evaluating recruiting efforts. If openings are filled quickly with qualified candidates, the work and productivity of the organization are not delayed by vacancies.

In summary, the effectiveness of recruiting sources will vary, depending on the nature of the job being filled and the time available to fill it. But unless calculated, the effectiveness may not be entirely obvious.

NATURE OF SELECTION

Selection is the process of choosing qualified individuals from an applicant pool to fill jobs in an organization. Without qualified employees, a healthcare organization is in a much poorer position to succeed. The JCAHO feature details the importance of a comprehensive selection process for healthcare employees.

THE JOINT COMMISSION ON ACCREDITATION OF HEALTHCARE ORGANIZATIONS

Joint Commission Standards on Recruitment and Selection

Healthcare organizations that comply with the JCAHO process of review to ensure the delivery of safe, competent care should be keenly aware of the standards that relate to recruitment and selection. These standards require healthcare organizations to maintain a system that ensures staff competency, by having an effective selection process.

Recruitment and Selection Process

Policies on recruitment and selection should be developed and maintained and contained in the HR policy manual for dissemination to individuals involved in the process. Key elements of the process should include the following:

▶ Interview
▶ Pre-employment testing, where appropriate
▶ Reference and background checking
▶ Pre-placement physical assessments
▶ Review of license, registration, or certification, as required

Consistently adhering to an effective selection process, as detailed above, is critical to ensuring the employment of the most qualified and competent candidates. Failure to follow a process can result in significant employment issues and liabilities for healthcare organizations.

Selection is much more than just choosing the best available person. Selecting the appropriate set of KSAs—which come packaged in a human being—is an attempt to get a "fit" between what the applicant can do and wants to do, and what the organization needs. Fit between the applicant and the organization affects both the employer's willingness to make a job offer and an applicant's willingness to accept a job. Fitting a person to the right job is called **placement.** More than anything else, placement of human resources should be seen as a *matching process.* Whether an employer uses specific KSAs or the more general approach, effective selection of employees involves understanding *criteria* and *predictors* of job performance.

Criteria, Predictors, and Job Performance

At the heart of an effective selection system is knowledge of what constitutes appropriate job performance and what characteristics in employees are associated with that performance. Once the definition of employee success (performance) is known, the employee specifications required to achieve that success can

FIGURE 6-3   Job Performance, Selection Criteria, and Predictors

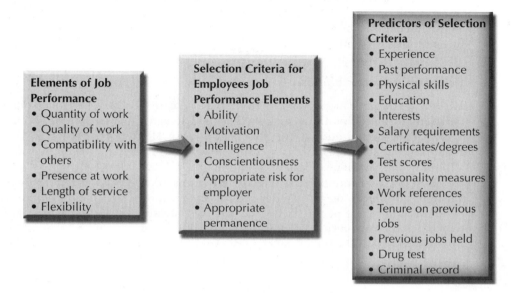

be determined. A **selection criterion** is a characteristic that a person must have to do the job successfully. Figure 6-3 shows that ability, motivation, intelligence, conscientiousness, appropriate risk, and permanence might be good selection criteria for many jobs. To predict whether a selection criterion (such as motivation or ability) is present, employers need to identify **predictors** as visable indicators of the selection criteria.

Legal Concerns

Generally, employers use a variety of pre-employment steps and predictors to ensure that applicants will fit available jobs. Selection is subject to all EEO concerns.

It is increasingly important for employers to define carefully exactly who is an applicant, given the legal issues involved. If there is no written policy defining conditions that make a person an applicant, anyone who sends unsolicited resumes might later claim that he or she was not hired because of illegal discrimination. A policy defining *applicant* might include the following aspects:

▶ Applications are accepted only when there is an opening.
▶ Only individuals filling out application blanks are considered applicants.
▶ A person's application ceases to be effective after a designated date.
▶ Only a certain number of applications will be accepted.
▶ People must apply for specific jobs, not "any job."

The **Immigration Reform and Control Act (IRCA) of 1986,** as revised in 1990, requires that within seventy-two hours of hiring, an employer must determine whether a job applicant is a U.S. citizen, registered alien, or illegal alien. Those not eligible to work in this country must not be hired. The I-9 form is used by employers to identify the status of potential employees.

Selection Responsibilities

Healthcare organizations vary in how they allocate selection responsibilities between HR specialists and managers. Selection activities may be centralized into a specialized organizational unit that is part of an HR department. In smaller organizations, such as clinics (especially those with fewer than 100 employees), a full-time employment specialist or unit might be impractical.

Most organizations take certain common steps to process applicants for jobs. Variations on this basic process depend on organizational size, nature of jobs to be filled, number of people to be selected, and pressure of outside forces. The selection process shown in Figure 6-4 is typical in a large healthcare organization. However, all or some of the components of the process are easily utilized in smaller organizations, such as physician or dental practices.

Reception and Job Preview/Interest Screening

In addition to matching qualified people to jobs, the selection process has an important public-relations dimension. This is especially true for healthcare employees. Discriminatory hiring practices, impolite interviewers, unnecessarily long waits, inappropriate testing procedures, and lack of follow-up letters can produce unfavorable impressions of an employer.

In some cases, it is appropriate to have a brief interview, called an *initial screening* or a *job preview/interest screen,* to see if the applicant is likely to match any jobs available in the organization after allowing the individual to fill out an application form. In certain cases healthcare organizations conduct the preview/interest screen interview by phone. The job preview/interest screen also can be done effectively by computer. Computerized processing of applicants can occur on several different levels. Computers can search resumes or application blanks for key words. Hundreds of large healthcare organizations use types of artificial-intelligence (AI) or *text-searching* software to scan, score, and track resumes of applicants. A second means of computerizing screening is conducting initial screening interviews electronically. Computer-assisted interviewing techniques can use tools such as videotaped scenarios to which applicants react.

The purpose of a **realistic job preview (RJP)** is to inform job candidates of the "organizational realities" of a job so that they can more accurately evaluate their own job expectations. By presenting applicants with a clear picture of the job, the organization hopes to reduce unrealistic expectations, thereby reducing employee disenchantment and ultimately employee dissatisfaction and turnover. A review of research on RJP's found that they tend to result in applicants having lower job expectations.[17]

FIGURE 6-4   Selection Process Flowchart

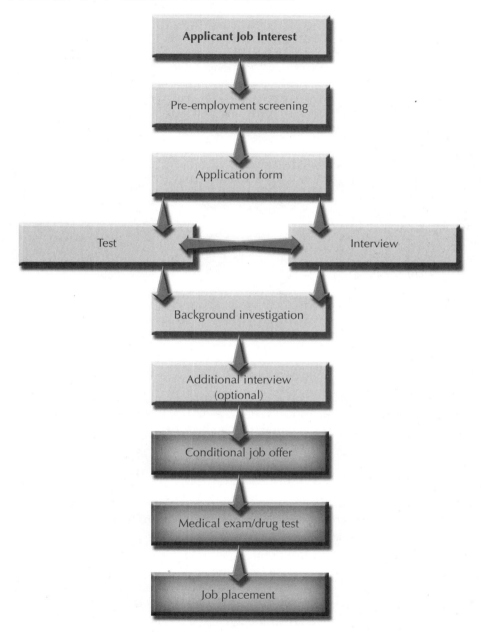

FIGURE 6-5   Psychology of Selection

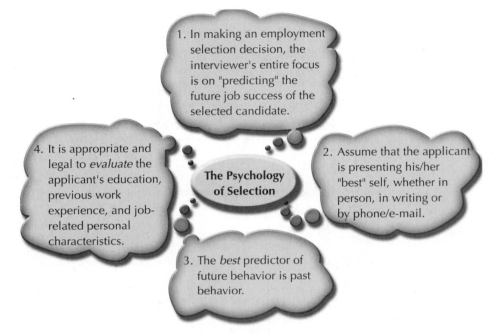

1. In making an employment selection decision, the interviewer's entire focus is on "predicting" the future job success of the selected candidate.

4. It is appropriate and legal to *evaluate* the applicant's education, previous work experience, and job-related personal characteristics.

The Psychology of Selection

2. Assume that the applicant is presenting his/her "best" self, whether in person, in writing or by phone/e-mail.

3. The *best* predictor of future behavior is past behavior.

The psychology of selection is depicted in Figure 6-5. The components described in Figure 6-5 provide a useful way to think about the way a selection decision should be approached and ultimately made.

Application Forms

Application forms are widely used. A sample application is available on the book's Web site: *http://flynn.swlearning.com.* Properly prepared, an application form serves four purposes:

1. It is a record of the applicant's desire to obtain a position.
2. It provides the interviewer with a profile of the applicant that can be used in the interview.
3. It is a basic employee record for applicants who are hired.
4. It can be used for research on the effectiveness of the selection process.

Application Disclaimers and Notices   Application forms need disclaimers and notices so that employers state appropriate legal protections. Recommended disclosures and notices appearing on applications include:

▶ *Employment-at-Will*—Indicates the right of the employer or applicant to terminate the employment relationship at any time with or without notice or cause (where applicable by state law).

▶ *Employment Testing*—Notifies applicants of required drug tests, physical exams, or other tests.

▶ *Reference Contacts*—Requests permission to contact references listed by applicants.

▶ *Application Time Limit*—Indicates how long applications are active (typically six months), and that individuals must reactivate applications after that period.

▶ *Information Falsification*—Conveys to an applicant signing the form that falsification of application information is grounds for termination.

Resumes   One of the most common methods applicants use to provide background information is the resume. Technically, a resume used in place of an application form must be treated by an employer as an application for EEO purposes. However, substituting a resume for an application form is discouraged. The application form, if properly designed, should require the applicant's signature attesting to the accuracy and truthfulness of the information provided by the applicant. When organizations rely exclusively on resumes they do not have those assurances to legally act upon in the event of misrepresentation by the applicants.

Selection Testing

According to the Uniform Selection Guidelines issued by the EEOC, any employment requirement is a "test." Some employers purchase prepared tests, while other employers develop their own tests. Many people feel that formal tests can be of great benefit in the selection process when properly used and administered.

Interpreting test results is not always straightforward, even if the test is valid. Individuals trained in testing and test interpretation should be involved in establishing and maintaining a testing system. Furthermore, the role of tests in the overall selection process must be kept in perspective.

Ability and Aptitude Tests   **Ability tests** assess the skills that individuals have already learned. **Aptitude tests** measure general ability to learn or acquire a skill.

Data entry tests are commonly given at many healthcare organizations to applicants for positions in registration and medical transcription. These tests are a form of ability tests. Other widely used tests measure mechanical ability and manual dexterity.

Mental ability tests measure reasoning capabilities. Some of the abilities tested include spatial orientation, comprehension and retention span, and general and conceptual reasoning. The General Aptitude Test Battery (GATB) is a widely used test of this type.

Assessment Centers An **assessment center** is not necessarily a place, but a series of evaluative exercises and tests used for selection and development. The assessment uses multiple exercises and multiple raters. In one assessment center, candidates go through a comprehensive interview, pencil-and-paper test, individual and group simulations, and work exercises. The candidates' performances are then evaluated by a panel of trained raters. It is crucial to any assessment center that the tests and exercises reflect the job content and types of problems faced on the jobs for which individuals are being screened.

Psychological/Personality Tests Personality is a unique blend of individual characteristics that affect interaction with the environment and help define a person. Historically, predictive validity has tended to be lower for personality tests used as predictors of performance on the job. However, some studies have shown that carefully chosen personality tests that logically connect to work requirements can help predict the interpersonal aspects of job success.

Physical Ability Tests Physical ability tests measure individual abilities such as the applicant's strength, endurance, and muscular movement. At a nursing home, nursing assistants must routinely lift or move residents. Testing the applicant's mobility, strength, and other physical attributes is job-related. A type of physical ability test, *functional capacity testing*, measures such areas as range of motion, strength and posture, cardiovascular fitness, and other facets.[18] As noted later, care should be taken to limit physical ability testing until after a conditional job offer is made in order to avoid violating the provisions of the Americans with Disabilities Act (ADA).

Different skill-based tests can be used, including **psychomotor tests** that measure a person's dexterity, hand–eye coordination, arm–hand steadiness, and other factors. Such tests as the MacQuarie Test for Mechanical Ability can measure manual dexterity for biomedical repair technician's skills.

Selection Interviewing

A selection interview is designed to identify information on a candidate and clarify information from other sources. This in-depth interview is designed to integrate all the information from application forms, tests, and reference checks, so that a decision can be made. Because of the integration required and the desirability of face-to-face contact, the interview is the most important phase of the selection process in many situations. Conflicting information may have emerged from tests, application forms, and references. As a result, the interviewer must obtain as much pertinent information about the applicant as possible during the limited interview time and evaluate this information against job standards. Figure 6-6 details the "do's" and "don'ts" of employment interviewing. Finally, a selection decision must be made, based on all of the information obtained in the preceding steps.

The interview is not an especially valid predictor of job performance, but it has high "face validity"—that is, it seems valid to employers and they like it. Virtually all employers are likely to hire individuals using interviews.

FIGURE 6-6   Interview Questions Do's and Don'ts

Do not ask	Do ask

Do not ask

- Do you have any physical or other limitations?
- Do you have any disabilities?
- Have you ever filed for or collected workers' compensation?
- How many times were you absent due to illness in the past two years?
- Have you been treated for any of the following medical conditions?
- Do you have any family members with health problems or history of illness or disabilities?
- Why are you using crutches, and how did you become injured?
- Have you ever seen a psychiatrist?
- When did you develop your disability?

Do ask

- Can you perform the essential functions of the job for which you are applying with or without accommodation? Please describe any accommodations needed.
- How would you perform the essential tasks of the job for which you applied?
- If hired, how would you perform the tasks outlined in the job description you reviewed?
- Describe your attendance record on your last job.
- Describe any problems you would have reaching the top of a six-foot filing cabinet.
- What did your prior job duties consist of, and which ones were the most challenging?

Structured Interview   The **structured interview** uses a set of standardized questions that are asked of all applicants. Every applicant is asked the same basic questions, so that comparisons among applicants can more easily be made. This type of interview allows an interviewer to prepare job-related questions in advance and then complete a standardized interviewee evaluation form. Completion of such a form provides documentation if anyone, including an EEO enforcement body, should question why one applicant was selected over another.

Behavioral Event Interview   When responding to a **behavioral event interview,** applicants are required to give specific examples of how they have performed a certain procedure or handled a problem in the past. Consistent with information detailed earlier, behavioral event interviews provide insight on how the applicant will perform in the future based on how they have performed in the past. For example, a behavioral event interview question for clinic manager applicant might be: "Describe how you have handled difficult employee relations situations in your past supervisory positions; include examples and outcomes in your response." An applicant's response to this question could provide important insight regarding how they would handle future employee relations situations they were confronted with, and whether their approach is compatible with the approach the organization they are interviewing with would utilize. Like other structured selection methods, behavioral event interviews generally provide better validity than unstructured interviews.

Panel Interview   Usually, applicants are interviewed by one interviewer at a time. But when an interviewee must see several people, many of the interviews are redundant and therefore unnecessarily time-consuming. In a **panel interview,** several interviewers interview the candidate at the same time. All the interviewers hear the same responses. On the negative side, applicants are frequently uncomfortable with the group interview format.

Background Checking

Due to the very nature of providing patient care and the close personal and physical contact many healthcare workers have with patients, residents, or clients, healthcare organizations have a special duty to conduct background checks. This duty is to ensure that the patient caregivers in their employment have no previous record involving crimes of violence or sexual misconduct.[19]

Background checking may take place either before or after the in-depth interview. It costs the organization some time and money, but it is generally well worth the effort. Unfortunately, some applicants misrepresent their qualifications and backgrounds.

Legal Constraints   Various federal and state laws have been passed to protect the rights of individuals whose backgrounds may be investigated during pre-employment screening. States vary in what they allow employers to investigate. In some states, healthcare employers can request information directly from law enforcement agencies on applicants. In Ohio, for example, healthcare organizations and daycare centers must submit the fingerprints of applicants to determine if the applicants have disqualifying criminal histories.

Fair Credit Reporting Act   Some healthcare employers check applicants' credit histories. The logic is that individuals with poor credit histories may signal irresponsibility. This assumption may be questioned, however, and firms that check applicants' credit records must comply with the federal Fair Credit Reporting Act. This act basically requires disclosing that a credit check is being made, obtaining written consent from the person being checked, and furnishing the applicant a copy of the report. Some state laws also prohibit employers from getting certain credit information.

Credit history checking should be done on applicants for jobs in which use, access, or management of money is an essential job function. Commonly, healthcare organizations check credit histories on employees who handle money or are responsible for sensitive financial information, such as accountants or business office personnel.

Giving References on Former Employees   In a number of court cases, individuals have sued their former employers for slander, libel, or defamation of character as a result of what the employers said to other potential employers that prevented the individuals from obtaining jobs. Because of such problems, lawyers advise organizations who are asked about former employees to give out only name, employment date, and title; many organizations have adopted policies restricting the release of reference information.

Under the Federal Privacy Act of 1974, a governmental employer must have a signed release from a person before it can give information about that person to someone else. The recommendation is that all employers obtain a signed release from individuals during exit interviews authorizing employers to provide reference information in the future.

Clearly, employers are in a difficult position. Because of threats of lawsuits, they must obtain information on potential employees but are unwilling to give out information in return. To address these concerns, thirty-five states have laws that protect employers from civil liability when giving reference information in good faith that is objective and factual in nature.[20]

Risks of Negligent Hiring   The costs of failing to check references may be high. Some organizations have become targets of lawsuits that charge them with negligence in hiring workers who have committed violent acts on the job. Lawyers say that an employer's liability hinges on how well it investigates an applicant's background. Prior convictions and frequent moves or gaps in employment should be cues for further inquiry. Details provided on the application form by the applicant should be investigated to the greatest extent possible, so the employer can show that due diligence was exercised. Also, employers should document their efforts to check background information by noting who was contacted, when, and what information was or was not provided. This documentation can aid in countering negligent hiring claims.

Medical Examinations and Inquiries

Medical information on applicants may be used to determine the individual's physical and mental capability for performing jobs. Physical standards for jobs should be realistic, justifiable, and geared to the job requirements. Workers with disabilities can perform satisfactorily in many jobs. However, in many places, they are rejected because of their disabilities, rather than being screened and placed in appropriate jobs.

ADA and Medical Inquiries   The Americans with Disabilities Act (ADA) prohibits the use of pre-employment medical exams, except for drug tests, until a job has been conditionally offered. Also, the ADA prohibits a company from rejecting an individual because of a disability and from asking job applicants any question relative to current or past medical history until a conditional job offer is made. Assuming a conditional offer of employment is made, then some organizations ask applicants to complete a pre-employment health checklist or are given a physical examination paid for by the employer.[21]

Drug Testing Drug testing may be a part of a medical exam, or it may be done separately. Using drug testing as a part of the selection process has increased in the past few years, although some employers facing tight labor markets have discontinued drug testing. If used, employers should remember that the accuracy of drug tests varies according to the type of test used, the item tested, and the quality of the laboratory where the test samples are sent. Because of the potential impact of prescription drugs on test results, applicants should complete a detailed questionnaire on this matter before the testing. If an individual tests positive for drug use, then an independent medical laboratory should administer a second, more detailed analysis. Whether urine, blood, saliva, or hair samples are used, the process of obtaining, labeling, and transferring the samples to the testing lab should be outlined clearly and definite policies and procedures established.

Genetic Testing Another controversial area of medical testing is genetic testing. Employers that use genetic screening tests do so for several reasons. First, the tests may link workplace health hazards and individuals with certain genetic characteristics. Second, genetic testing may be used to make workers aware of genetic problems that could occur in certain work situations. The third use is the most controversial: to exclude individuals from certain jobs if they have genetic conditions that increase their health risks. Because people cannot change their genetic makeup, the potential for illegal discrimination based on genetic predisposition to future health issues is very real.

Making the Job Offer

The final step of the selection process is making a job offer. Often extended over the phone, many job offers are formalized in letters and sent to applicants. It is important that the offer document be reviewed by legal counsel and that the terms and conditions of employment be clearly identified. Care should be taken to avoid vague, general statements and promises about bonuses, work schedules, or other matters that might change later. These documents also should provide for the individuals to sign an acceptance of the offer and return it to the employer, who should place it in the individual's personnel files. Once selected, new employees may require relocation assistance.

Relocation Assistance

Healthcare employers may provide relocation assistance for individuals selected who live away from the new job site. Such relocation assistance often includes sales of existing homes, moving expenses, house-hunting trip costs, automobile transportation, and new home mortgage assistance. Regardless of the type of relocation assistance, the nature and extent of relocation assistance sets a tone for the way new employees view their new jobs. Such assistance also aids in the adjustment of the employees' family members. Relocation assistance enables new employees to become more productive more quickly in their new locations.[22]

CASE

Excelsior Nursing and Care Centers (Excelsior) is an eighty-five-bed geriatric care center. Like many nursing and extended care facilities, Excelsior has been struggling to attract applicants for many of its open positions. Its current vacancy rates for key positions includes the following: a) LPNs 20% b) Nursing aides 40% c) Housekeeping assistants 20%

In the past its external recruitment efforts have been to utilize the traditional methods of newspaper ads and notifying the local high schools and trade schools of openings. Internally, Excelsior posts all open positions and encourages employees to monitor the postings and refer their friends and relatives for consideration. However, the lack of applicants for open positions is reaching a critical point. A moratorium was instituted for any new patient admissions. Also, for new residents, Excelsior has been forced to utilize temporary staffing agencies for LPNs to cover open night and weekend shifts.

To deal with this crisis a task force composed of department heads has been established. The role of the task force is to evaluate the recruitment situation and make recommendations.

Questions

1. Identify a strategic approach to developing recruitment methods.
2. What other methods of recruitment should the task force consider?

END NOTES

1. Jan Greene, "The Goal: Helping Employees Help Their Careers," *Hospitals & Health Networks* (Winter 2002), 44–47.
2. David B. Friend, "Healthcare.com RX for Reform," *Watson Wyatt Worldwide* (2000), 2.
3. "Labor/Staffing Issue Now CEO's Top Concern," *AHA News Now*, (August 2, 2001). *http://www.AHAnews.com.*
4. Bureau of Labor Statistics, U.S. Department of Labor, 2002–03 *http://www.BLS.gov.*
5. Kennard T. Wing, "When Flex Comes to Shove: Staffing and Hospital Census," *Nursing Management* (January 2001), 43–46.
6. Mary Chris Jaklevic, "Wanted: A Few Good Leaders," *Modern Healthcare* (October 2, 2000), 38.
7. John R. Hall, "Recruiting Via The Internet," *Air Conditioning, Heating & Refrigeration News* (April 9, 2001), 26.
8. Internet Recruiting Newsletter, (March 9, 2001). Available at *http://www.recruitersnetwork.com.*
9. Kate Dale, "Making the New Work," *HR World* (May–June 2000), 32–36.

10. Bill Leonard, "Online and Overwhelmed," *HR Magazine* (August 2000), 37–42.

11. C. Glenn Peace and Tracey L. Tuten, "Internet Recruiting in The Banking Industry," *Business Communications Quarterly* (March 2001), 9–18.

12. Peter Cappelli, "Making the Most of Online Recruiting," *Harvard Business Review* (March 2001), 139–146.

13. Skip Corsini, "Wired to Hire," *Training* (June 2001), 50–54.

14. "Online Recruiting: What Works, What Doesn't," *HR Focus* (March 2000), 1+.

15. Peter Kuhn and Mikal Skuiterud, "Job Search Methods: Internet Versus Traditional," *Monthly Labor Review* (October 2000), 3–11.

16. "Red Carpet Clinical Rotations," *Health Care Advisory Board: Competing for Talent Recovering America's Hospital Workforce* (2001), 309–320.

17. Jean M. Phillips, "Effects of Realistic Job Previews on Multiple Organizational Outcomes," *Academy of Management Journal* 41 (1998), 673–690; and *Peter W. Horn, et al.,* "An Exploratory Investigation Into Theoretical Mechanisms Underlying Realistic Job Previews," *Personnel Psychology* 51 (1998), 421.

18. Craig S. Philson, "Functional Capacity Testing," *Occupational Health and Safety* (January 2000), 78–84.

19. Walter J. Flynn, "Pre-employment Background Checks," *Employment Benefits Planner* (Third Quarter 2001), 18–19.

20. Carolyn Hirschman, "Laws Protect Reference Checks," *HR Magazine* (June 2000), 91.

21. Peter J. Petesch, "Popping the Disability Related Question," *HR Magazine* (November 2000), 161–172.

22. Thomas Philbin, "Give Your Movers A Performance Review," *HR Magazine* (January 2001), 81–84.

CHAPTER 7

Organizational Relations and Employee Retention in Healthcare

Learning Objectives

After you have read this chapter, you should be able to:

▶ Explain the factors affecting the relationship between employees and healthcare organizations.

▶ Discuss the importance of employee retention for healthcare organizations.

▶ Identify the common reasons employees voluntarily leave organizations.

▶ Define the various organizational retention determinants.

▶ Describe how to compute the cost of organizational turnover.

Healthcare HR Insights

Poudre Valley Health System in Fort Collins, Colorado reports an RN vacancy rate of 4.6% out of 650 nursing positions. This vacancy rate is less than 50% the national average, even though Poudre Valley must compete with hospitals in nearby Denver and Greeley. Poudre Valley's nursing retention plan includes five key efforts:

▶ Poudre Valley invests $1 million a year to support a low patient-to-nurse ratio—two to three medical/surgical patients during day shift and up to six patients per nurse at night.

▶ $350,000 is donated annually to a nearby nursing school for scholarships. In return, the system receives the commitment of placing ten new nurses a year in its facility.

▶ The CEO and Board of Trustees support efforts to discourage disruptive physician behavior by encouraging effective communications between physicians and nursing staff members.

▶ Experienced nurses receive extra pay for helping to orient new hires.

▶ Some nurses also receive higher pay if they serve as clinical coordinators or patient coordinators.

Not only have Poudre Valley's efforts yielded a low RN vacancy rate, but it has also been selected as a "magnet hospital" by the American Nurses Association's (ANA) credentialing center. This ANA program recognizes what it deems as excellence in nursing management philosophy and practices.[1]

Retaining competent clinical professionals is a critical requirement for all healthcare providers. Given the difficulty of recruiting clinical professionals from an aging workforce and declining new graduate pool, it is imperative that healthcare providers focus attention on retaining their current clinical professionals.[2]

RELATIONSHIPS

At one time, loyalty and long service with one healthcare organization was considered an appropriate individual/organizational relationship. Recently, changes have been noted in both loyalty and length of service, with employees leaving more frequently. Additionally, various surveys have found that only about half of the workers in U.S. organizations are relatively satisfied with their jobs, a decline of 10% from five years ago. The biggest decline occurred with workers ages 45 to 54. Even more concerning is that about one-fifth of employees in some surveys are so turned off about their jobs that they negatively affect other employees.[3]

The long-term economic health of healthcare organizations depends on the efforts of employees with the appropriate capabilities and motivation to perform their jobs well. Organizations that are successful over time have understood that individual relationships do matter and should be managed.

FIGURE 7-1 The New Psychological Contract

EMPLOYERS PROVIDE:	EMPLOYEES CONTRIBUTE:
▶ Competitive compensation and benefits	▶ Continuous skill improvement
▶ Career development opportunities	▶ Reasonable time with organization
▶ Flexibility to balance work and home life	▶ Extra effort when needed

The Psychological Contract

One concept that has been useful in discussing employees' relationships with organizations is that of a **psychological contract,** which refers to the unwritten expectations that employees and employers have about the nature of their work relationships. Because the psychological contract is individual and subjective in nature, it focuses on expectations about "fairness" that may not be defined clearly by employees.

Both tangible items (such as wages, benefits, employee productivity, and attendance) and some intangible items (such as loyalty, fair treatment, and job security) are encompassed by psychological contracts between employers and employees in healthcare organizations of all types.

Changing Psychological Contract This psychological contract has changed over the years. In the "good old days," employees exchanged their efforts and capabilities for a secure job that offered rising pay, comprehensive benefits, and career progression within the organization. But as healthcare organizations have downsized and cut workers who have given long and loyal service, a growing number of employees question whether they should be loyal to their employers. Closely related to the psychological contract is the concept of *psychological ownership*. When individuals feel that they have some control and perceived rights in the organization, then they are more likely to be committed to the organization.[4]

The transformation in the psychological contract mirrors an evolution in which organizations have moved from employing individuals just to perform tasks, to employing individuals expected to produce results. Rather than just paying them to follow orders and put in time, increasingly employers are expecting employees to utilize their skills and capabilities to accomplish organizational results. As Figure 7-1 depicts, both employers and employees are affected by the new psychological contract.

Factors Affecting the Individual/Organizational Relationship

The relationship between individuals and healthcare organizations is influenced by outside forces. Four of the biggest influences are economic changes, the expectations of different generations of individuals, loyalty, and changing career expectations for women. These factors affect the psychological contracts in a number of ways.

Economic Changes   One major factor affecting employee expectations is the ebb and flow of the economy. Just consider the employment world when the dot-com and technology boom was underway. Many individuals, especially younger ones with technology backgrounds, expected and demanded high starting salaries, hiring bonuses, flexible scheduling, relaxed and casual workplaces, and frequent career promotions or changes.[5] These expectations frequently competed with the realities of the healthcare work place, which demands 24/7 coverage, some high-tech, but more high-touch care, combined with stressful environments.

Generational Differences   Much has been written about the differing expectations of individuals in different generations. It should be recognized that many of these observations are anecdotal and give generalizations about individuals in the various age groups. Some of the common generational labels are

▶ The Matures (born before 1945)
▶ Baby Boomers (born 1945–1965)
▶ Generation X (born 1966–1980)
▶ Generation Y (born 1980–1990)

Rather than identifying the characteristics cited for each of these groups, it is most important here to emphasize that people's expectations differ between generations, as well as within these generation labels. For employers, the differing expectations present challenges. For instance, many of the baby boomers and matures are concerned about security and experience, whereas the younger Generation Ys often are seen as the "why" generation who expect to be rewarded quickly, are very adaptable, and tend to be more questioning about why managers and organizations make the decisions they do.[6]

Also, consider the dynamics of a mature manager directing Generation X and Y individuals, or Generation X managers supervising older, more experienced baby boomers. These generational differences are likely to continue to create challenges and conflicts in organizations because of the differing expectations that various individuals have.[7] One of the most common areas of difference is seen in loyalty to organizations.

Loyalty   Employees *do* believe in psychological contracts, and hope their employers will keep their sides of the "agreement." Many employees still want security and stability, interesting work, a supervisor they respect, and competitive pay and benefits. When they are not provided, employees may feel a diminished need to contribute to organizational performance. When organizations merge, lay off large numbers of employees, outsource work, and use large numbers of temporary and part-time workers, employees see fewer reasons to give their loyalty to employers in return for this loss of job security. Healthcare employers are finding that in any type of labor market, especially tight labor markets, turnover of key people occurs more frequently when employee loyalty is low, and they have concluded that a loyal and committed workforce is important.

One important organizational value that affects employee loyalty is *trust*. Employees who believe that they can trust their managers, co-workers, and the organizational justice systems are much less willing to leave their current employers. One study that surveyed more than 600 employees found that trust and organizational values were noted as factors which most influenced intentions by employees to stay with their current employers.[8]

Career Expectations for Women   Closely aligned with the generational differences are changing career expectations for women. Many women have far more career opportunities than the traditional teaching and nursing pathways. Hospitals and nursing homes are not viewed as attractive places to work. The hours are unpredictable, the work can be dangerous and physically taxing, and workers fail to garner respect from physicians and administrations.[9] Both the design and the nature of work, as well as the characteristics of the employer, can affect the willingness of women to seek employment in healthcare organizations.

JOB SATISFACTION AND ORGANIZATIONAL COMMITMENT

In its most basic sense, **job satisfaction** is a positive emotional state resulting from evaluating one's job experiences. Job *dis*satisfaction occurs when these expectations are not met. For example, if a lab tech expects clean and safe working conditions in the lab, then the tech is likely to be dissatisfied if the lab is dirty and dangerously unsafe.

Job satisfaction has many dimensions. Commonly noted facets are: satisfaction with the work itself, wages, recognition, rapport with supervisors and co-workers, and opportunities for advancement. Each dimension contributes to an individual's overall feeling of satisfaction with the job itself.

There is no simple formula for predicting an individual employee's job satisfaction. Furthermore, the relationship between productivity and job satisfaction is not entirely clear. The critical factor is what employees expect from their jobs and what they are receiving as rewards from their jobs. Although job satisfaction itself is interesting and important, perhaps the "bottom line" is the impact that job satisfaction has on organizational commitment, which affects employee turnover and organizational performance.[10]

As Figure 7-2 depicts on the next page, the individual's ability, motivation, and support are brought to the job. Based on how the interaction of the individual and the job differs, levels of job satisfaction or dissatisfaction and organizational commitment result. Those two factors provide influences that can impact the performance of the individual and the organization.

If employees are committed to an organization, they are more likely to be productive. **Organizational commitment** is the degree to which employees believe in and accept organizational goals and desire to remain with the organization. Various research studies have revealed that the people who are relatively satisfied with their jobs will be somewhat more committed to the organization. Also, people who are relatively committed to the organization are more likely to have greater job satisfaction.

FIGURE 7-2   Model of Individual/Organizational Performance

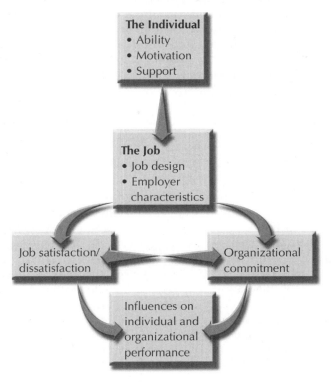

A logical extension of organizational commitment focuses specifically on *continuance commitment* factors, which suggests that decisions to remain with or leave an organization ultimately are reflected in employee absenteeism and turnover statistics. Individuals who are not as satisfied with their jobs or who are not as committed to the organization are more likely to withdraw from the organization, either occasionally through absenteeism or permanently through turnover.

RETENTION OF HUMAN RESOURCES

Retention of employees has become a primary concern in healthcare organizations for several reasons. Every healthcare worker who is retained means one less worker to have to recruit, select, and train. Also, organizational and individual performance is enhanced when there is continuity with employees who know their jobs, co-workers, organizational service, and patient/resident or client. Continuity of employees provides better employee image for attracting and retaining other individuals. There is also a link between patient satisfaction and employee retention. Staffing shortages in healthcare have increased patient complaints and decreased patient satisfaction.[11]

Healthcare providers who understand the relationship between patient satisfaction and employee satisfaction resulting in high levels of retention are counted among the nation's 100 Best Companies. Annually, *Fortune* magazine develops a list of the "100 Best Companies To Work For," and a number of hospitals recently made the list. Honorees included East Alabama Medical Center, number 18 on *Fortune*'s list, whose employees receive a financial bonus when patient satisfaction is high. "They didn't install hot tubs or pool tables in the employee lounge to win the honor. Instead, they found that improving customer service to patients resulted in a happier workforce."[12]

Importance of Retention

The importance of retention is seen in a number of ways. A survey of Chief Executive Officers found that the greatest contribution to organizational success over the next five years will be to get and retain employee talent.[13] For example, St. Elizabeth's Medical Center (St. E's) in Northern Kentucky has been ranked by the Healthcare Advisory Board as one of five "destination hospitals" for nurses in the nation. The criteria for selection to this prestigous list include low nurse turnover and vacancy rates, location in a competitive market, a strategic approach to management, excellent reputation for patient care, and viewed as an outstanding place to work among peers. The Advisory Board's evaluation included a survey of St. E's nurses, the results of which were compared to national satisfaction averages. St. E's enjoys an excellent reputation as both a high-quality patient care provider and employer competing successfully for both patients and employees with health systems and medical centers in nearby Cincinnati, Ohio.[14]

Retention as a Continuing Concern Healthcare managers face a growing crisis in how to take care of more patients with fewer employees, as turnover and a tight labor market increasingly hobble the healthcare industry. Healthcare employee shortages are coming at a particularly bad time. The elderly, who typically require more healthcare services than other age groups, represent the fastest-growing segment of the population.

Further, consumers are becoming more informed about their healthcare choices and are increasingly advocating more for themselves when receiving services. This leads to greater demands on healthcare workers, especially nurses, who have the most interaction with patients. These increased demands cause significant stress, increasing the likelihood that healthcare employees will seek less stressful work environments.[15] Therefore, it is imperative that healthcare organizations and managers recognize that retention must be a continuing HR emphasis.

Retention as a Supervisory and Management Measure Another sign of the importance of employee retention is that a growing number of healthcare employers have identified retention as a significant responsibility for their supervisors' and managers.' Healthcare providers of all types and sizes are placing more emphasis on their supervisor's and manager's roles in retention.

Even more directly, healthcare organizations are evaluating managers and supervisors on retention as part of their performance reviews. More and more, the performance reviews of healthcare managers not only includes criteria for budget, safety and operations, but also how effective are the managers at recruiting and retaining workers. In a survey of America's top 100 hospitals listed by HCIA–SACHS, a healthcare information company, survey respondents had measurable management objectives that included decreasing voluntary turnover by 15 percent by the year 2010. In general, the survey found that healthcare organizations that had measurable turnover objectives for managers experienced lower turnover rates.[16]

Retention Officer   Often an individual in the HR department is assigned the responsibility of focusing on retention to ensure that it receives high priority and the efforts needed to increase employee retention.[17] Some healthcare employers have placed such a high priority on employee retention that they have designated an individual in HR as the *retention officer* for the organization. United Hospital in St. Paul, Minnesota, one of the country's best fifty hospitals according to *Modern Maturity* magazine,[18] has developed and staffed such an employee retention specialist position. As depicted in Figure 7-3 the employee

---

F I G U R E   7 - 3   Employee Retention Specialist

EMPLOYEE RETENTION SPECIALIST

POSITION PURPOSE
Provide hospital-wide and job-specific retention strategies, planning and retention measurement and trending so that overall and key employee retention is improved.

RESPONSIBILITIES
▶ Work with leaders and employees to create and update department retention plans.
▶ Co-ordinate activities with leaders and employee groups to create and update position-specific retention plans.
▶ Assist recruitment specialists to understand factors that will improve retention of new hires and to provide feedback to recruiters that will assist in attracting talent to the organization.
▶ Be responsible for comprehensive exit interview process, data compilation, reporting, and feedback systems.
▶ Analyze employee turnover, providing detailed diagnosis related to turnover statistics.
▶ Identify career ladder opportunities and the education/training necessary to implement; be responsible for working with leaders to identify, support mentoring, and monitor the progress of promotable employees.
▶ Work with employee relations specialists to improve retention efforts and provide them with status updates for business partner reporting.
▶ Work with employee relations specialists when retention planning involves addressing issues that may involve policy and/or union contracts.
▶ Work with leaders to identify employees who are at risk for terminating and identify effective interventions to decrease turnover.
▶ Identify factors that keep employees at the hospital and the factors that make them leave; utilize employee survey results, focus groups, and individual interviews.

retention specialist's job purpose and responsibilities specifically focus on retention strategies, planning, and measurement.

Why People Stay or Leave

There are many reasons why individuals stay or leave their jobs and organizations. Obviously, individuals who are terminated leave at the request of the organizations. But the bigger issue in many healthcare organizations is why employees voluntarily leave.

Several different studies provide some consistent patterns and insights. One study found that the most important factors were career opportunities and competitive compensation/benefits. Of the remaining areas cited, several were personal, and less controllable by employers (relocation, returning to school, etc.).

Another survey done by McKinsey and Company, a large international consulting firm, emphasized the importance of retention by concluding that employers face "a war for talent."[19]

Retention Determinants

Reviewing a wide range of studies and situations faced by healthcare employers and employees, it appears that there are some common areas that affect employee retention. Figure 7-4 depicts retention determinants, as the figure depicts, there are some broad organizational components that are important. Assuming those organizational components are being delivered appropriately to individuals, then there are other factors that affect retention. Surveys of employees consistently show that career opportunities and compensation are the two most important determinants of retention. Finally, the job design/work factors and fair and supportive employee relationships with others inside the organization contribute to retention. If all of these components are present to meet individual employee expectations, then there is a greater likelihood that voluntary and controllable turnover will be lower, thus increasing employee retention.

Organizational Components

There are a number of organizational components that impact decisions by individuals to stay or leave their employers. Research indicates that organizations that have positive, distinctive cultures and values have fewer turnovers, as the earlier discussion on *Fortune*'s "100 Best Companies" indicates.

Organizational Culture and Values   **Organizational culture** is a pattern of shared values and beliefs giving members of an organization meaning and providing them with rules for behavior. These values are inherent in the ways organizations and their members view themselves, define opportunities, and plan strategies. Much as personality shapes an individual, organizational culture shapes its members' responses and defines what an organization can or is willing to do.

FIGURE 7-4 Retention Determinants

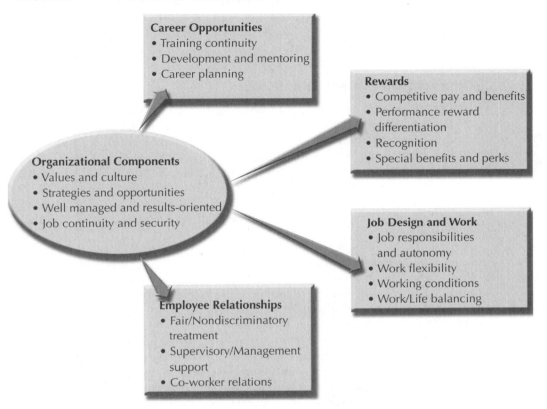

Numerous examples can be given of key employees leaving organizations because of cultures that seem to devalue people and create barriers to the use of individual capabilities. In contrast, by creating a culture that values people highly, some healthcare employers have been very successful at attracting and retaining employees.

One health system well-known for its culture and values is The Mayo Clinic. Mayo focuses considerable effort on instilling its values of high-quality patient care and employee excellence in customer service and employee involvement through its HR efforts. These efforts have paid off in Mayo's performance in retaining employees and being widely seen as an "employer of choice" in the healthcare industry.

Job Continuity and Security   Many healthcare employees have seen a decline in job security over the past decade. All of the downsizings, layoffs, mergers and acquisitions, and organizational restructuring have affected employee loyalty and retention. Also, as co-workers have been affected by layoffs and job reductions, the anxiety levels of the employees that are still employed rises.[20] Consequently, employees start thinking about leaving before they, also, get cut. However, employees who work in organizations where job continuity and security is high tend to have higher retention rates.

Organizational Career Opportunities

Surveys of workers in all types of jobs consistently find that career opportunities and development efforts provided in their organizations are most often cited as affecting employee retention. A Workforce Commitment Survey conducted annually by AON Consulting has found that *opportunities for personal growth* lead the reasons why individuals took their current jobs and why they stay there. This ranks ahead of compensation and work/family balance.[21] This is even more true for technical professionals and those under age 30, where opportunities to develop skills and promotions rank above compensation as a retention concern.[22]

Career Development   Career opportunities and development are dealt with by organizations in a number of ways. Tuition aid programs typically offered as benefits by many healthcare employers allow employees to pursue additional educational and training opportunities. Employees who participate in tuition assistance programs have been found to have higher retention rates than individuals who do not do so. However, just offering such a program is not sufficient. Organizations must also identify ways to use the employees' new knowledge and capabilities inside the organization. Otherwise, employees are more likely to take their new capabilities to another employer because they feel their increased "value" is not being recognized.[23] Overall, the thrust of organizational career development efforts is designed to meet many employees' expectations that their employer is committed to keeping their knowledge, skills, and abilities current.

An example of an effective career development program is seen at Tampa's General Hospital. Tampa General designed and implemented a clinical ladder program that encourages its RNs to remain at the bedside as clinical nurses with specialized knowledge. The clinical ladder is a four-level process, with each level consisting of four areas of specialized knowledge. This program has had the twofold effect of enhancing Tampa General's ability to provide specialized care and encouraging its RNs to stay at the bedside providing patient care.[24]

Career Planning   Healthcare organizations also increase employee retention by having formal career planning efforts. Employees and their managers mutually discuss career opportunities within the organization and what career development activities will enhance employees' future growth. Job posting programs have proven to be an especially effective HR program for healthcare organizations for facilitating both inter- and intra-departmental transfers and promotions. These programs encourage employees to pursue new opportunities without leaving their current organizations.

Rewards and Retention

The tangible rewards that people receive for working come in the form of pay, incentives, and benefits. This compensation is what provides the economic means for individuals to meet their financial obligations. Numerous surveys and experiences of HR professionals reveal that one important key to retention is to have *competitive compensation practices.* Many managers believe that money is the prime retention factor (89% in one survey) and many employees cite better pay or higher compensation as reasons when they leave an employer.[25] However, the reality is a bit more complex.

Pay and benefits must be competitive, which means they must be "close" to what other employers are providing and what individuals believe to be consistent with their capabilities, experience, and performance. If compensation is not close, often defined as within 10% of the "market," then turnover is likely to be higher.

This is especially true for individuals making lower rates of pay, such as those with less than $25,000 to $30,000 annual income. Simply put, their living costs and financial requirements make how much they are compensated crucial. Therefore, if these lower-paid workers can get $1 per hour more or get employer-paid family health benefit coverage elsewhere, they are more likely to leave. However, for more highly paid individuals, especially those paid $60,000 and higher, their retention is affected by having compensation relatively competitive. Then other considerations are more likely to enter into decisions to stay or leave. In fact, money might be why some people leave a job, but other factors might be why many stay.

Competitive Benefits   Another compensation issue affecting employee retention is having competitive benefits programs. Offering health insurance, 401(k) retirement, tuition assistance, and many other benefits commonly offered by competing employers is vital. A nationwide survey of healthcare HR managers revealed that healthcare facilities offer a wide array of benefits to employees. Most hospitals provide basic benefits, such as group health, disability and dental insurance, to nearly all employees.[26]

Employers also are learning that having some *benefits flexibility* aids retention.[27] When employees choose how much and what benefits they will have from a "cafeteria" of choices, given a set sum of money available from the employer, the employees can tailor the benefits to what they want. For instance, a married worker who has health insurance coverage under a spouse's health plan at another organization may instead prefer to contribute more to a 401(k) or 403(b) plan or purchase additional group life insurance. By giving employees more choice, employees feel more "individual" and "in control," thus reducing their desire to move to another employer.[28]

Special Benefits and Perks   A number of healthcare employers have used a wide range of special benefits and perks to attract and retain employees. As an example, at Baptist Hospital in Miami, employees have access to a day care center, hair salon, post office, and dry cleaners to make their lives easier.[29] By offering these special benefits and perks, healthcare employers hope to reduce the time employees spend after work on personal chores and to thus be seen as more desirable employers where individuals will remain for longer stays. The healthcare HR manager survey noted earlier also included data on other perks, including reserved parking and paid membership in civic clubs, which are typically reserved for administrative personnel. Flextime, signing bonuses, and relocation cost reimbursement are frequently offered to employees in areas of critical shortage (such as RNs, therapists, pharmacists, computer personnel).

Performance Differentiation of Compensation   Many individuals expect their rewards to be differentiated from others based on performance. For instance, if an employee receives about the same pay increase and overall pay as others who have lower productivity, more absenteeism, and work fewer hours, then the lack of differences in compensation may create a feeling of "unfairness," and may lead to the individual deciding to look for another job that pays more money and where differences lead to differential compensation amounts.

When healthcare organizations have surveyed their employees many have found that individuals are more satisfied with the levels of their pay than the processes used to determine pay. That is why the performance management system and performance appraisal processes in healthcare organizations must be linked to compensation increases. If some individuals receive high performance ratings, but compensation only changes similarly to others, then their desire to stay with the organization may diminish.

To achieve greater links between individual performance and compensation, a growing number of healthcare organizations are using variable pay and incentives programs. These programs in the form of cash bonuses or lump sum payments are one mechanism used to reward extra performance.

The introduction of variable pay programs has been viewed in a controversial light for nonprofit healthcare organizations. Critics argue that extreme levels of variable pay for executives or employed physicians are inappropriate and contribute to the rising cost of healthcare. However, healthcare organizations frequently compete for the same talent with private-sector firms who can offer a wide range of variable pay options, including stock options.

Recognition   Employee recognition as a form of reward can be both tangible and intangible. The tangible recognition comes in many forms, such as employee of the month, perfect attendance, or other special awards. Recognition also can be intangible and psychological in nature. Feedback from managers and supervisors that acknowledges extra effort and performance of individuals provides recognition, even though monetary rewards are not given. For instance, many nursing homes use both tangible and intangible recognition as part of employee retention efforts. Employees who receive a recognition card from either residents or co-workers are recognized in newsletters or banquets held in their honor.

Job Design, Selection, and Retention

Another fundamental factor affecting employee retention is the nature of the jobs and work to be done. First, retention is affected by the *selection process* that tries to achieve a *person/job match* whereby individuals' knowledge, skills, and abilities are matched to the demands of the jobs they could be hired to perform.

A number of organizations have found that high employee turnover rates in employees' first few months of employment often are linked to inadequate selection screening efforts. Figure 7-5 illustrates the importance of sound selection processes. St. Lucie Medical Center, a 150-bed hospital located in Port St. Lucie, Florida, concluded that dedication to high performance begins with a strict candidate selection process that identifies applicants with the greatest potential to be both top performers and a good fit for St. Lucie, increasing the chances they will stay longer.[30]

Once individuals have been placed into jobs, several job/work factors affect retention. Because individuals spend significant time at work, they expect *working conditions* to be good, given the nature of the work. Such factors as space, lighting, temperature, noise, layout, and other physical and environmental factors affect retention of employees. Also, employees expect to work with modern equipment and technology.

Additionally, there needs to be a *safe work environment,* whereby risks of accidents and injuries have been addressed. This is especially true for healthcare employers where safety risks can include exposure to disease, harmful chemicals and radiation.

Work Flexibility   The ability to have flexibility in work schedules and how work is done has grown in importance.[31] Flexibility extended to HR policies such as casual dress also has been useful as retention aids.

FIGURE 7-5 Setting a Higher Standard Contributes to Retention

EMPLOYEE SELECTON

▶ Organization commits to using standard selection tool.
▶ Management defines specific selection criteria for hospital and individual units based on current high performers' scores on tool.
▶ Managers receive extensive training on selection criteria, interviewing process, and scoring method.
▶ Managers interview candidates by phone and score their interviews.
▶ Only candidates reaching threshold scores are invited for face-to-face interviews with management and unit staff.
▶ Hospital only hires candidates possessing desired traits.
▶ Expectation is that each new hire maintains or increases performance levels.

Source: Adapted from Competing for Talent, Recovering America's Hospital Workforce, Healthcare Advisory Board (2001), 473.

Work flexibility is particularly vital as organizational workload pressures have increased due to organizational restructurings and rightsizing. These efforts have resulted in the remaining employees having heavier workloads, more work hours, and less time for personal and family issues. Approximately a third of all U.S. employees surveyed said they often felt overworked or were "overloaded." Women cited being overworked more frequently, and managers and professionals indicated feeling more overworked than other occupational groups.[32] It is crucial that healthcare employers wishing to retain employees monitor the workload levels placed on employees. If these demands become too great, then employees are more likely to change jobs to reduce their workloads.

One way healthcare employers have provided work flexibility is through the use of a variety of *work scheduling alternatives*. These alternatives include telecommuting for administrative employees, whereby employees can work from home or other locations, alternative arrangements such as flextime, and compressed work weeks (4 days/10 hours, 3 days/12 hours, etc.). The growth of work schedule flexibility is illustrated in Figure 7-6.

Many studies demonstrate that work flexibility aids in retention. As an illustration, a two-year study of work place flexibility found that 76% of managers and 80% of employees reported that flexible working relationships impacted retention positively. The study also found that work flexibility led to higher work quality and productivity.[33] Perhaps the greatest benefit of work flexibility is that it meshes well with work/family efforts by employers.

Balancing Patient Care Needs with Work Schedule Flexibility   Healthcare managers are very aware of the need to balance patient care delivery staffing

FIGURE 7-6   **Work Schedule Flexibility**

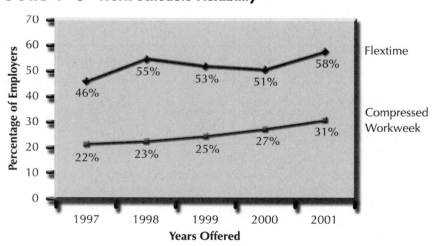

Source: Based upon data in *2001 SHRM Benefits Survey* (Alexandria, VA: Society for Human Resource Management, 2001).

requirements and work schedule flexibility. Patient care must come first, but the lack of predictability of patient census in environments such as in-patient nursing units or emergency rooms requires significant scheduling flexibility that can frustrate even the most flexible workers. Healthcare professionals frequently cite this issue as the reason for leaving the healthcare workplace, especially hospitals, and finding positions in workplaces with less scheduling variability.

Hospitals, clinics, physician and dental offices, and nursing homes have become very creative in dealing with this issue. Their strategies have included the following:

▶ *Staffing with Part-Time and Casual Workers*—Replacing one or two full-time employees with multiple part-time and casual employees can provide the necessary flexibility. Part-time employees may be scheduled for sixteen to thirty-two hours per week, but with the opportunity to pick-up additional hours if patient care needs necessitate additional staff. Casual employees are called in if they are needed.

▶ *Developing Patient Census Prediction and Staffing Models*—Although it is difficult to predict with 100% accuracy, some healthcare providers have become proficient at predicting patient care needs and developing staffing requirements that closely match those needs. These models typically predict the *core* staffing needs of the unit, clinic or departments and based on such variables as the time of year, surgery demands or seasonal infectious disease patterns allow for higher levels of *variable* staffing. Based on good historical data, these staffing models can be surprisingly accurate.

Work/Life Balancing   The changing demographics of the U.S. workforce have led to many individuals having to balance work responsibilities, family needs, and personal life demands. With more single parent families, dual-career couples with children, and workers' responsibilities for aging elderly relatives, balancing work and family roles may sometimes be very difficult. Such factors as work and family time demands and resources all must be considered.[34]

Work/life programs offered by employers can include a wide range of items. Some include work/job options, such as flexible work scheduling, job sharing, or telecommuting. Others include benefits program components, such as flexible benefits, on-site fitness centers, childcare or elder-care assistance, veterinarian care for pets, flexible timeoff, and sick leave policies. The purpose of all these offerings is to communicate to individuals that the employer cares about the employees and recognizes the challenges of balancing work/life demands.[35]

Organizational and Employee Relationships

A final set of factors found to affect retention is based on the relationships that employees have in organizations.Healthcare organizations have long been aware

FIGURE 7-7 Supervisory Retention Efforts

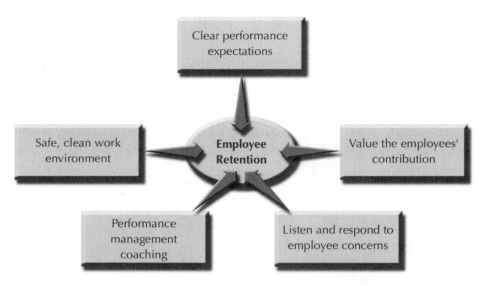

of how poor supervisory skills and attitudes have affected employee retention. A poor supervisor can outweigh all the other positive efforts extended by the organization. Figure 7-7 depicts what the supervisor can do to contribute to employee retention.

One expectation that employees have is that they will be treated fairly at work. Such areas as the reasonableness of HR policies, the fairness of disciplinary actions, and the means used to decide work assignments and opportunities all affect employee retention. If individuals feel that policies are unreasonably restrictive or applied inconsistently, then they might be more likely to look at jobs offered at other employers.

Particularly important with the increasing demographic diversity of U.S. workplaces is that all employees, regardless of their gender, age, and other factors, have *nondiscriminatory treatment.* Organizational commitment and job satisfaction of ethnically diverse individuals may be affected by perceived discriminatory treatment.[36]

Other concerns that affect employee retention are supervisory/management support and co-worker relations. Many individuals build close relationships with those with whom they work. In a survey of individuals of a variety of ages and working in a variety of industries, the most positively cited factor about going to work was the relationships with co-workers.[37] Coupled with co-worker relationships is having supportive supervisory and management relationships.[38] A supervisor builds positive relationships and aids retention by providing clear performance expectations, providing a safe, clean work environment, valuing the employee's contribution, and providing coaching. However, as defined by individual employees, having a "good" boss means that communication is likely to be more open and the supervisor listens and responds to the employees' concerns.[39]

RETENTION MANAGEMENT PROCESS

Having just identified the determinants of retention, it is important that HR professionals and their organizations have processes in place to manage retention of employees. Left to chance or infrequent attention, retention of employees is not as likely to be as successful. The retention management process contains three primary phases, each of which is discussed next.

Retention Measurement and Assessment

To ensure that appropriate actions are taken to enhance retention and reduce turnover, it is important that management decisions be made using data and analyses, rather than subjective impressions, anecdotes of selected individual situations, or panic reactions to the loss of a few key people. That is why having several different types of measures and analyses is important.

Measures of Turnover   The turnover rate for an organization can be computed in different ways. The following formula from the U.S. Department of Labor is widely used where *separation* means leaving the organization.

$$\frac{\text{Number of employee separations during the month}}{\text{(Total number of employees at midmonth)}} \times 100$$

Turnover figures can range from almost zero to over 100% per year, and normal turnover rates vary among industries. Organizations that require entry-level employees to have few skills are likely to have higher turnover rates among those employees than among managerial personnel. Often a part of human resource information systems, turnover data can be gathered and analyzed in a number of ways, including the following:

▶ Jobs and job level
▶ Departments, units, and location
▶ Reason for leaving
▶ Length of service
▶ Demographic characteristics
▶ Education and training
▶ Skills and abilities
▶ Performance ratings/levels

   Several examples illustrate why detailed analyses of turnover is important. One long-term care organization had an organization-wide turnover rate that was not severe—but 80% of the turnover occurred in one unit. This imbalance indicated that some action was needed to resolve problems in that unit. At a family practice clinic there was 20% annual turnover, with 60% of that turnover occurring in the first sixty days. By analyzing turnover rates by length of service, the HR manager of the clinic learned that the recruiting, selection, and training processes needed to be changed. By reducing the number of individuals hired who could not successfully complete training and perform satisfactorily after training, turnover was reduced significantly. A medical center found that its greatest turnover in registered nurses occurred twenty-four to thirty-six months after hire, so the organization instituted a two-year employee recognition program and expanded the career development and training activities for employees with at least two years of service. In all of these examples, the turnover rates declined as a result of the actions taken based on the turnover analyses done.

Costs of Turnover   Determining turnover costs can be done relatively simply or in a complex manner, depending on the nature of the efforts and data used. Figure 7-8 is a simplified costing model. In that model if a job pays $25,000 (A) and benefits cost 30% (B), then the total annual cost for one employee is $32,500. Assuming ten employees quit in the previous year (D) and that it takes three months for the employee to be fully productive, the calculation in (F) results in a per-person turnover cost of $3,217.50. Overall, this means that the annual turnover cost would be $32,175.00 for the ten individuals who left. It should be noted that this simplified model likely is very conservative, but it makes the point that turnover is costly. For instance, if the job is a nursing assistant in a large nursing home and 150 people leave in a year, the conservative model results in turnover costs more than $500,000 per year.

More detailed and sophisticated turnover costing models consider a number of factors. Some of the most common areas considered include the following:[40]

▶ *Hiring Costs*—Includes recruiting and advertising expenses, search fees, HR interviewer and staff time and salaries, employee referral fees, relocation and

---

F I G U R E   7 - 8   Simplified Turnover Costing Model

JOB TITLE _____

A. Typical annual pay for job
B. Percentage of pay for benefits times (x) annual pay   ____
C. Total employee annual cost (add A + B)   ____
D. How many employees voluntarily quit in this job in the past 12 months? ____
E. How long does it take for one employee to become fully productive (in months)? ____
F. Per person turnover cost:
   (Multiply E ÷ 12 × C × 30%*)   ____
G. Annual turnover cost for this job:
   (Multiply F × D)   ____

*Assumes 30% productivity throughout the learning period (E).

moving costs, supervisor and managerial time and salaries, employment testing costs, reference checking time, pre-employment medical expenses, etc.

▶ *Training Costs*—Includes paid orientation time, training staff time and salaries, costs of training materials, supervisors' and managers' time and salaries, co-worker "coaching" time and salaries, etc. ›

▶ *Productivity Costs*—Includes lost productivity due to "break-in" time of new employees, loss of customer knowledge and contacts, unfamiliarity with organizational products and services, more time to use organizational resources and systems, etc.

▶ *Separation Costs*—Includes HR staff and supervisor time and salaries to prevent separations, exit interview time, unemployment expenses, legal fees for separations challenged, etc.

Employee Surveys   Employee surveys can be used to diagnose specific problem areas, identify employee needs or preferences, and reveal areas in which HR activities are well received or are viewed negatively. For example, questionnaires may be sent to employees to collect ideas for revising a performance appraisal system or to determine if employees are satisfied with their benefits programs. Regardless of the topic of the survey, obtaining employee input provides managers and HR professionals with data on the "retention climate" in an organization.

One specific type of survey used by many organizations is an **attitude survey** that focuses on employees' feelings and beliefs about their jobs and the organization. By serving as a means to obtain data on how employees view their jobs, their supervisors, their co-workers, and organizational policies and practices, these surveys can be starting points for reducing turnover and increasing employee retention for longer periods of time. Some employers conduct attitude surveys on a regularly scheduled basis (such as every year), while others do so intermittently. As the use of the Internet has spread, more organizations have begun conducting attitude surveys electronically.[41]

Attitude surveys can be conducted using surveys developed by consulting firms, academicians, or others. Also, they can be custom-designed to address specific issues and concerns in an organization. But regardless of the type of surveys used, only surveys that are valid and reliable can measure attitudes accurately.[42] Often a "research" survey developed in-house is poorly structured, asks questions in a confusing manner, or leads employees to respond in ways that will give "favorable" results.

By asking employees to respond candidly to an attitude survey, management is building up employees' expectations that action will be taken on the concerns identified. Therefore, a crucial part of conducting an attitude survey is to provide feedback to those who participated in it. It is especially important that even negative survey results be communicated to avoid fostering the appearance of hiding the results or placing blame. Generally, it is recommended that employee feedback be done through meetings with managers, supervisors, and employees; often, this is done in small groups to encourage interaction and discussion.[43]

That approach is consistent with the most common reason for conducting an attitude survey—to diagnose strengths and weaknesses so that actions can be taken to improve the HR activities in an organization.

Exit Interviews   One widely used data source on turnover is the **exit interview,** in which those who are leaving the organization are asked to identify the reasons for their departure. One survey of employers found that 87% of them conduct exit interviews, and over half of them have used the information gathered to make changes to aid retention.[44] A wide range of issues can be examined in exit interviews.

Retention Interventions

Based on what the measurement and assessment data reveals, a variety of HR interventions can be undertaken to improve retention. Turnover can be controlled and reduced in several ways.[45] During the *recruiting process,* the job should be outlined and a realistic preview presented, so that the reality of the job matches the expectations of the new employee. By ensuring that the expectations of potential employees match what the organization is likely to offer, voluntary turnover may be reduced.

Another way to eliminate turnover is to improve the *selection process* in order to better match applicants to jobs. By fine-tuning the selection process and hiring people who will not have disciplinary or performance problems or whose work histories suggest higher turnover potential, employers can reduce turnover. Once selected, individuals who receive effective orientation and training are less likely to leave.

Other HR factors are important as well. *Compensation* is important because a competitive, fair, and equitable pay system can help reduce turnover. Inadequate benefits also may lead to voluntary turnover, especially if other employers are offering significantly higher compensation levels for similar jobs. *Career development* and *planning* can help an organization keep employees. If individuals believe they have few opportunities for career development advancement, they are more likely to leave the organization. *Employee relations,* including fair/nondiscriminatory treatment and enforcement of HR policies, can enhance retention, also.

Healthcare organizations can adopt such programs to enhance their retention efforts. Given the large percentage of females in healthcare organizations retention interventions that impact on female retention is especially important.

One example of successful retention interventions has been experienced at Deloitte & Touche, a national accounting and consulting firm. An HR study at the firm found that it was losing many talented female employees after several years with the firm. Because the firm had invested significant time and funds in training and developing the women, a special program throughout Deloitte & Touche was established to focus on retaining all employees, especially women, who had significantly higher turnover rates. Key portions of the program include workshops on "Men and Women as Colleagues," enhanced career mentoring programs, revised family/work policies and alternatives, and establishing a women's leadership program.[46]

Healthcare HR professionals should use the information on retention determinants and the assessment information to identify what changes are needed to improve retention. Usually, a multifaceted approach is needed, rather than just focusing on one area. For example, just changing benefits without considering the recruitment and selection processes may not result in attracting and hiring individuals more likely to stay longer. That is why it is important to evaluate and follow up to see if retention intervention efforts have produced lower turnover rates and extended the stays of existing employees.

Evaluation and Follow-Up

Once retention intervention efforts have been implemented, it is important that they be evaluated and that appropriate follow-up and adjustments be made. Regular *review of turnover data* can identify when turnover increases or decreases among different employees classified by length of service, education, department, gender, or other factors.

Tracking intervention results also should be part of evaluation efforts. Some healthcare organizations may use pilot programs to see how turnover is affected before extending the changes to the entire organization. For instance, to test the effect of flextime scheduling on employee turnover, a clinic might allow flexible scheduling in one department on a pilot basis. If the turnover rate of the employees in that department drops in comparison with the turnover in other departments still working set schedules, then the experimental pilot project may indicate that flexible scheduling can reduce turnover. Next, the clinic might extend the use of flexible scheduling to other departments.

Retention of employees can be increased through use of a coordinated process. Numerous examples of healthcare organizations that have focused on retention management illustrate that attracting and retaining human resources can contribute significantly to organizational success.

CASE

Clarion Medical Clinic (CMC) is a fourteen-physician family practice clinic with 185 employees. CMC's patient care model included the use of medical assistants (MAs) working directly with the M.D.s and nurse practitioners providing patient assessment, diagnostic, and well care.

Management at CMC had prided themselves on providing a positive work environment; market-based pay and benefits; and flexible work schedules. This approach to managing CMC human resources had consistently resulted in high staff morale and low turnover. Management tracked turnover rates for the overall clinic and the major organizational divisions on an annual basis to monitor any issues that might emerge. A recent study on turnover analysis found the following:

ORGANIZATIONAL UNIT	TURNOVER PERCENTAGE
Nursing	10%
Laboratory	16%
Business office	7%
Medical records	8%
Registration and scheduling	5%
CMC total organization	8%

Management had been aware of some issues in the laboratory department, but was surprised by the significantly higher turnover rate indicated on the report. The HR manager was charged with determining what factors might be contributing to the high turnover in the laboratory department.

Questions

1. What might be some of the reasons for the higher turnover in the laboratory department versus the rest of the organization?
2. What should the HR manager do to determine what retention efforts should be initiated in the laboratory department?

END NOTES

1. Terese Hudson Thrall, "Skipping Gimmicks, Keeping Nurses," *Hospitals & Health Networks* (September 2001), 18–20.
2. Jodi Spiegel Arthur, "Curing a Crisis," *Human Resource Executive* (August 2001), 61–65.
3. "Disengaged at Work," *The Wall Street Journal* (December 2000), 7; and Shari Caudron, "The Myth of Job Happiness," *Workforce* (April 2001), 32–36.
4. Jon L. Pierce, Tatiana Kostova, and Kurt T. Dirks, "Toward a Theory of Psychological Ownership in Organizations," *Academy of Management Review* 26 (2001), 298–310.
5. Joan Hamilton, "The Harder They Fall," *Business Week* (May 14, 2001), EB14–16.
6. "Generation Y Brings Challenges to Workplace," *Bulletin to Management* (May 10, 2001), 145.
7. James B. Lathrop, Jr., "Employers Can Expect Greater Conflict in Four-Generation Workforce," *HR News* (February 2001), 23.
8. "Survey Says that Trust is the basis for Employee Retention," *HR Focus* (February 2001), 8.
9. Clark W. Bell, "Our Valuable Caregivers," *Modern Healthcare* (March 5, 2001), 28.
10. Daniel J. Koys, "The Effects of Employee Satisfaction, Organizational Citizenship Behavior, and Turnover on Organizational Effectiveness," *Personnel Psychology,* 54 (2001), 101–114.
11. Jeff Tieman, "A Grim Outlook," *Modern Healthcare* (February 4, 2002), 18.
12. Jan Greene, "A Happy Workforce," *Hospitals and Health Networks* (April 2002), 22–26.
13. Shannon Reilly and Keith Simmons, "What Are CEO's Thinking?" *USA Today* (May 3, 2001), 1B.
14. "St. Elizabeth Ranked One of Five Destination Hospitals for Nurses," *The Cincinnati Enquirer* (January 2, 2002).
15. Michael Abrams, "Employee Retention and Turnover: Holding Managers Accountable," *Trustee* (March 2002), T1–T4.

16. Rita E. Numerof, "Retaining Employees: Lessons From the Best," *Healthcare Executive,* (March/April 2001), 62–63.

17. Jodi Spiegel Arthur, "Title Wave," *Human Resource Executive* (October 2, 2000), 115–118.

18. "50 Top Hospitals," *Modern Maturity,* see *http://www.AARP.org.*

19. *War for Talent* (New York: McKinsey & Company, 1998).

20. Steve Gibbons, "Down to a System: Keeping Employee Morale and Retention High," *The Journal of Quality and Participation* (March/April, 2000), 20–22.

21. *United States @ Work,* AON Consulting, 2000, *http://www.aon.com.*

22. "Survey Finds Top-Performing Employees Want Opportunities for Advancement and Skill Development," *Watson-Wyatt Worldwide Global News & Issues* (December 18, 2000). *http://www.watsonwyatt.com.*

23. Maureen Hannay and Melissa Northam, "Low-Cost Strategies for Employee Retention," *Compensation and Benefits Review* (July/August 2000), 65–72.

24. Deborah L. Ressler, "Experienced RNs Remain at Patient's Bedside," *Vital Signs Magazine* (September 12, 2000), *http://www.vsigns.com.*

25. Hara Marks, "Money—That's Not What They Want," *HR-eSource Newsletter* (May 7, 2001).

26. Jerry Kinard, "An Examination of Employer Provided Benefits in the Healthcare Industry," *The Healthcare Manager* (June 2000), 55–62.

27. David Kelly, "When It Comes to Benefits, One Size Does Not Fit All," *HR-esource* (May 14, 2001), *http://www.hr-esource.com.*

28. Christopher Ryan, "Employee Retention—What Can the Benefits Professional Do?" *Employee Benefits Journal* (December 2000), 18–22.

29. Maureen Glabman, "Nurses Needed—STAT," *Trustee* (June 2001), 8–23

30. *Competing for Talent, Recovering America's Hospital Workforce,* Healthcare Advisory Board, 2001, 473.

31. Crayton Harrison, "Flexible Programs Help Companies Maintain Talent," *Dallas Morning News* (April 1, 2001), 11L.

32. Ellen Galinsky, Stacy S. Kim, and James T. Bond, *Feeling Overworked: When Work Becomes a Burden* (New York: Families and Work Institute, 2001).

33. Margaret M. Clark, "More Companies Offering Flextime," *HR News* (June 2001), 1+.

34. Jeffrey R. Edwards and Nancy P. Rothbard, "Mechanisms Linking Work and Family: Clarifying the Relationship Between Work and Family Constructs," *Academy of Management Review,* 25 (2000), 178–199.

35. Daniel B. Moskowitz, "Care Package," *Human Resource Executive* (May 1, 2001), 1, 30–36.

36. Ellen A. Ersher, Elisa J. Grant-Vallore, and Stewart I. Donaldson, "Effects of Perceived Discrimination on Job Satisfaction, Organizational Commitment, Organizational Citizenship Behavior, and Grievances," *Human Resource Development Quarterly,* 12 (2001), 53–72.

37. "Worker Dissatisfaction Rising, Studies Indicate," *Omaha World-Herald* (May 20, 2001), 5G.

38. Paul R. Bernthal and Richard S. Wellins, *Retaining Talent: A Benchmarking Study* (Pittsburgh, PA: Development Dimensions International, 2001).

39. Mark Enger and Laura Beeth, "Survive or Thrive," *Minnesota Physician* (October 2000), 1.

40. Wayne F. Cascio, *Costing Human Resources* (Cincinnati: South-Western Publishing, 2000), 73–75.

41. David Zatz, "Create Effective E-Mail Surveys," *HR Magazine* (January 2000), 97–103.

42. For information on books on attitude surveys, see David W. Bracken, "Designing and Using Organizational Surveys . . . " *Personnel Psychology* 53 (2000), 206–209.

43. Kevin Sheridan, "Making the Most of Your Post-Survey Action Planning and Communications Process," *New Solutions* (Winter/Spring 2001), 3.

44. *SHRM Retention Practices Survey* (Alexandria VA: Society for Human Resource Management, 2000), 10.

45. D. Mitchell, "How to Reduce the High Cost of Turnover," *http://www.ijob.com/news,* October 30, 2000.

46. Charlene Marmer Solomon, "Cracks in the Glass Ceiling," *Workforce* (September 2000), 86–94.

CHAPTER 8

Training and Development in Healthcare Organizations

Learning Objectives

After you have read this chapter, you should be able to:

▶ Discuss how job performance and training can be integrated.

▶ Identify how organizational and training strategies are linked.

▶ Define various learning styles.

▶ Describe the orientation, training, and staff development requirements of the Joint Commission.

▶ Explain the unique aspects of healthcare employee development.

Healthcare HR Insights

Jewish Home and Hospital, a nursing home in New York with a 150-year history, has a remarkable employee retention rate. Not only do employees stay with Jewish Home and Hospital, they stay for a long time. Employees with tenure of twenty years are the norm, and the nursing home also reports having employees with as much as forty years of service.

What makes Jewish Home and Hospital so unusual is that high employee retention and long-tenured employees are not typical for the nursing home industry. The work is labor intensive, and it is both physically and emotionally draining. The residents are often frail, sick, and confused. Many employees receive low pay and substandard benefits. All of these factors and others often lead to high turnover and short employment stays in many nursing homes.

Jewish Home and Hospital accounts for its employee retention success being due to several factors. Some key ones include:

▶ Competitive, fair wages
▶ Respected and celebrated employees
▶ Training and educational opportunities
▶ Career guidance and promotion opportunities
▶ Effective communication between employees and management

According to Jewish Home and Hospital's CEO, Sheldon Goldberg:

> The issue of training and educating nursing care workers is critical and must be considered essential for maintaining staff, as well as providing an atmosphere where advancing one's knowledge is valued. We encourage our employees to go to school, return to school for higher levels of training, take courses that will enhance their skills or qualify them for new ones and seek any instruction that will elevate them professionally.

In addition, Jewish Home and Hospital provides financial aid through scholarships or loans and allows its employees to tailor their schedules to accommodate classes. Researchers are also encouraged to use its facilities in their projects, and students engaged in medical education, nursing, social work, therapy and other human services professions are welcome.[1]

Not only is training and employee development important to ensure the competence of healthcare workers it is also a key element in retaining a competent workforce. In this chapter, we will review the key aspects of healthcare training and employee development.

Training and development are critical in healthcare organizations to ensure the ongoing delivery of safe, competent care. **Training** is a process whereby people acquire capabilities to aid in the achievement of organizational goals. Because this process is tied to a variety of organizational purposes, training can be viewed either narrowly or broadly. In a limited sense, training provides employees with specific, identifiable knowledge and skills for use on their current jobs. **Employee development** is broader in scope and focuses on individuals gaining new capabilities useful for both current and *future jobs*.

NATURE OF TRAINING IN HEALTHCARE ORGANIZATIONS

Currently, U.S. employers are spending an estimated $60 billion annually on training. According to the American Society of Training and Development (ASTD), the average expenditure per employee for all firms in its database and for leading-edge firms were $650 and $1,966, respectively. Unfortunately, the Healthcare industry ranks at the bottom, spending only an average of $345 per employee, effectively 1.2% of payroll on training. In contrast, organizations like Motorola and General Electric spend between 3% and 4% of their payroll on training. These and other leading-edge companies recognize the importance of training and development as integral to organizational effectiveness.[2] Training in healthcare organizations is offered in many different areas and different ways, as noted in Figure 8-1.

As part of strategic competitiveness, employees whose capabilities stay current and who receive regular training are better able to cope with the challenges and changes occurring in healthcare. Compare the healthcare environment of today to five years ago, with all of the new technologies, the explosion of web technology, and cost pressures. Without continual training, healthcare organizations may not have staff members with the KSAs needed to provide care and manage organizations.

Training also assists organizational competitiveness by aiding in the retention of employees. As emphasized previously, a primary reason why many individuals stay or leave organizations is career training and development opportunities. Healthcare employers that invest in training and developing their employees do so in part as retention efforts.

FIGURE 8-1 Common Types of Healthcare Training

- ▶ New employee orientation
- ▶ Conducting performance appraisals
- ▶ Personal computer courses
- ▶ Team building
- ▶ Customer service
- ▶ Leadership skills
- ▶ Sexual harassment prevention
- ▶ Selection interviewing
- ▶ Patient safety
- ▶ Operating new equipment
- ▶ Diversity awareness

Something else is changing as well. An old axiom in HR management traditionally has been, "When times get tough, training is the first expenditure to be cut." Accordingly, training expenditures often are reduced significantly at times. But a growing number of healthcare employers have recognized that training is not just a cost; it is an investment in the human capital of the organization that benefits the entire organization longer-term. Although training expenditures may decline as organizational cost-cutting occurs, more progressive healthcare organizations seldom reduce training efforts significantly.

Integration of Job Performance, Training, and Learning

Job performance, training, and employee learning must be integrated to be effective. First, because training interventions are best when moved closer to the job in order to achieve real-time learning, the linkage between training and job performance is vital. Consider the following example. As a new respiratory therapist receives orientation to the Intensive Care Unit (ICU), the trainee works closely with an experienced respiratory therapist. The experienced therapist serves in the role of preceptor, providing the new therapist with guidance and hands-on training. Trainees can watch the trainer (preceptor) perform procedures in the proper manner, attempt to safely replicate the actions, and receive real-time feedback in the actual work setting.

Second, organizations prefer more authentic (and hence more effective) training experiences for their trainees, using real organizational problems to advance employee learning. Rather than separating the training experience from actual job performance context, trainers who incorporate everyday operations as learning examples increase the realism of training exercises and scenarios. Many healthcare organizations, such as Gulf Breeze Hospital, in Gulf Breeze, Florida, have initiated customer service training for their employees. The objective of Gulf Breeze Hospital's customer service training is to provide actual customer situations to the trainees and teach them how to react and respond. During the training, talking scripts are provided. The scripts have been developed as best practice approaches to dealing with various customer service scenarios.[3] This is an example of another way the lines between training, learning, and job performance have become more integrated. As a result, training becomes more performance focused.

Training as Performance Consulting

Performance consulting is a process by which a trainer (either internal or external to the organization) and the organizational client work together to boost workplace performance.[4] Performance consulting is based on desired and actual organizational results being compared to desired and actual employee performance. Once these comparisons are made, then performance consulting considers all the factors in dealing with performance issues:

▶ Focusing on identifying and addressing *root causes* of performance problems
▶ Recognizing the *interaction of individual and organizational factors* that work together to influence employee performance
▶ Comparing the *actions and accomplishments of high performers* with actions of more typical performers.[5]

Regardless of whether the trainer is internal to the organization or an outside training consultant, training cannot automatically solve every employee performance problem. Instead, training must be viewed as one piece of a larger *bundled* solution. For instance, some employee performance issues might be resolved by creating a training program for employees, while other situations might call for compensation or job design changes.

The following illustrates the performance consulting approach. Assume you are the HR training specialist in a large medical center and the Director of Patient Care contacts you about creating a training program for the nurses on the patient care units. Over the last six months, the director has received various complaints about the nurses' interactions and communications with personnel from other medical center departments that support the units. The Director asks you to develop a customized training program on effective communications and collaborative working relationships.

Instead of just developing a training program, users of performance consulting gather more information in order to identify: (1) the root causes of the communication problems; (2) the various individual RNs and organizational factors that are contributing to this issue; and (3) the primary reasons for the gap between effective RNs and lower performance RNs on the units. Obtaining all of this information helps in determining whether *any* form of training will play a role in your integrated performance improvement solution. Perhaps recent changes in patient volumes has resulted in higher work demands on the RNs and has contributed to their need to demand more responsiveness from support department personnel. Whatever the causes, a tailored and comprehensive approach is needed to get to the root of the communications and interaction issues.

Integrating Training Responsibilities

One of the most important implications resulting from the performance consulting approach is that HR staff members and trainers work as partners with operating managers to integrate training that bolsters both individual employee and organizational performance. A typical division of training responsibilities is shown in Figure 8-2. The HR unit can serve as a source of expert training assistance and coordination. The unit often has a more long-range view of employee careers and the development of the entire organization than do individual operating managers. The difference is especially true at lower levels in the organization.

However, managers are likely to be the best source of technical information used in skills training. They also are in a better position to decide when employees need training or retraining. Because of the close and continual interaction they have with their employees, it is appropriate that managers determine and

FIGURE 8-2   Typical Division of HR Responsibilities: Training

HR UNIT

▶ Prepares skill-training materials
▶ Conducts the organizational new employee orientation
▶ Coordinates training efforts
▶ Conducts or arranges for off-the-job training
▶ Coordinates career plans and employee development efforts
▶ Provides input and expertise for organizational development
▶ Maintains organizational training records (Safety and Joint Commission)

HEALTHCARE MANAGERS

▶ Conduct departmental new employee orientation
▶ Provide technical information
▶ Monitor training needs
▶ Conduct on-the-job training
▶ Continually discuss employees' growth and future potential
▶ Participate in organizational change efforts
▶ Determine on-going training needs for their areas of responsibility

discuss employee career possibilities and plans with individual employees. There-fore, a training partnership between the HR staff members and operating managers must develop.

LEGAL ISSUES AND TRAINING

There are a number of legal issues that must be considered when designing training. The primary one is to ensure that the criteria and practices used to select individuals for inclusion in training programs are job related and must not unfairly restrict the participation of protected-class members. Another concern is differences in pay based on training to which protected-class members have not had equal access. A third is the use of training as a basis for selecting individuals for promotions, particularly if protected-group individuals have not had adequate opportunities for the training needed. Failure to accommodate individuals with disabilities to participate in training also has led to EEO lawsuits.

Another contemporary legal issue is the use of *training contracts* whereby employers require employees participating in expensive training to sign such contracts in order to protect the costs and time invested in specialized employee training. For instance, a hospital that paid $15,000 to have a therapist certified used a training contract whereby one-fourth of the cost is forgiven for each year the therapist stays with the organization following the training. If the therapist leaves sooner, then the hospital can use the contract to collect the unpaid balance.

Strategic Training

Training adds value to an organization by linking training strategy to organizational objectives, goals, and business strategies. **Strategic training** focuses on efforts that develop individual worker competencies and can produce ongoing value and competitive advantages for the organization. This basically means that training must be based on organizational plans and HR planning efforts. Strategic training also implies that HR and training professionals need to be involved in organizational change and strategic planning in order to develop training plans and activities that support top management's strategic decisions. Thus, training must help the organization create competitive advantage. Ultimately, to the extent that organizational training efforts are inherently difficult for competitors to imitate or copy, training can be considered a strategic asset.

A strategic training mindset also reduces the idea that training can solve most employee or organizational problems. As in the earlier situation where the Director of Patient Care was convinced her employees needed communications skills training, it is not uncommon for operating managers, HR professionals, and trainers to react to problems by saying, "I need a training program on X." With a strategic training focus, it is more likely that there will be an assessment of such requests to determine what training and/or non-training solutions should be used to address the performance issues. Such a focus also encourages that performance and training expectations be set and then measurement of the training results occur.

THE TRAINING PROCESS

Effective training requires the use of a systematic training process. Figure 8-3 depicts the training process as having four phases: *assessment, design, delivery,* and *evaluation.* Using such a process reduces the likelihood of unplanned, uncoordinated, and haphazard training efforts occurring that may significantly reduce the learning that should happen. A discussion of each phase of the training process follows next.

Assessment of Training Needs

Because training should be designed to help the organization accomplish its objectives, assessing organizational training needs is the diagnostic phase of setting training objectives. **Assessment** considers employee and organizational performance issues to determine if training can help. Using the performance consulting approach mentioned earlier, managers must consider non-training factors as well, such as compensation, organization structure, job design, physical work settings, and others. But if training is necessary, then the assessment efforts lead to analyzing the need for training and specifying the objectives of the training effort.[6] For example, looking at the performance of clerks in a billing department, a manager might believe that their data-entry and keyboard abili-

FIGURE 8-3 Training Process

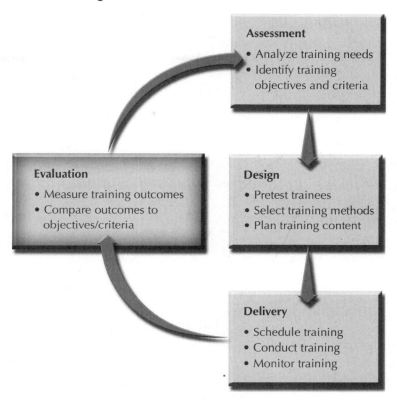

ties are weak and that they would profit by having instruction in these areas. As part of assessment, the clerks might be given a keyboard data-entry test to measure their current skills. An objective of increasing the clerks' keyboard entry speed to sixty words per minute without errors might be established. The number of words per minute without errors is the criterion against which training success can be measured, and it represents the way in which the objective is made specific. Figure 8-4 on the next page shows the three sources for obtaining training-needs assessment analyses.

Establishing Training Objectives and Priorities   Once the training needs have been identified using the various analyses, then training objectives and priorities should be established. All of the gathered data is used to compile a **gap analysis,** which identifies the distance between where an organization is with its employee capabilities and where it needs to be. Training objectives and priorities are set to close the gap.

The success of training should be measured in terms of the objectives set. Useful objectives are measurable. For example, an objective for a new Medicare

FIGURE 8-4 Sources of Training Needs Assessment

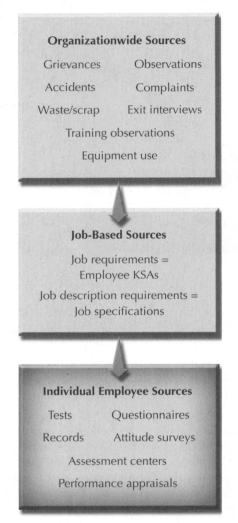

biller might be to "demonstrate the ability to explain the various billing processes in the department within two weeks." This objective serves as a check on internalization, or whether the person really learned and is able to use the training.

Because training seldom is an unlimited budget item and there are multiple training needs in an organization, it is necessary to prioritize needs. Ideally, training needs are ranked in importance on the basis of organizational objectives. The training most needed to improve the performance of the organization should be done first in order to produce visible results more quickly.

Training Design

Once training objectives have been determined, **training design** can be done. Regardless of whether the training is job specific or broader in nature, designing the training determines how the assessed needs are to be addressed. Effective training design considers learning concepts, legal issues, and different types of training.

Learning: The Focus of Training   Working in organizations should be a continual learning process, and learning is at the heart of all training activities. Different learning approaches are possible, but learning is a complex psychological process that is not fully understood by practitioners or research psychologists. There are three primary considerations when designing training: (1) determining learner readiness, (2) understanding different learning styles, and (3) designing training for transfer. Each of these elements must be considered in order for the training design to mesh together.[7]

Adult Learning   The classic work of Malcolm Knowles on adult learning suggests five principles for designing training for adults. This and subsequent work suggest that adults:[8]

1. Have the need to know why they are learning something.
2. Have a need to be self-directed.
3. Bring more work-related experiences into the learning process.
4. Enter into a learning experience with a problem-centered approach to learning.
5. Are motivated to learn by both extrinsic and intrinsic factors.

Because adults compose most learners in healthcare organizations, there are many implications for training design from Knowles' principles. For instance, trainers cannot expect to do a brain dump of material (i.e., the *fire-hose approach*) without giving trainees the context or bigger picture of why the participants need to know the training information. This concept is referred to as **whole learning** or **Gestalt learning.** As applied to job training, this means that instructions should be divided into small elements, but only *after* employees have had the opportunity to see how all the elements fit together.

Reinforcement and Immediate Confirmation   The concept of **reinforcement** is based on the **law of effect,** which states that people tend to repeat responses that give them some type of positive reward and avoid actions associated with negative consequences. Closely related is another learning concept called **immediate confirmation:** People learn best if reinforcement and feedback is given as soon as possible after training.

Transfer of Training   Finally, training interventions should be designed for the highest positive transfer of training. Transfer occurs when trainees actually use on the job what they have learned in training. Estimates of transfer in corporate training are fairly dismal—organizations with one hundred or more employees collectively spend about $60 billion on training each year, but of that total amount, only about $6 billion, or 10%, is thought to result in positive training transfer.[9]

Effective **transfer of training** meets two conditions. First, the trainees must be able to take the material learned in training and apply it to the job context in which they work. Second, use of the learned material must be maintained over time on the job.

There are a number of ways to increase the transfer of training.[10] One useful way is to ensure that the training is as much like the job as possible. In training, trainees should be able to experience the types of situations they can expect on the job. For example, training healthcare managers to be better interviewers should include role playing with *applicants* who respond in the same way that real applicants would. Also, offering trainees an overview of the training and how the training will be done seems to help with both short-term and longer-term training transfer.[11]

TYPES OF TRAINING

Training can be designed to meet a number of different objectives. Consequently, several types of training must be designed. One useful classification tool is to view training as being of several types:

▶ *Required and Regular Training*—Done to comply with various mandated legal requirements (e.g., OSHA, EEO), and as training for all employees (new employee orientation)
▶ *Job/Technical Training*—Done so that employees can perform their jobs, tasks, and responsibilities well (e.g., customer service, word processing, machine operations)
▶ *Interpersonal and Problem-Solving Training*—Conducted to address both operational and interpersonal problems and improving organizational working relationships (e.g., team building, conflict resolution)
▶ *Developmental and Innovative Training*—Long-term focused to enhance individual and organizational capabilities for the future (e.g., organizational change, creative thinking)

As described in the JCAHO feature on the next page, staff orientation, training and development are important components of healthcare efforts to ensure competency.

Orientation: Training for New Employees

All newly employed healthcare employees must attend orientation. All employees who routinely rotate to different areas of the health facility should also receive orientations to each of the areas. Examples of employees who rotate include RNs, respiratory therapists, agency nurses, and other contingency staff employees. Additionally, orientation is required for employees who have been reemployed, transferred, or promoted to new duties and employees who have been impacted by departmental or organizational redesigns.

THE JOINT COMMISSION ON ACCREDITATION OF HEALTHCARE ORGANIZATIONS

Joint Commission Standards and Orientation, Training, and Development

The Joint Commission on Accreditation of Healthcare Organizations (JCAHO) standards have a significant focus on staff orientation, training, and development. As depicted below, the standards require a process for the ongoing and continuous effort of assuring staff competency through orientation, training and development, and encouraging self-development. In addition, the standards require that data on competence patterns be monitored to identify trends and respond to employees' learning needs. These factors work together to ensure staff competency.

Identify Competence Trends and Respond to Employees' Learning Needs

In addition to the training described above, the Joint Commission also requires organizations to monitor patient care and safety incidents to determine employee-learning needs. As an example, a medical center evaluates the number of incidents of inadvertent needlesticks on each of the patient care units and determines if any special training would be required on a particular unit based on an exceptionally high number of sticks in comparison to other units. Training focusing on remedying competence issues is an extremely important in meeting Joint Commission HR standards. Monitoring trends and initiating training efforts designed to deal with issues should be well documented and "showcased" during a Joint Commission review.

Orientation is an important component of the organizational HR training strategy. It requires cooperation between individuals in the HR unit and other managers and supervisors. In a small organization without an HR department, such as a clinic, the new employee's supervisor or manager has most of the responsibility for orientation. In large organizations, managers and supervisors, as well as the HR department, should work as a team in employee orientation. Many organizations use checklists so that both HR staff and operating managers can coordinate what is covered during new employee orientations.

There are several key purposes of orientation. The most important ones are to

▶ Establish a favorable employee impression of the organization and the job
▶ Provide organization and job information
▶ Enhance interpersonal acceptance by co-workers
▶ Accelerate new employees' socialization and integration into the organization
▶ Ensure quicker employee performance and productivity

Effective orientation efforts contribute to both short-term and longer-term employment success. Various research studies and employer surveys have found that the socialization of new employees and their initial commitment to the organization are positively affected by orientation.[12] This socialization helps with enhancing the "person–organization fit," which also reinforces the positive views of the jobs, co-workers, and the organization.[13] Another key value of orientation is that healthcare employers have found that employee retention rates are higher when new employees receive effective orientation. Successful orientations speed up the adaptation process by helping new employees feel comfortable in the organization and by making them more productive on the job. This process approach to orientation results in reduced employee turnover.[14]

One way that orientations are being made more effective is through the use of electronic orientation. Employers place general employee orientation information on company intranets or on corporate Web sites. New employees can log on and go through much of the general material on organizational history, structure, products and services, mission statements, and other background information instead of having to sit in a classroom where the information is delivered in person or by videotape. The more specific questions and areas can be addressed by HR staff and others after the Web-based information has been reviewed by the new employees. Figure 8-5 shows the typical components of organizational and departmental orientations. As noted, many of the topics would lend themselves to Web-based presentation complemented by group meetings.

Unfortunately, many new employee orientation sessions are seen as boring, irrelevant, and a waste of time by both new employees and their department supervisors and managers. Many healthcare organizations are reconsidering their approach to new employee orientations in an effort to make the event more interesting and relevant. As an example, a large home health agency conducts their new employee orientation at a breakfast meeting, with extensive use of videos and presenters that incorporate humor and real-situation information in their presentations.

FIGURE 8-5 Typical Components of Healthcare Orientations

Organizational Orientation	Departmental Orientation
▶ Mission vision and values	▶ Departmental structure
▶ Organizational ethics	▶ Patient/work flow
▶ Organizational structure	▶ Tour of area
▶ Customer service requirements	▶ Job responsibilities
▶ Patient safety	▶ Performance standards
▶ Hazardous materials wastes management	▶ Departmental relationships
▶ Maintaining confidentiality	▶ Unit-specific safety
▶ Infection control practices	▶ Department policies
▶ Patient rights	
▶ Benefits, compensation and HR policies	
▶ Security and fire safety	

Encourage Self-Development

Not all of the training and education needs of healthcare employees can be met through organizational, departmental, or supervisory guided training. Employee training needs are often individualized and require the employee to take the initiative to meet their own needs. However, the organization must encourage and provide the employees with the resources and encouragement to pursue self-development. Encouraging and facilitating self-development can take many forms including the following ones:

▶ Resource libraries or learning labs where employees can research information or develop procedural skills in a self-paced manner
▶ Computer-based training (CBT) that employees can access either at the health facility or from their home computers
▶ Opportunities to attend professional society meetings that offer a variety of workshops and educational forums
▶ Tuition reimbursement or stipends to pursue technical or college-level course work

Beyond the importance of encouraging self-development for purposes of ensuring staff competency, a healthcare organization's investment in the self-development efforts described above can contribute to staff retention. As an example, at Griffin Hospital in Derby, Connecticut, which is considered one of the "100 Best Companies To Work For" according to *Fortune* magazine, staff development is a focal point of their employee retention efforts.[15] Retention of competent staff further contributes to safe, high-quality patient care.

On-going Training and Development

Training and development take many forms in the healthcare setting. These include, among others, on-the-job preceptorship by the supervisor or another proficient employee, in-service education on new procedures, policies or processes; continuing education classes and professional development workshops or seminars. The general objectives of these training and development efforts are to continually ensure employee competence and to enhance the employee's overall knowledge of their job duties, department, and organization. The specific objectives include the following:

▶ Correcting performance or competence deficiencies
▶ Provide training on new technology, techniques, or processes
▶ Meet safety or regulatory compliance requirements on such areas as blood-borne pathogens or fire safety standards
▶ Preparing employees for new job duties or promotional opportunities

Ensuring on-going training and development of healthcare employees is typically the responsibility of the employees' supervisors or department heads. However, HR plays a significant role in helping supervisors' monitor attendance at organizational-level training such as safety training and providing processes for documenting attendance at these programs.

Delivery of Training

The amount of each type of training done varies by organization, depending on the strategic plans, resources, and needs identified in various organizations. One of the most important and widely conducted types of regular training is new employee orientation.

Once training has been designed, the actual delivery of training can begin. It is generally recommended that the training be pilot-tested or conducted on a trial basis in order to ensure that the training meets the needs identified and that the design is appropriate. However, regardless of the type of training done, there are a number of different approaches and methods of training that can be used. The growth of training technology has expanded the choices available.

Regardless of the approaches used, there are a variety of considerations that must be balanced when selecting training approaches and methods. The common variables considered are:

▶ Nature of training
▶ Subject matter
▶ Number of trainees
▶ Individual versus team
▶ Self-paced versus guided
▶ Training resources
▶ Costs
▶ Geographic locations
▶ Time allotted
▶ Completion timeline

To illustrate, supervisory training for a large clinic with three locations in different, but close geographic areas may bring supervisors together for a two-day workshop once a quarter. However, a large, multistate nursing home system may use Web-based courses to reach supervisors throughout the country.

There are a number of different approaches to training. Frequently, training is conducted internally, but there are other types of training that make use of external or technological training resources.

Internal Training

Training internally tends to be viewed as being very applicable to the job. It is also popular because it saves the cost of sending employees away for training, and it often avoids the cost of outside trainers. Often, skills based technical training is conducted inside organizations. Technical training is usually skills based (e.g., training to run laboratory equipment). Due to rapid changes in technology, the building and updating of technical skills have become crucial training needs. Basic technical skills training is also being mandated by federal regulations in areas where the Occupational Safety and Health Administration (OSHA), the Environmental Protection Agency (EPA), and other agencies have regulations. Web-based training and intranets also are growing as internal means of training.

▶ *Informal Training*—One internal source of training is **informal training,** which occurs through interactions and feedback among employees. Much of what employees know about their jobs they learn informally from asking questions and getting advice from other employees and their supervisors, not from formal training programs.

▶ *On-the-Job Training (OJT)*—The most common type of training at all levels in an organization is **on-the-job training (OJT).** Different from informal training that often occurs spontaneously, OJT should be planned. The supervisor or manager doing the training must be able to teach, as well as to show, the employee what to do. On-the-job training is by far the most commonly used form of training because it is flexible and relevant to what the employee is doing.

External Training

External training is used extensively by organizations of all sizes. In large organizations, external training may be used because the absence of needed internal training capabilities or need to train many people quickly. External training may be the best option for training in smaller firms due to limitations in the size of their HR staffs and in the number of employees who may need various types of specialized training.

Training Outsourcing   The **outsourcing** of training to external training firms, consultants, and other entities is used by many employers of all sizes. According to data from ASTD, approximately 20% of training expenditures go to outside training sources. Interestingly, over a three-year period outsourcing of training has been declining, especially in firms with fewer than 500 employees.[16] The reasons for the decline may be due to cost concerns, greater emphasis on internal linking of training to organizational strategies, or others.

One external source that is popular is to use vendors and suppliers to train employees. Several different computer software vendors offer employees technical certifications on their software. For example, being a Microsoft Certified Product Specialist gives employees credentials that show their level of technical expertise. The certifications also provide employees items to put on their resumes should they decide to change jobs. These certifications also benefit employers, who can use the certifications as job specifications for hiring and promotion purposes.

E-Learning: Training Online

E-learning is defined as the use of the Internet or an organizational intranet to conduct training online. Many people are quite familiar with the Internet, given that it has so dramatically altered the way people do business, locate information, and communicate. An *intranet* is similar to the Internet, but it is a private organizational network behind "firewall" software that restricts access to authorized users, which includes employees participating in e-learning.

The growth of e-learning is seen in a number of statistics. One study forecasted that U.S. spending on e-learning is increasing 400% every three years and is expected to total about $15 billion by 2004. Adding in global employers raises this figure even higher.[17] Another indicator comes from ASTD, which found that the firms surveyed delivered about 8.4% of their training using e-learning. Although e-learning has leveled off some in smaller firms, larger firms are making the most use of e-learning where almost 14% of their training is done using e-learning. This is understandable because larger firms have more resources, and they also benefit most from the savings in distribution and travel costs due to the economies of scale provided by e-learning. As an example, Eckerd Pharmacy, a retail drug store chain, has developed an e-learning system to enable its pharmacists and pharmacy technicians to fulfill continuing education requirements in order for them to maintain their state licenses and certifications.[18]

There are a number of training methods many of which use technology:

▶ *Instructor-Led Classroom and Conference Training*—Instructor-led training is still the most prevalent method of training. Employer-conducted short courses, lectures, and meetings usually consist of classroom training, whereas numerous employee development courses offered by professional organizations, associations, and educational institutions are examples of conference training. Particularly important in classroom training is to recognize that adults in classroom training have different expectations and learning styles than do younger students.

▶ *Distance Training/Learning*—The e-learning presence in training departments is similar to what has happened in distance training and learning. A growing number of college and university classes use some form of Internet-based course support. Blackboard and WebCT are two of the more popular support packages that thousands of college professors are using to make their lecture content available to students. These packages enable virtual chat and electronic file exchange among course participants, and facilitate enhanced instructor–student contact. Many colleges and universities are using interactive two-way television to present classes. The medium allows an instructor in one place to see and respond to a "class" in any number of other locations. If a system is fully configured, employees can take courses from anywhere in the world.

▶ *Technology and Training*—The use of technology in the training arena has escalated substantially in the past few years.[19] This is to be expected, as information technology has revolutionized the way in which all individuals work. Today, computer-based training is able to involve a wide array of *multimedia technologies*—including sound, motion (video and animation), graphics, and hypertext—to tap multiple learner senses. *Video streaming* allows video clips of training materials to be stored on a firm's network server. Employees then can access the material using the firm's intranet. *Interactive video training* with the use of optical disks, CD-ROMs, or DVDs provides full-motion video to portray a situation in which the trainee views the correct use of a procedure or behavior. The learner then attempts to duplicate the behavior and a video camera records their facial expressions and verbal responses. The session can be taped for feedback purposes and later critiqued by a course facilitator. Interactive video training has been found to be effective, for example, in teaching interview and presentation skills.

Computer-supported *simulations* also are being used in organizational training to replicate the psychological and behavioral requirements of a task, often in addition to providing some amount of physical resemblance to the trainee's work environment. From highly complicated surgical simulations replicating difficult surgical scenarios, to training that helps phlebotomists draw blood, the main advantages of simulations are that they allow for safe training when the risks associated with failure are high.[20] Computer-based simulators also incorporate sound learning principles, such as immediate feedback reinforcement, self-directed learning, and work-relevant problems.

New technologies are being incorporated into training delivery, design, administration, and support of training. For example, healthcare organizations are investing in electronic registration and record-keeping systems that allow trainers to register participants, record exam results, and monitor learning progress. To support training, there are computer applications providing requested information, advice, and/or skills training, known as *electronic performance support systems* (EPSS). These computer-based systems allow continuous learning on the job and aid in training transfer. For example, a hospital uses an electronic system to provide additional support to clinical engineers when using a diagnostic system to identify and repair equipment troubles.

Generally speaking, what is occurring is a movement from technology taking center stage in training to "technology in the background," whereby technology becomes embedded in learning and training.[21] As learning and work merge even closer in the future, technology likely will become seamlessly integrated into more employees' work environment. This integration will allow trainers, training managers, and training designers to concentrate on learning rather than on technology, so that employees will spend less time in the future learning how to use technology, and more time on the desired learning content.

Evaluation of Training

Evaluation of training compares the post-training results to the objectives expected by managers, trainers, and trainees. Too often, training is done without any thought of measuring and evaluating it later to see how well it worked. Because training is both time-consuming and costly, evaluation should be done.

Cost–Benefit Analyses   One way to evaluate training results is to examine the costs associated with the training and the benefits received through a cost–benefit analysis. Figure 8-6 shows some costs and benefits that may result from training. Although some benefits (such as attitude changes) are hard to quantify, comparison of costs and benefits associated with training remains a way to determine if training is cost effective.[22] For example, one hospital evaluated a traditional safety training program and found that the program did not lead to a reduction in accidents. Therefore, the training was redesigned so that better safety practices resulted. However, careful measurement of both the costs and the benefits may be difficult.

Return on Investment (ROI)   In organizations today, training is expected to produce a return on investment in the training costs. Like other parts of organizations, HR and training must be justified on the value-added for the training investments made. Unfortunately, in too many circumstances, training is justified because employees like it, not because of beneficial use of resources.[23]

F I G U R E 8 - 6   Balancing Costs and Benefits of Training

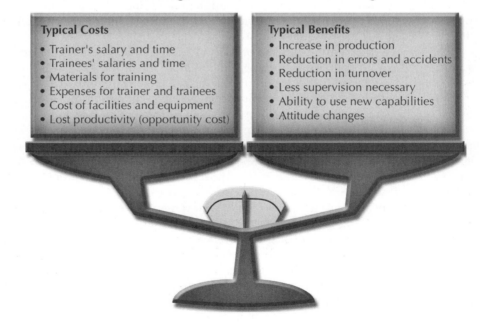

Typical Costs
- Trainer's salary and time
- Trainees' salaries and time
- Materials for training
- Expenses for trainer and trainees
- Cost of facilities and equipment
- Lost productivity (opportunity cost)

Typical Benefits
- Increase in production
- Reduction in errors and accidents
- Reduction in turnover
- Less supervision necessary
- Ability to use new capabilities
- Attitude changes

Benchmarking Training   Rather than doing training evaluation internally, some organizations are using benchmark measures of training that are compared from one organization to others. To do benchmarking, HR professionals in an organization gather data on training and compare it to data at other organizations in the industry and of their size. Comparison data are available through the American Society of Training and Development (ASTD) and its Benchmarking Service. This service has training-related data from more than 1,000 participating employers who complete detailed questionnaires annually. Training also can be benchmarked against data from the American Productivity and Quality Center and the Saratoga Institute.[24] In addition, here are a number of private healthcare benchmarking services that provide benchmark studies for individual hospitals, clinics, and other providers.

Evaluation Designs   If evaluation is done internally because benchmarking data are not available, there are many ways to design the evaluation of training programs to measure improvements. Depending on the nature of the program or material presented post-measure and pre-/post-measures may be effective approaches to consider.

▶ *Post-Measure*—The most obvious way to evaluate training effectiveness is to determine after the training whether the individuals can perform in an more effective manner or their knowledge has increased. As an example, assume that a nursing manager has twenty health unit coordinators (HUCs) who need to improve their data entry speeds. They are given a one-day training session and then given a test to measure their speeds. If the HUCs can all type at the required speed after training, was the training beneficial? It is difficult to say; perhaps most of them could have done as well before training. It would be difficult to know whether the typing speed is a result of the training or could have been achieved without training.

▶ *Pre-/Post-Measure*—By designing the data entry evaluation differently, the issue of pre-test skill levels could have been considered. If the nursing manager had measured the data entry speed before and after training, she could have known whether the training made any difference. However, a question remains. If there was a change in speed, was the training responsible for the change, or did these people simply work faster because they knew they were being tested? People often perform better when they know they are being tested on the results.

DEVELOPING HUMAN RESOURCES

Development represents efforts to improve employees' abilities to handle various assignments and to cultivate capabilities beyond those required by the current job. Development benefits both organizations and individuals. The employees and managers with their experiences and abilities may enhance organizational competitiveness and the ability to adapt to a changing environment. In the development process, individuals' careers also may evolve and gain new or different focus.[25]

Development differs from training. It is possible to train most people to run a copy machine, answer customer service questions, or operate a computer. However, development in areas such as judgment, responsibility, decision making, and communications presents a bigger challenge. These areas may or may not develop through life experiences by individuals. A planned system of development experiences for all employees, not just managers, can help expand the overall level of capabilities in a healthcare organization.

Development starts with the HR plans of an organization because these plans analyze, forecast, and identify current and future organizational needs for human resources. HR planning anticipates the movement of people in the organization due to retirements, promotions, and transfers. Further, it helps identify the capabilities needed by the organization in the future and the development necessary for people to be available to meet those needs.

Developing Specific Capabilities

Exactly what kind of development a given individual might need to expand his or her capabilities depends on both the person and the capabilities needed. However, some important and common management capabilities often include action orientation, quality decision making, ethical values, and technical skills. Team building, developing subordinates, directing others, and dealing with uncertainty are equally important, but much less commonly developed capabilities for successful managers.

One point is clear about development, however. In studies that asked employees what they want out of their jobs, training and development ranked at or near the top. Because the assets of individuals are their knowledge, skills, and abilities (KSAs), many people view the development of their KSAs as an important part of their organizational package.[26]

Development Needs Analyses

As with training, employee development begins with analyses of the needs of both the organization and individuals. Evidence indicates that these analyses of individuals' development needs frequently receive insufficient attention in many organizations.

Either the organization or the individual can analyze what a given person needs by way of development. The goal, of course, is to identify strengths and weaknesses. Methods used by organizations to assess development needs include use of assessment centers, psychological testing, and performance appraisals.

Succession Planning

Succession planning is planning for the succession of key executives, managers, and other employees is an important part of HR development. **Succession planning** is a process of identifying a longer-term plan for orderly replacement of key employees.

FIGURE 8-7 **Succession Planning Process**

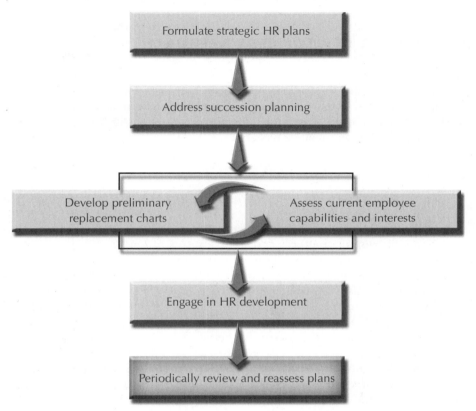

The need to replace key employees results from promotions, transfers, retirements, deaths, disability, departures, or other reasons. Succession planning often focuses on top management, such as ensuring a CEO successor. However, limiting succession planning just to top executive jobs is one of the greatest mistakes made.[27] For instance, identifying successors for admissions supervisors, IT technicians, physical therapists, and other key jobs is just as crucial as succession planning for the top executive jobs in a healthcare institution. For example, a large clinic whose director of nursing is planning retirement must consider the implications for maintaining continuity in delivering competent patient care and nursing leadership. The need to plan for and eventually replace this key manager is *a strategic HR issue.* The succession planning process depicted in Figure 8-7 is recommended.

Two coordinated activities begin the actual succession planning process. First, the development of preliminary replacement charts ensures that the right individuals with sufficient capabilities and experience to perform the targeted jobs are available at the right time. These charts both show the backup "players" for each position and they identify positions without a current qualified backup. The charts identify who could take over key jobs if someone leaves, retires, dies unexpectedly, or otherwise creates a vacancy, and the development necessary to ready some of the others to do so.

CHOOSING A DEVELOPMENT APPROACH

Common development approaches can be categorized under two major headings—**job-site development** and **off-site development.** Both are appropriate in developing managers and other employees. Investing in human intellectual capital, whether at work or off the job, becomes imperative for organizations as "knowledge work" aspects increase for almost all employers.

Development Approaches: Job-Site Methods

A number of job-site development methods are available. However, all too often unplanned and perhaps useless activities pass as development on the job. To ensure that the desired development actually occurs, managers must plan and coordinate development efforts, and several means can be used.

The oldest on-the-job development technique is **coaching,** which is the observation and feedback given to employees by immediate supervisors. Coaching involves a continual process of learning by doing. For effective coaching, a healthy and open relationship must exist between employees and their supervisors or managers. Many firms conduct formal training courses to improve the coaching skills of their managers and supervisors.

Committee Assignments/Meetings Assigning promising employees to important committees may broaden their experiences and can help them understand the personalities, issues, and processes guiding the organization. For instance, employees on a safety committee can gain a greater understanding of safety management, which would aid them to become supervisors. They may also experience the problems involved in maintaining employee safety awareness. However, managers need to guard against committee assignments that turn into time-wasting activities.

Job Rotation The process of shifting an employee from job to job is **job rotation.** In some organizations, job rotation is unplanned. However, other organizations follow elaborate charts and schedules, precisely planning a rotation program for each employee's development. When opportunities for promotion are scarce, job rotation through use of lateral transfers may be beneficial in rekindling enthusiasm and developing employees' talents. The best lateral moves do one or more of the following:

▶ Move the person into the core business
▶ Provide closer contact with patients/residents/clients
▶ Teach new skills or perspectives

Despite its benefits, job rotation can be expensive. Furthermore, a substantial amount of time is taken when trainees change positions, because they must become acquainted with different people and techniques in each new unit.

"Assistant-To" Positions   Positions Some firms create "assistant-to" positions, which are staff positions immediately under a manager. Through such jobs, trainees can work with outstanding managers they might not otherwise have met. Some organizations set up "junior boards of trustees" or "management cabinets" to which trainees may be appointed. These assignments provide useful experiences if they present challenging or interesting assignments to trainees.

Development Approaches: Off-Site Methods

Off-the-job development techniques give individuals opportunities to get away from the job and concentrate solely on what is to be learned. Moreover, contact with others who are concerned with somewhat different problems and come from different organizations may provide employees with new and different perspectives. Various off-site methods are used.

Classroom Courses and Degrees   Most off-the-job development programs include some classroom instruction. Most people are familiar with classroom training, which gives it the advantage of being widely accepted. But the lecture system sometimes used in classroom instruction encourages passive listening and reduced learner participation, which is a distinct disadvantage. Often trainees have little opportunity to question, clarify, and discuss the lecture material. The effectiveness of classroom instruction depends on multiple factors: group size, trainees' abilities, instructors' capabilities and styles, and subject matter.

Organizations often send employees to externally sponsored seminars or professional courses, such as those offered by the American Hospital Association. Many healthcare organizations also encourage continuing education by reimbursing employees for the costs of college tuition courses. Such programs provide incentive for employees to study for advanced degrees, such as MHAs, through evening and weekend classes, outside of their regular workdays.

Human Relations Training   This type of training attempts to prepare supervisors to deal with "people problems" brought to them by their employees. The training focuses on the development of the human relations skills a person needs to work well with others. Most human relations training programs typically are aimed at new or relatively inexperienced first-line supervisors and middle managers. Content areas covered include motivation, leadership, employee communication, and other behavioral topics.

The most common reason managers fail after being promoted to management is poor teamwork with subordinates and peers. Other common reasons for management failure include not understanding expectations, failure to meet goals, difficulty in adjusting to management responsibilities, and inability to balance work and home life.

Sabbaticals and Leaves of Absence   A **sabbatical leave** is paid time off to develop and rejuvenate oneself. These have been popular for many years in academic environments but sabbaticals have also been adopted in other areas of healthcare as well. Some organizations give employees three to six months off to work on socially desirable projects. Such projects have included leading training programs in urban ghettos or participating in corporate volunteer programs to aid non-profit organizations.

As an example, United Way and Community Chest organizations have "Executive-on-loan" programs that are excellent opportunities for both the healthcare executive and the healthcare organization. The executive gets to learn and do new and different things and the organization gets to contribute in a high value and unique way to the community.

Organizations that offer sabbaticals speak well of the results. They say sabbaticals help prevent employee burnout, offer advantages in recruiting and retention, and boost individual employee morale. One obvious disadvantage of paid sabbaticals is the cost. Also, the nature of the learning experience generally falls outside the control of the organization, leaving it somewhat to chance.[28]

Leaves of absence for educational purposes may or may not be provided with pay. Some healthcare organizations allow employees the opportunity to access vacation time or continue benefits while on leaves of this nature. An educational leave of absence is typically granted to allow employees the time to commit full attention and effort to their education where there is a likelihood that such employees will be able to utilize their education to enhance their job performance when they return.

Management Development

Although development is important for all employees, it is essential for managers. Effective management development imparts the knowledge and judgment needed by managers. Without appropriate development, managers may lack the capabilities to best deploy and manage resources (including employees) throughout the organization. Necessary capabilities are often a focus of management development include leadership, dealing with change, coaching and advising subordinates, controlling operations, and providing performance feedback.

Experience plays a central role in management development. Indeed, experience often contributes more to the development of senior managers than classroom training does, because much of their experience occurs in varying circumstances on the job over time. Yet, despite a need for effective managers, finding such managers for middle-level jobs is often difficult. At the middle-management level, some individuals refuse to take management jobs. Many very talented healthcare professionals such as RNs, respiratory therapists, or pharmacists that could potentially make excellent managers refuse to do so because it would remove them from day-to-day patient care responsibilities. Sometimes the increase in pay is not enough to compensate for the increased work load and responsibility. Many are also disenchanted with the "thanklessness" of the job, commenting that they would be caught between unhappy employees and nonsupportive senior management.

Managerial Modeling   A common adage in management development says that managers tend to manage as they were managed. In other words, managers learn by behavior modeling, or copying someone else's behavior. This tendency is not surprising, because a great deal of human behavior is learned by modeling. Children learn by modeling the behaviors of their parents and older children. Management development efforts can take advantage of natural human behavior by matching young or developing managers with appropriate models and then reinforcing the desirable behaviors exhibited. Note that the modeling process involves more than straightforward imitation, or copying; it is considerably more complex. For example, one can learn what not to do by observing a model who does something wrong. Thus, exposure to both positive and negative models can benefit a new manager.

Management Coaching   Coaching combines observation with suggestions. Like modeling, it complements the natural way humans learn. A brief outline of good coaching pointers often includes the following:

▶ Explaining appropriate behavior
▶ Making clear why actions were taken
▶ Accurately stating observations
▶ Providing possible alternatives/suggestions
▶ Following up/reinforcing

In the context of healthcare management development, coaching involves a relationship between two managers for a period of time as they perform their jobs. Effective coaching requires patience and good communication skills.

Mentoring

Mentoring is a relationship in which experienced managers aid individuals in the earlier stages of their careers. Such a relationship provides an environment for conveying technical, interpersonal, and organizational skills from the more-experienced to the less-experienced person. Not only does the inexperienced employee benefit, but also the mentor may enjoy the challenge of sharing his or her wisdom.

However, mentoring is not without its problems. Young minority managers frequently report difficulty finding mentors. Also, men generally show less willingness than women to be mentors. Further, mentors who are dissatisfied with their jobs and those who teach a narrow or distorted view of events may not help a young manager's development. Fortunately, many managers have a series of advisors or mentors during their careers and may find advantages in learning from the different mentors. For example, the unique qualities of individual mentors may help less-experienced managers identify key behaviors in management success and failure. Further, those being mentored may find previous mentors to be useful sources for networking.[29]

SPECIAL ISSUES IN HEALTHCARE EMPLOYEE DEVELOPMENT

The healthcare industry is a diverse collection of various types and sizes of organizations. From an employment perspective, the jobs and careers within the industry are even more diverse. From physician to medical assistant, CEO to line supervisor, architect to repair technician, every conceivable type of position and profession is represented in the healthcare industry. There are·a number of important considerations in healthcare employee development, including the size and sophistication of the organization, academic and credential requirements, and organizational strategies.

Depending on the type of facility or entity within the healthcare industry, employee development can be non-existent or unplanned and haphazard or be very well developed and thoroughly planned. In small facilities, such as clinics or rural nursing homes, the organizational structures are very flat with minimal opportunities for promotion or even lateral transfers, consequently employee development is typically not a priority. Conversely, large integrated systems such as Kaiser-Permanente, Intermountain Healthcare, and Henry Ford Hospitals carefully craft employee development plans aimed at identifying and developing the best and the brightest for future clinical management and executive positives within their organizations.[30]

Academic and Credential Requirements

For many healthcare environments advancement is entirely dependent on academic attainment and credentials. As an example, nurses cannot be promoted to physicians because they lack the appropriate educational background. Although this example seems an almost absurd observation, this reality and others like it are important considerations in healthcare employee development. Although physicians are rarely provided with management or leadership skills development, they often find themselves in positions of leadership. Since they provide medical direction and leadership and/or own the practice, clinic or hospital, it follows that they would also provide leadership in non-medical areas.

The key criterion for their leadership role is their academic preparation as an M.D., without which they could not be in their position. In many of the clinical and administrative management roles, similar situations occur. Figure 8-8 provides examples of other healthcare management positions that normally require specific academic preparation or credentials.

F I G U R E   8 - 8   Samples of Healthcare Positions and Academic Preparation/Credentials

POSITION	ACADEMIC PREPARATION/CREDENTIAL
Clinical	
Director of Pharmacy	Pharm D.
Director of Nursing	RN, MSN
Director or Respiratory Care	B.S. Respiratory Care, Registered Respiratory Therapist (RRT)
Administrative	
Nursing Home Administration	Certification in Nursing Home Administration
Facilities Director	Professional Engineer (P.E.)
Director of Finance	Certified Public Accountant (CPA)
Director of Health Information	Registered Health Information Administrator (RHIA)

HR Development and Organizational Restructuring

When healthcare organizational strategies involve restructurings and downsizing, it is difficult to know what a career is, much less how to develop one. Further, some employers wonder why they should worry about career "development" for employees when the future likely holds fewer internal promotion opportunities and more movement in and out of organizations by individuals. Even though these views may seem extreme, employee development has changed recently in three significant ways:

1. The middle management "ladder" in healthcare organizations now includes more horizontal than upward moves.
2. Many organizations target their efforts to ensure that their focus is on core competencies.
3. The growth of project-based work makes careers a series of projects, not just steps upward in a given organization.

Traditionally, career development efforts targeted managerial personnel to look beyond their current jobs and to prepare them for a variety of future jobs in the organization. But development for all employees, not just managers, is necessary for organizations to have the needed human resource capabilities for future growth and change.

Mergers, acquisitions, restructurings, and layoffs all have influenced the way healthcare employees and organizations look at careers and development. In the "new career," the individual—not the organization—manages his or her own development. Such self-development consists of personal educational experiences, training, organizational experiences, projects, and even changes in occupational fields. Under this system, the individual defines career success, which may or may not coincide with the organizational view of success.

CASE

Associated Community Health Centers (ACHC), a family practice clinic with 250 employees and nine locations servicing the suburbs of a large city, is facing a variety of HR issues. The HR manager conducted an HR audit in order to evaluate the problems and make recommendations for improvement. Her findings fell into four categories: a) retention issues; b) staff complaints; c) patent concerns; and d) clinical incidents.

▶ *Retention Issues*—Focusing specifically on RN staffing, one of the most critical positions for ACHC, the current RN turnover rate is 26%. The RN vacancy rate, or the percentage of open positions for RNs is 20%.

▶ *Staff Complaints*—The HR Manager, through staff interviews, learned that ACHC's employees were concerned about a variety of issues including late performance reviews, a lack of promotional opportunities and poor communications between supervisors and staff.

▶ *Patient Concerns*—The HR manager evaluated patient feedback forms to gain insight into the HR issues. From the patient feedback a number of related HR issues were identified. These consisted of rude behavior on the part of patient schedulers, inattentiveness to patients by reception staff and long waits by patients without explanation.

▶ *Clinical Incidents*—In order to evaluate the effect of the HR issues on the quality of patient care being provided by ACHC, the HR manger reviewed data on clinical incidents. Two important categories of clinical incidents were noted:

    ▶ 20% of x-rays taken had to be retaken due to poor quality.

    ▶ 15% of laboratory test result reports were lost or mis-filed, requiring either re-tests or a delay in reporting.

The HR manager was very concerned about the findings. However, she was confident that with effective HR efforts, the issues detailed above could be addressed.

Questions

1. Which of ACHC's issues could be improved through orientation, training, or staff development programming?
2. Based on your answer to question 1, detail the types of programming that could be effective in dealing with the issues you identified.

END NOTES

1. Sheldon L. Goldberg, "Keys to Retaining Staff: The Jewish Home and Hospital Experience," *Nursing Homes* (May 2000), 24–28.
2. Steven Berger, "Training Shouldn't Be the First to Go," *Modern Healthcare* (February 21, 2000), 35.
3. Brenda Paik Sundo, "Results Oriented Customer Service Training," *Workforce* (May 2001), 84–90.
4. For example, see James Robinson, *The Evolving Performance Consultant Job* (Pittsburg, PA.: Partners in Charge, Inc., 2000).
5. Michael Wykes, J. March-Swets, and L. Rynbrandt, "Performance Analysis: Field Operations Management," in J. Phillips (ed.), *In Action: Performance Consulting and Analysis* (Alexandria, Va.: American Society of Training and Development, 2000), 135–153.
6. Elwood F. Holton III, Reid A. Bates, and Sharon S. Naquin, "Large-Scale Performance-Driven Training Needs Assessment: A Case Study," *Public Personnel Management,* 29 (2000), 249–267.
7. Jennifer J. Salopek, "The Young and the Rest of Us," *Training and Development,* February 2000, 26–30.
8. Shawn B. Merriam and Rosemary Caffarella, *Learning in Adulthood: A Comprehensive Guide,* 2nd ed. (San Francisco: Jossey-Bass, 1999).
9. Kathryn Tyler, "Hold On to What You've Learned," *HR Magazine* (May 2000), 94–102.
10. For a detailed discussion on transfer of training, see Raymond A. Noe, *Employee Training & Development* (New York: Irwin McGraw-Hill, 1999, 109–128.
11. Marvin L. Schroth, "The Effects of Type and Amount of Pre-training on Transfer in Concept Formation," *The Journal of General Psychology,* 127 (2000) 261.
12. Howard J. Klein and Natasha A. Weaver, "The Effectiveness of an

Organizational-Level Orientation Training Program in the Socialization of New Hires," *Personnel Psychology* 53 (2000), 47–66.

13. Daniel M. Cable and Charles K. Parsons, "Socialization Tactics and Person–Organization Fit," *Personnel Psychology* 54 (2001), 1.

14. "Successful Orientation Programs," *Training and Development* (April 2000), 59.

15. Thomas C. Dolan, "Do You Still Walk the Halls at Night?" *Healthcare Executive* (March/April 2001), 4.

16. Mark E. Van Buren, *ASTD State of the Industry Report, 2001* (Alexandria, Va.: ASTD, 2001) 11–12.

17. Rob Eure, "On the Job: Corporate E-Learning Makes Training Available, Anytime, Anywhere," *The Wall Street Journal* (March 12, 2001), R33.

18. Simone Karp, "E-learning and The Enterprise," *Health Management Technology* (December 2001), 32–34.

19. For a more detailed review of Training Technology, see Larry A. Pace, "Technological Advancements in Training Design, Delivery, Support and Administration." In Burke, *High-Impact Training Solutions* (Westport, CT: Quorum Publishers, 2001).

20. Cinda Becker, "Students Can Learn at High-Tech Surgery Lab," *Modern Healthcare* (November 6, 2000), 94.

21. H. W. Hodgins, *Into the Future: A Vision Paper,* American Society for Training & Development and the National Governor's Association Commission on Technology and Adult Learning (Washington, D.C.: American Society for Training & Development, 2000.)

22. Robert W. Rowden, "A Practical Guide to Assessing the Value of Training in Your Company," *National Productivity Review,* (Autumn 2000), 9–13.

23. Ben Worthen, "Measuring the ROI of Training," *CIO* (February 15, 2001), 128–136.

24. For information, go to the following Web sites: *http://www.astd.org, http://www.apqc.org,* and *http://www.saratogainstitute.com.*

25. Scott E. Seibert, *et al.,* "A Social Capital Theory of Career Success," *The Academy of Management Journal,* 44 (2001), 219–237.

26. Kevin Sweeney, "Top of the Class," *Employee Benefit News* (March 2001), 33–35; and Harley Frazis, "Correlates of Training," *Industrial and Labor Relations Review,* 53 (2000), 443.

27. Scot T. Fleischmann, "Succession Management for the Entire Organization," *Employment Relations Today* (Summer 2000), 53–62.

28. Vicky Uhland, "Sabbatical Is Icing on Cake," *The Denver Rocky Mountain News* (August 20, 2000), J1.

29. Monica C. Higgins and Kathy E. Fram, "Reconceptualizing Mentoring at Work: A Developmental Network Perspective," *Academy of Management Review,* 26 (2001), 264.

30. Gail L. Warden and John R. Griffith, "Ensuring Management Excellence in the Healthcare System," *Journal of Healthcare Management* (July/August 2001), 228–237.

CHAPTER 9

Performance Management in Healthcare Organizations

Learning Objectives

After you have read this chapter, you should be able to:

▶ Discuss the importance of the performance appraisal process.

▶ Compare and contrast the administrative and development uses of performance appraisals.

▶ Review the informal versus systematic appraisal processes.

▶ Identify who should conduct appraisals.

▶ Describe the various methods of appraising performance.

▶ Identify the various rater errors that occur during the appraisal process.

Healthcare HR Insights

A major urban health system of hospitals and clinics located in the midwest had to confront some significant employee performance issues. The health system went through a series of changes over the past several years to improve the quality of patient care. Many of the changes have resulted in initiatives to improve the knowledge, skills, and abilities (KSAs) of its employees.

One change initiative was named "Pursuit of Excellence," which included the development of a new employee appraisal system. The new appraisal system included three steps: agreeing on performance criteria, informal reviews throughout the year, and a formal process based on data from the entire year. This comprehensive review represented a positive change because managers and employees participated equally in job-criteria development. Under the new appraisal system, performance reviews were conducted annually. Also, managers were encouraged to review performance informally as needed.

The new initiative required the development of job standards for each position, which were tied to the Excellence values (including cooperation, teamwork, accountability, fairness, and dignity). All Excellence values were weighted equally with the exception of the *value of accountability,* which was weighted higher because of its importance in the Excellence initiative. The performance-appraisal process also identified job standards to evaluate performance and developmental opportunities for employees who needed to improve their KSAs.

APPRAISAL FORM

The revised appraisal form contained five sections: employee demographics, job prerequisites, Excellence values, narrative comments by the manager and employee, and signatures of their acknowledgment. The heart of the appraisal process is measuring employees' performance against the Excellence values. Using the revised performance appraisal form, a rating scale describes the employees' achievements compared to three performance levels: role model (the highest), fully effective and needs improvement.

The Excellence values support the performance-appraisal process by describing job expectations using behavioral examples. One Excellence value is dignity, which the appraisal document defines as "treating patients, visitors, and fellow employees with dignity," and asks, "to what extent does the employee demonstrate the value of dignity?" This provides managers with a concrete description of the value and a guide for assessing behaviors.

Results of this new approach have been very positive. Employees have had a better understanding of job expectations, which has resulted in higher levels of job satisfaction and has decreased turnover significantly. Also, the appraisal system has identified development opportunities for employees. As a consequence, since the inception of the program, employees have participated in a number of development classes.

Employee performance is important for organizations that are counting on their employees to help meet organizational goals. Part of achieving satisfactory employee performance is an effective performance management system. HR professionals implement performance management systems that identify, encourage, measure, evaluate, and improve employee work performance.

Performance management is a vital link between organizational strategy and its outcomes. For example, if a nurse practitioner in a clinic has the ability to perform her duties but the organization does not support her with the appropriate equipment and technology, she will not succeed in her position. In many cases, some of performance factors are present but if any of the factors are missing, individuals will not be able to perform according to their job standards.

Organizations develop performance management systems to define expectations for employees and to manage their performance. These systems identify job expectations, measure, evaluate, and reward performance, and provide for improvement where needed.

Based on organizational goals, healthcare managers need to organize their employees' jobs to provide care and services that patients/residents/clients value. Employee performance is monitored to ensure that each job is performed successfully to help organizations meet their objectives. Employee performance is measured by job standards defined by job criteria.

Job Criteria

Job criteria identify factors employees must meet for satisfactory job performance. Criteria in most jobs are weighted for importance. As an example, a laboratory technician's job may have several criteria, but those that require the technician to do quality-control checks on lab results may receive greater weight. Recall that at the University of Chicago Hospital, excellence received a weight of 60% compared with other job criteria.

Criteria may be classified as trait-based, behavior-based, and/or results-based. **Trait-based criteria** identify subjective personal traits, such as having a positive attitude, that may contribute to job success. **Behavior-based criteria** identifies behaviors, such as persuasion skills, that may lead to successful completion of job expectations. In some cases, both trait-based and behavior-based qualities are difficult to identify and evaluate objectively. **Results-based criteria,** such as completing projects on time, are easier to identify and evaluate.

Criteria Relevance When developing systems to measure performance, managers should include criteria that are relevant to the job. Job criteria relevance is determined by job description accuracy and its translation into performance standards. For example, measuring the performance of a nurse anesthetist for presentation skills would not be relevant, but measuring their anesthesia management abilities would be relevant because they are tied to a primary job responsibility. Reviewing the job description and the criteria before doing a performance appraisal helps to eliminate criteria that are not vital for use.

Potential for Criteria Problems   All jobs are a compilation of duties and tasks. Some organizations develop job descriptions and performance appraisals, and some may not be relevant to the job. When the measurement process omits significant criteria, the measures are **deficient.** For example, if an appointment scheduler was not measured for the ability to meet patient, physician, and staff needs when scheduling appointments, the criteria for evaluation would be considered deficient. If irrelevant criteria are included in the measurement process, it is **contaminated.** The same scheduler should be measured for scheduling accuracy, but measuring the scheduler's ability to program a computer would be an illustation of contaminated criteria. HR professionals and managers should review job descriptions and performance appraisals regularly to prevent using deficient or contaminated criteria.

Performance Standards

Each job is assigned a set of standards with which to compare employees' performance levels. HR professionals and managers determine performance standards for each job before employees begin work. Employees should be given performance standards when they are hired because they will be evaluated during performance appraisals on how they meet those standards.[1]

PERFORMANCE APPRAISAL

One of the most important managerial duties is to evaluate employees' performance. During performance reviews, managers should discuss how well employees are meeting their job standards. The process of evaluating an employee's performance is called the **performance appraisal.**

Evaluating an employee's performance is one of the most important HR processes. In one healthcare system, the Vice-President of HR realized that both managers and employees did not like the performance-appraisal system. Employees thought it was too subjective and department managers were reluctant to complete the appraisals. A new system was designed that simplified the rating system, standardized the evaluation criteria, and streamlined the process.[2]

Another important consideration in the development and implementation of a healthcare organizational performance appraisal process is compliance with JCAHO standards. The JCAHO feature on the next page details the standards that impact the performance appraisal process.

THE JOINT COMMISSION ON ACCREDITATION OF HEALTHCARE ORGANIZATIONS

Joint Commission Standards and Performance Evaluation

A number of JCAHO standards affect performance appraisals:

▶ Management of human resources
▶ Leadership
▶ Improving organization performance

The common objective of these standards is to ensure the ongoing competence and appropriate performance of employees. Also, a healthcare organization should have policies and programs in place to monitor deficiencies and to evaluate improvement efforts when necessary.

The components of a JCAHO-acceptable performance appraisal system include the following characteristics:

▶ Job descriptions identifying duties and required competencies
▶ A performance evaluation process and supporting documents
▶ Competency assessment checklists

Performance evaluation and competency assessment are two different, but related processes. Some healthcare organizations conduct performance evaluations and competency assessments simultaneously, and others treat them as separate processes. Performance evaluations are used to determine how well employees are performing the duties and responsibilities of their positions as described on the job descriptions. Competency assessments are used to determine whether the employees have the knowledge, skills, ability, training, education, and licensure to meet the requirements of their position.[3]

Performance appraisals have two major, sometimes conflicting uses in healthcare organizations, they include both administrative and development uses. Figure 9-1 illustrates the two potentially conflicting roles for performance appraisal.

Administrative Uses

Performance appraisal results can be used administratively to determine the amount of a pay adjustment an employee receives. Pay increases awarded as a result of performance are called merit-based or performance-based. Because performance is tied to compensation, employees need to believe that performance appraisals are being done equitably.

The performance appraisal process is also used administratively for promotions, terminations, and layoffs. Managers use performance appraisals to con-

FIGURE 9-1   Conflicting Roles for Performance Appraisal

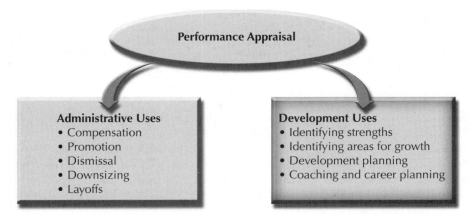

sider employees for promotion. Performance appraisals can also be used to sup-plement other documentation about performance deficiencies that may lead to termination. Some organizations use performance appraisals to determine who is laid off when downsizing is necessary. Any time managers make decisions that differentiate employees for promotions, dismissals, and layoffs, they should use performance appraisals to support their decisions.

Legal Issues and Performance Appraisals   Performance appraisals have increased in importance to organizations as employees have increasingly pur-sued their legal rights through Federal and State compliance agencies and courts that hear employee complaints.[4] The major legal challenges are about dis-criminatory practices in performance appraisals. To avoid charges of discrimi-natory practices, performance appraisals must be objective and job related.

Healthcare managers and HR professionals must adhere to legal restrictions that affect the rights of employees and employers. Topics to consider before a significant performance management intervention include discrimination, pub-lic-policy issues, contractual issues, and tort-liability issues.[5] These legal issues typically provide a basis for employee claims made against employers.

Development Uses

Performance appraisals are also used to help identify development plans for employees. Performance appraisals should contain information that describes where the employee needs development to meet job expectations. The manager and employee usually agree to the development plan. When an employee does not meet job expectations, the manager is still responsible for providing feed-back about unsatisfactory work.[6] The appraisal presentation meeting should be constructive and supportive for the employee by suggesting a development plan and resources to improve performance.

Because managers are ultimately the judges of performance, they must play a key role in designing and assessing the development-plan components and provide advice and support to help the employee improve. When a development plan has been established, the manager and employee should regularly review the employee's progress toward improving performance.[7]

Informal versus Systematic Appraisal

Supervisors can conduct performance appraisals formally or informally. The **informal appraisal process** is conducted at the manager's discretion. The informal appraisals can be used to praise good work or motivate an employee to improve behavior. Informal appraisals are generally given when the performance occurs to assure its maximum effectiveness. Informal feedback should be documented and retained for the annual review.

A **formal appraisal process** systematically defines an organization's policies and procedures. This type of system involves using an official form that documents the important aspects of the job and contains information about an employee's performance. The formal appraisal process begins when the HR staff and managers develop an appraisal form that documents the current responsibilities for the job. The manager uses the job criteria to collect information, summarize the data, and conduct the review.

Appraisal Responsibilities The responsibility for completing the appraisal process usually rests with the manager, but the HR staff plays a role in assisting the manager. Both managers and HR professionals monitor completed performance appraisals in order to improve the process by revising it where necessary.

In some healthcare organizations, managers have developed performance-appraisal systems that require a lengthy review every other year and a shortened checklist review for the off year. Other healthcare organizations have developed performance reviews, called *exception-based reviews*. This kind of review shortens the process and is viewed positively because it recognizes behaviors that exceed the job standards and identifies behaviors that can be improved.

When to Conduct Appraisals Most healthcare organizations develop policies that require formal appraisals once a year, and they are usually scheduled on the employees' anniversary dates in their jobs. Data collection usually begins about a month before the appraisal meeting and should include information from the entire year. Employees may also receive a *probationary* or *introductory review* in their first few months on their job. This type of evaluation helps managers decide whether or not employees should continue employment.

Appraisals and Pay A recent trend in the healthcare industry is to link pay with the appraisal. This type of HR program is typically refered to as *pay-for-performance*. This approach to performance appraisal and compensation administration is an important HR strategic decision that requires extensive training of managers to administer. Many healthcare HR professionals believe that linking pay to performance is the best way to influence performance.[8]

WHO CONDUCTS APPRAISALS

It is important to determine who is involved in appraisals in an organization. As indicated in Figure 9-2, there are a variety of means used to conduct appraisals.

Supervisory Rating of Subordinates

In most healthcare organizations, the immediate supervisor typically conducts the performance review for the employee. When the review is completed, the manager and the employee develop annual goals for performance. The most common way to conduct this review is during a face-to-face meeting between the supervisor and the employee. When reviewing the employee's performance from the previous year, the manager and employee should be involved in a conversation about the performance. Problem-solving and goal-setting for the coming year are typical components of the evaluation process.

In order to do an effective job of reviewing the employee's performance, the manager must collect information about the employee's performance. Collecting information from co-workers, other supervisors, and patients/residents/clients are common ways to receive information. Information from all of these sources may result in a performance appraisal that is referred to as a 360-degree evaluation.[9]

FIGURE 9-2 **Who Conducts Performance Appraisals**

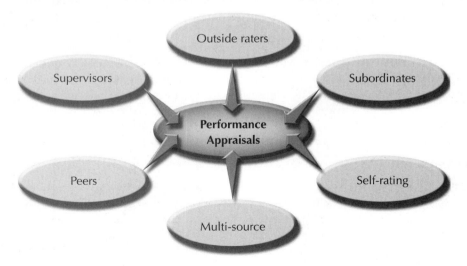

FIGURE 9-3 **Performance Checklist for a Nurse Manager**

PERFORMANCE CHECKLIST FOR A NURSE MANAGER
COMPLETED BY REGISTERED NURSES

- ☐ Effectiveness of the clinical orientation to the nursing unit
- ☐ Staff communications through staff meetings
- ☐ Clinical skills feedback to registered nurse staff
- ☐ Fairness to staff on work issues
- ☐ Employee relations skills and maintaining a positive work environment
- ☐ Promotion of teamwork
- ☐ Sets clear work expectations through job descriptions
- ☐ Effective and efficient nursing operations
- ☐ Advocating for the needs of the staff

Employee Rating of Managers

In some healthcare organizations, the performance-appraisal philosophy has been expanded to include the performance rating of managers by their employees. Figure 9-3 depicts an example of a rating form to be completed by an RN to evaluate the RN's supervisor (Nurse Manager). This method of appraising performance takes advantage of the fact that employees frequently have first-hand knowledge of the manager's performance.

Team/Peer Ratings

A common performance-rating approach in healthcare is **team** or **peer rating.** Healthcare organizations are generally organized around large departments of employees that make observing individual employees difficult. In these situations, processes are developed to help managers collect performance information by using teams and peers that the employee has worked with during the evaluation period.

The team and peer ratings are advantageous because they offer the benefit of direct feedback about performance. The downside includes potential disagreements within employee groups. The system may not work when employees do not feel that they can offer honest feedback about their colleagues. Most of the team- and peer-evaluation programs are anonymous in order to encourage more candid feedback.

Self-Rating

Another way to gather information about an employee's performance is to ask the employee to conduct a **self-rating.** The self-rating method is helpful for employees because it requires them to examine their own strengths and weaknesses. This kind of evaluation involves employees in constructing development plans. Self rating is helpful, but usually is supplemental to other forms of information gathering.

Outside Raters

In some situations, an organization may employ an **outside rater** to evaluate employee performance. One of the advantages of using an outside rater to evaluate performance is that the rater offers a different perspective. The outsider will likely bring an objective view to the process that might not be possible with internal staff members. Outside raters are usually hired on contract by Boards of Directors to rate top executives' performance.[10] Board members who participate on executive committees also evaluate executives. For example, the members of a hospital's Board finance committee may be involved in appraising the performance of the CFO.

Multi-Source Ratings

As noted, the popular term for this type of rating is a **360-degree appraisal.**[11] This process involves getting performance evaluations from many of the individuals with whom the staff member works with or supports. Input from staff members and managers is crucial to a full understanding of an employee's performance. In this process, the manager collects and collates the performance information from peers, subordinates, the employee (self evaluation), and the manager.

Most healthcare organizations have executive and management goals that include patient satisfaction. Patients/Residents/Clients provide valuable outside rater information about facilities. Most healthcare organizations measure satisfaction by surveying patients when they are discharged. This information is summarized by an outside agency and communicated to executives and managers.

METHODS OF APPRAISING PERFORMANCE

Many healthcare organizations use one of the following methods as depicted in Figure 9-4 on the next page to conduct appraisals: Category methods, comparative methods, behavioral and objective methods, and narrative methods.

Category Methods

Performance appraisals apply rating methods such as rating scales and checklists. The appraiser rates an employee on a **graphic-rating scale,** or a continuum, of scores from unacceptable to acceptable to exemplary. This type of appraisal is easy to use but may have limitations, including: combined job criteria, descriptive words that require interpretation, and loosely defined rating-scale descriptors, such as outstanding, average, and poor.

The **checklist method** of appraising performance offers a list of words or statements that describe employees' performance. The managers evaluate these statements and checks those that describe the employees' behavior. Some examples of these statements are, "On time for work," "Completes assignments on time," "Works well with other employees," "Has pursued self development,"

FIGURE 9-4 **Performance Appraisal Methods**

Category Rating Methods
• Graphic rating scale
• Checklist

Comparative Methods
• Ranking
• Forced distribution

Performance Appraisal Methods

Behavioral/Objective Methods
• Behavioral rating approaches
• Management by objectives (MBO)

Narrative Methods
• Critical incident
• Essay
• Field review

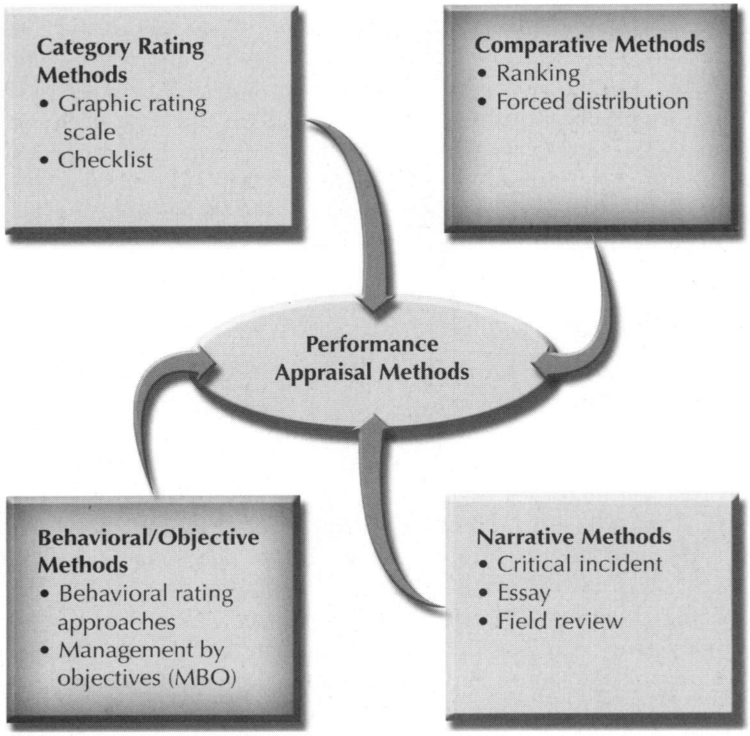

and "Has good conflict-management skills." The checklist method, while easy to use, limits both the manager and employee because the performance rating information can be interpreted in a variety of ways.

Comparative Methods

This method of performance appraisal requires managers to compare the performance of one employee against another. Comparative appraisal methods include **ranking** all employees, paired comparison of employees from a full list, and ranking employees in a **forced distribution** along a bell curve.[12]

Narrative Methods

The **narrative** performance-appraisal method provides comments using essays, documentation of critical incidents, or field reviews. The *essay* describes employees' performance during the evaluation period. This appraisal usually contains a few general performance areas for which managers document their comments. This method allows managers significant flexibility in describing employees' work performance. In the **critical-incident narrative,** managers document incidents that are highly favorable or unfavorable representations of employees' work performance. The incidents are documented throughout the year and are summarized at the time of the appraisal. The **field-review** may be conducted by an outside professional. This person reviews the manager's comments about each employee's performance. Based on these comments, the outside reviewer rates each employee.

Behavioral/Objective Methods

Several performance approaches measure behaviors rather than job characteristics. This approach is most commonly associated with *behaviorally anchored rating scales* (*BARS*), that provide behavioral descriptions of employee actions on the job. This method compares standardized behavioral descriptions to the employee's actual performance. The behavioral standards are measured against a scale of performance levels.

Management by objectives (MBO) develops performance goals that an employee and the manager agree to complete within a defined period. The goals are usually tied to organizational objectives. The basic assumption underlying MBO is that planning and mutual goal setting will result in higher performance. MBO clearly defines goals and objectives, which makes it more measurable than other appraisal methods.

Combination of Methods

Combining methods of appraisal is very common in healthcare organizations. Some strengths of each method may be advantageous to incorporate into the performance-appraisal system. Organizations that want an appraisal that is easy to administer may develop a checklist. Organizations that want to tie performance to strategies may use the behavioral methods. Combined methods often include a checklist, a narrative method for development, and an MBO approach.

For healthcare organizations that subscribe to the JCAHO, performance appraisals must meet JCAHO standards. These standards encourage the organization to link the job description to the performance appraisal. The job description must be a specific and accurate description of the duties, rather than simply general observations about all jobs.

RATER ERRORS

For employees to benefit from feedback during the appraisal process, managers should be trained to avoid evaluation errors. Figure 9-5 illustrates some of the common types of errors that occur in appraisals. A discussion of each follows.

FIGURE 9-5 Common Rater Errors

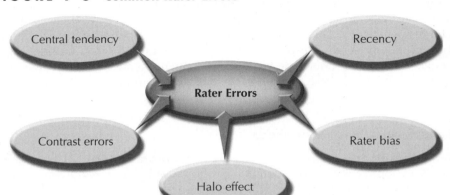

Recency

One of the most common errors managers make when conducting appraisals is to use only recent events to judge employees' performance. To avoid this error, managers need to keep information about employees' performance throughout the year and use that information during the annual review. Reviewers should keep both negative and positive information from the entire evaluation period.

Central Tendency, Leniency, and Strictness Errors

Managers who tend to rate all of their employees within a narrow range are referred to as **central-tendency raters.** In this error, managers would not distinguish among poor, average, and above average performers.

Managers who give all of their employees high ratings are described as **lenient raters.** Conversely, managers who give their employees low ratings make the mistake of being overly **strict raters.** In all of these situations, managers undermine the performance appraisal process, leaving employees without ideas about where they really stand. Not evaluating each employee with objectivity against performance standards is more likely to result in frustration among employees.

Rater Bias

Rater bias occurs when a manager has a bias against a certain employee or employee group based on the manager's own values or prejudices. Biased appraisals may be associated with age, gender, or religion, among others. In these cases, the manager's supervisor should also be involved in the process before the manager meets with the employee.

Halo Effect

The **halo effect** occurs when a manager rates an employee high or low on all job standards based on one characteristic. For example, if a hospital housekeeping employee is always willing to assume extra shifts, the manager may rate that employee highly on all aspects of their performance, based entirely on that one characteristic. Another example of the halo effect would be if an employee who admits patients provides excellent customer service but is divisive with co-workers. The manager, in this example of the halo effect, would give a favorable overall rating based only on the employee's excellent customer skills, ignoring the divisive behaviors that lead to departmental problems.

Contrast Errors

Contrast errors in the performance-review process occur when a manager compares employees to each other rather than to job performance standards. Managers should rate employees against job requirements, not other employees.

Basic supervisory training courses should include appropriate use of the performance-appraisal process. Supervisors should be oriented to performance-appraisal policies, practices, and documentation. During the training, supervisors should study actual cases and learn how to avoid common rater mistakes.

APPRAISAL FEEDBACK

It is important to communicate appraisal information to employees to leave them with a clear understanding about how they are performing. Most managers deliver the performance feedback during a personal meetings with individual employees. At each feedback meeting, any misunderstanding about an employee's performance should be clarified. The manager should coach the employee about performance and provide development opportunities. Providing education and development is an important reason that employees are willing to stay with an organization. The performance feedback meeting should be interactive and mutually beneficial to the manager and employee. While the performance-appraisal process provides information to an employee annually, a manager must use performance management programs to address daily performance issues. The annual performance-appraisal contains information from the daily performance-management program.[13]

Feedback Systems

Feedback systems have three components: collecting data, evaluating the data, and taking action based on the data.[14] As shown in Figure 9-6, collecting data is how a manager gathers information about an employee's performance. The actions, consequences, and outcomes of an employee's performance result in data that a manager needs to review performance. For example, if a ward clerk in a hospital can

FIGURE 9-6 Feedback Process

process significantly higher numbers of doctors' orders for lab tests, that data might lead the manager to give high marks for performance. But if the employee accomplishes this task at the expense of responding to questions from other staff members or patient families, the performance rating might be different.

The final step in the feedback system is taking action based on the results of the appraisal. In some cases, the action is processing a salary increase. In other cases, the action is a development plan. For many employees, the action is recognition of performance and encouragement to continue to perform well.

Appraisal Interview

The interview, when the employee and the manager meet to discuss the employee's performance, is a critical event for both parties. Employees are concerned about their evaluation, while managers understand that they need to communicate information about performance and maintain a working relationship with the employee. The key to an effective appraisal interview is preparation. Having all of the information is important and communicating it to the employee effectively is critical to the value of the appraisal.

Reactions of Managers

Many managers do not like to do performance appraisals.[15] The preparation and delivery time of performance appraisals requires a significant time commitment, and managers may not like to be ultimate decision makers. Judging performance and supporting the employee who needs development and mentoring are difficult and contradictory responsibilities for managers. Managers who have difficulty with the appraisal process should be supported with supervisory training.

Reactions of Employees

Employees who are being appraised demonstrate a variety of reactions to the appraisal process. Some employees become defensive as they imagine how the manager will appraise their performance. If the review is positive, this type of defensive feeling dissipates. When the discussion is about making improvements, the employee may become defensive and challenge the reviewer about the data collected and its evaluation.[16]

To be effective at delivering performance appraisals, supervisors should use a variety of appraisal methods, but emphasizing self-development and performance improvement is most effective with employees. In this case, the manager's role of helpful coach and mentor may have a positive impact on the employee.

FIGURE 9-7   Dealing with Performance Problems

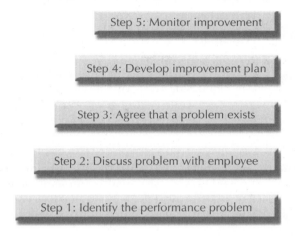

Step 5: Monitor improvement

Step 4: Develop improvement plan

Step 3: Agree that a problem exists

Step 2: Discuss problem with employee

Step 1: Identify the performance problem

EFFECTIVE PERFORMANCE MANAGEMENT

Managing employees' performance is a crucial issue for organizations that count on employees to achieve goals and objectives. With labor shortage in the healthcare industry projected for the next two decades, managers must dedicate organizational resources to programs that manage and improve employees' performance.

An effective performance management program identifies and resolves employee performance problems. Managers use tools such as job descriptions, performance appraisals, and progressive discipline process to improve employees' performance. The program should follow a sequence when dealing with performance management issues including identifying the problem, meeting with the employee to review the issue, and developing a performance improvement plan. Figure 9-7 shows the steps in dealing with performance problems.

Identifying Performance Problems

One of managers' most important responsibilities is to identify and resolve staff performance problems. Sources of information about each employee's performance include performance appraisals, disciplinary actions, feedback from staff including supervisors, and feedback from customers and the public.[17]

Meeting with the Employee

When managers have information about performance problems, they should meet with each individual employee to review the issue. The managers' purpose is to discuss the employee's performance and find options to develop a performance-improvement plan.

Agree Problem Exists

If the manager and the employee can agree that there is a problem and clearly articulate it, they are ready to develop the improvement plan. A performance improvement plan should be developed, and it is important to get "buy-in" from the employee.

Developing a Performance Improvement Plan

Performance improvement plans are based on information managers receive about an employees' performance. The plan is implemented when the manager and the employee meet to discuss job expectations and construct the improvement plan. The typical components of an improvement plan include the following:

▶ Description of the problem
▶ Clear job expectations
▶ Plan that improves performance
▶ Resources available to the employee
▶ Process to evaluate performance
▶ Timeline for improvement
▶ Consequences if performance does not improve

The employee should receive a copy of the documented performance improvement plan, and another copy should be placed in the employee's personnel file. Ideally, the plan is signed by the employee and the manager, but many employees won't sign this type of document, especially when they dispute the evaluation. Managers should also document the employee's refusal to the sign the plan. The employee's refusal to sign does not change the requirement for the employee to follow the improvement plan.

Monitoring Improvement

The support that managers give to their employees, as well as the influence that managers have, can affect any improvements in employees' performance. Helping employees develop skills and knowledge about their job usually results in a performance issue being improved. Managers who excel at performance improvement maybe able to retain valuable and loyal employees.

Developing a performance improvement plan is complex and sometimes confrontational, leading many managers to avoid this important responsibility. It is important for employees to receive guidance, development, and training to meet their performance standards. HR professionals and managers must strive to create and implement effective performance-appraisal systems. Providing employees with the opportunity to improve is a critical part of a performance appraisal process.[18]

CASE

Center City Clinic is an established multi-specialty clinic with 200 employees, which has never had a performance-appraisal process. The clinic is owned by thirty-five physicians whose Board of Directors includes the administrator and the president of the medical group.

The clinic administrator, who is new to the clinic, has decided to implement a performance appraisal system. The management staff, consisting of fifteen department directors, have resisted a performance-appraisal system. They are concerned about the administrator's enthusiasm for such a system.

Some of the clinic's employees who have not been interested in a performance appraisal system, have approached the physicians to lobby against establishing it. The clinic administrator has led meetings and information sessions for both employees and directors about the benefits of a performance appraisal system. For the employees, he noted the value of regular feedback to them on their performance and the opportunity to increase their productivity, which could result in developmental opportunities. For the directors, he described the value a performance appraisal system would provide in helping them manage their employees more effectively.

Questions

1. Why would the directors and employees of Center City Clinic object to the development and implementation of a performance appraisal system?
2. Given the concerns of the directors and employees what would be the most effective performance appraisal system to implement?

END NOTES

1. Gail Dutton, "Making Reviews More Efficient and Fair," *Workforce* (April 2001), 76–81.
2. Dick Grote, "The Secrets of Performance Appraisal: Best Practices from the Masters," *Across the Board* (May 2000), 14–20.
3. John M. Herringer, "Once Isn't Enough When Measuring Staff Competence," *Nursing Management* (February 2002), 22–23.
4. Gillian Flynn, "Getting Performance Reviews Right," *Workforce* (May 2001), 76–78.
5. Peggy Anderson and Marcia Pulich, "Managing the Temperamental Employee," *The Health Care Supervisor* (June 1999), 28–36.
6. Dayton Fandray, "The New Thinking in Performance Appraisals," *Workforce,* (May 2001), 36–40.
7. Peggy Anderson and Marcia Pulich, "A Positive Look at Progressive Discipline," *The Health Care Manager* (September 2001), 1–9.
8. Andrew Sikula Sr., "The Five Biggest HRM Lies," *Public Personnel Management* (Fall 2001), 419–428.
9. G. Patrick Connors and T. Wayne Munro, "360-Degree Physician Evaluations," *Healthcare Executive* (September/October 2001), 58–59.
10. J. Larry Tyler and Erroll L. Biggs, "Practical Governance: CEO Performance Appraisal," *Trustee* (May 2001), 18–21.

11. Andie Evans, "From Every Angle," *Training* (September 2001), 22.

12. Peter Flynn and Barry J. Gibbons, "You Are Simply Average," *Across the Board* (March/April 2001), 51–55.

13. Russell C. Coile Jr., "Magnet Hospitals Use Culture, Not Wages, to Solve Nursing Shortage," *Journal of Healthcare Management* (July–August 2001), 224–227.

14. Kathy Williams, "New Developments in Performance Management," *Strategic Finance* (April 2002), 19, 22.

15. David H. Freed, "One More Time: Please Fire Marginal Employees," *The Health Care Manager* (March 2000), 45–51.

16. Dick Grote, "Performance Appraisals: Solving Tough Challenges," *HR Magazine* (July 2000), 145–150.

17. "A Manager Asks: Dealing with the Troublesome Employee," *The Health Care Manager* (June 2002), 78–86.

18. Jonathan A. Segal, "86 Your Appraisal Process?" *HR Magazine* (October 2000), 199–206.

CHAPTER 10

Employee Relations in the Healthcare Industry

Learning Objectives

After you have read this chapter you should be able to:

▶ Review the common components of an employment agreement.

▶ Define Employment-At-Will and identify exceptions to this concept.

▶ Describe due process and explain alternative dispute resolution processes.

▶ Explain the whistleblower doctrine and apply the concepts to the healthcare industry.

▶ Discuss issues associated with drug testing for healthcare employees.

▶ Identify elements common to employee handbooks.

▶ Outline the progressive discipline process.

Healthcare HR Insights

A medical center located in the southern U.S. conducted an employee survey to measure employee perceptions of their work environment. Several survey responses requested a formal program to recognize the contributions of staff-level employees.

An advisory council of employees was formed to implement suggestions made in the survey, including a recognition program. Since its implementation, the program has been giving special recognition to staff employees for their exceptional service to patients, their families, and other employees. A selection committee developed criteria to evaluate nominations submitted by the individual departments. Only staff employees and volunteers are eligible; managers, supervisors, administrators, and physicians are not eligible.

Some of the award winners have created special events for long-term patients and their families by planning field trips outside of the hospital. Other winners have volunteered to give parents of chronically ill children periods of respite from full-time care giving. Employees have been recognized for helping peers when they are overwhelmed by high patient census and for a wide variety of actions that have affected families and children. The employees use creativity to find new ways to champion the special needs of children.

Winners may be individual employees or groups, who receive up to $250.00. The program has generated more than 160 winners from across the medical center. Several employees have won recognition more than once. Because of the organization's interest in developing positive employee relations and its willingness to listen to employees, this successful employee relations program is continuing to recognize outstanding caregivers.

Healthcare organizations can manage their relationships with employees through a series of HR policies, procedures, and practices. Employers also base their relationships with employees upon a series of rights that are defined and mandated by federal, state, and local compliance agencies and the justice system. In addition, employers and employees often define their rights and obligations with contractual agreements. Regardless, organizations either purposefully or by inference develop philosophies and practices that define the nature of their relationship with employees.

NATURE OF EMPLOYER EMPLOYEE RELATIONS

Each healthcare organization must carefully craft an employee relations philosophy which is beneficial to the organization. The **employee relations philosophy** includes all aspects of how an organization treats and responds to its employees, including how it communicates with its employees. How this philosophy is used strategically serves as an important differentiation that may cause an employee to select one organization over another. As noted in Chapter 7, employee satisfaction has become a retention issue as well. Managers, employees, and employee candidates might consider the following questions as they evaluate whether to take a job or remain employed at an organization:

▶ Is the work environment too legalistic and governed by too many policies and procedures?

▶ Is the organization willing to manage the relationship with a minimum of rules and regulations?

An organization may elect to develop an employee relations philosophy statement that outlines the rights and responsibilities for both the employer and the employees. The HR department manages the process for developing the statement and the organization uses policies and procedures to manage its relationship with its employees. In healthcare organizations, employee relations philosophies are more important than ever because the shortage of healthcare personnel requires organizations to adopt policies that provide a positive work environment, which may result in lower turnover and higher-levels of productivity.

RIGHTS AND RESPONSIBILITIES

There are two types of employee rights: those guaranteed by law and those governed by contracts. Figure 10-1 depicts the key laws, regulations, and agreements that affect the rights and responsibilities for both employees and employers.

Statutory Rights

Existing laws, legislation, and evolving case law protect healthcare employees' rights. In addition to general **statutory rights,** other regulations apply specifically to healthcare workers. An example of a law specific to healthcare employ-

---

FIGURE 10-1 **Rights and Responsibility of Employees and Employers**

STATUTORY RIGHTS	CONTRACTUAL RIGHTS
❑ Federal and state regulations	❑ Employment contracts/agreements
❑ Equal employment opportunity (EEO)	❑ Separation agreements
❑ Health and safety regulations (OSHA)	❑ Retention agreements
❑ Employee benefits law (ERISA)	❑ Training contracts
❑ Wage and hour law (FLSA)	❑ Drug testing permissions
❑ Case law	
❑ Professional association guidelines	
❑ Workers' compensation	
❑ Unemployment compensation	

ees is the Vulnerable Adults Acts, which requires professional care givers to report incidents of abuse or neglect for people who are unable to speak up for themselves or defend themselves against abuse. Although this statutory requirement is healthcare-specific, most statutory rights apply to workers in all industries.

Many of the general rights guaranteed for employees in all industries have been created to allow employees to assert their rights and be heard by external agencies, such as the Equal Employment Opportunity Commission, The National Labor Relations Board, and OSHA (Occupational Safety and Health Act). These rights are a matter of law and employers must recognize them, but employers and employees are free to dispute the intent of any regulation. Employers and employees sometimes disagree with the intent of regulations and negotiate clarifications as they resolve their differences.

In addition, professional regulatory bodies for healthcare workers generate rules that define and govern the conduct of its members. In some professions, such as registered nurses, states have implemented nurse practice standards and professional behavior requirements. These standards usually define clinical competency and professional behavior. As an obligation of a nurse practice standard, nurses in a given state may be required to report unsafe staffing issues that could lead to patient injuries.

Contractual Rights

Rights of employees may be extended by a contract based on terms and conditions agreed to by employers and employees. These contracts specifically define and formalize the working relationship.

A formal agreement between an employer and an employee about their working relationship is called an **employment contract.** The contract, in most cases, is a written document prepared by an attorney who represents the organization.[1] In most organizations, employment contracts are reserved for executives. Employment contract provisions for executives may include compensation, general benefits, performance-based incentive and bonus provisions, executive benefits such as additional retirement benefits, severance pay, benefit continuation, outplacement services, and others. However, in the healthcare industry, employment agreements have been used to attract and retain employees for hard-to-fill positions.

Employment agreements often include provisions identifying job expectations, length of employment, termination rights, and protection from claims based on federal and state laws. In some contracts, provisions prohibit the employees from competing with the organization when they leave voluntarily. These **non-compete provisions** are usually offered in exchange for substantial benefits and economic security during employees' search for their next jobs.[2] Figure 10-2 describes common elements in an employment contract.

Retention Agreements   Another type of agreement is a **retention agreement,** designed to retain key employees during mergers, consolidations, or changes in

FIGURE 10-2 **Employment Contract Contents**

Employment Contract Contents

- Terms of the contract—Duration
- Provisions for renewing the contract —Automatic or mutually agreed
- Duties and responsibilities—Job description
- Compensation—Salary and variable pay
- Benefits—Group and individual
- Severance benefit—Continuation of salary and benefits after job ends
- Noncompete clauses—Restriction on choice of future employers
- Nonsolicitation clauses—Raiding clients and staff after job ends
- Dispute-resolution clauses—Settling contract disputes
- Change-in-control clauses—Change of ownership, board, mangement
- Termination and resignation clauses—Immunity from state and federal laws

organizational leadership and Board representation. In healthcare organizations, retention agreements help to provide stable leadership and management during times of change. Retention agreements usually provide for monetary benefits to the recipients for staying with the employer during a time of change or instability.

Contract Clauses that Protect Employees   In most agreements, a prospective employee has certain rights and responsibilities, generally known as **review and rescission rights.** These rights allow the employee time to review the agreement and rescind it even after agreeing. Federal and state laws define the time periods; a minimum review period is seven days and may be extended to twenty-one days in some legal jurisdictions. After the contract is signed, the rescission period is usually seven to fourteen days.

Implied Contracts

Employees without agreements are subject to the employer's policies and procedures, including employee handbooks, which have been held to be implied contracts defining the employment relationship.[3] Unwritten agreements between employers and employees are called **implied contracts.** Sometimes, an employee will argue that they had an implied contractual agreement when hired. Implied contracts often are the focus of disputes between the employers and employees. If an employer hires an employee for an undefined period or promises job security and no document is written and signed, a court may decide whether an implied contract exists. If an employee believes that the terms of the employment agreement were implied in conversations or through an oral job offer, the employee may sue to achieve the implied terms that were denied.

Employment Practices Liability Insurance

A new type of liability insurance protects healthcare organizations against costly lawsuits initiated by their employees. This insurance is known as **employment practices liability insurance** (EPLI). The key goal of EPLI is to offer legal and risk-management advice to organizations to minimize their legal exposure and negotiate settlements to employee claims. In organizations, general liability insurance policies do not include suits filed by employees based on employment-related claims.[4] The types of claims typically filed include discrimination, sexual harassment, wrongful termination, and breach of contract. To obtain EPLI coverage, an organization must submit to an HR audit of policies and practices, including policy manuals, employee handbooks, employment forms, and other HR practices.[5]

EMPLOYEE RELATIONS AND RIGHTS OF EMPLOYEES

Employees' rights and organizational employee relations philosophies may clash when employees think their contractual or implied-contractual rights have been violated. Several doctrines—employment-at-will, just cause and due process—affect both employees and employers when settling disputes.

Employment-At-Will

Hiring and firing employees has always been the employer's right. Several employment law cases, however, have challenged that right and employers and their attorneys respond by establishing **Employment-At-Will provisions** in their employee handbooks. The Employment-At-Will statements are usually contained in the employee handbook or in policy and procedure manuals. The statement says that employers have the right to hire, fire, and promote whomever they chose. In exchange for the employer's right to Employment-At-Will, employees receive the right to terminate their employment at any time for any reason. Typical Employment-At-Will verbiage is shown in Figure 10-3.

Exceptions to the At-Will Doctrine   Over time and because of lawsuits, the legal system has identified three exceptions to the at-will doctrine: *public-policy decisions, implied contractual disputes,* and *good faith and fair dealing.* These arguments are raised to assert employees' rights when they believe their rights have been violated and many legal jurisdictions have recognized the following exceptions to Employment-At-Will Doctrine.

FIGURE 10-3 **Employment-at-Will Language**

Employment-At-Will Language

I understand that my employment is At-Will with no specific duration, which means that no contractual agreement limits my right to terminate my employment. I also understand that my company retains the right to terminate my employment or change any term or condition of employment at any time, with or without cause or proper notice.

I understand that the employee handbook I received from my company is not a contract or legal document and nothing in the handbook should be construed to be a contract whether expressed or implied. I also understand that only the CEO and the vice-president of human resources have the ability to promise or agree to any substantive terms or conditions of employment.

I have been informed of my At-Will status and have been given an opportunity to ask questions of my supervisor.

Signed _____

Dated _____

Witnessed _____

▶ A **public-policy violation** occurs when an employee is fired for reporting illegal activities by the employer as required by federal or state law.
▶ An **implied contract** might suggest that an employee will be employed indefinitely or might seem to promise continued employment as long as an employee performs the job satisfactorily.
▶ A **good faith** and **fair dealing** exception provides that the employer and the employee have entered into a relationship whose objective is treating each other fairly. If the employer is treating the employee unfairly by being unreasonable, such as assigning difficult work on inconvenient shifts, the employee can assert that the employer is not acting in good faith.

FIGURE 10-4 **Documentation for Wrongful Discharge Lawsuits**

New Employee Orientation Materials	Discharge Letter with Reason for Termination
Employee Handbook	Performance Appraisals
At-Will Employment Statement—Signed	Job Description
Departmental Orientation Documents	Discipline Process Documentation
Documentation of Employee Meetings	Performance Management Activities (counseling statements, warnings, and suspensions)

Wrongful Discharge and the Importance of Documentation

One of the most prevalent claims against employers by disgruntled former employees is that of *wrongful discharge,* which occurs when employers discharge their employees for reasons that are illegal, improper, or are inconsistent with organizational policies, procedures, and/or rules. To avoid wrongful discharge claims by former employees, organizations must ensure that discharged employees are dealt with properly by following applicable policies and procedures that relate to discharge. For example, if a clinic has a process for discipline, the employee should be discharged only after that process has been followed to conclusion. If the process is not followed, the clinic could be accused of not providing the employee with due process.

Wrongful discharge suits have become a major issue for many healthcare organizations. Insurers offer risk management services designed to reduce the risk of wrongful discharge. The items listed in Figure 10-4 are commonly used to defend healthcare organizations against wrongful-discharge lawsuits, including some of the key ones discussed next.

New Employee Orientation Materials   Employees receive orientation information as they begin their employment. Included in the information that employees receive in their orientation packets are policies that are very important for healthcare organizations to communicate to their employees. Sexual harassment policies, appropriate use of the Internet and e-mail policies, and smoking policies are usually included in the new employee orientation packets. The employee handbook is in the packet and employees may be required to sign a form at orientation that they have read the handbook and agree to follow the employer's policies and procedures.

In the healthcare industry *patient confidentiality policies* are part of the orientation materials. Confidentiality of patient information is a highly held value by healthcare organizations and employees sign a statement guaranteeing confidentiality. The documentation mentioned may be used in discharge decisions by the employer and used to defend against a wrongful discharge claim.

Employee Handbooks   The employee handbook in most organizations acts a guideline for employees about the work rules that need to be followed. Job expectations and behaviors are also explained in the handbook and employees are required to acknowledge that they will, as a condition of employment, follow the handbook.

Discharge Letters   Discharge letters document the reason and conditions of the discharges. Some states require the disclosure of the reasons for discharges to employees within a set time period.

Performance Appraisals   Employee performance appraisals are used by organizations as a method to improve employees' performance. An effective performance appraisal system also provides a legal defense for termination decisions.

Job Description   Job descriptions contain vital information about the job duties and responsibilities for employees. In many cases employees are given their job descriptions and sign a document acknowledging that they have received a copy.

Discipline Process and Performance Management   The majority of information that is used to defend an employer against wrongful discharge suits are generated through discipline and performance management policies and programs. Documentation of discipline decisions and the performance management process helps employers explain the reasons for discharge decisions.

Just Cause

Just cause is typically defined by whether the organization acted reasonably, fairly, and impartially in administering discipline, including discharge. The facts and circumstances of each case usually determine whether there was just cause for the action taken by the organization. Courts typically must determine whether the employer acted appropriately in terminating the employee. Figure 10-5 contains points that determine just cause.

Constructive Discharge

When a healthcare employer creates impossible working conditions that force an employee to resign, **constructive discharge** has occurred. Sometimes an organization will wage a purposeful campaign against an employee, whose managers have decided must leave. Work schedules are changed or work assignments are unfavorable or supervisors just make the job difficult. When courts have ruled that constructive discharge has occurred, an employee may be awarded compensation, including back pay and punitive damages. Constructive discharge claims are becoming more frequent, and employers should be aware of this issue when "encouraging" employees to resign.

FIGURE   1 0 - 5   Just-Cause Determinants

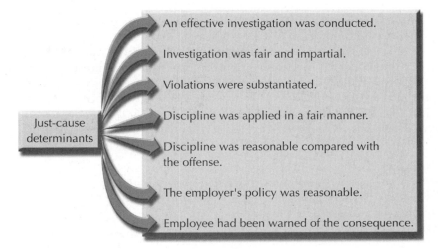

Just-cause determinants

- An effective investigation was conducted.
- Investigation was fair and impartial.
- Violations were substantiated.
- Discipline was applied in a fair manner.
- Discipline was reasonable compared with the offense.
- The employer's policy was reasonable.
- Employee had been warned of the consequence.

Due Process

Healthcare employees may contest disciplinary action if they feel they are not given due process. Employees have successfully argued that they were not afforded **due process,** which is the opportunity to explain and defend their actions against charges of misconduct or other reasons in their disciplinary process. Due process is a way in which employees can question discipline against them. In deciding whether due process has occurred, an external investigation should be conducted to determine whether the employee was afforded all avenues of recourse allowed by the employer's policies. The investigation should also determine how the employee was informed of his or her rights and if valid documentation exists to support the employer's position.

Managers need to be certain that employees' due-process rights are maintained to avoid negative decisions by outside investigators. The following are key questions:

- ▶ Is an employee complaint process available to employees?
- ▶ Did the organization offer the complaint process to the employee?
- ▶ Did the employee use the process?
- ▶ Did the employee voice any concerns about potential retaliation?
- ▶ Were there any current policies that impacted the outcome of the complaint?
- ▶ Were there any past precedents that affected the outcome of the complaint?
- ▶ If this complaint was reviewed by EEOC or human rights agencies, how would the case have been decided?
- ▶ What decision was ultimately made based on the facts of the case?

Resolving Employee Complaints

As part of ensuring due process, many employers have established problem resolution policies that define the employee complaint process. Having an internal problem resolution process in place is advantageous when outside agencies, such as EEOC or OSHA, review employees' complaints. In a unionized setting, a union contract usually includes a grievance procedure that must be followed.

Resolving differences between employees and their employers is an everyday occurrence in the workplace. When issues cannot be resolved, one effective option to utilize is **alternative dispute resolutions** (ADR). The ADR methods include arbitration, peer-review panels, and company ombudsmen.[6]

Arbitration Using a third party to resolve disputes has gained popularity as both employees and employers try to avoid time-consuming and expensive legal proceedings. Some organizations have elected to use **arbitration,** which requires an employer and employee to present their case to a neutral third party for a binding decision.

Peer Review Panels Some healthcare organizations utilize a **peer review panel**, which is an internal committee of employees who review employee complaints and make recommendations about complaints. Panel members receive training in peer review techniques. HR managers typically facilitate the peer review process. In some healthcare organizations the committee is limited to making recommendations to management; in other healthcare organizations, the panel may make decisions about complaint resolution.

Federal and State agencies and courts frequently view peer review panels positively when employees file claims against their healthcare employers. Such panels are often viewed by courts as enhancing due process. However, existence of such panels does not guarantee that employers will prevail in these cases.

Employee Ombudsman Some healthcare organizations use an ombudsman to help resolve employees' problems. Ombudsmen are usually staff employees but not part of the formal management hierarchy. They receive special training to administer their roles in a way that is fair to both the employer and employees.

BALANCING EMPLOYER SECURITY AND EMPLOYEE RIGHTS

Many employees have exercised their rights to privacy in the workplace, and employers have been forced to agree that some employee information is private and confidential and cannot be used for or against employees. Balancing employer security with employee rights requires managers to review HR policies and practices regularly.

FIGURE 1 0 - 6   Personnel File Contents

INCLUDE:

▸ Application for employment
▸ New employee orientation information—Checklist
▸ Letter offering the job
▸ Employee group insurance benefit forms
▸ Compensation records
▸ Performance appraisals
▸ Performance management documentation

DO NOT INCLUDE:

▸ Employee health files
▸ Performance comments by co-workers

Employee Records

The **Privacy Act of 1974** issued regulations that affect HR record-keeping systems, policies, and procedures for governmental employers. In some states, laws have been passed regarding employee records issues.

Many healthcare organizations have responded to federal and state laws by developing policies regarding access to personnel records. The purpose of these policies is to protect employee information. Often, such policy statements include who has access to the employee record and how employees can dispute information in their personnel file. Figure 10-6 lists documents that should and should not be included in personnel files.

Other policies that govern personnel files deal with information available through Human Resources Information Systems (HRIS). An HRIS is an electronic record system. Access to the HRIS should be restricted and protected by confidential passwords and access codes.

Employees' Right to Free Speech

Employees have challenged employers' right to enforce policies that limit free speech. Several areas of conflict between employers and employees are discussed next.

Whistleblowing   An employee's free speech is protected when reporting employer public-policy violations. Employees who report such activity are called *whistleblowers,* and statutes that allow employees to report illegal activities by their employers protect them. A common area for healthcare whistleblowers is Medicare fraud and abuse.[7] Healthcare employees are encouraged to report improprieties. Legislation has been developed to protect whistleblowing healthcare workers from retaliation, such as discipline and termination. Under current federal legislation, employees may receive payment for reporting fraud and abuse that is verified by federal agencies. The award to the employee can be up to 10% of the penalty assessed against the organization.[8]

Employers may not retaliate against employees who speak out. Most large healthcare organizations provide some process, such as a confidential telephone hotline number to call, to bring the alleged impropriety forward within the organization before the whistleblower seeks help from federal or state agencies. Employees in healthcare organizations that have internal processes are not required to use them, but they are encouraged by their employers to do so.

Monitoring E-mail and Voicemail   Growth in technological capabilities has caused healthcare organizations to define employer rights and employee privacy rights. Monitoring employees' e-mail and voicemail is a privacy issue that organizations must keep in mind as they write policies to protect business interests. Policy statements include limiting technology use for business purposes only, restricting personal e-mail and voicemail use, prohibiting shared passwords, and retaining a right to monitor or search all e-mail and voicemail.

Healthcare organizations also want to prevent using e-mail and voicemail to transmit information that would violate HR policies, including transmitting jokes and cartoons that may be discriminatory based on gender, religion, or race. HR staff must address these issues with policies and consistent enforcement.

To protect themselves, healthcare organizations must establish a policy, train employees frequently, and enforce the policy consistently. Many healthcare organizations have developed statements as screen savers to remind employees about appropriate and inappropriate computer use. Firms may also require employees to sign forms at the end of orientation or training that acknowledge that the employee understands the policy and the consequences for failing to comply with it.

Tracking Internet Use   Healthcare employers may encourage Internet use for business purposes, but most are concerned about reduced productivity when employees spend work time "surfing the net." In addition, some employers are concerned that employees might view inappropriate Web sites that may tarnish the company's image. Employers are especially concerned about Web sites with pornographic content. Many organizations have installed software that tracks Internet use and prevents access to certain Web sites.

Honesty in the Workplace

Workers in healthcare organizations have access to drugs and are responsible for the well-being of their patients. Especially because of their position of trust, healthcare organizations must ensure that employees are honest.

One of the most significant problems facing employers is theft by employees. All theft is serious, but in healthcare organizations drug theft is particularly disconcerting. Drug theft can occur when drugs are taken from locked cabinets; however, a more serious violation occurs when staff divert drugs from patient use.

Most healthcare employers use some form of background check to screen new employees. Managers, security personnel, and pharmacy staff should cooperatively develop a plan to prevent the theft of drugs, especially narcotics. Elaborate systems, including inventory checks after each shift, have reduced theft of drugs from supply cabinets, but diverting patients' medications is more difficult to discover. The best protection against potential theft by employees with drug dependencies is a thorough background check on applicants that have access to drugs.

Performance Surveillance   An employer is allowed to search an employee's work area if a manager has legitimate business reasons for doing so, such as suspicion of theft or illegal activities. Employees are not protected from monitoring and searches if there is reason to believe they are engaged in activities that violate the employer's work rules.

Employer Investigations   Healthcare employers have typically conducted investigations when employees were suspected of theft; however, healthcare employers are now concerned about a variety of issues including theft, illegal drug use, workplace violence, and workers' compensation fraud.

Investigations are conducted by security personnel when the organization is large enough to have a security department. In other cases, managers or HR professionals investigate employees' activities. It is important to conduct thorough inquiries to avoid concerns about improper or incomplete investigations.

An organization can develop rules that facilitate investigations. Some examples of these rules follow: Have at least one witness present when confronting an employee. Don't touch or restrain the employee. Inform the employee that he or she is free to leave the meeting at any time. Have at least one witness of the same gender present to avoid harassment claims. If the employee refuses to respond or participate, make clear that such behavior is insubordination and that disciplinary action will be taken if the incident warrants it. Figure 10-7 illustrates techniques for investigations.

Since in a healthcare setting some of the more commons types of investigations include the illegal use of drugs and theft, some of the issues investigated by healthcare managers need to be reported to the agencies that license healthcare professionals.

Polygraph-and-Honesty Testing

Pre-employment polygraph testing to judge an employee's truthfulness is prohibited under the Polygraph Protection Act. The polygraph test measures the subject's stress reaction to questions posed by an examiner. The presence of stress indicates that the subject might be less than honest about a question.

Honesty/Integrity Testing   Testing prospective employees using an honesty or integrity test is one method used by employers. Healthcare organizations should review state court cases before administering the tests because some courts have held that the tests aren't reliable or valid for job-related purposes.

FIGURE 10-7 **Methods of Workplace Investigations**

Off-the-Job Behavior

Employers are reluctant to monitor employees' off-the-job behaviors unless the activities have definite job-related consequences. For example, a healthcare employer would want to know that an employee will miss work because they are incarcerated, particularly if the employee is in the final stages of progressive discipline for attendance problems. However, the situation becomes more complex if the employee is jailed for public intoxication during chemical dependency rehabilitation.

Healthcare employers are typically not concerned about their employees off-the-job behavior unless it becomes a problem. If the behavior disrupts the work environment and jeopardizes patient care, the employer must take action. Some organizations establish employee assistance programs to help employees with on- and off-the-job behaviors that threaten their jobs. Employee assistance programs provide counseling and other help to employees who have emotional, physical, or personal problems.

Employee Substance Abuse and Employer Drug Testing Policies

Healthcare organizations have shown leadership in designing policies and practices to provide a drug-free workplace. These policies are consistent with the **Drug-Free Workplace Act of 1988** whose purpose is to make workplaces safe, healthy, and efficient for employees, patients, and visitors. Policy violations in healthcare organizations may include unlawful possession, use, distribution, or manufacture of a controlled substance at the facility or on facility grounds. Policy statements prohibit employees from arriving at work under the influence of drugs, including alcohol. Many healthcare organizations have adopted drug-testing policies that help to ensure that the workplace is free from drug use. Many healthcare employers test for drugs during pre-employment screening, "for cause," randomly, or after an injury or incident.[9] Most healthcare organizations will withdraw conditional job offers to candidates who fail the test.[10]

HUMAN RESOURCE POLICIES, PROCEDURES, AND RULES

All organizations have policies, procedures, and rules that govern their employer–employee relationships. In most cases, these documents are recorded and organized into an HR policy and procedure manual. The employee handbook is a condensed version of the larger policy-and-procedure manual, and employees are encouraged to use the policy and procedure manual if their handbook doesn't answer their questions.

There are differences between policies, procedures, and rules, as follows:

▶ Policies are general statements about the organization's position on an issue.
▶ Procedures define the customary way an organization deals with the policy issue.
▶ Rules define expected behaviors of employees at work.

Effective policies protect organizations from lawsuits and complaints. When an employee has a specific issue related to his or her employment, managers and HR staff should refer employees to the HR policies and procedures.[11]

Coordinating Policies and Procedures

Coordinating, implementing, and using policies in healthcare organizations is an important responsibility. Agencies that monitor and periodically review policies in the healthcare industry include the State Department of Health, Health Care Finance Administration, and The Joint Commission on Accreditation of Healthcare Organizations. Several steps assure successful development and implementation of policies and procedures. The process includes identifying the need for a policy, developing a draft, formally reviewing the draft by key stakeholders and the leadership team, reviewing by outside legal counsel, distributing the policy, training the management group to use the policy for its intended purpose, and implementing the policy. Developing policies that are accessible and easy to use encourages application by managers.

Policies are usually drafted in a standard format and contain a policy statement, procedures, and definitions. Cross-referencing policies helps managers who want additional or related information. HR practitioners usually provide consultative services to managers about how to interpret and implement procedures.

Employee Handbook

Most employees receive a copy of a handbook at their initial orientation. The handbook can be an effective method to communicate pertinent organizational information. As policies change, the *employee handbook* should be updated with several factors in mind, including readability, accessibility, and legal issues. All employees should receive copies of each new handbook with a notice that it replaces the previous one.[12] Employee handbooks are now available in many healthcare organizations to employees and managers via the Intranet or Internet.

Other Internal Communications

Keeping the lines of communication open between management and employees is very important, especially when the organization has made important decisions, such as adding new services or building new facilities. Communicating HR information is also very important. Healthcare employers want workers to know about HR changes, such as training and development opportunities, benefit enrollment information, and salary increases, among many others. In the past, employees have relied on memos, newsletters, and meetings with management to get information about the organization. With newer communication technologies, such as teleconferencing, organizations can hold a meeting with employees at more than one location. Also, e-mail has grown in use, along with computer message boards.

A form of upward communication is a *suggestion system*. This kind of program encourages employees to offer ideas that might improve the organization and its operations. Suggestion systems often include recognition and financial rewards to employees who provide cost-saving or process-improvement ideas.

EMPLOYEE DISCIPLINE

Following established HR policies, procedures, and regulations, and maintaining high-quality job performance are required for organizations to deliver excellent products and services. Healthcare Organizations develop discipline systems to help employees meet their job responsibilities, improve their performance, and establish a successful employee-employer working relationship.

Although they usually represent a small number, problem employees can be disruptive to the work environment, and their performance must be dealt with in a timely manner. In these cases, management provides training and feedback to employees with the expectation that their behavior and performance will improve. Typical discipline issues include absenteeism, tardiness, interpersonal issues, insubordination, inability to meet job standards, and productivity.

To determine when to use the discipline process, managers must evaluate each issue on a case-by-case basis to determine which type of discipline to administer. When the issue is easily resolved, no disciplinary action may be necessary.

A common employee-discipline process is called **progressive discipline,** which utilizes a series of identifiable steps to communicate concerns to employees. Each step is separate and distinct and is designed to warn the employee to change their work performance or behavior or further discipline will occur. Figure 10-8 depicts a typical progressive discipline system.

Counseling   The goal of this step is to tell the employee what job expectations are not being met and talk about how to make improvements in performance. The employee may be unaware of a problem, therefore, counseling by the manager should be positive and encouraging. As an example, if a laboratory technician fails to follow appropriate safety guidelines in the laboratory, counseling from the manager may be needed.

Verbal Warning   The second step is a verbal warning, which represents an escalation in the process. If the employee has not improved work performance, the manager then issues a verbal warning. The goal of this step is to point out the performance deficiencies and to explain the importance of improving performance. In this step, the manager decides whether to offer any additional training to help the employee meet performance expectations. In the laboratory

FIGURE 10-8   Progressive Discipline Procedure

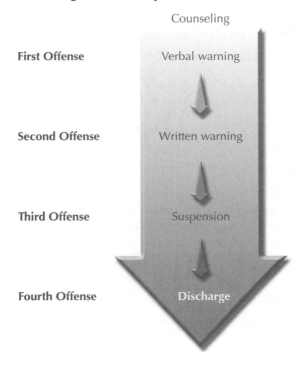

	Counseling
First Offense	Verbal warning
Second Offense	Written warning
Third Offense	Suspension
Fourth Offense	Discharge

technician example, the manager might initiate a verbal warning and require the technician to read the safety guidelines for the laboratory.

Written Warning   If the employee does not improve performance, the manager conducts another performance conference in which job expectations are outlined and documented in writing. Additional resources including training may be offered to help the employee achieve the expected performance. This step is a warning that performance needs to improve to avoid the next step in the disciplinary process. If the technician continues to disregard safety guidelines, the manager would give a written warning, clearly stating the reason for discipline, the steps that must be taken to improve, or the consequences if disregard for safety procedures continues. Specifically, if disregard for safety procedure continues, the technician will be suspended and then discharged.

Suspension   An employee will be suspended if performance has not improved. The length of the suspension depends on the severity of the performance deficiency. This step is critical for the employee because the next step is final—discharge.

Discharge   When an employee cannot or will not perform satisfactorily, termination may be necessary. The final stage in the discipline process and must be managed very carefully. This stage is used when an employee's behavior is so egregious that termination is appropriate consistent with the progressive discipline process.

Reasons for Not Using Discipline

Managers may be reluctant to use discipline for a variety of reasons. The most common reasons for not using discipline include fear of lawsuits, lack of support from the organization, fear of retaliation from employees, not being liked by employees, guilt, loss of friendship, and the time and energy to manage the discipline process. To counter these reasons, healthcare organizations should train managers about the effective use of discipline.

Training Managers

Management training programs should be designed to include the basics of discipline, including treating employees with respect and dignity. Building supervisory skills to facilitate discussions and counsel employees is especially important. Performance discussions should provide positive assistance so that employees can improve their job performance.

Employee Termination Decisions

The final step in the discipline process—as noted—discharge—is difficult for both employees and employers. Managers must use a firm, respectful, and focused manner when discharging an employee. Except in serious situations, employees have received warnings so the discharge should not be a surprise. The manager should clearly define why the employee is being discharged. The discharge meeting should be carefully planned and is often attended by an HR representative. All wage and benefit information should be communicated in writing in the event the employee doesn't remember all of the discussion. It is important to end the meeting and help the employee leave the building in a dignified way.

INNOVATIVE EMPLOYEE RELATIONS STRATEGIES

In addition to all of the policies, procedures, rights and responsibilities, and discipline procedures, most organizations strive to affect their employees positively by using innovative strategies. Some of the more common strategies follow.

Employee Attitude Surveys

When an organization makes a commitment to perform employee attitude surveys, they may be scheduled as often as once per year. However, most healthcare organizations conduct surveys every two to three years. Conducting an attitude survey encourages feedback from employees about their work environment and measures their morale. Surveys help organizations gather information from their employees about potential problems that may be developing. For example, a hospital might wish to conduct an attitude survey when the administrator determines that employee issues may lead to difficulties in recruiting new staff members. Healthcare administrators might want survey information analyzed by departments or shifts. Information from the survey is interpreted and translated into an action plan to make the appropriate improvements.

In a survey conducted by Walker Information Research, healthcare employees' responses indicated they were "as" or "more" satisfied than workers from other industries. These high satisfaction responses were influenced by the employees' commitment to patient care. In fact, healthcare employees scored higher on commitment to their work, satisfaction with their jobs, and feeling a sense of achievement. The study reported that employers could even improve employees' commitment further by allowing them to think independently to solve problems, by valuing them, and by providing necessary tools and resources.[13]

Employee Assistance Programs

Organizations provide employee assistance programs (EAPs) to help their employees cope with personal life management issues that affect their work. Initially, the most common use of EAPs was to deal with drug and alcohol abuse but EAPs have been extended to include legal, financial, marital, and interpersonal issues. The services may be offered two ways: through internal programs staffed by company employees, or by an outside sevice.[14] EAP programs whether offered internally or externally, are designed to help employees with problems that may affect their productivity. EAP counselors must be qualified to treat and refer employees.[15]

Employer of Choice (EOC) Programs

Organizations interested in becoming an "employer of choice" must redefine their HR practices to clearly demonstrate their commitment to their employees. A successful employer-of-choice philosophy requires a plan with the following components:

▶ Long-term top management commitment to becoming an EOC
▶ Defined organizational purpose
▶ Innovative and competitive compensation and benefit programs
▶ Staff-development opportunities
▶ Rewards for innovation and creativity
▶ Rewards aligned with performance
▶ Culture that respects diversity, encourages staff participation, and rewards employee and organizational success[16]

Reward and Recognition

Another strategy that has experienced renewed interest is employee reward and recognition programs.[17] In one study, 86% of the organizations surveyed reported having a program that recognized employees' contributions in the work setting. Recognition programs have been used successfully to attract and retain employees. Employees' sense of commitment and loyalty is likely to increase when they receive recognition from their managers or peers.[18]

Standards of Behavior

Another popular method to improve organization-employee relationships is to develop a series of expectations the organization has for all employees. The standards of behavior, or the rules of conduct, have become popular as a means to clearly identify behavioral and performance expectations. Standards are usually developed and aligned to organizational values communicated continuously. The standards should define how the expectations affect employees on a daily basis.[19] The standards may include the following expectations:

▶ Respect
▶ Excellence
▶ Cooperation
▶ Compassion
▶ Communication
▶ Fairness and Equity
▶ Self care
▶ Personal accountability

CASE

Clifton Health Clinic is a multi-specialty clinic with 20 physicians and 75 employees. As currently organized, the Clinic has been in business for 5 years.

The Clinic has a very informal approach to HR activities, with the Administrator or *any* of the physicians responding situationally to employee questions or concerns. Over time, employees have become used to inconsistencies in management and HR decisions, depending on who made the decisions.

As the Clinic has grown, the employees, many of whom have worked at other facilities with clearly defined HR policies and procedures, have complained that the inconsistencies in important HR decisions are unfair and frustrating. As an example, the employees in the x-ray department of the Clinic are allowed to leave early on Fridays when their work is finished, with full pay. The Chief Radiologist made this decision without consulting with the other physicians or the Administrator. Conversely, no other department of the Clinic

is allowed the same opportunity to leave with pay, even though there are parallel staffing situations in other departments. This inconsistent approach in staffing and pay practice has caused significant unrest among the employees and physicians outside of the x-ray department.

In answer to the concerns raised by this situation, a small group of physicians have met to determine what needs to be done. As a result of their deliberations, they have decided to retain an HR consultant to assist them in developing an employee handbook.

Questions

1. How will an Employee Handbook assist the Clinic in dealing with their HR issues?
2. What are the advantages and disadvantages to the development and implementation of an Employee Handbook for Clifton Health Clinic?

END NOTES

1. Steve Harris and Alisa McMillan, "Employment Contract: Get it in writing!" *Financial Executive* (December 2001), 28–31.
2. Clifford M. Koen Jr. and William H. Reinhardt Jr., "Employment Contracts: Preventative Medicine for Post-Termination Disputes," *Supervision* (July 2000), 5–9.
3. Larry L. Hansen, "Don't Sign the New Employment Contract!" *Occupational Hazards* (August 2000), 27–30.
4. Lisa Bee and Gerald L. Maatman Jr., "Fair Treatment in Firings Avoids Suits," *National Underwriter* (February 25, 2002), 20–23.
5. Michael Barrier, "EPLI Providers Turn Up the Heat," *HR Magazine* (May 2002), 46–50.
6. John W. Cooley, "A Dose of ADR for the Health Care Industry," *Dispute Resolution Journal* (February–April 2002), 14–20.
7. Thomas H. Stanton, "Fraud-and-Abuse Enforcement in Medicare:

Finding Middle Ground," *Health Affairs* (July–August 2001), 28–42.

8. Roy L. Simpson, "Government Cracks Down on Billing Fraud," *Nursing Management* (July 2001), 10–11.

9. Lee Fletcher, "Employer Drug Testing Has Pitfalls, *Business Insurance* (October 23, 2000), 1 and 69.

10. Eugene F. Ferraro, "Is Drug Testing Good Policy?" *Security Management* (January 2000), 166–168.

11. Gillian Flynn, "Take Another Look at the Employee Handbook," *Workforce* (March 2000), 132.

12. Gale Cutler. "Tom Confronts Lab Rage," *Research Technology Management* (July–August 2001), 60–61.

13. "Are Health Care Workers Committed?" *Trustee* (November–December 2001), 6–7.

14. Abby Ellin, "Traumatized Workers Look for Healing on the Job," *New York Times* (September 30, 2001), 3.10.

15. Rudy M. Yandrick. "The EAP Struggle: Counselers or Referrers?" *HR Magazine* (August 1998), 90–96.

16. Gary Mecklenberg. "Helping Hospitals be 'Employers of Choice,'" *AHA News* (December 10, 2001), 7–8.

17. Bridget McCrea. "Putting Employees First," *Warehousing Management* (December 2000), 41–44.

18. Jeremy Handel. "Recognition: Pats on the Back Motivate Employees," *Workspan* (December 2001), 36–38.

19. *Standards of Behavior*, Children's Hospitals and Clinics, Minneapolis and St. Paul, Minnesota, 1995.

CHAPTER 11

Labor Relations and Healthcare Organizations

Learning Objectives

After you have read this chapter, you should be able to:

▶ Explain the labor relations challenges facing the healthcare industry.

▶ Describe the National Labor Relations Act, including the unique healthcare provisions.

▶ Outline the stages of the unionization process.

▶ Discuss the collective bargaining process.

▶ Identify the contract negotiations process in the healthcare industry.

Healthcare HR Insights

Recently in Hawaii a number of nurses went on strike at several hospitals. The strike reflected the frustrations and concerns experienced by nurses in Hawaii and many other states. Led by the Hawaii Nurses' Association (the union representing the nurses), intensive negotiations with management failed to reach settlements. Thus the impasses lead to strikes at The Queen's Medical Center, St. Francis Medical Center, and Kuakini Medical Center. The strikes were of varying length, with one lasting three weeks.

The core issues at each of these hospitals were similar: nurses were concerned more about their excessive hours of work and scheduling required, than their level of pay or the benefits they were receiving. For instance, at Kuakini, unionized nurses wanted to end mandatory overtime, where nurses working 12-hour shifts had been required to work 4 hours more on a number of days, resulting in 16-hour workdays. The union's concern was that these long shifts resulted in worker fatigue, which reduced the quality of patient care and increased the possibilities for patient-care mistakes. At St. Francis, the union fought a plan to eliminate nine nursing positions as part of management's efforts to reduce the hospital's $29 million operating loss the year before.

To counter the strike and continue to provide patient care, several approaches were used by management, including hiring temporary nurses brought in from California, assigning management staff to nursing duties, and reducing admissions of patients. These actions further angered the unions and led to picketing, public protests, and extensive news media coverage. However, hospital managers argued that such actions were necessary to continue care for existing patients.

After a three-week period, strikes at all of the hospitals were settled. Most of the issues won by the unions were in scheduling and other issues they claimed that affected the quality of patient care. However, pay and benefits increases of 20% or more over a four-year period were also part of the settlements. For management at each organization, provisions in the final contract allowed more flexibility in making work assignment arrangements and in scheduling. Overall, while each side "won" some points, there remain concerns about the continuing effect of employee-management relations at Hawaii Hospitals.[1]

A union is a formal association of workers that promotes its members' interests through collective bargaining. It is the official employee representative, and it executes its responsibilities by negotiating labor contracts and administering the contracts until they expire.

Membership in unions in the United States has declined by about 9% over the past ten years to about 16 million in the year 2000. Unions represent only about 13.5% of the total U.S. civilian workforce. To offset the decline unions are targeting the service sector for their membership drives.[2] Healthcare is a major employer in the service sector, so HR practitioners in the industry are and should be increasingly concerned about unionizing attempts.

UNIONS IN THE HEALTHCARE INDUSTRY

Union activity in healthcare has been heavily concentrated in metropolitan areas and on the east and west coasts of the United States. Also, unions tend to be more successful in northern states—in part, because these areas have a long history of unionism. Unions tend to win more representation elections in healthcare than in any other industry. In hospitals, the average "win rate" is 62% to 73%.[3] Even Physicians are forming unions to negotiate their compensation through contractual agreements.[4]

Increased unionism in the future of healthcare seems likely. Physicians employed by large healthcare organizations have tried to unionize in several states, and unions are eager to help with organizing attempts. Service workers in healthcare organizations are seeking union protection and nurses are organizing and local nurses' unions are merging with larger national unions to enhance their protection. Unions that typically have not represented healthcare workers are making organizing attempts as they see opportunities in healthcare.

Why Employees Unionize

The process of unionizing an employee group can be initiated either by employees or union organizers. The union assesses the potential for success before it commits union resources to a costly organizing campaign. Once the union decides there is potential interest by a group of employees, representatives begin the campaign.

Some healthcare employees seek union assistance because they believe that their employers have not treated them respectfully and they believe a union can negotiate financial and job security and better working conditions. Financial concerns may cause employers to find ways to deliver care more cost effectively, but some of the new systems result in lower staffing ratios that may affect quality of patient care.[5] Employees involved in patient-care professions have worried about changes in staff-to-patient ratios and have asked unions to represent them and to negotiate staffing ratios with their employers.[6]

A survey by the American Organization of Nurse Executives found that registered nurses were satisfied with their employment and employers for the following reasons: peer relationships, performance recognition, independent decision making, inter-departmental and intra-departmental communications, contributions to the decision-making process, and support from management. In the same study, nurses indicated specific reasons for satisfaction in the workplace, including competitive compensation, flexible work schedules, continuing education, and respect from management.[7] Figure 11-1 shows the reasons for nurse job satisfaction and dissatisfaction.

FIGURE 11-1   **Registered Nurses' Job Satisfiers and Dissatisfiers**

JOB SATISFIERS	JOB DISSATISFIERS
▶ Peer relationships	▶ Poor working conditions
▶ Performance recognition	▶ Lack of recognition
▶ Effective communication	▶ Job stress
▶ Input into decisions	▶ Lack of career opportunities
▶ Competitive compensation	▶ Competing personal family commitments
▶ Support from management	
▶ Flexible work schedules	
▶ Continuing education opportunities	
▶ Management respect	
▶ Independent decision making	

In a related study, researchers recorded reasons that contributed to why registered nurses' leave their jobs: unhappiness with the work environment, job-related stress and anxiety, lack of recognition of professional status, lack of expanded career opportunities, and personal commitments and responsibilities.[8] The risk of unionization decreases significantly when an organization adopts positive policies and supportive HR practices for employees.[9] The studies show that healthcare workers want to be informed, respected, and included in decision making. Also, they want to participate in care decisions for patients. Healthcare administrators must understand their workers' reasons for job satisfaction and dissatisfaction when they develop HR policies, if their goal is to avoid unionization.

Organizations can avoid unionization by adopting HR strategies, including competitive compensation and benefit programs. Recognizing employees' accomplishments and responding to employee concerns also can reduce the risk of unionization. Adopting a philosophy of participation in decision making may have a positive effect on employees and their commitment to the organization. In addition, employers may conduct employee surveys to determine their employees' level of satisfaction and implement policies and programs to deal with areas of employee dissatisfaction.

LABOR-RELATIONS PHILOSOPHY

In healthcare organizations that have unions, union and management representatives adopt strategic positions about the types of relationships they will have with each other. As a product of these positions, the union-management relationship is developed and a philosophy emerges that mirrors past relationships.

Union–management relationships exist somewhere on a philosophical continuum between **adversarial** and **collaborative.** It is important for both sides to determine what they want their relationship to be as negotiations and contract management occur.

Adversarial Relationships

Traditionally, many relationships between healthcare organizations and unions have been adversarial, an atmosphere in which both parties try to control the process and relationship by winning beneficial contracts for the organization or the workers.

Decisions made in adversarial relationships are usually not favorable for long-term relationships, especially when one party perceives that it is continually compromising to maintain the relationship. Both parties are suspicious and may use information and communication selectively to gain a negotiating advantage. The organization controls the economics, while the union has the power to call a strike when a satisfactory agreement is not reached.

Collaborative Relationships

In some healthcare organizations, a philosophy emerges that supports collaborative relationships. The goal of these non-adversarial relationships of shared responsibility is to address the mutual interests and issues of both sides. They openly share information and make decisions in a collaborative manner. A fundamental belief is that decisions made by consensus are more durable than decisions resulting from compromise.[10]

A healthcare organization's philosophy of labor relations reflects a strategic decision whether to have a relationship that is adversarial, collaborative, or between the two. Upper management must support the philosophy, middle management must agree to implement the intent of the philosophy, and supervisors should be trained to deal effectively with employees and unions, whether the philosophy is adversarial, collaborative, or somewhere in between.

LEGAL FRAMEWORK FOR UNION–MANAGEMENT RELATIONS

There are three major laws that created the "National Labor Code," as illustrated in Figure 11-2 on the next page. A discussion of each follows.

National Labor Relations Act (NLRA)

In 1935, Congress passed the **National Labor Relations Act,** also known as the **Wagner Act,** to provide more specific guidelines to govern the relationship between organizations and employees. Section 7 of the Act provides for the right to bargain collectively. Section 8a of the Act describes **unfair labor practices** by organizations. Section 8b, added later, covers unfair labor practices by unions.

National Labor Relations Board   The Act also established the **National Labor Relations Board (NLRB),** whose purpose is to enforce the provisions of

FIGURE 11-2   National Labor Code

the Act for both unions and organizations. The **NLRB** is a federal agency comprised of five members who interpret and enforce the NLRA. Two major functions of the board are to conduct representation elections and to investigate and resolve unfair labor practices by either organizations or the union.

Federal Mediation and Conciliation Services   A provision in the National Labor Relations Act created the **Federal Mediation and Conciliation Services (FMCS),** an agency charged with mediating labor negotiations when asked by negotiating parties or assigned by the FMCS Director. The Director makes assignments when disputes substantially threaten to interrupt healthcare services. The FMCS trains managers and union representatives to negotiate collaboratively. The agency also mediates conflicts during adversarial negotiations.

Taft–Hartley Act   The **Taft–Hartley Act,** passed in 1947, equalized the effects of the NLRA by defining and prohibiting unfair labor practices by unions. Because unions had grown significantly with the passage of the NLRA, the U.S. Congress responded to pressure by employers to hold unions to the same fair labor practices that employers were required to follow.

Landrum–Griffin Act   The **Landrum–Griffin Act,** passed in 1959, was designed to curtail corrupt union practices, including officials using pension funds for their personal use and making threats and using physical force against members to retain their elected positions. The act, in essence, protects workers from the unions that represent them. It requires unions to develop bylaws, financial reports, and bills of rights for union members under the supervision of the U.S. Secretary of Labor.

NLRA and the Healthcare Industry

Prior to 1974, the healthcare industry was not included in the National Labor Relations Act. That year, Congress repealed the clause that had exempted the healthcare industry from employee unionization.

During the mid-1970s, the healthcare industry was growing rapidly, and union leaders saw an opportunity to recruit a large number of members, many of whom believed their wage and benefits programs were not competitive. In Congress, lawmakers were concerned that if healthcare workers were allowed to organize, there could be a disruption in vital healthcare services. In response, lawmakers added several provisions to the NLRA that would protect communities in case of union strikes during contract negotiations. Important provisions in the law include a ten-day strike notice and a requirement to use federal and state mediation services.

Ten-Day Strike Notice   One of the provisions passed in 1974 required unions to give ten-days' notice of their intent to strike. In most cases, the ten-day notice coincides with the contract expiration. If a union fails to give the ten-day notice to the employer, the NLRB is not required to protect striking workers, leaving healthcare employers the option of hiring permanent replacement workers.

Although this provision was created to provide healthcare organizations with some warning about an impending strike, most healthcare organizations begin planning well in advance. The ten-day notice is built into negotiation work plans and is usually coordinated with the contract ratification vote. If the members reject the contract and vote to strike, the ten-day notice is issued.[11]

Negotiation Notification   The act also requires organizations and unions to inform the FMCS of the parties' intent to begin negotiations ninety days before the contract expires. The notification process allows the mediation service to assign a mediator to the negotiations and offer any training the negotiating parties might need.

Impasse   Another provision in the act helps to expedite the negotiating process when an **impasse** occurs. If the negotiating parties have a dispute they cannot resolve, they must report the situation to FMCS. A mediator is assigned to facilitate a resolution. In healthcare organizations that use collaborative labor relations, a mediator is usually included in the negotiations from the initial meeting.

Strikes and the Board of Inquiry   When negotiations have failed and a strike is possible, the FMCS Director may appoint a **board of inquiry** to investigate, report, and recommend to the Director solutions to resolve the contractual disputes. In this case, the current labor contract must be extended for thirty days while the board of inquiry completes its work. The use of a board of inquiry is a last step in the process to settle a contract dispute.

THE UNIONIZATION PROCESS IN HEALTHCARE

The process of unionizing healthcare employees has been relatively unchanged since 1974, when healthcare employees gained the right to bargain collectively. Unions typically conduct campaigns in organizations if the relationship between employees and managers has been negative. The most common way to measure the potential of a union campaign is to assess those relationships. Unionizing is frequently a vote against management rather than a vote for the union. The role of the manager in creating a positive work environment is essential for the organization that is interested in a non-union work environment. Managers interact with employees on a daily basis and have the opportunity to build positive working relationships that negate the need for union representation. If the organization and management fail to develop proactive policies and practices and fail to practice preventive labor relations, the employees may seek representation by the union.

To unionize, it must be shown that a majority of employees who vote want union representation. A number of steps comprise the unionization process, and they are shown in Figure 11-3.

Organizing Campaign

The campaign to form a union usually begins when a group of employees, who are dissatisfied with their employer, approaches a union to seek its expertise in organizing workers into a union. Alternatively, a union may target an organization or a group of employees about their potential interest in being represented.

FIGURE 11-3 Union Campaign Process

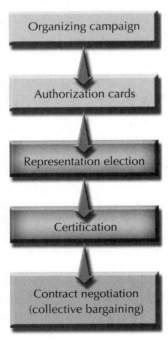

Unions make an early determination of whether there is sufficient interest in representation before they agree to invest resources in an organizing campaign.

If a union decides interest is sufficient, it conducts informational meetings with the employees at an off-site location to share information about the union and its capabilities. The meetings, often unknown to managers, provide opportunities for employees to air concerns about their working conditions, which helps the union to assess the likelihood of a successful campaign. Union representatives also present data about wage and benefit contracts in the industry and other organizations to help convince workers that union representation will be financially beneficial for them.

Authorization Cards   To prove that a sufficient number of employees are interested in union representation, the NLRB requires the union to get signatures on **authorization cards** from employees to indicate their interest. The union must have signed cards from at least 30% of the employee group. Employees who sign the authorization cards have authorized the union to seek a representation election that could formalize the union's role in negotiating labor contracts on behalf of the employee group.

When the union has signatures from at least 30% of the employees, it can make a formal request to the NLRB to authorize a representation election. If the NLRB agrees that the union has met the 30% requirement, it orders an election. Some unions prefer at least a 50% signature rate or they will not file with the NLRB unless they have the higher number of authorization card signatures.

Official notification to management occurs when the union requests an election. Management is given an opportunity to review and perhaps contest the union's request. The NLRB will hold a hearing, if necessary, to hear arguments from both sides.

Bargaining-Unit Determination   Management will typically argue that the union is trying to organize a group that has not been determined to be an appropriate bargaining unit according rules developed by the NLRB in 1991. If the organization can prove that the union is not following the NLRB rules, the request for the representation election will be denied.[12]

Healthcare and Bargaining Units

As the healthcare industry began to unionize, disputes occurred about the composition and number of unions. In response, Congress asked the NLRB to make recommendations about the appropriate number of and types of unions a healthcare facility could have. The NLRB determined that hospitals have eight distinct employee groups that could be considered bargaining units as depicted in Figure 11-4.

When management challenges a union's formation, the NLRB determines whether an employee group is part of the appropriate bargaining group. When a union begins an organizing drive, it must limit its campaign to one of the eight groups listed in the figure. Despite this rule, disputes about unit determination still

FIGURE 11-4 Appropriate Bargaining Units in Healthcare

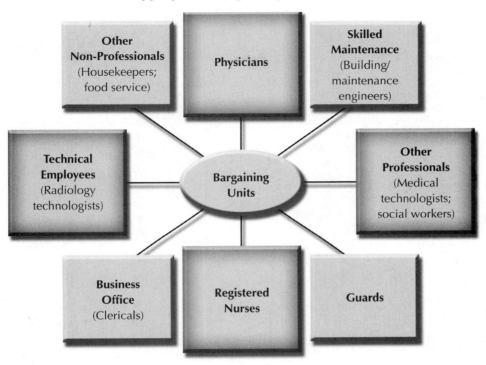

occur and the NLRB is asked to resolve these issues. Typically, organizations prefer fewer groups with larger numbers of employees. Unions usually are interested in smaller groups, which often leads to more successful organizing campaigns.

Representation Elections

If the NLRB is satisfied that the union has received enough authorization cards and that the employees who seek representation are an appropriate bargaining unit, it orders an election, supervised by an NLRB official and representatives from both the union and management. A union election is determined by a **simple majority**—50% plus one—of the employees who voted on the election day.

Management and the union encourage employees to vote because the employees who vote on election day determine whether the union will be sanctioned as the official bargaining agent for all of the employees in that group. A high turnout of voters usually is beneficial for management because non-involved employees are more likely to vote against the union.

If the union or management thinks the election was handled improperly or unfair labor practices occurred during the election, they may challenge the

FIGURE 11-5 **Unfair Labor Practices**

MANAGEMENT	UNIONS
▶ Interfering with, restraining, or coercing employees in the exercise of their right to organize or bargain collectively	▶ Interfering with restraining or coercing employees in the exercise of their right to organize or to bargain collectively
▶ Dominating or interfering with the formation or administration of any labor organization	▶ Causing an employer to discriminate or discourage union membership
▶ Encouraging or discouraging membership in any labor organization by discriminating with regard to hiring, tenure, or conditions of employment	▶ Refusal to bargain in good faith
	▶ Conducting secondary boycotts
	▶ Organization or recognition picketing by a union where the employer has recognized another union as the official bargaining agent
▶ Discharging or otherwise discriminating against an employee because he or she filed charges or gave testimony under the Act	
▶ Refusing to bargain in good faith	

results. If the NLRB determines no violations occurred, it rules on the election results. If the union does not win the election, it is prohibited from conducting another organizing campaign for 12 months.

Unfair Labor Practices   One of the major roles of the NLRB is resolving unfair labor practices. *Unfair labor practices* are defined in Section 8a and 8b of the National Labor Relations Act:[13] Figure 11-5 illustrates the unfair labor practices for both management and unions. Most charges of unfair labor practices are filed by unions.

It is important for organizations to avoid unfair labor practices. Therefore, managers should receive training about unfair labor practices. Most organizations provide a list of dos and don'ts, described in Figure 11-6, during unionization campaigns and when the contract is in place. A good general rule is to avoid making any promises or threats to employees during an organizing campaign.

Certification—Decertification

If the union receives the necessary votes and is **certified** by the NLRB, it then becomes the exclusive bargaining representative of the employee group, and the employer is required to negotiate in good faith with the union. As the certified employee representative, the union is now ready to negotiate the initial contract. Throughout union negotiations and contract administration, the union must be involved in discussions with employees about anything considered a subject of bargaining. The organization has lost the opportunity to deal directly with its employees.

FIGURE 11-6   Legal Dos and Don'ts for Unionization Campaigns

DO (LEGAL)	DON'T (ILLEGAL)
• Tell employees about current wages and benefits and how they compare with those in other firms • Tell employees that the employer opposes unionization • Tell employees the disadvantages of having a union (especially cost of dues, assessments, and requirements of membership) • Show employees articles about unions and relate negative experiences elsewhere • Explain the unionization process to employees accurately • Forbid distribution of union literature during work hours in work areas • Enforce disciplinary policies and rules consistently and appropriately	• Promise employees pay increases or promotions if they vote against the union • Threaten employees with termination or discriminate when disciplining employees • Threaten to close down or move the company if a union is voted in • Spy on or have someone spy on union meetings • Make a speech to employees or groups at work within 24 hours of the election (before that, it is allowed) • Ask employees how they plan to vote or if they have signed authorization cards • Encourage employees to persuade others to vote against the union (such a vote must be initiated solely by the employee)

Decertification   When an employee group decides that the union no longer meets its needs, it can **decertify** the union. Only employees can initiate a decertification process because management must stay out of the process all together or risk an unfair labor charge. Decertification is rare in the healthcare industry because employees believe their powerful unions will continue to protect them against employers who are unwilling to make significant workplace improvements.

The process for decertifying a current union is much like the certification process. Employees, without help from their employer, must obtain signatures from at least 30% of the employees who are union members. The NLRB conducts an election and decertifies the union when it determines that a **simple majority**—50% plus one—of employees want decertification. Six months must pass after certification before employees can decertify their union.

Collective Bargaining

Negotiating the initial contract can be difficult and time-consuming because both parties must start without any contract language about working conditions, wages, and benefits, among other issues. Developing an effective initial contract requires significant attention to detail because it will be the foundation for union-management relationships.

COLLECTIVE BARGAINING AND THE NEGOTIATING PROCESS

The collective-bargaining process begins when the NLRB notifies the management and union that the union has the official right to represent the employees. Both sides are required to bargain in good faith; that is, they must meet and exchange information about contractual issues, including economic and workplace policies and procedures. The labor contract finally agreed to by both parties is a legal document and supervisors and managers, as agents of the organization, must follow the contract provisions to avoid grievances or unfair labor practice charges.

Contract Components

Most labor contracts contain common clauses that provide some degree of consistency among contracts. Common clauses appear in the following:

▶ Management rights clauses
▶ Union security clauses
▶ Wages and benefits
▶ Working conditions

Management Rights Clauses   **Management rights clauses** are generally consistent from contract to contract and contain language that gives management the exclusive right to manage, direct, and control its business. Most such clauses give organizations the right to manage any issue not covered in the contract.

The management rights clause becomes more limited over time as each new contract identifies and documents some of the issues that the labor contract might not have covered previously. When management implements a practice that has not been covered by the clause and to which the union objects, the practice may become the subject of negotiations. The union might try to extend the contract or connect an issue to a related contract clause. For example, a union might contend that smoking on the facility grounds is a contractual benefit and that any attempt to enforce a new no-smoking policy would need negotiation. In this case, because there was no language in the current contract about smoking, it is likely that the next contract negotiations will include proposals that clarify the issue before management implements the policy.

Union Security Clauses   The **union security clause** recognizes the exclusive right of the union to bargain on behalf of the employees represented by the union. It also allows the union to contact current and new employees who would

FIGURE 11-7 Negotiation Process

be union members. A **dues check-off process** to pay union dues automatically through payroll deductions is also part of the union security clause.

Wages and Benefits   Union contract clauses about wages may include statements about base pay, premium pay, shift differential pay, and incentive pay for union members. Benefit clauses in the contract typically include health, dental, life, and disability insurance.

Working Conditions and Scheduling   Healthcare contracts usually contain significant language about the employer's ability to schedule its employees' work. Staffing requirements for individual patient-care units are usually the subject of substantial discussion during negotiations. In addition to scheduling clauses, many contracts include language about workplace safety issues that are designed to protect union members from occupational hazards in the workplace.

Negotiation Process

The process for negotiating a labor contract varies from organization to organization, but certain steps must be followed to make the process successful. The four major steps in the negotiations process are listed in Figure 11-7.

Data Collection   When the collective-bargaining process begins, both parties collect data and develop competitive wage and benefit information that will support the positions they promote.

Conflicts about data collection are common as the two parties compare other organizations' wage and benefits packages. Both the union and management benefit from a contract that is competitive in the local job market. They collect the following information:

▶ *Base Pay*—Hourly pay for work performed
▶ *Premium Pay*—Additional pay for evening, night, and weekend work
▶ *Employee Benefits*—Health, dental, life, and disability insurance
▶ *Retirement Benefits*—Partial income after retirement
▶ *Staffing and Scheduling Practices*—Staff-to-patient ratios and work times
▶ *Economic and Working Conditions*—Compared with other union and non-union groups
▶ *Workplace Issues*—Health, safety, and security
▶ *Employee Grievances*—Finding trends that convert to demands

During data collection, management negotiators meet with managers to collect data on issues that they want negotiated into the contract. Likewise, the union meets with employees to collect information to be converted into contract demands. Each party develops a formal presentation of contract demands or interests to begin the negotiations.

Negotiations   During the initial negotiating meeting, the two parties agree on how they will conduct negotiations. Developing a schedule and proposed agenda, while allotting sufficient time to resolve issues, can contribute to effective negotiations. The parties must determine how much time and how many meetings need to be scheduled to resolve the contract before the current one expires.

During the negotiations, the parties will review the current agreements, present new economic and noneconomic demands, provide data and information for each contract demand, discuss each issue, propose solutions, come to agreement, and document the agreement. When an agreement is reached on a demand, the proposed language is drafted and reviewed by both parties. They repeat this process for all issues that the parties raise.

Interest-Based Bargaining   A new technique that has been used effectively in the negotiating process is **interest-based bargaining,** which emphasizes problem solving and consensus building. Employers and unions may receive training from the FMCS about how to facilitate discussing issues, interests, options, and solutions. The typical steps to interest-based bargaining are as follows:

1. Select an issue
2. Clarify the issue
3. Discuss each party's interests (not positions or demands)
4. Generate options through brainstorming
5. Evaluate options
6. Select options that meet mutual needs
7. Document agreed solutions

Interest-based bargaining has been successful in some situations, but it requires both sides to be open to collaborative relations.

Tentative Agreement   A **tentative agreement** is reached when both parties agree to move forward with a recommended contract. Union representatives are required to take the proposal to their membership for a ratification vote. If the negotiation team for the employees believes that the contract offered by management is fair, the negotiating team will recommend contract passage.

During difficult discussions, the negotiating team may not recommend contract ratification but explain the contract as offered and let the members decide. If the members reject the contract, they can authorize sending the negotiating team back to the table for more discussions or authorize a strike.

Settlement or Impasse   Throughout the negotiation, to prove that they have bargained in good faith, each party demonstrates that it has met, exchanged proposals, and reviewed and considered the offers of the other party. In many cases, the parties agree on resolutions that are good for both sides.

In some cases, however, the parties bargain to impasse and a contract agreement is not reached. Bargaining to impasse does not necessarily mean that the parties have not negotiated in good faith, but rather that despite their best efforts, they couldn't come to an agreement. When they bargain to impasse, a strike is possible.

Planning for Strikes

Because of the complexities of doing business, both union and management representatives must plan well in advance of a strike. Although it might seem contrary to the mission of contract negotiations, planning for a strike begins at about the same time negotiations start. Crucial concerns are listed in the Figure 11-8. Unions prepare members for economic and emotional realities of a work stoppage while managers prepare to care for patients during the strike. Managers and union officials have a variety of challenges and concerns to deal with when a strike is imminent. Managers are concerned about patient care, covering work schedules, diverting patients and services during the strike, the economic impact of the

FIGURE 11-8   Strike Concerns

MANAGEMENT	UNION
▶ Communicating to the community, physicians, and non-striking employees about the contingency plan	▶ Communicating to NLRB and management of intent to strike
▶ Training managers and supervisors to provide patient care	▶ Communicating strike authorization to members
▶ Determining how many patients the reduced staff can cover	▶ Planning logistics of maintaining the picket line
▶ Contacting temporary staffing agencies to provide temporary workers during the strike	▶ Scheduling pickets
▶ Deciding where patients will be referred to other non-striking providers	▶ Providing information hotline to update striking members
▶ Determining how to treat staff members who cross the picket line	▶ Planning public relations to influence public opinion
▶ Securing the facility and grounds to avoid disruptions	
▶ Arranging for supplies and equipment deliveries across the picket line	
▶ Contracting vendors with union contracts to assure no sympathy strike by other unions	

strike on the organization, the conflict between striking and nonstriking employees, and its public image.

Union officials are also faced with critical challenges that require time and thought in the event of a strike: lost wages of striking members, solidarity of striking workers, emotional conflicts of care-giving union members, replacement workers, quality of patient care, relationships with nonstriking employees, and its public image.

Professional healthcare employees face several dilemmas in a strike situation. Among these is a reluctance about participating in a work stoppage when it means stopping patient care. But when a strike is called, each union member must decide whether to honor the strike or cross the picket line. Management's challenges include finding a balance in how managers treat striking workers, who will eventually return to work, and in negotiating a contract that is fair and equitable.

If the number of patients remains the same during the strike, other nonstriking caregivers will likely have to fill in where striking staff members are absent. Assigning substitutes to care for patients is complex because managers must consider quality issues, including credentialed staff replacements, levels of authority for substitute caregivers, and appropriate staff-to-patient ratios. Conflict and resentment build in these situations. Long strikes cause even greater conflict. Because healthcare is labor intensive and specialized, the likelihood that managers and supervisors can continue to carry the workload alone is unrealistic during a long strike.

The emotional impact of a strike or difficult negotiations must not be minimized when an organization finally negotiates a contract. When the issues are resolved and the workforce returns to work, rebuilding relationships with the employees who were on strike will be vital to meeting organization objectives. In most cases, the objective of both parties is to come to a satisfactory settlement and return to work.

Formalizing the Agreement

When the negotiations are complete, the parties draft a contract agreement and each reviews it for approval. The final contract is important because it governs the relationship between management and employees during the life of the contract, usually three years or more. Tentative agreements have been reached on individual issues throughout negotiations, and contract language has been documented.

The bargaining parties must present the tentative language to their constituents for review and a ratification vote. This is a crucial stage in the negotiation process, because if the members vote to reject the contract agreement, the parties will return to the table or the members will vote to strike. If the members ratify the tentative agreement, it will be converted into the final contract. The last stage in the negotiation process is writing an official version of the agreements. When the contract is in final form and approved, authorized representatives of the union and management formally sign the agreement.

CONTRACT ADMINISTRATION

Implementing the labor contract on a daily basis is the next critical issue that labor and management face. The contract is a legal agreement that must be followed during its term, and it must be implementable by managers who might not have been involved in the negotiations. During bargaining, negotiators must keep contract administration issues in mind and anticipate conflicts and contract interpretation issues to avoid administration problems.

Labor–Management Committees

Labor–management committees are comprised of management representatives, union members, and bargaining agents and meet regularly. Union members are elected by their colleagues; management representatives are assigned by organization leaders. Managers and union members communicate issues to the committee as a result of their daily interactions. Labor–management committees should be based entirely on cooperation and an interest in equal partnership.[14]

Grievance Procedures

Because it is difficult to anticipate all of the issues that may come up during the life of the contract, special clauses deal with disputes. A grievance procedure is commonly used to resolve unforeseen contract disputes.

A **grievance procedure** is a formal process used to resolve issues that arise out of daily interactions between managers and workers. Most healthcare HR professionals strive to resolve issues internally before grievances are filed.[15]

The procedure, outlined in the contract, comprises several steps that allow employees to present their disputes to management. A grievance process is outlined in Figure 11-9 on the next page. The general steps in the figure may be supplemented by additional steps, depending on the union agreement.

In most cases, the employee typically uses a union representative to help present the issues in each step of the grievance process. In some contracts, the process ends with binding arbitration. **Arbitration** requires the two parties to present their cases to a mutually selected arbitrator from a list provided by the American Arbitration Association. The arbitrator hears the grievance and makes a binding decision. **Mediation** is a process that involves a third party who facilitates discussions and proposes resolutions to the two parties. The mediator's suggestions are never binding however.

EFFECTIVE UNION-MANAGEMENT RELATIONS IN HEALTHCARE ORGANIZATIONS

If the unionization process is successful, organizations and unions must collaborate. Partnerships must be forged and issues that affect one party must be resolved by both parties.

FIGURE 11-9 Employee Grievance Process

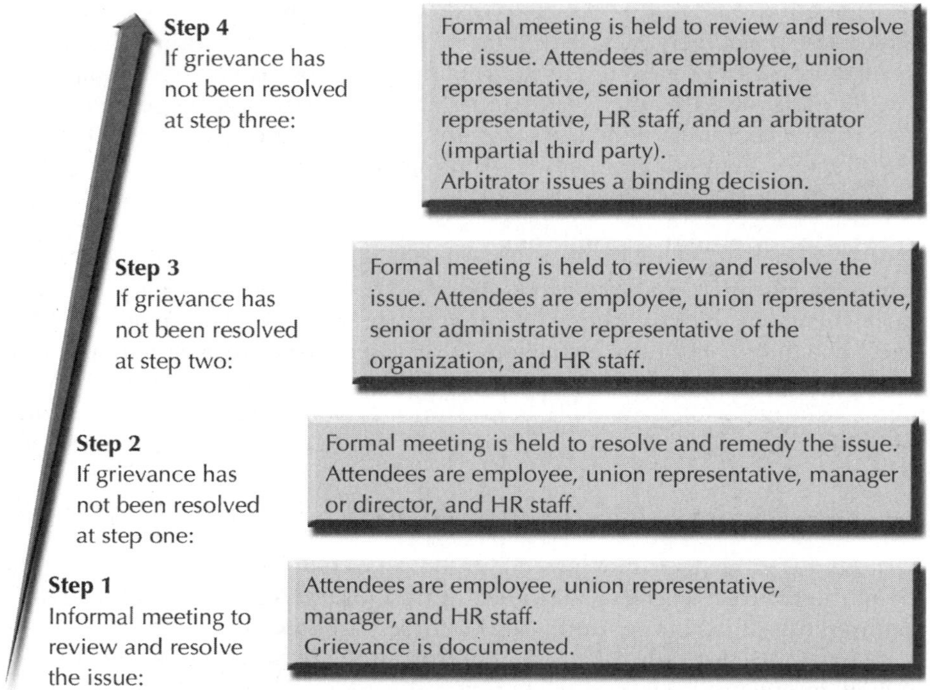

Step 4
If grievance has
not been resolved
at step three:

Formal meeting is held to review and resolve
the issue. Attendees are employee, union
representative, senior administrative
representative, HR staff, and an arbitrator
(impartial third party).
Arbitrator issues a binding decision.

Step 3
If grievance has
not been resolved
at step two:

Formal meeting is held to review and resolve the
issue. Attendees are employee, union representative,
senior administrative representative of the
organization, and HR staff.

Step 2
If grievance has
not been resolved
at step one:

Formal meeting is held to resolve and remedy the issue.
Attendees are employee, union representative, manager
or director, and HR staff.

Step 1
Informal meeting to
review and resolve
the issue:

Attendees are employee, union representative,
manager, and HR staff.
Grievance is documented.

Labor management relationships are always evident when the parties meet to negotiate new contracts. If both parties have had a good relationship during the years between contract negotiations, the negotiating process will progress more rapidly than if the sides had been uncommunicative or adversarial. Both parties must be interested in working on issues that will improve the organization and the healthcare industry.

Competing in the marketplace and improving organizations' economic health must be a goal shared by both organizations and unions.[16] The largest expense in labor-intensive healthcare facilities is employees' wages and benefits, so improvements to the budget usually mean that wages and benefits will be affected. The most promising way to facilitate changes and maintain functional relationships will be a strong commitment to positive labor relations and problem solving.[17]

CASE

A specialty clinic, with four unions representing 40% of the employees has been notified that the Teamsters' Union has been contacted by an employee group to conduct a unionization campaign to represent some of the employees, including service workers, clerical workers, and all levels in the accounting department. The clinic's labor-relations philosophy would be characterized as traditional and noncollaborative. It has decided to resist the union's attempt to organize the employees.

The four groups of employees who are currently represented by unions include technical employees, registered nurses, pharmacists, and maintenance workers. Some 70 employees are represented by the current contracts. The registered nurses constitute 40% of the 70 union members.

The group that has been proposed in the organizing attempt includes 45 employees, and the service workers (housekeeping, food service, and nursing assistants) constitute 75% of the proposed members.

Management is concerned about the organizing campaign. Relationships with the current unions have not been very productive, and further unionization will lead to more distrust between management and employees. Management is concerned about the union's ability to call strikes in the future, which may require the organization to severely limit services and could greatly affect its financial health.

Management must decide whether to mount a campaign to prevent the union from organizing. If it decides to mount a campaign, management must develop a strategy to present arguments to the employees for not having union representation.

Questions

1. What steps must the Teamsters' Union follow to cause an election to occur?
2. During the union campaign how should the managers conduct themselves to avoid being accused of committing unfair labor practices?

END NOTES

1. Robbie Dingeman, "New Pacts for Nurses May Bring Cost Cuts," *The Honolulu Advertiser,* January 12, 2003, A28, 30.
2. Robert L. Mathis and John H. Jackson, *Human Resource Management,* 9th ed. (Cincinnati, Ohio: South-Western College Publishing, 2000), 606.
3. Satish Deshpande, "Hospitals and Union Elections," *The Health Care Manager* (December 2000), 8–12.
4. Deanna Bellandi, "Labor Flexes Muscle," *Modern Healthcare* (July 2, 2001), 8.
5. Paul F. Clark, Darlene A. Clark, David V. Day, and Dennis O'Shea, "Healthcare Reform and the Workplace Experience of Nurses: Implications for Patient Care and Union Organizing," *Industrial and Labor Relations Review* (October 2001), 133–148.
6. Ed Lovern, "The Right Ratio," *Modern Healthcare* (October 16, 2000), 3.
7. Bonny Friedrich, "Staying Power," *Nursing Management* (July 2001), 26–28.
8. D. Clark, P. Clark, D. Day, and D. Shea, "The Relationship between Health Care Reform and Nurses' Interest in Union Representation: The Role of Workplace Climate," *Journal of Professional Nursing* (2000), 16(2), 92–96.
9. Melissa Fitzpatrick, "Collective Bargaining: Vulnerability assessment," *Nursing Management* (February 2001), 40–42.

10. Deanna Bellandi, "Provider Disunity on Labor," *Modern Healthcare* (October 9, 2000), 22–24.

11. National Labor Relations Board Fact Sheet, *NLRB Web site,* *http://www.nlrb.gov.*

12. Michael H. LeRoy, "Is the NLRB Still Relevant? A Performance Review," *Journal Labor of Research* (Fall 2001), 781–794.

13. Mary Kathryn Zachary, "Labor Law for Supervisors: Union Campaigns Prove Sensitive for Supervisory Employees," *Supervision* (May 2000), 23–26.

14. John H. Sheehan, "Labor's Achievement, Weakness, and Future Goals: Labor Day Did Not Happen by Accident," *Vital Speeches of the Day* (September 15, 2001), 732–735.

15. Mable H. Smith, "Grievance Procedures Resolve Conflict," *Nursing Management* (April 2002), 13.

16. Sheehan, 732–735.

17. Saul Rubenstein, "Union as Value Adding Networks: Possibilities for the Future of U.S. Unionism," *Journal of Labor Research* (Summer 2001), 581–598.

CHAPTER 12

Healthcare Compensation Practices

Learning Objectives

After you have read this chapter, you should be able to:

▶ Describe the differences between an entitlement compensation philosophy and a performance-focused compensation philosophy.

▶ Define the issues confronting the healthcare industry in complying with the Fair Labor Standards Act (FLSA).

▶ Discuss the various methods of administering a compensation process.

▶ Identify the steps in the compensation administration process.

▶ Explain the issues associated with awarding pay increases.

▶ Discuss the five components of executive compensation.

Healthcare HR Insights

At Madelia Community Hospital (MCH), a small rural hospital, balancing RN staffing requirements and payroll according to the Fair Labor Standards Act (FLSA)—the major federal law that covers the payment of overtime wages—was a challenge. MCH struggled with the need to provide adequate RN staffing levels to ensure high quality care with fluctuating patient census. MCH treated RNs as non-exempt employees who receive overtime after 40 hours of work in a week. This created a significant overtime payment amount due to the fluctuating staffing requirements. MCH also had to staff its inpatient care units on a 24/7 basis, and RNs were required to work every other weekend. If MCH implemented an alternative weekend staffing schedule for the RNs to avoid the every other weekend requirement, it would be required to pay excessive amounts of overtime, which the hospital's budget could not tolerate.

The RNs were becoming increasingly dissatisfied with the weekend coverage requirements. In response to the RNs' scheduling concerns, nursing leadership, in concert with HR, explored a variety of staffing and pay practice options. After much study, the decision was reached to move the RNs to a salaried-exempt status and institute 12-hour shifts for weekend coverage, which is allowable under the FLSA for RNs.

Moving the RNs to exempt status allowed for the scheduling flexibility that would facilitate 12-hour shifts and weekend coverage requirement for RNs on every third weekend. The full-time RNs were placed on a salary base that included their hourly rate times their scheduled and past overtime pay, and began working 12-hour shifts. However, the adjustment to a base salary and not being compensated for overtime was a significant adjustment for the RNs. But the trade-off from working every other weekend to working every third weekend was a motivating factor to accept the new pay practice.

This hospital and other healthcare providers often find that the FLSA is a difficult act to comply with when it comes to maintaining staffing flexibility without incurring higher costs due to overtime payments. Later in this chapter, the FLSA is discussed in detail.

Source: Adapted with permission from Madelia Community Hospital, Madelia, Minnesota.

In developing compensation strategies, healthcare organizations are confronted with a dilemma. Consumer groups, insurance companies, HMOs, and federal and state governments are demanding higher-quality care at lower or contained costs. Further, the demand for healthcare in this country is accelerating at an unprecedented rate as the baby-boom generation ages, yet fewer individuals are pursuing healthcare careers. In order to attract and retain competent and motivated workers, healthcare organizations must aggressively compete with each other and with other industries for skilled workers. The net effect is that healthcare HR compensation strategies must do the impossible, balance these competing factors and priorities and deliver compensation systems that meet the needs of their organizations.[1]

HEALTHCARE COMPENSATION RESPONSIBILITIES

Compensation costs represent significant expenditures in most healthcare organizations. For instance, at one large clinic, employee payroll and benefits expenditures make up about 60% of all costs. Although actual compensation costs can be easily calculated, the value derived by employers proves more difficult to identify.

Healthcare HR professionals guide the development and administration of an organizational compensation system, including responsibilities for developing base pay programs, pay structures, and compensation administration policies. Healthcare HR professionals may or may not do actual payroll processing. This labor-intensive responsibility is typically among the first to be outsourced. However, today many healthcare organizations are retaining in-house processing because of improvements in software and Internet processing. Operating managers evaluate the performance of employees and consider their performance when deciding compensation increases within the policies and guidelines established by the HR unit and upper management.

Compensation systems in healthcare organizations must be closely linked to organizational objectives and strategies. An effective compensation program addresses four objectives:

1. Legal compliance with all appropriate laws and regulations
2. Cost-effectiveness for the organization
3. Internal, external, and individual equity for employees
4. Performance enhancement for the organization

Healthcare employers must balance compensation costs at a level that both ensures organizational competitiveness and provides sufficient rewards to employees for their knowledge, skills, abilities, and performance accomplishments. In order to attract, retain, and reward employees, employers provide several types of compensation.

NATURE OF COMPENSATION

Compensation is an important factor affecting how and why people choose to work at one organization over others. Healthcare employers must be reasonably competitive with several types of compensation to attract and retain competent employees.

Rewards can be both intrinsic and extrinsic. **Intrinsic rewards** often include praise for completing a project or meeting performance objectives. Other psychological and social effects of compensation are reflected in the intrinsic rewards.[2] **Extrinsic rewards** are tangible and take both monetary and nonmonetary forms.

FIGURE 12-1 Components of a Compensation Program

Compensation	
Direct	**Indirect**
Base Pay • Wages • Salaries **Variable Pay** • Bonuses • Incentives • Stock options	**Benefits** • Medical/life insurance • Paid time off • Retirement pensions • Workers' compensation • Others

Compensation Components

Tangible components of a compensation program are of two general types (see Figure 12-1). With direct compensation, the employer exchanges monetary rewards for work done. Employers provide indirect compensation—like health insurance—to everyone simply based on membership in the organization. *Base pay* and *variable pay* are the most common forms of direct compensation. Indirect compensation commonly consists of employee *benefits*.

Base Pay   The basic compensation that an employee receives, usually as a wage or salary, is called **base pay.** Many organizations use two base pay categories, *hourly* and *salaried,* which are identified according to the way pay is distributed and the nature of the jobs. Hourly pay is the most common means of payment based on time, and employees paid hourly receive **wages,** which are payments directly calculated on the amount of time worked. In contrast, people paid **salaries** receive consistent payments each period regardless of the number of hours worked. Being salaried typically has carried higher status for employees than being paid wages. However, healthcare employees still must pay overtime to certain employees as defined by federal and state pay laws.

Variable Pay   Another type of direct pay is **variable pay,** which is compensation linked directly to individual, team, or organizational performance. The most common types of variable pay for most employees take the form of bonuses and incentive program payments. Executives often receive longer-term rewards such as deferred compensation. Variable pay is discussed in Chapter 13.

Benefits   Many organizations provide numerous extrinsic rewards in an indirect manner. With indirect compensation, employees receive the tangible value of the rewards without receiving the actual cash. A **benefit** is an indirect reward—health insurance, vacation pay, or retirement pensions—given to an employee or group of employees as a part of organizational membership, regardless of performance.

Healthcare Compensation Approaches

Healthcare organizations regard pay as an important tool for recruiting, motivating, and retaining good people. Indeed, those goals have changed little over time, but the ways in which some healthcare organizations approach them differ dramatically from previous approaches. Performance-based pay, tailored to the strategic circumstances of each organization, may consist of base pay, an annual bonus, and a choice of various other benefits. Such a "total rewards" package would have been uncommon for a worker in 1950, but it is increasingly common today.[3] Figure 12-2 presents some of the choices organizations must make regarding compensation approaches.

Traditional Compensation Approach   For some organizations a traditional compensation approach makes sense and offers certain advantages in specific competitive situations. It may be more legally defensible, less complex, and viewed as more "fair" for average and below-average employees. However, the total rewards approach helps retain top performers, can be more flexible when the economy goes up or down, and is favored by top-performing organizations.[4] It clearly will *not* work in every situation.

Traditional compensation systems have evolved over a period of time to reflect a logical, rational approach to compensating employees. Job descriptions identify tasks and responsibilities and are then used to decide which jobs are more valuable. These systems calculate the value that each job contributes to the organization based on job evaluation. That value is used to establish a pay range that reflects a person's progression as he or she grows and presumably gets better at the job.

FIGURE 12-2   Compensation Approaches: Traditional versus Total Rewards

Traditional Compensation Approach	Total Rewards Approach
Compensation is primarily base pay.	Variable pay is added to base.
Bonuses/perks are for executives only.	Annual/long-term incentives are provided to executives, managers, and employees.
Fixed benefits are tied to long tenure.	Flexible and portable benefits are offered.
Pay grade progression is based on organizational promotions.	Knowledge/skill-based broadbands determine pay grades.
Organization-wide standard pay plan exists.	Multiple plans consider job family, location, and business units.

Total Rewards Approach   The total rewards approach tries to place a value on individuals rather than just the jobs. Managers factor in elements such as how much an employee knows or how much competence an employee has when determining compensation. The need for such an approach becomes more evident in trying to pay people with high demand clinical skills such as radiology technologists, pharmacists, and RNs.

Currently, some healthcare organizations incorporate variable pay programs as part of a total rewards approach for all levels of employees. Widespread use of various incentive plans, team bonuses, organizational gainsharing programs, and other designs serves to link growth in compensation to results. However, management must address three main issues when using variable pay systems:

1. Should performance be measured and rewarded based on individual, group, or organizational performance?
2. Should the length of time for measuring performance be short-term (less than one year) or longer-term (more than one year)?
3. Are variable-pay programs compatible with the mission and values of the organization?

The various types and facets of variable pay are discussed in the next chapter. But it is important to recognize the shift toward compensation being allocated through such plans, rather than the organization relying solely on base pay to reward employees at all levels for attaining strategic organizational objectives.

Compensation Philosophies

The two basic compensation philosophies lie on opposite ends of a continuum. At one end of the continuum in Figure 12-3 is the *entitlement* philosophy; at the other end is the *performance-oriented* philosophy.[5] Most compensation systems fall somewhere in between.

Entitlement Orientation   Many traditional organizations that give automatic increases to their employees every year practice the entitlement philosophy. Further, most of those employees receive the same or nearly the same percentage

FIGURE 1 2 - 3   Continuum of Compensation Philosophies

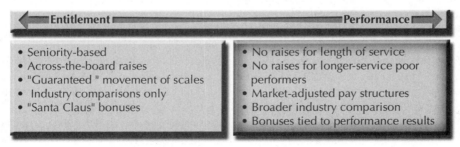

increase each year. Employees and managers who subscribe to the entitlement philosophy believe that individuals who have worked another year are *entitled* to a raise in base pay. They also believe all incentives and benefit programs should continue and be increased, regardless of changing industry or economic conditions. Commonly, in organizations following an entitlement philosophy pay increases are referred to as *cost-of-living* raises, even if they are not tied specifically to economic cost-of-living indicators.

Following an entitlement philosophy ultimately means that as employees continue their employment lives, employer's costs increase, regardless of employee performance or organizational competitive pressures. Market data will be monitored, but will not necessarily drive compensation strategy decisions unless significant recruitment or retention issues are identified for a particular job, group, or position (e.g., RNs or nurse anesthetists).

Hospitals and medical centers have especially struggled with the entitlement orientation of their long-term employees. Today's market pressures on healthcare organizations and the declining revenues described in earlier chapters would argue for a merit- or performance-based approach to paying annual increases. However, two factors have contributed to the entitlement orientation: 1) decades of paying automatic increases and 2) collective bargaining agreements that require automatic step increases.

Performance Orientation Where a performance-oriented philosophy is followed, organizations do not guarantee additional or increased compensation simply for completing another year of organizational service. Instead, pay and incentives reflect performance differences among employees. Employees who perform well receive larger compensation increases; those who do not perform satisfactorily see little or no increase in compensation. Thus, employees who perform satisfactorily maintain or advance in relation to market compensation levels, whereas poor or marginal performers may fall behind. Bonus compensation may be paid on the basis of individual, team, or organizational performance.

Decisions about Healthcare Compensation Levels

Even though healthcare organizations might wish to pay the top wages and salaries relative to their competition, that might not be possible because of the significant pressure healthcare organizations face to control their costs. Three basic approaches to healthcare compensation include market-based pay, competency-based pay, and team pay. Next is presented an overview of each approach.

Market-Based Pay Some healthcare organizations establish specific policies about where they wish to be positioned in the labor market. These policies use a *quartile strategy,* as illustrated in Figure 12-4. Data in pay surveys reveal that the actual dollar difference between quartiles is generally 15% to 20%.

Most employers choose to position themselves in the *second quartile,* in the middle of the market (median), based on pay survey data of other employers'

FIGURE 12-4   Market-based Compensation Strategies

Third Quartile: Above-Market Strategy

> (Employer positions pay scales so that
> 25% of firms pay above and 75% pay below)

Second Quartile: Middle-Market Strategy

> (Employer positions pay scales so that
> 50% of firms pay above and 50% pay below)

First Quartile: Below-Market Strategy

> (Employer positions pay scales so that
> 75% of firms pay above and 25% pay below)

compensation plans. Choosing this level attempts to balance employer cost pressures and the need to attract and retain employees by providing mid-level compensation levels.

An employer using a *first-quartile* approach might choose to pay below market compensation for several reasons. The employer might be experiencing a shortage of funds, making it unable to pay more and still meet objectives. Also, when an abundance of workers is available, particularly those with lower skills, a below-market approach can be used to attract sufficient workers at lesser cost. The downside of this strategy is that higher turnover of workers is more likely. If the labor market supply tightens, then attracting and retaining workers becomes more difficult.

A *third-quartile* approach uses an aggressive pay-above-market emphasis. This strategy generally enables an organization to attract and retain sufficient workers with the required capabilities and to be more selective when hiring. However, because it is a higher-cost approach, organizations often look for ways to increase the productivity of employees receiving above-market wages.

In many cases, depending on the availability of workers with certain skills (e.g., pharmacist or certified nurse anesthetists), organizations may adopt a strategy to utilize a third-quartile approach for those positions, yet pay at first- or second-quartile levels for less hard-to-fill positions. This approach entails a "market-driven" philosophy for the hard-to-fill positions.[6]

Competency-Based Pay   The design of most compensation programs rewards employees for carrying out their tasks, duties, and responsibilities. The job requirements determine which employees have higher base rates. Employees receive more for doing jobs that require a greater variety of tasks, more knowledge and skills, greater physical effort, or more demanding working conditions.[7]

However, some healthcare organizations are emphasizing competencies rather than tasks. Competencies such as the ability to perform a particular clinical procedure or the attainment of a clinical credential such as a certified emergency nurse. A number of organizations are paying employees for the competencies they demonstrate rather than just for the specific tasks performed. Paying for competencies rewards employees who exhibit more versatility and continue to develop their competencies.

In knowledge-based pay (KBP) or skill-based pay (SBP) systems, employees start at a base level of pay and receive increases as they learn to do other jobs or gain other skills and therefore become more valuable to the employer. For example, in an RN clinic ladder program RNs will have the opportunity to move two or more pay levels based on their ability to demonstrate higher levels of clinical competency. Figure 12-5 depicts the pay structure of a clinical nursing ladder program. The success of competency plans requires managerial commitment to a philosophy different from the traditional one in organizations.[8] This approach places far more emphasis on training employees and supervisors. Due to the extensive commitment to training and the need to monitor the competencies of employees that competency-based pay systems require, they are more likely to be implemented in larger healthcare organizations. Also, workflow must be adapted to allow workers to move from job to job as needed.

When a healthcare organization moves to a competency-based system, considerable time must be spent identifying the required competencies for various jobs. Progression of employees must be possible, and they must be paid appropriately for all of their competencies. Any *limitations* on the numbers of people who can acquire more competencies should be clearly identified. *Training* in the appropriate competencies is particularly critical. Also, a competency-based system needs to acknowledge or certify employees as they acquire certain competencies, and then to verify the maintenance of those *competencies*. In summary, use of a competency-based system requires significant investment of management time and commitment.

Individual versus Team Rewards As healthcare organizations have shifted to using work teams, they face the logical concern of how to develop compensa-

FIGURE 12-5 **Pay Structure of a Nursing Clinical Ladder Program**

POSITION	GRADE	RANGE (HOURLY)	
		MINIMUM	MAXIMUM
Clinical Nurse I	10	$22.00	$31.00
Clinical Nurse II	11	$25.00	$35.00
Clinical Nurse III	12	$28.00	$39.00

tion programs that build on the team concept. At issue is how to compensate the individual whose performance may also be evaluated on the basis of team achievement. Paying everyone on teams the same amount, even though they demonstrate differing competencies and levels of performance, obviously creates equity concerns for many employees.[9]

Many organizations use team rewards as variable pay added to base pay. For base pay, individual compensation is based on competency- or skill-based approaches. Variable pay rewards for teams are most frequently distributed annually as a specified dollar amount, not as a percentage of base pay. Rather than substituting for base pay programs, team-based rewards appear to be useful in rewarding performance of a team beyond the satisfactory level. More discussion on team-based incentives is contained in the next chapter.

Compensation System Design Issues

Compensation decisions must be viewed strategically. Because so many organizational funds are spent on compensation-related activities, it is critical for top management and HR professionals to match compensation practices with what the organization is trying to accomplish. Consider the following examples. The compensation program for a new physician practice will probably be different from a mature, well-established clinic. If a new practice wishes to accelerate its capabilities to grow and expand, it may offer higher-than-market wages and recruitment bonuses in order to attract extremely talented workers who can quickly contribute to the success of the practice. However, for a large, stable clinic, with a well-established patient referral base, more structured pay and benefit programs will be more common.

Organizations must make a number of important decisions about the nature of a compensation system. Some decisions include the following: What philosophy and approach will be taken? How will the firm react to market pay levels? Is the job to be paid on the person's level of competence? Will pay be individual or team-based?

Perceptions of Pay Fairness

Most people in healthcare organizations work in order to gain rewards for their efforts. Except in volunteer organizations, people expect to receive fair value in the form of tangible compensation for their efforts. Whether considering base pay, variable pay, or benefits, the extent to which employees perceive compensation to be fair often affects their performance and how they view their jobs and employers.

Pay Openness An important equity issue concerns the degree of openness or secrecy that organizations allow regarding their pay systems. Pay information kept secret in "closed" systems includes how much others make, what raises others have received, and even what pay grades and ranges exist in the organization.[10]

A growing number of healthcare organizations are opening up their pay systems to some degree by informing employees of compensation policies, providing a general description of the compensation system, and indicating where an individual's pay is within a pay grade. Such information allows employees to make more accurate equity comparisons. The crucial element in an open pay system is that managers be able to explain satisfactorily the pay differences that exist.[11]

External Equity   If an employer does not provide compensation employees view as equitable compared to organizations, that employer is more likely to experience higher turnover. Other drawbacks include greater difficulty in recruiting qualified and high-demand individuals. Also, by not being competitive the employer is more likely to attract and retain individuals with less knowledge, skills, and abilities, resulting in lower overall organizational performance. Organizations track external equity by using pay surveys, which are discussed later in the chapter.

LEGAL CONSTRAINTS ON PAY SYSTEMS

Compensation systems must comply with a myriad of government constraints. Important areas addressed by the laws include minimum wage standards and hours of work. The following discussion examines the laws and regulations affecting base compensation; laws and regulations affecting incentives and benefits are examined in later chapters.

Fair Labor Standards Act (FLSA)

The major federal law affecting compensation is the Fair Labor Standards Act (FLSA), which was passed in 1938. Amended several times to raise minimum wage rates and expand employers covered, the FLSA affects both private- and public-sector employers.

Compliance with FLSA provisions is enforced by the Wage and Hour Division of the U.S. Department of Labor. To meet FLSA requirements healthcare employers must keep accurate time records and maintain these records for three years. Compliance investigations from the Wage and Hour Division investigate complaints filed by individuals who believe they have not received the overtime payments due them. Also, certain industries that historically have had a large number of wage and hour violations can be targeted, and firms in those industries can be investigated.

Penalties for wage and hour violations often include awards of back pay for affected current and former employees for up to two years. For example, a large medical center had allowed the nursing supervisors to arbitrarily pay overtime wages to some permanent charge nurses, who had been classified as exempt employees, to encourage them to pick up additional shifts. Some of the charge nurses who had not been recipients of the overtime pay complained to the Wage and Hour Division. Upon investigation, the division determined that the payment of indiscriminate overtime wages to otherwise exempt employees nullified their exempt status, and the Division subsequently negotiated a $750,000 back-pay award for the charge nurses.

Some argue that the 60+ year-old law does not reflect today's economy or meets the needs of the healthcare industry. Its complexity creates great difficulties for healthcare employers trying to follow all the requirements of the law. Also, the burden of proof and record-keeping requirements "falls squarely on the employer" a management attorney notes.[12] However, because little agreement can be reached on to how to change the FLSA, it is unlikely to happen. The act focuses on the following three major objectives:

1. Establish a minimum wage floor.
2. Discourage oppressive use of child labor.
3. Encourage limits on the number of weekly hours employees work through overtime provisions (exempt and nonexempt status).

Minimum Wage   The FLSA sets a minimum wage to be paid to the broad spectrum of covered employees. The actual minimum wage can be changed only by congressional action. A lower minimum-wage is set for "tipped" employees, such as restaurant servers, but their compensation must be equal to or exceed the minimum wage when average tips are included. Minimum wage levels continue to spark significant political discussions and legislative maneuvering.

Child-Labor Provisions   The child-labor provisions of the FLSA set the minimum age for employment with unlimited hours at 16 years. Individuals 14 to 15 years old may work outside school hours, with certain limitations. Many healthcare employers require age certificates for employees because the FLSA makes the employer responsible for determining an individual's age. A representative of a state labor department, a state education department, or a local school district generally issues such certificates.

Exempt and Non-Exempt Status Under the FLSA   Employees are classified as exempt or non-exempt. Exempt employees hold positions classified as *executive, administrative, professional,* or *outside sales,* to which employers are not required to pay overtime. Non-exempt employees must be paid overtime under the Fair Labor Standards Act.

In base pay programs, employers often categorize jobs into groupings that tie the FLSA status and the method of payment together:

▶ Hourly
▶ Salaried non-exempt
▶ Salaried exempt

Hourly jobs require employers to pay overtime to comply with the FLSA. Employees in positions classified as *salaried non-exempt* are covered by the overtime provisions of the FLSA and therefore must be paid overtime. Salaried non-exempt positions sometimes include secretarial, clerical, and salaried blue-collar positions. *Salaried exempt* employees are not required by the FLSA to be paid overtime, although some organizations have implemented policies to pay a straight rate for extensive hours of overtime. For instance, some hospitals pay pharmacists extra using a special rate for extra hours worked during staffing emergencies.

Three major factors determine whether an individual holds an exempt position:

1. Discretionary authority for independent action
2. Percentage of time spent performing routine, manual, or clerical work
3. Earnings level

Figure 12-6 shows the impact of these factors on each type of exemption. Note that earnings levels are basically meaningless, because they have not changed in years despite increases in the minimum wage. These inconsistencies result from political disagreement among employers, unions, legislators, and federal regulators.

Computer-Related Occupations   Due to the growth of information systems and computer jobs, a special category of professionals was added in 1990. For those working in computer-related occupations that are paid at least the equivalent of $27.63 per hour on a salaried basis, the FLSA does not require overtime pay. Because the wage level in this case is set at approximately $58,000 per year, a limited number of jobs and individuals are affected.[13] For all other occupations, the FLSA has no set dollar level above which overtime is not required.

Overtime Provisions   The FLSA establishes overtime pay requirements. Its provisions for *healthcare organizations* set overtime pay at one and one-half times the regular pay rate for all hours in excess of 40 per week or 8 hours in a day or 80 hours in a pay period.

The most difficult part of compliance with the act for healthcare organizations is distinguishing who is and is not exempt. Some recent costly settlements have prompted more workers to sue for overtime pay.

The problem for most healthcare organizations that struggle with determining who is and is not exempt revolves around the issue of scheduling variability. Non-exempt employees must be paid for *all* hours worked. If the hours worked are in excess of 40 hours in one week, for those employees paid on a 40-hour basis, or in excess of 8 in a day (or 80 in a pay period, for those employees paid on an 8/80 basis), they must receive overtime wages. Exempt employees may be required to work significant amounts of time over a standard 40-hour week. Yet they cannot be compensated on an hourly basis and remain in an exempt status.

Consequently, many healthcare employees struggle with the need to provide adequate coverage and pay their exempt employees consistent with requirements of the act. This results in the treatment of what would otherwise be an exempt position (e.g., RN, pharmacist, occupational therapist) as non-exempt to avoid staffing problems and wage and hour compliance issues.[14]

Compensatory Time Off   Often called *comp-time*, compensatory time off is given in lieu of payment for extra time worked. However, unless it is given to non-exempt employees at the rate of one and one-half time for the hours worked over a 40-hour week, comp-time is illegal in the private sector. Also, comp-time cannot be carried over from one pay period to another.

FIGURE 12-6   Wage/Hour Status Under Fair Labor Standards Act

Exemption Category	A Discretionary Authority	B Percent of Time	C Earning Levels
Executive	1. Primary duty is managing 2. Regularly directs work of at least two others 3. Authority to hire/fire or recommend these	1. Must spend 20% or less time doing clerical, manual, routine work (less than 40% in retail or service establishments)	2. Paid salary at $155/wk or $250/wk if meets A1-A2
Administrative	1. Primarily responsible for nonmanual or office work related to management policies 2. Regularly exercises discretion and independent judgment and makes important decisions 3. Regularly assists executives and works under general supervision	1. Must spend 20% or less time doing clerical, manual, routine work (less than 40% in retail or service establishments)	1. Paid salary at $155/wk or $250/wk if meets A1-A2
Professional	1. Performs work requiring knowledge of an advanced field *or* creative and original artistic work *or* works as a teacher in educational system 2. Must do work that is predominantly intellectual and varied	1. Must spend 20% or less time doing nonprofessional work	1. Paid salary at least $170/wk or $250/wk if meets A1
Outside Sales	1. Customarily works away from employer site *and* 2. Sells tangible or intangible items *or* 3. Obtains orders or contracts for services	1. Must spend 20% or less time doing work other than outside selling	2. No salary test

FIGURE 12-7   **The IRS Test for Employees and Independent Contractors**

AN EMPLOYEE	AN INDEPENDENT CONTRACTOR
▶ Must comply with instructions about when, where, and how to work ▶ Renders services personally ▶ Has a continuing relationship with an employer ▶ Usually works on the premises of the employer ▶ Normally is furnished materials, and other equipment by the employer ▶ Can be fired by an employer ▶ Can quit at any time without incurring liability	▶ Can hire, supervise, and pay assistants ▶ Generally can set own hours ▶ Usually is paid by the job or on straight commission ▶ Has made a significant investment in facilities or equipment ▶ Can make a profit or suffer a loss ▶ May provide services to two or more unrelated persons or firms at the same time ▶ Makes services available to the public

Source: U.S. Internal Revenue Service.

Independent Contractor Regulations

The growing use of contingent workers by many organizations has focused attention on another group of legal regulations—those identifying the criteria that independent contractors must meet. Figure 12-7 illustrates some of the key differences between an employee and an independent contractor.

Classifying someone as an independent contractor rather than an employee offers two primary advantages for the employer. First, the employer does not have to pay Social Security, unemployment, or workers' compensation costs. These additional payroll levies may add 10% or more to the costs of hiring the individual as an employee. Second, if the person is classified as an employee and is doing a job considered non-exempt under the federal Fair Labor Standards Act, then the employer may be responsible for overtime pay at the rate of time-and-a-half for any week in which the person works more than 40 hours. Most other federal and state entities rely on the criteria for independent contractor status identified by the Internal Revenue Service (IRS).

Equal Pay and Pay Equity

Various legislative efforts address the issue of wage discrimination on the basis of gender. The Equal Pay Act of 1963 applies to both men and women and prohibits using different wage scales for men and women performing substantially the same jobs. Pay differences can be justified on the basis of merit (better performance), seniority (longer service), quantity or quality of work, or factors other than gender. Similar pay must be given for jobs requiring equal skills, equal effort, or equal responsibility or jobs done under similar working conditions.

Pay equity is an issue different from equal pay for equal work. Pay equity is the concept (similar to comparable worth) that the pay for all jobs requiring comparable knowledge, skills, and abilities should be the same even if job duties and market rates differ significantly. States with such laws for public-sector jobs include Hawaii, Iowa, Maine, Michigan, Minnesota, Montana, Ohio, Oregon, Washington, and Wisconsin. Such an approach in Canada has been deemed unsuccessful.[15] However, simply showing the existence of pay differences for jobs that are different has not been sufficient to prove discrimination in court in most cases.[16]

State Laws

Many state and municipal government bodies have enacted modified versions of federal compensation laws. If a state has a higher minimum wage than that set under the Fair Labor Standards Act, the higher figure becomes the required minimum wage.

Garnishment Laws

Garnishment of an employee's wage occurs when a creditor obtains a court order that directs an employer to set aside a portion of one employee's wages to pay a debt owed a creditor. Regulations passed as part of the Consumer Credit Protection Act established limitations on the amount of wages that can be garnished and restricted the right of employers to discharge employees whose pay is subject to a single garnishment order. All fifty states have laws applying to wage garnishments.

DEVELOPMENT OF A BASE PAY SYSTEM

As Figure 12-8 on the next page shows, development of a base wage and salary system assumes that accurate job descriptions and job specifications are available. The job descriptions then are used for *job evaluation* and *pay surveys*. These activities are designed to ensure that the pay system is both internally equitable and externally competitive. The data compiled in these two activities are used to design *pay structures*, including *pay grades* and minimum-to-maximum *pay ranges*. After the development of pay structures, individual jobs must be placed in the appropriate pay grades and employees' pay adjusted based on length of service and performance. Finally, the pay system must be monitored and updated.

Job Evaluation

Job evaluation provides a systematic basis for determining the relative worth of jobs within an organization.[17] It flows from the job analysis process and relies on job descriptions and job specifications. In a job evaluation, every job is examined and ultimately priced according to the following features:

▶ Relative importance of the job
▶ Knowledge, skills, and abilities (KSAs) needed to perform the job
▶ Difficulty of the job

Healthcare employers want their employees to perceive their pay as appropriate in relation to pay for jobs performed by others.[18] Because jobs vary

FIGURE 12-8 **Compensation Administration Process**

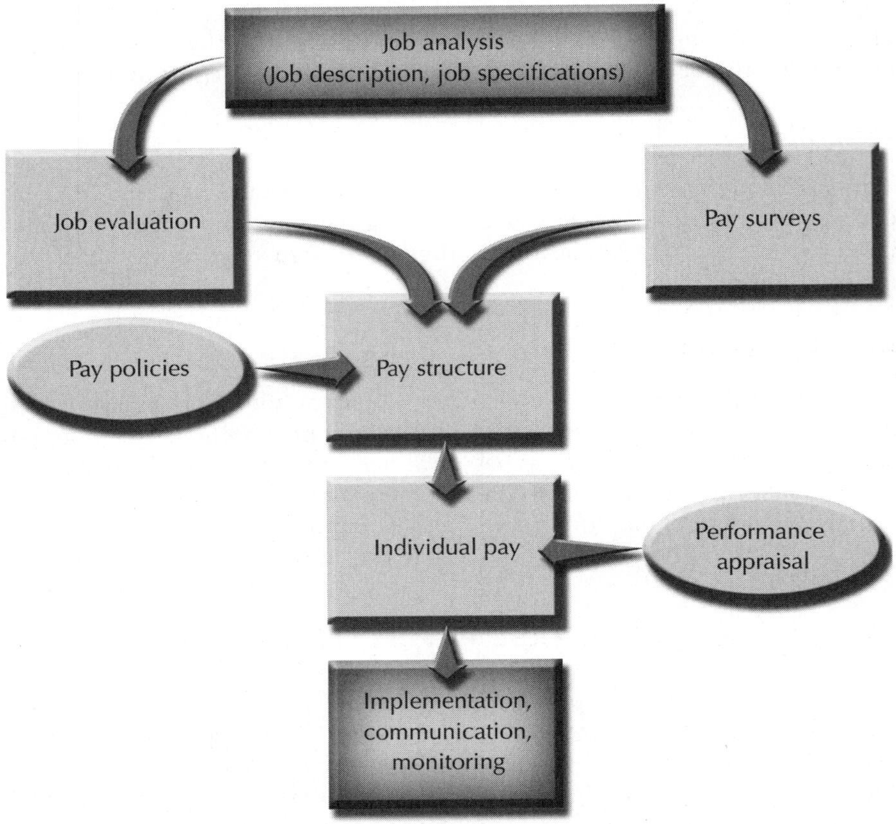

```
                    Job analysis
              (Job description, job specifications)
```

Job evaluation   Pay surveys

Pay policies   Pay structure

                      Individual pay   Performance
                                              appraisal

                   Implementation,
                   communication,
                   monitoring

widely in healthcare organizations, it is particularly important to identify **benchmark jobs**—jobs that are found in other healthcare organizations and performed by several individuals who have similar duties that are relatively stable and that require similar KSAs. For example, benchmark jobs commonly used in a hospital patient financial services department are biller, collector, and cash application clerk. Benchmark jobs are used with the job evaluation methods discussed here because they provide "anchors" against which unique jobs can be evaluated.

Given the diversity of healthcare organizations, there are a variety of methods used to determine internal job worth through job evaluation. All methods have the same general objective, but they differ in complexity and means of measurement. Regardless of the method used, the intent is to develop a usable, measurable, and realistic system to determine compensation in an organization:

▶ *Ranking Method*—The ranking method is one of the simplest methods of job evaluation. It places jobs in order, ranging from highest to lowest in value to the organization. The entire job is considered rather than the individual components. Several different methods of ranking are available, but all present problems.

▶ *Classification Method*—In the classification method of job evaluation, descriptions of each class of jobs are written, and then each job in the organization is put into a grade according to the class description it best matches.

▶ *Point Method*—The point method, the most widely used job evaluation method, is more sophisticated than the ranking and classification methods. It breaks down jobs into various compensable factors and places weights, or *points,* on them. A compensable factor identifies a job value commonly present throughout a group of jobs. Consequently, the compensable factors used and the weights assigned must reflect the nature of the jobs under study.[19] A special type of point method used by a consulting firm, the Hay Group, has three major factors. The three factors and their subfactors are identified as follows:

KNOW-HOW	PROBLEM SOLVING	ACCOUNTABILITY
▶ Functional expertise	▶ Environment	▶ Freedom to act
▶ Managerial skills	▶ Challenge	▶ Impact of end results
▶ Human relations		▶ Magnitude

▶ *Factor Comparison*—The factor-comparison method is a quantitative and quite complex combination of the ranking and point methods. It involves first determining the benchmark jobs in an organization, selecting compensable factors, and ranking all benchmark jobs factor by factor. Next, a comparison of jobs to market rates for benchmark jobs results in the assignment of monetary values for each factor. The final step is to evaluate all other jobs in the organization by comparing them with the benchmark jobs.

▶ *Integrated and Computerized Job Evaluation*—Increasingly, organizations are linking the components of wage and salary programs through computerized and statistical techniques. Using a bank of compensable factors, employers can select those factors most relevant for the different job families in the organization. Because of the advanced expertise needed to develop and computerize the integrated systems, management consultants are the primary source for them. These systems really are less a separate method and more an application of information technology and advanced statistics to the process of developing a wage and salary program.

Legal Issues and Job Evaluation

Employers usually view evaluating jobs to determine rates of pay as a separate issue from selecting individuals for those jobs or taking disciplinary action against individuals. Because job evaluation affects the employment relationship, specifically the pay of individuals, it involves legal issues that must be addressed.

Job Evaluation and the Americans with Disabilities Act (ADA)   The Americans with Disabilities Act (ADA) requires employers to identify the essential functions of a job. However, all facets of jobs are examined during a job evaluation. For example, a materials management job in a community hospital requires a distribution clerk to stock and distribute stock carts to the patient units. Every two hours the clerk must deliver a cart, which might weigh 100 pounds or more, to a unit. The movement of the cart probably is not an essential function. But if job evaluation considers the physical demands associated with pushing the cart, then the points assigned may be different from the points assigned if only the essential functions are considered.

Job Evaluation and Gender Issues   Critics have charged that traditional job evaluation programs place less weight on knowledge, skills, and working conditions for many female-dominated jobs in office and clerical areas than on the same factors for male-dominated jobs in craft and manufacturing areas. As discussed earlier, advocates of pay equity view the disparity in pay between men's jobs and women's jobs as evidence of gender discrimination. These advocates also have attacked typical job evaluations as being gender biased. Employers counter that because they base their pay rates heavily on external equity comparisons in the labor market, they are simply reflecting rates the market economy sets for jobs and workers, rather than engaging in discrimination. Undoubtedly, with further court decisions, government actions, and research, job evaluation activities will face more pressures to address gender differences.

Pay Surveys

Another part of building a pay system is surveying the pay that other healthcare organizations provide for similar jobs. A **pay survey** is a collection of data on compensation rates for workers performing similar jobs in other organizations. An employer may use surveys conducted by other organizations, or it may decide to conduct its own survey.[20]

Whether available electronically or in printed form, national surveys on many jobs and industries come from the U.S. Department of Labor, Bureau of Labor Statistics, and through national trade associations.[21] Many healthcare employers participate in wage surveys sponsored by various healthcare trade associations, such as the Medical Group Management Association (MGMA).

Properly using surveys from other sources requires that certain questions be addressed:

▶ *Participants*—Is the survey a realistic sample of those employers with whom the organization competes for employees?

▶ *Broad-based*—Is the survey balanced so that organizations of varying sizes, industries, and locales are included?

▶ *Timeliness*—How current are the data (determined by the date when the survey was conducted)?

▶ *Methodology*—How established is the survey, and how qualified are those who conducted it?

▶ *Job Matches*—Does it contain job summaries so that appropriate matches to job descriptions can be made?

The results of the pay survey usually are made available to those participating in the survey in order to gain their cooperation. Most surveys specify confidentiality, and data are summarized to assure anonymity. Different job levels often are included, and the pay rates are presented both in overall terms and on a regional basis to reflect regional pay differences. Figure 12-9 depicts a section of a clinic survey on the next page.

Legal Issues and Pay Surveys

One reason for employers to use outside consultants to conduct pay surveys is to avoid charges that the employers are attempting "price-fixing" on wages. The federal government has filed suit in the past, alleging that by sharing wage data, employers may be attempting to hold wages down artificially, in violation of the Sherman AntiTrust Act.

A key case involved the Utah Society for Healthcare Human Resource Administration (USHHRA) and nine hospitals in the Salt Lake City area. Although the USHHRA was not found guilty of any wrongdoing, a consent decree resulted that prohibited all healthcare facilities in Utah from designing, developing, or conducting a wage survey. The hospitals can participate in surveys conducted by independent third-party firms only if privacy safeguards are met. Specifically, only aggregate data that are summarized may be provided, and no data from an individual firm may be identified. As a result, it is likely that fewer healthcare firms will conduct their own surveys, and the use of outside consultants to do pay surveys will continue to grow.

Different Pay Structures

In organizations that have a number of different job families, pay survey data may reveal different levels of pay resulting from market factors that may lead to the establishment of several different pay structures, rather than just one structure. Examples of some common pay structures include: (1) hourly and salaried; (2) office, technical, professional, and managerial; (3) clinical allied health and support; and (4) clerical, information technology, professional, supervisory, management, and executive. The nature and culture of the organization are considerations for determining how many and which pay structures to have.

Establishing Pay Grades   In the process of establishing a pay structure, organizations use **pay grades** to group individual jobs having approximately the same job worth. Although no set rules govern establishing pay grades, some

FIGURE 12-9 Sample Survey Data
Average Hourly Salaries and Salary Administration Program Pay Ranges for Selected Clinic Positions

POSITION	REGION	RANGE OF REPORTED HOURLY RATES	INCUMBENTS				PAY RANGE—SALARY ADMINISTRATION PROGRAM AVERAGES		
			AVERAGE HOURLY RATE	NUMBER OF EMPLOYEES	NUMBER OF FULL TIME EQUIVALENTS	NUMBER OF ORGANIZATIONS REPORTING INCUMBENT RATES	MINIMUM HOURLY RATE	MIDPOINT HOURLY RATE	MAXIMUM HOURLY RATE
Medical Records Clerk	All	7.00–16.33	9.53	571	433.14	36	8.57	10.42	11.92
	Metro	7.25–16.33	10.83	168	134.55	23	9.63	11.66	13.58
	Non Metro	7.00–16.00	8.97	403	289.59	13	7.95	9.60	10.95
	Central	7.15–11.60	8.76	81	67.15	6	7.76	9.45	10.59
Medical Secretary/ Transcriptionist	All	8.40–19.16	12.15	398	349.04	33	10.32	12.51	14.40
	Metro	9.50–19.16	14.37	86	73.43	18	12.32	14.74	16.62
	Non Metro	8.40–15.60	11.56	312	275.61	15	9.32	11.28	13.29
	Central	8.40–15.50	11.56	90	81.65	9	9.07	11.40	12.92
LPN	All	7.00–24.00	13.21	689	569.10	36	11.29	13.62	15.65
	Metro	11.73–24.00	14.89	170	147.99	19	13.55	15.82	18.01
	Non Metro	7.00–18.56	12.69	519	421.11	17	10.48	12.52	14.59
	Central	9.51–18.56	12.38	256	208.75	9	10.64	12.77	14.60

Source: Used with permission, Langan and Flynn, LLC, St. Paul, MN.

overall suggestions can be useful. Generally, from eleven to seventeen grades are used in small and medium-sized healthcare organizations with fewer than five hundred employees.

Broadbanding   **Broadbanding** is the practice of using fewer pay grades with much broader ranges than in traditional compensation systems. Combining many grades into these broadbands is designed to encourage horizontal movement and therefore more skill acquisition.[22]

The primary reasons for broadbanding are: (1) creating more flexible organizations, (2) encouraging competency development, and (3) emphasizing career development. However, broadbanding is not appropriate for every healthcare organization, as seen in survey results that found only about 15 percent of employers use broadbanding.[23] Many healthcare organizations operate in a relatively structured manner, and the flexibility associated with broadbanding is not consistent with the traditional culture in many healthcare organizations.

Pay Ranges

The pay range for each pay grade also must be established. Using the market line as a starting point, the employer can determine minimum and maximum pay levels for each pay grade by making the market line the midpoint line of the new pay structure.[24] For example, in a particular pay grade, the maximum value may be 20% above the midpoint located on the market line and the minimum value 20% below it.

As Figure 12-10 shows, a smaller minimum-to-maximum range should be used for lower-level jobs than for higher-level jobs, primarily because employees in lower-level jobs tend to stay in them for shorter periods of time and have greater promotion possibilities. For example, a clerk-typist might advance to the position of secretary or word-processing operator. In contrast, a pharmacist likely would have fewer possibilities for upward movement in an organization. However, using the same percentage range at all levels can make administration of a pay system easier in small firms. If broadbanding is used, then much wider ranges, often exceeding 100%, may be used.

Compensation experts recommend having an overlap between grades. This structure means that an experienced employee in a lower grade can be paid more than a less-experienced employee in a job in the next pay grade. With pay

FIGURE 12-10   **Typical Pay Range Widths for Healthcare Positions**

TYPES OF JOBS	RANGE ABOVE MINIMUM	% AROUND MIDPOINT
Executives	50%–70%	+ or –20–25%
Mid-Management/Professionals	40%–50%	+ or –16–20%
Technicians/Skilled Craft & Clerical	30%–40%	+ or –13–16%
General Clerical/Others	25%–35%	+ or –11–15%

grade overlap, an individual in the higher-grade job, for example grade 4, may be paid less than someone in a grade 3 job, but has more room for pay progression. Thus, over time the pay of a person in the grade 4 job may surpass the pay of a person in grade 3, who may "top out" because of the pay grade 3 maximum. Compensation experts have suggested that the same monetary amounts can appear in as many as four different pay grades.

Once pay grades and ranges have been computed, then the current pay of employees must be compared to the draft ranges. If the pay of a significant number of employees falls outside the ranges, then a revision of the pay grades and ranges may be needed. Also, once costing and budgeting scenarios are run in order to assess the financial impact of the new pay structures, then pay policy decisions about market positioning may have to be revised, by either lowering or raising the ranges.

Individual Pay

Once managers have determined pay ranges, they can set the pay for specific individuals. Setting a range for each pay grade gives flexibility by allowing individuals to progress within a grade instead of having to be moved to a new grade each time they receive a raise. A pay range also allows managers to reward the better-performing employees while maintaining the integrity of the pay system.

Rates Out of Range

Regardless of how well constructed a pay structure is, there usually are a few individuals whose pay is lower than the minimum or higher than the maximum. These situations occur most frequently when organizations that have had an informal pay system develop a new, more formalized one.

Red-Circled Employees   A **red-circled employee** is an incumbent who is paid above the range set for the job. For example, assume that an employee's current pay is $12.00 per hour but the pay range for that grade is $6.94 to $10.06. The person would be red circled. Over time, management would attempt to bring the employee's rate into grade.

Several approaches can be used to bring a red-circled person's pay into line. Although the fastest way would be to cut the employee's pay, that approach is not recommended and is seldom used. Instead, the employee's pay may be frozen until the pay range can be adjusted upward to get the employee's pay rate back into the grade. Another approach is to give the employee a small lump-sum payment but not adjust the pay rate when others are given raises; this is referred to as a red-circled bonus.

Green-Circled Employees   An individual whose pay is below the range is a **green-circled employee.** Promotion is a major cause of this situation. Generally, it is recommended that the green-circled individual receive pay increases to get them to the pay grade minimum fairly rapidly. Frequent increases should be considered if the increase to minimum would be substantial.

Pay Compression

One major problem many healthcare employers face is **pay compression,** which occurs when the pay differences among individuals with different levels of experience and performance becomes small. Pay compression occurs for a number of reasons, but the major one involves situations in which labor market pay levels increase more rapidly than current employees' pay adjustments. Such situations are prevalent in many occupational areas (e.g., the information technology field), depending on specific market conditions.[25]

In response to competitive market shortages of particular job skills, managers occasionally may have to deviate from the priced grades to hire people with scarce skills. For example, suppose the worth of a radiological special procedures technician's job is evaluated at $48,000 to $58,000 annual salary in a hospital, but qualified individuals are in short supply and other employers are paying annual salaries of $70,000. The hospital must pay the higher rate to attract new technicians. Suppose also that several technicians who have been with the hospital for several years started at $48,000 and have received 6% increase each year. These current employees will still be making less than salaries paid to attract and retain new technicians from outside with less experience, causing a significant pay compression issue between the current employees and the new hires.

ISSUES INVOLVING PAY INCREASES

Decisions about pay increases often are critical ones in the relationships among employees, their managers, and the organization. Individuals express expectations about their pay and about how much increase is "fair," especially in comparison with the increases received by other employees. There are several ways to determine pay increases.

Pay Adjustment Matrix

Many employers profess to have a pay system based on performance. But relying on performance appraisal information for making a pay adjustment assumes that the appraisals are accurate and done well, which is not always the case. Consequently, some system for integrating appraisals and pay changes must be developed and applied equally. Often, this integration is done through the development of a **pay adjustment matrix,** or *salary guide chart.* Using pay adjustment matrices, adjustments are based in part on a person's **compa-ratio,** which is the pay level divided by the midpoint of the pay range. To illustrate from Figure 12-11 on the next page, the compa-ratio for two employees is:

$$\text{Employee A} = \frac{\$25.00 \text{ (current pay)}}{\$24.00 \text{ (midpoint)}} \times 100 = 104$$

$$\text{Employee B} = \frac{\$22.00 \text{ (current pay)}}{\$24.00 \text{ (midpoint)}} \times 100 = 92$$

FIGURE 12-11 Performance-Based Pay-Adjustment Matrix

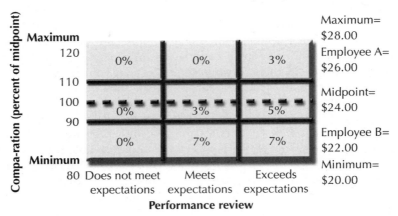

Such charts can facilitate a person's upward movement in an organization, which depends on the person's performance, as rated in an appraisal, and on the person's position in the pay range, which has some relation to experience as well. Notice that as employees move up the pay range, they must exhibit higher performance to obtain the same percentage raise as those lower in the range performing at the "meets performance expectations" level. This approach is taken because the firm is paying above the market midpoint but receiving only satisfactory performance rather than above expectations performance. Charts can be constructed to reflect the specific pay-for-performance policy and philosophy in an organization.

Seniority

Seniority, or time spent in the organization or on a particular job, can be used as the basis for pay increases. Many employers have policies that require a person to be employed for a certain length of time before being eligible for pay increases. Pay adjustments based on seniority often are set as automatic steps once a person has been employed the required length of time, although performance must be at least satisfactory in many nonunion systems.

Step systems, which use pay increases based solely on the attainment of a designated period of employment (typically 2,080 hours) continue to be a popular method of awarding pay increases in healthcare organizations, especially in states where there is significant unionization of healthcare employees. Figure 12-12 depicts a step system. Each step represents the pay adjustment for employees as they attain one full-time equivalent year of employment (2,080 hours), after their first 6 months.

FIGURE   1 2 - 1 2   Step System

	GRADE 1
	STEP
Start:	$ 8.00
6 mos:	8.24
Step 1:	8.49
Step 2:	8.74
Step 3:	9.00
Step 4:	9.27
Step 5:	9.55
Step 6:	9.84
Step 7:	10.14
Step 8:	10.44
Step 9:	10.75
Step 10:	11.07

Cost-of-Living Adjustments (COLA)

A common pay-raise practice is the use of a *standard raise* or **cost-of-living adjustment (COLA).** Giving all employees a standard percentage increase enables them to maintain the same real wages in a period of economic inflation. Often, these adjustments are tied to changes in the consumer price index (CPI) or some other general economic measure. However, numerous studies have revealed that the CPI overstates the actual cost of living.

Unfortunately, some healthcare employers give across-the-board raises and call them **merit raises,** which they are not. If all employees get the same increase, it is legitimately viewed as an across-the-board adjustment that has little to do with good performance. For this reason, employers should reserve the term *merit* for any amount above the standard raise, and they should state clearly which amount is for performance and which is the COLA adjustment.

Lump-Sum Increases (LSI)

Most employees who receive pay increases, either for merit or seniority, first have their base pay adjusted and then receive an increase in the amount of their regular monthly or weekly paycheck. For example, an employee who makes $15.00 per hour and then receives a 3% increase will move to $15.45 per hour.

In contrast, a lump-sum increase (LSI) is a one-time payment of all or part of a yearly pay increase. The pure LSI approach does not increase the base pay. Therefore, in this example the person's base pay remains at $15.00 per hour. If an LSI of 3% is granted, then the person receives $936.00 (45¢ per hour for 2,080 working hours in the year.) However, the base rate remains at $15.00 per hour, which slows down the progression of the base wages. It also allows for the amount of the "lump" to be varied, without having to continually raise the base rate. Some organizations place a limit on how much of a merit increase can be taken as a lump-sum payment. Other organizations split the lump sum into two checks, each representing one-half of the year's pay raise.

EXECUTIVE COMPENSATION

As Figure 12-13 shows, the common components of executive compensation are salaries, annual bonuses, long-term incentives, supplemental benefits, and perquisites.

Executive Salaries

Salaries of executives vary by type of job, size of organization, region of the country, and industry. On average, salaries make up about 40% to 60% of the typical top executive's annual compensation total.

Executive Bonus Plans

Executive performance may be difficult to determine, but bonus compensation must reflect some performance measures if it is to be meaningful. As an example, a major medical center ties annual bonuses for senior managers to cost reductions and employee retention. The bonuses have amounted to as much as 25% of each senior manager's base salary.

FIGURE 12-13 **Executive Compensation Components**

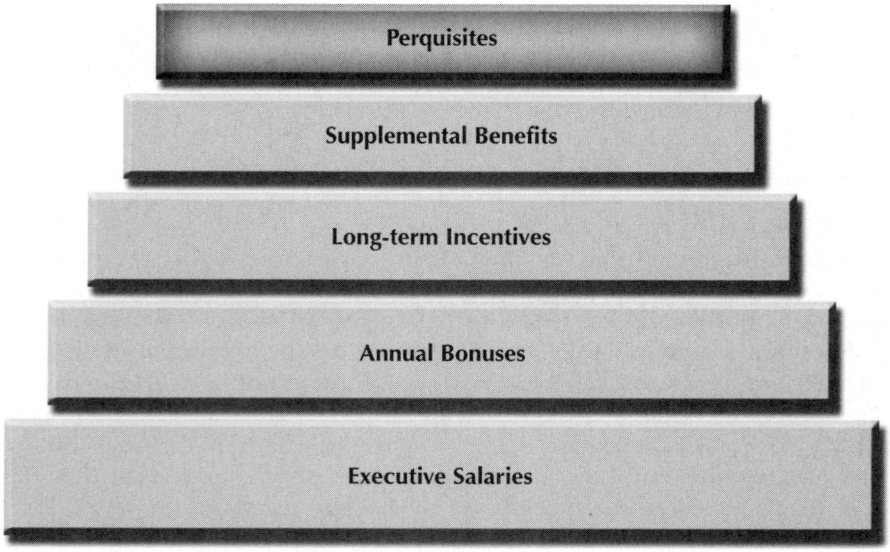

Perquisites

Supplemental Benefits

Long-term Incentives

Annual Bonuses

Executive Salaries

Bonuses for executives can be determined in several ways. A discretionary system whereby bonuses are awarded based on the judgments of the Chief Executive Officer and the Board of Directors is one way. However, the absence of formal, measurable targets detracts significantly from this approach. Also, as noted, bonuses can be tied to specific measures, such as return on investment, earnings per share, or net profits before taxes. More complex systems create bonus pools and thresholds above which bonuses are computed. Whatever method is used, it is important to describe it so that executives trying to earn bonuses understand the plan; otherwise, the incentive effect will be diminished.[26]

Performance Incentives: Long Term versus Short Term

Performance-based incentives attempt to tie executive compensation to the long-term growth and success of the organization. However, whether the emphasis is really on the long term or merely represents a series of short-term rewards is controversial. Short-term rewards based on quarterly or annual performance may not result in the kind of long-run-oriented decisions necessary for the organization to continue to do well.[27]

Benefits for Executives

As with benefits for non-executive employees, executive benefits may take several forms, including traditional retirement, health insurance, vacations, and others. However, executive benefits may include some items that other employees do not receive. For example, executive health plans with no co-payments and with no limitations on deductibles or physician choice are popular among small and middle-sized businesses. Organizational-owned life insurance on the life of the executive is popular and pays both the executive's estate and the company in the event of death. Trusts of various kinds may be designed by the organization to help the executive deal with estate issues. Deferred compensation offers another possible means of helping executives with tax liabilities caused by incentive compensation plans.

Executive Perquisites

In addition to the regular benefits received by all employees, executives often receive benefits called perquisites. **Perquisites (perks)** are special executive benefits—usually noncash items. Perks help tie executives to organizations and demonstrate their importance to their companies. Many executives value the status enhancement of perks because these visible symbols of status allow executives to be seen as "very important person's (VIPs) both inside and outside their organizations. In addition, perks can offer substantial tax savings because many perks are not taxed as income.[28] Figure 12-14 lists some commonly used executive perks in the healthcare industry.

The history of executive compensation shows that a combination of events has created today's situation in the United States.[29] Strong demand, the tax structure, performance, and pay-for-performance notions have all contributed. Many

FIGURE 12-14   Common Executive Perks

healthcare organizations, especially large ones, administer executive compensation differently from compensation for lower-level employees. Healthcare executives—typically someone in the top two levels of an organization, such as Chief Executive Officer (CEO), Administrator, President, or Senior Vice-President—are paid very well. Pay for female executives continues to be less than pay for their male counterparts. Female executives earn about 45% less than that of men until adjusted for age and experience; and then nationally the gap shrinks to about 5% or less.[30]

Current Nature of Healthcare Executive Compensation

In most healthcare organizations, the Board is the major policy-setting entity. For publicly traded companies covered by federal regulatory agencies, such as the Securities and Exchange Commission (SEC), the Board must approve executive compensation packages. Even for many nonprofit organizations, Internal Revenue Service regulations require the Board to review and approve the compensation for top-level executives.

The **compensation committee of the board of directors** usually is a subgroup of the Board composed of Directors who are not officers of the firm. Compensation committees generally make recommendations to the Board of Directors on overall pay policies, salaries for top officers, supplemental compensation such as bonuses, and additional perquisites for executives.

Determining "Reasonableness" of Executive Compensation

The reasonableness of executive compensation is often justified by comparison to compensation market surveys, but these surveys usually provide a range of compensation data that requires interpretation. Various questions have been suggested for determining if executive pay is "reasonable" in a specific instance, including the following:

▶ Would another organization hire this person as an executive?
▶ How does the executive's compensation compare with that for executives in similar organizations in the industry?
▶ Is the executive's pay consistent with pay for other employees in the organization?

Boards must address the need to continually link organizational performance with variable pay rewards for executives and other employees. There is certainly more controversy about executive compensation in other industries, but healthcare Boards of Directors must also be mindful of the reasonableness of executive pay and benefits.

In the next chapter, the other key components of compensation (benefits and variable pay) are discussed. Consistent with the discussion in this chapter, the reader is encouraged to consider wages, benefits, and variable pay plans as interrelated components of a healthcare organization's total compensation program.

CASE

Dr. Clark, along with three of his physician colleagues, decided to leave their positions with Community Care Plan, a regional HMO, and start their own family medicine practice. Dr. Clark had been a department head with Community Care Plan and was confident that his knowledge of administration and HR would equip him well to quickly develop the policies and programs necessary to make the new practice successful. He knew one of his first challenges would be recruiting the necessary non-physician employees to staff his new organization.

The healthcare employment market where the new practice was to be located was very competitive due to the number of healthcare employers, especially for experienced clinical professionals such as RNs, X-ray technicians, and medical technologists. Many healthcare employers in the area paid individuals in these positions exclusively on a "market" basis. As an example, it was not unusual for pay increases to exceed 6% and to occur more than once a year for RNs.

Dr. Clark was fully aware of these pay issues and decided that the new practice required the most skilled and experienced staff he could recruit. This recruitment and staffing strategy was motivated by his and his colleagues' desire to quickly achieve high levels of patient referrals and grow the new practice to a positive margin in the first two years of operation.

Questions

1. Given Dr. Clark's organizational strategy of quickly establishing the new practice, what compensation approaches would you recommend?
2. What type of wage increase program would you recommend that would also be compatible with the compensation approaches?

END NOTES

1. J. Duncan Moore, Jr., "Healthcare Compensation Rises," *Modern Healthcare* (July 17, 2000), 29–36.
2. Paul W. Mulvey et al., "Rewards of Work," *WorldatWork Journal* (Third Quarter 2000), 6.
3. George T. Milkovich and Jennifer Stevens, "From Pay to Rewards: 100 Years of Change," *ACA Journal* (First Quarter 2000), 6–18.
4. Diane J. Gherson, "Getting the Pay Thing Right," *Workspan* (June, 2000), 47.

5. Gerald E. Ledford and Elizabeth J. Hawk, "Compensation Strategy," *ACA Journal* (First Quarter 2000), 28.

6. Demand Pushing Nurse Anesthetists' Salaries to All-time High," *Omaha World Herald* (June 2, 2002), CRI.

7. Bobette M. Gustafson, "Skill-based Pay Improves PFS Staff Recruitment, Retention and Performance," *Healthcare Financial Management* (January 2000), 62–63.

8. Jörgen Sandberg, "Understanding Competence at Work," *Harvard Business Review* (March 2001), 24.

9. B. L. Kirkman, "Understanding Why Team Members Won't Share," *Small Group Research* 31, no. 2, n.d. 175–209.

10. Talking About Pay," *The Wall Street Journal* (June 27, 2000), A1.

11. Kemba J. Dunham, "Employers Ease Bans on Workers Asking, 'What Do They Pay You?' " *The Wall Street Journal* (May 1, 2001), B10.

12. Simon J. Nodel, "Living with FLSA Not Easy," *Bulletin to Management* (June 22, 2000), 199.

13. Robert Greenberger, "More Web Workers Claim Unfair Labor Practices," *The Wall Street Journal* (October 17, 2000), B1; and Victoria Roberts, "Think All Computer Workers Are Exempt? Think Again," *Bulletin to Management* (November 30, 2000), 383.

14. Caryn Pass, "Dealing with the FLSA's Gray Areas," *HR Focus* (January 2002), 7, 10.

15. Charles Fay and Howard Risher, "Comparable Worth Redux?" *Workspan* (July 2000), 41.

16. Karen Caldwell, "Comparable Worth Comparisons Called Unfair," *HR News* (May 2001), 23.

17. Deborah M. Figart, "The Role of Job Evaluation in an Evolving Social Norm," *Journal of Economic Issues* (March 2000), 1.

18. Robert McNabb and Keith Whitfield, "Job Evaluation and High Performance Work Practices," *Journal of Management Studies* (March 2001), 293.

19. Robert L. Heneman, "Work Evaluation," *WorldatWork Journal* (Third Quarter 2001), 65–70.

20. "How Reliable are Online Salary Data?" *HR Focus* (October 2001), 5–6

21. Maury Gittleman and William Wiatrowski, "The BLS Wage Query System: A New Tool to Access Wage Data," *Monthly Labor Review* (October 2001), 22–27.

22. Dawne Shand, "Broadbanding the IT Worker," *Computer World* (October 9, 2000), 58.

23. "Broadbanding Pay Structures Do Not Receive Flat-Out Support," *Bulletin to Management* (January 13, 2000), 11.

24. David Westman, "A Story About STEP," *Workspan* (March 2001), 49.

25. Carol Hymowitz, "Managers Face Battle to Keep Salaries Fair in a Tight Job Market," *The Wall Street Journal* (March 21, 2000), B1.

26. M. C. Struman and J. C. Short, "Lump-Sum Bonus Satisfaction: Testing the Construct Validity of a New Pay Satisfaction Dimension," *Personnel Psychology,* (53 (2000) 673–700.

27. "Organizations Are Diversifying Executive Incentive Pay Plans," *Bulletin to Management* (October 19, 2000), 332.

28. "Benefits Policies," *Bulletin to Management* (June 22, 2000), 196.

29. Bruce Ellig, "CEO Pay: A 20th Century Review," *WorldatWork Journal* (Third Quarter 2000), 71–78.

30. Michael McKee, "History, Age Push at Ceiling," *The Denver Post* (October 21, 2000), C1.

13

The Management of Benefits and Variable Pay in Healthcare

Learning Objectives

After you have read this chapter, you should be able to:

▶ Describe the challenges that confront healthcare employers in providing benefits and variable pay programs.

▶ Discuss why healthcare employers must offer competitive benefits programs to their employees.

▶ Identify various types of benefits.

▶ Explain the role that healthcare HR professionals must play in administering benefits.

▶ Compare and contrast individual and team-based incentives.

Healthcare HR Insights

Benedictine Health System (BHS), like other healthcare organizations has recognized the importance of offering competitive benefits programs to its employees in order to increase the effectiveness of organizational recruitment and retention efforts. BHS has more than sixty operating entities, including hospitals and long-term care facilities throughout the U.S. Management began a comprehensive review of employee health insurance plans and 401(k) plans with the multiple goals of stabilizing their employees' costs, improving their employees access to care, and improving the administration of the plans.

BHS undertook the review after conducting a comprehensive analysis of its current plans, which were widely different for each of its facilities. As a product of its review, BHS developed the following objectives:

1. Contribute to the Benedictine Health System's strategic objective of being a "Healthcare Employer of Choice," which will increase BHS's ability to recruit and retain a skilled, motivated workforce.
2. Achieve the competitive advantages of integrated healthcare and retirement plans across the system, which will result in the following:
   - ▶ Consistency in the benefits offered across the BHS System
   - ▶ Consolidated administration of the plans
   - ▶ Increase in the number of employees actively participating in the plans
   - ▶ Increased participant satisfaction in the employee benefits plans
   - ▶ Enhanced ability to maintain the quality and regulatory compliance of the plans
   - ▶ Cost containment and reduction capabilities

BHS's Board of Trustees and executive management recognized the importance of effective employee benefits program administration. Accordingly, significant financial and HR resources have been dedicated to this initiative. BHS developed a project team facilitated by external consultants to study this initiative and to examine the marketplace for health plans and 401(k) service providers that could meet their needs.

As a result of the project team's efforts, BHS will ultimately have one healthcare insurance plan with three levels of coverages for their employees. In addition, the system will reduce the number of 401(k) plans and service providers. BHS corporate management is confident that the objectives of the integration initiative will be fully achieved over time.

The challenges of recruiting and retaining skilled workers have caused healthcare organizations to consider every aspect of their HR program. Significant opportunities exist in dealing with these challenges through effective management of employee benefits programs.

Source: Adapted with permission from the Benedictine Health System, Duluth, Minnesota.

Developing and implementing compensation strategies for healthcare organizations are critically important for healthcare HR professionals. Whether considered as a part of a total compensation approach or viewed separately, developing and implementing employee benefits and variable pay programs for healthcare organizations are challenging.

Healthcare employers provide employee benefits to their workers for being part of the organization. A **benefit** is a form of indirect compensation. Benefits often include retirement plans, vacations with pay, health insurance, educational assistance, and other programs.

Benefits clearly influence employees' decisions about which particular employer to work for, whether to stay or leave employment, and when they might retire. However, the unique characteristics of benefits sometimes make them difficult to administer. For example, government involvement in benefits continues to expand. Federal and state governments *require* that certain benefits be offered (Social Security, workers' compensation and unemployment insurance), and government regulate many of the non-required benefits as well (retirement, family leave, and flexible benefits).

Further, employees tend to take benefits for granted. For instance, so many organizations offer health insurance that employees expect it. However, benefits are also complex, and as a result, employees might not understand them, or in many cases might not even know what benefits exist. Yet benefits are costly to employers, averaging 30% to 40% of payroll costs over the past several years (for required and voluntary benefits together). These characteristics of benefits suggest that healthcare HR professionals should carefully consider the strategic role of benefits in their organizations.[1]

STRATEGIC PERSPECTIVES ON BENEFITS

For many healthcare employers, providing employee benefits represents a double-edged sword. On one side, employers know that in order to attract and retain employees with the necessary capabilities, they must offer appropriate benefits that can have significant expense to the overall operation of the organization.[2] On the other side, they know the importance of controlling or even cutting costs. Benefits comprise a significant part of the total compensation package offered to employees. Total compensation includes money paid directly (such as wages and salaries) and money paid indirectly (such as benefits). Too often, both managers and employees think of only wages and salaries as compensation and fail to consider the additional costs associated with benefits expenditures.

Total compensation costs for labor amounts to as much as 60% of total operating costs in healthcare organizations. Healthcare employers also find themselves on both sides of the healthcare insurance cost debate—as employers that must provide competitive benefit programs, including healthcare insurance, and as healthcare providers that must negotiate with the various insurance carriers for whom they receive reimbursement. There are times when this dual role provides competing objectives. Specifically, healthcare employers must negotiate for the most cost-effective coverage possible for their employees with their insurance company. As a providers, they must defend the highest possible reimbursement for the health services they provide, often with the same insurance companies.

Because of their sizable proportion of organizational costs, the compensation components of base pay, variable pay, and benefits require serious and realistic assessment and planning. Figure 13-1 shows where each benefit dollar typically is spent, on average, based on various surveys conducted regularly.

Goals for Benefits

Benefits should be looked at as part of the overall compensation strategy of the organization. For example organizations can choose to compete for employees by providing base compensation, variable pay, or benefits, or perhaps all three. Which approach is chosen depends on many factors, such as the competition, organizational life cycle, and corporate strategy.[3] For example, a new clinic may

FIGURE 13-1 Typical Benefit Dollar Spending

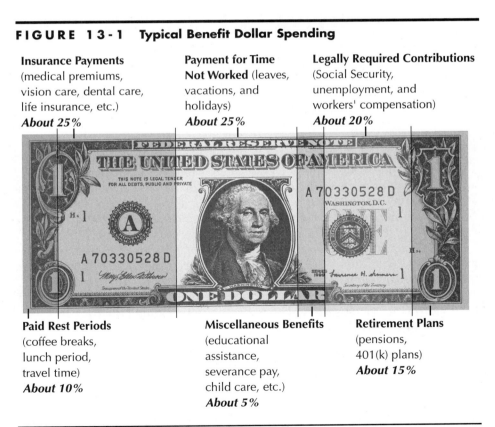

Insurance Payments
(medical premiums, vision care, dental care, life insurance, etc.)
About 25%

Payment for Time Not Worked (leaves, vacations, and holidays)
About 25%

Legally Required Contributions
(Social Security, unemployment, and workers' compensation)
About 20%

Paid Rest Periods
(coffee breaks, lunch period, travel time)
About 10%

Miscellaneous Benefits
(educational assistance, severance pay, child care, etc.)
About 5%

Retirement Plans
(pensions, 401(k) plans)
About 15%

Source: Based on information in Employee Benefits, 2000 Edition (Washington, D.C.: U.S. Chamber of Commerce, 2000.)

choose to have lower base pay, and use high variable incentives to attract new employees, but keep the cost of benefits as low as possible for a while. Or a hospital that hires predominately female employees might choose a family-friendly set of benefits including on-site childcare to attract good employees.[4]

Benefits Needs Analysis

Given the current challenges healthcare employers face in recruiting and retaining skilled workers, understanding what employees want in a benefit program is critical. A **benefits needs analysis** includes a comprehensive look at all aspects of benefits in an organization. Done periodically, such an analysis is more than simply deciding what benefits employees might want. In order to make certain that the mix of benefits is doing what it should, someone doing a benefits needs analysis might consider the following issues:

▶ How much total compensation, including benefits, should be provided?
▶ What part should benefits comprise of the total compensation of individuals?
▶ What expense levels are acceptable for each benefit offered?
▶ Why is each type of benefit offered?
▶ Which employees should be given or offered which benefits?
▶ What is being received by the organization in return for each benefit?
▶ How does having a comprehensive benefits package aid in minimizing turnover or maximizing recruiting and retention of employees?
▶ How flexible should the package of benefits be?

Funding Benefits

Total benefits costs can be funded both by contributions made by the employer and contributions made by the employee. If the employer fully subsidizes a benefit, the cost to the employee would be zero. But if an employer chooses to pay $650 per month toward an employee's health insurance premium while the employee pays $100, then the employee contributes to covering benefits costs.

Benefit plans also can be funded by purchasing insurance from an insurance provider. Premiums to be paid reflect the predicted claims and will be adjusted based on actual claims. Some large healthcare employers choose to "self-fund" and are their own insurers—they set aside money to cover benefits costs. Self-funding by large employers has been effective in containing the overall costs of providing this benefit.

TYPES OF BENEFITS

Employers offer some benefits to aid recruiting and retention, some because they are required to do so, and some because doing so reinforces the organization's HR philosophy.[5] For example, life insurance can be purchased at a better rate if the purchaser is a large employer that qualifies for a group rate. Further, tax laws provide beneficial tax treatment of some benefits for employees that

FIGURE 13-2   Types of Benefits

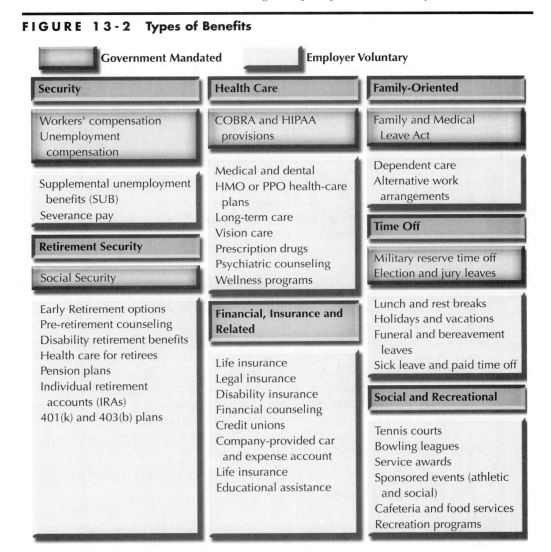

| Government Mandated | Employer Voluntary |

Security

Workers' compensation
Unemployment
  compensation

Supplemental unemployment
  benefits (SUB)
Severance pay

Retirement Security

Social Security

Early Retirement options
Pre-retirement counseling
Disability retirement benefits
Health care for retirees
Pension plans
Individual retirement
  accounts (IRAs)
401(k) and 403(b) plans

Health Care

COBRA and HIPAA
  provisions

Medical and dental
HMO or PPO health-care
  plans
Long-term care
Vision care
Prescription drugs
Psychiatric counseling
Wellness programs

**Financial, Insurance and
Related**

Life insurance
Legal insurance
Disability insurance
Financial counseling
Credit unions
Company-provided car
  and expense account
Life insurance
Educational assistance

Family-Oriented

Family and Medical
  Leave Act

Dependent care
Alternative work
  arrangements

Time Off

Military reserve time off
Election and jury leaves

Lunch and rest breaks
Holidays and vacations
Funeral and bereavement
  leaves
Sick leave and paid time off

Social and Recreational

Tennis courts
Bowling leagues
Service awards
Sponsored events (athletic
  and social)
Cafeteria and food services
Recreation programs

they would not get if purchased by individuals. Figure 13-2 shows the many different benefits offered, classified by type.

Government-Mandated Benefits

There are many **mandated benefits** that employers in the United States must provide to employees by law. Social Security and unemployment insurance are funded through a tax paid by the employer based on the employee's compensation. Workers' compensation laws exist in all states. In addition, under the Family and Medical Leave Act (FMLA), employers must offer unpaid leaves to employees with certain medical or family difficulties. Other mandated benefits are available through Medicare, which provides healthcare for individuals who are age 65 and over. It is funded in part by an employer tax through Social Security. The Consolidated Omnibus Budget Reconciliation Act (COBRA) and the Health Insurance Portability and Accountability Act (HIPAA) mandate that an employer continue healthcare coverage paid for by the employees after they leave the organization, and that most employees be able to obtain coverage if they were previously covered in a health plan.

Voluntary Benefits

Employers voluntarily offer other types of benefits in order to compete for and retain employees.[6] By offering additional benefits, organizations are recognizing the need to provide greater security and benefit support to workers with widely varied personal circumstances. The following sections describe the different types of benefits that were shown in Figure 13-2.

Temporary and Part-Time Employee Benefits

Workers who are not regular full-time employees sometimes do not receive benefits, but that is changing. In one survey, 49% of employers said they offer health insurance to part-timers. The contribution is half the amount provided for full-timers.[7] The healthcare industry has been a leader in offering part-time benefits. Due to the variability of staffing needs for many healthcare employers, part-time employees are an important resource to meet those needs. In some cases, healthcare employers have had to staff with multiple part-time employees when full-time employees have not been available. Providing part-time employees with some or all of the benefits offered to full-time employees are critical for their effect on recruitment and retention.

SECURITY BENEFITS

A number of benefits provide employee security. These benefits include some mandated by laws and others offered by employers voluntarily. The primary benefits found in most organizations include workers' compensation, unemployment compensation, and severance pay.

Workers' Compensation

Workers' compensation provides benefits to persons injured on the job. State laws require most employers to provide workers' compensation coverage by purchasing insurance from a private carrier or state insurance fund or by providing self-insurance.

The workers' compensation system requires employers to give cash benefits, medical care, and rehabilitation services to employees for injuries or illnesses occurring within the scope of their employment.[8] In exchange, employees give up the right of legal actions and awards. However, it is in the interests of both employers and employees to reduce workers' comp costs through safety and health programs.[9]

Unemployment Compensation

Another benefit required by law is unemployment compensation, established as part of the Social Security Act of 1935. Because each U.S. state operates its own unemployment compensation system, provisions differ significantly from state to state. Employers finance this benefit by paying a tax on the first $7,000 (or more, in 37 states) of annual earnings for each employee. The tax is paid to state and federal unemployment compensation funds. The percentage paid by individual employers is based on *experience rates,* which reflect the number of claims filed by workers who leave.

Severance Pay

Severance pay is a security benefit voluntarily offered by employers to some employees who lose their jobs. Severed employees may receive lump-sum severance payments if the employer terminates their employment.

Some healthcare employers have offered reduced amounts of cash severance and replaced some of the severance value by offering continued health insurance and outplacement assistance. Through *outplacement* assistance, ex-employees receive resume writing instruction, interviewing skills workshops, and career counseling.

RETIREMENT SECURITY BENEFITS

Few people set aside sufficient financial reserves to use when they retire; instead, they count on retirement benefits for a large part of their income. Except for some employers with fewer than one hundred employees, most employers offer some kind of retirement plan. Generally, private pensions make up a critical portion of income for people after retirement. With the baby-boomer generation in the United States closing in on retirement, pressures on such funds are likely to grow.

Retirement Benefits and Age Discrimination

As a result of a 1986 amendment to the Age Discrimination in Employment Act (ADEA), most employees cannot be forced to retire at a specific age. As a result, employers have had to develop different policies to comply with these regulations. In many employer pension plans, "normal retirement" is the age at which employees can retire and collect full pension benefits. Employers must decide whether individuals who continue to work past normal retirement age (perhaps age 65) should receive the full benefits package, especially pension credits. As possible future changes in Social Security may increase the age for full benefits past 65, modifications in policies are likely.

Early Retirement Many healthcare organizations offer pension-plan provisions for **early retirement** in order to give workers opportunities to leave their jobs. After spending twenty-five to thirty years working for the same employer, some individuals may wish to use their talents in other areas. Phased-in and part-time retirements offer an alternative to individuals and firms.

Some healthcare employers have used early-retirement buyout programs to cut back their workforces and reduce costs. Healthcare employers must take care to make these early retirement programs truly voluntary. Forcing workers to take advantage of an early retirement buyout program led to the passage of a federal law titled the Older Workers Benefit Protection Act (OWBPA).

Given the current state of healthcare staffing, some healthcare employers are rethinking incentives for early retirement. Some employers are moving to a concept referred to as **phased retirement,** defined as a program that helps employees retire in stages. These programs include options that allow employees to reduce the number of hours worked, take a different job, or be hired into a different capacity after retirement.[10]

Social Security

The Social Security Act of 1935, with its later amendments, established a system providing *old age, survivors, disability,* and *retirement benefits.* Administered by the federal government through the Social Security Administration, this program provides benefits to previously employed individuals or their dependents. Employees and employers share in the cost of Social Security through a tax on employees' wages or salaries.

Since the system's inception, Social Security payroll taxes have risen to 15.3% currently, with employees and employers each paying 7.65% up to an established maximum. In addition, Medicare taxes have more than doubled, to 2.9%. But benefits also became increasingly generous during the 1960s and 1970s.[11]

Pension Plans

Pension plans are retirement benefits established and funded by employers and employees. Organizations are not required to offer pension plans to employees, and they cover only 40% to 50% of U.S. workers for all employers. Smaller organizations offer them less often than large ones.

Traditional Pension Plans "Traditional" pension plans, where the employer makes the contributions and the employee gets a defined amount each month upon retirement, are no longer the norm. In these **defined-benefit plans** the employees' contributions are based on actuarial calculations that focus on the *benefits* to be received by employees after retirement and the *methods* used to determine such benefits. A defined-benefit plan gives the employee greater assurance of benefits and greater predictability in the amount of benefits that will be available for retirement.

In a **defined-contribution plan,** the employer makes an annual payment to an employee's pension account. The key to this plan is the *contribution rate;* employee retirement benefits depend on fixed contributions and employee earnings levels. Because these plans hinge on the investment returns on the previous contributions, which can vary according to profitability or other factors, employees' retirement benefits are somewhat less secure and predictable.

Cash Balance Plans   Healthcare employers are increasingly changing traditional pension plans to **cash balance plans,** a hybrid based on ideas from both defined-benefit and defined-contribution plans. Cash balance plans define retirement benefits for each employee not on years of service and salary, but by reference to a hypothetical account balance.

Employee Retirement Income Security Act (ERISA)   The widespread criticism of how pension plans were administered and how the pension funds were protected led to the passage of the Employee Retirement Income Security Act (ERISA) in 1974. The purpose of this law is to regulate private pension plans in order to assure that employees who put money into them or depend on a pension for retirement funds actually receive the money when they retire.

Pension Terms and Concepts

Pension plans can be either contributory or noncontributory. In a **contributory plan,** both the employee and the employer pay in money for pension benefits. In a **non-contributory plan,** the employer provides all the funds for pension benefits. As would be expected, employees and unions generally prefer the use of non-contributory plans.

Certain rights are attached to employee pension plans. Various laws and provisions have been passed to address the right of employees to receive benefits from their pension plans. Called **vesting,** it assures employees of a certain pension, provided they work a minimum number of years. If employees resign or are terminated before they have been employed for the required time, no pension rights accrue to them except the funds that they have contributed. If employees stay the allotted time, they retain their pension rights and receive the funds contributed by both the employer and themselves.

Another feature of some employee pensions is **portability.** In a portable plan, employees can move their pension benefit from one employer to another. A growing number of firms offer portable pension plans. Instead of requiring workers to wait until they retire to move their traditional pension plan benefits, the portable plan takes a different approach. Once workers have vested in a plan for a period of time, such as five years, they can transfer their fund balances to other retirement plans if they change jobs.

Individual Retirement Options

The availability of several retirement benefit options makes the pension area more complex. The most prominent options are individual retirement accounts (IRAs), 401(k) and 403(b) plans, and 457 plans. These plans may be available in addition to organizational pension plans.

Individual Retirement Accounts (IRAs)   An **individual retirement account (IRA)** is a special account in which an employee can set aside funds that will not be taxed until the employee retires. The major advantages of an IRA are the ability to accumulate extra retirement funds and the shifting of taxable income to later years, when total income—and therefore taxable income—is likely to be lower. Federal law changes in 1997 authorized a special type of IRA, called the *Roth IRA,* which likely will increase the usage of IRAs.

401(k), 403(b) and 457 Plans   **401(k), 403(b) and 457 plans** allow individual employees to elect to reduce their current pay by a certain percentage, which is then used to fund a retirement plan. The 403(b) and 457 plans are only available to non-profit employers, while 401(k) plans are available to both non-profit and for-profit organizations.

HEALTHCARE BENEFITS

Many healthcare employers provide a variety of healthcare and medical benefits, usually through insurance coverage. The most common plans cover medical, dental, prescription drug, and vision care expenses for employees and their dependents. Basic healthcare insurance to cover both normal and major medical expenses is also desired and expected by most employees. Dental insurance is also important to many employees. Some dental plans include orthodontic coverage, which is a major expense for some families. Some employer medical insurance plans also cover psychiatric counseling, but many do not.

The costs of healthcare insurance have continued to escalate at a rate well in excess of inflation for several decades. By the end of the 1990s, the rise in healthcare costs forced many employers to make concerted efforts to control medical premium increases and other healthcare costs. Estimates are that the average healthcare cost per employee is more than $5,500 per year.[12] Although those cost-control efforts were successful for a while, the rate of increases in health-benefits costs has turned up again, as Figure 13-3 indicates. Currently many healthcare employers, especially small group practices and clinics, are reconsidering their ability to offer health insurance for their employees.

Controlling Healthcare Benefits Costs

There are a number of different approaches that can be used to control healthcare benefit costs. Two approaches that focus specifically on what employers pay are increasing co-payments and using defined-contribution plans.

FIGURE 13-3   Increases in Healthcare Benefits Costs to Employers

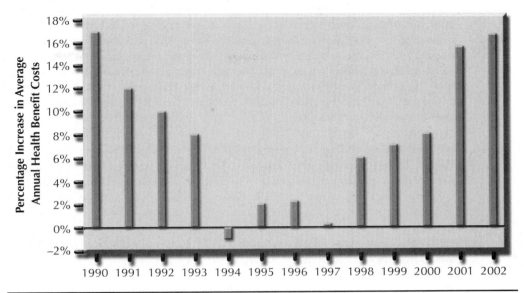

Source: U.S. Bureau of Labor Statistics, U.S. Department of Labor, 2002.

Co-Payment   In the past, many healthcare employers had *first-dollar coverage.* With this type of coverage, all expenses, from the first dollar of healthcare costs, were paid by the employee's insurance. Experts claim that when first-dollar coverage is included in a basic health plan, many employees see a doctor for every slight illness, which results in an escalation of the benefits costs.

As health insurance costs rise, employers have tried to shift some of those costs to employees. The **co-payment** strategy requires employees to pay a portion of the cost of both insurance premiums and medical care. Employers who have raised the deductible per person, from $50 to $250 have realized significant savings in healthcare expenses due to decreased employee usage of healthcare services.[13]

Defined-Contribution Plans for Health Benefits   Some employers have implemented *defined-contribution plans.* In this type of plan an employer makes a defined contribution of a set amount into each employee's "account." Then individual employees decide what type of healthcare coverage they want to select and pay for from the alternatives identified by the employer.

The advantage of such plans for employers is shifting more of the increases in healthcare benefits to be paid by employees.[14] However, as would be expected, negative reactions from employees may result. Therefore, implementing a defined-contribution plan for health benefits requires extensive planning and educational efforts with employees.[15]

Managed Care

Several other types of programs attempt to reduce healthcare costs paid by employers. **Managed care** consists of approaches that monitor and reduce medical costs through restrictions and market-system alternatives. These managed-care plans emphasize primary and preventative care, the use of specific providers who will charge lower prices, restrictions on certain kinds of treatment, and prices negotiated with hospitals and physicians. The most prevalent types of managed care are Preferred Provider Organizations (PPOs) and Health Maintenance Organizations (HMOs).

Preferred Provider Organizations (PPOs)   One type of managed care plan is the **preferred provider organization (PPO),** a healthcare provider that contracts with an employer or an employer group to provide healthcare services to employees at a competitive rate. Employees have the freedom to go to other providers if they want to pay the difference in costs.

Health Maintenance Organizations   A **health maintenance organization (HMO)** provides services for a fixed period on a prepaid basis. The HMO emphasizes both prevention and correction. An employer contracts with an HMO and its staff of physicians, medical personnel, and health facilities to furnish complete medical care. The employer pays a flat rate per enrolled employee or per family. The covered individuals may then go to the HMO for health care as often as they need to.

Utilization Review   Many employers, through their insurance company or healthcare plan administrator, find it useful to conduct some level of oversight of the type and frequency of the care provided to their employees and the charges related to that care. Unnecessary procedures or incorrect or improperly recorded care can result in higher costs to the employer. Consequently, both employers and insurance firms often require that medical work and charges be audited through a **utilization review.** This process may require a second opinion, review of procedures used, and review of charges for procedures done.

Wellness Programs   Wellness programs encourage employees to lead more healthy lifestyles. Often wellness programs include activities such as smoking-cessation classes, diet and nutrition counseling, exercise and physical fitness centers and programs, and health education.

Many healthcare employers also utilize programs to educate employees about healthcare costs and how to reduce them. Newsletters, formal classes, and many other approaches are all designed to help employees understand why healthcare costs are increasing and what they can do to control them. Some healthcare employers even are offering financial incentives to improve health habits. These programs reward employees who stop smoking, lose weight, and participate in exercise programs, among other activities.[16]

Healthcare Legislation

COBRA   Provisions Legal requirements in the **Consolidated Omnibus Budget Reconciliation Act (COBRA)** require that most employers (except churches and the federal government) with twenty or more employees offer extended healthcare coverage to the following groups:

▶ Employees who voluntarily quit, except those terminated for "gross misconduct"
▶ Widowed or divorced spouses and dependent children of former or current employees
▶ Retirees and their spouses whose healthcare coverage ends

Employers must notify eligible employees and/or their spouses and qualified dependents within 60 days after the employees quit, die, get divorced, or otherwise change their status. The coverage must be offered for 18 to 36 months, depending on the qualifying circumstances. The individual no longer employed by the organization must pay the premiums, but the employer may charge this individual no more than 102% of the premium costs to insure a similarly covered employee.

For most healthcare employers, the COBRA requirements mean additional paperwork and related costs. For example, employers must not only track the former employees but also notify their qualified dependents. The 2% premium addition generally does not cover all relevant costs; the costs often run several percentage points more.

HIPAA Provisions   The **Health Insurance Portability and Accountability Act (HIPAA)** of 1996 allows employees to switch their health insurance plan from one employer to another to get new health coverage, regardless of pre-existing health conditions. The legislation also prohibits group insurance plans from dropping coverage for a sick employee, and requires them to make individual coverage available to people who leave group plans.[17] Effective April 2003, healthcare providers, insurance companies and other organizations that had access to or knowledge of an individual's medical information, have a significantly higher requirement to maintain and protect medical record confidentiality. This will affect how employees deal with employee benefit information.

FINANCIAL, INSURANCE, AND OTHER BENEFITS

Healthcare employers may offer workers a wide range of special benefits: financial benefits, insurance benefits (in addition to health-related insurance), educational benefits, social benefits, and recreational benefits. These benefits can be useful in attracting and retaining employees. Workers like receiving special benefits, which often are not taxed as income.

Financial Benefits

Financial benefits include a wide variety of items. A *credit union* sponsored by the employer provides saving and lending services for employees. Employee *thrift savings plans* may be made available. Some employers match a portion of the employee's contribution. To illustrate, in a savings plan, the organization provides matching funds equal to the amount invested by the employee in the 401(k) plan. *Financial planning and counseling* are especially valuable services for executives, many of whom may need information on investments, tax shelters, and comprehensive financial counseling because of their higher levels of compensation. The importance of these financial planning benefits likely will grow as a greater percentage of workers approach retirement age.

Insurance Benefits

In addition to health-related insurance, some employers provide other types of insurance. These benefits offer major advantages for employees because many employers pay some or all of the costs. Even when employers do not pay any of the costs, employees still benefit because of the lower rates available through group programs.

Life Insurance   It is common for employers to provide *life insurance* for employees. Life insurance is bought as a group policy, and the employer pays all or some of the premiums, but the level of coverage is usually low and is tied to the employee's base pay. A typical level of coverage is one-and-a-half or two times an employee's annual salary. Some executives may get higher coverage as part of executive compensation packages. Healthcare employers frequently provide their employees' access to optional life insurance that the employee pays the full premium for, but at discounted group rates.

Disability Insurance   Other insurance benefits frequently tied to employee pay levels are *short-term* and *long-term disability insurance.* This type of insurance provides continuing income protection for employees who become disabled and unable to work. Long-term disability insurance is much more common because many employers cover short-term disability situations by allowing employees to accrue the sick leave granted annually. A growing number of healthcare employers are integrating their disability insurance programs with efforts to reduce workers' compensation claims. There are a number of reasons to have **integrated disability management programs,** such as cost savings and better coordination.[18]

Educational Benefits

Another benefit used by many healthcare employees is *educational assistance programs* to pay for some or all the costs associated with formal education courses and degree programs, including the costs of books and laboratory materials.

Some employers' pay for schooling on a proportional schedule, depending on the grades received; others simply require a passing grade of C or above.

Unless the education paid for by the employer meets certain conditions, employees must count the cost of educational aid as taxable income. Section 127 of the Internal Revenue Code received favorable treatment in federal tax legislation and now includes graduate education.[19]

Social and Recreational Benefits

Some benefits and services are social and recreational in nature, such as bowling leagues, picnics and parties, employer-sponsored athletic teams, organizationally owned recreational lodges, and other sponsored activities and interest groups. As interest in employee wellness has increased, more firms provide recreational facilities and activities. But employers should retain control of all events associated with their organizations because of possible legal responsibility.

Family-Oriented Benefits

The composition of families in the United States has changed significantly in the past few decades. The number of traditional families—in which the man is the primary or exclusive "bread winner" and the woman stays home to raise children—has declined significantly, while the percentage of two-worker families has more than doubled. The growth in dual-career couples, single-parent households, and increasing work demands on many workers has increased the emphasis some employers are placing on family-oriented benefits. To provide assistance, employers have established a variety of family-oriented benefits, and the federal government passed the Family and Medical Leave Act in 1993.

Family and Medical Leave Act (FMLA)

The Family and Medical Leave Act (FMLA) covers all employers with 50 or more employees who live within 75 miles of the workplace and includes federal, state, and private employers. Only employees who have worked at least 12 months and 1,250 hours in the previous year are eligible for leaves under FMLA.

FMLA Eligibility   The law requires that employers allow eligible employees to take a total of 12 weeks' leave during any 12-month period for one or more of the following situations:

▶ Birth, adoption, or foster-care placement of a child
▶ Caring for a spouse, child, or parent with a serious health condition
▶ Serious health condition of the employee

A **serious health condition** is one requiring inpatient, hospital, hospice, or residential medical care or continuing physician care. An employer may require an employee to provide a certificate from a doctor verifying such an illness as being covered.

FMLA provides for the following guidelines regarding employee leaves:

▶ Employees taking family and medical leave must be able to return to the same job or a job of equivalent status or pay.

▶ Health benefits must be continued during the leave at the same level and conditions.

▶ The leave taken may be intermittent rather than in one block, subject to employee and employer agreements, when birth, adoption, or foster childcare is the cause. For serious health conditions, employer approval is not necessary.

▶ Employees can be required to use all paid-up vacation and personal leave before taking unpaid leave.

▶ Employees are required to give 30-day notice, where practical.

Employer Reactions to FMLA   Since the passage of the act, several factors have become apparent. First, many employers have not paid enough attention to the law. Some employers are denying leaves or failing to reinstate workers after leaves are completed. However, the law does not protect one from layoff during or after leave. In fact, cutbacks are legitimate reasons for layoff regardless of FMLA, and courts have decided against employees in 74% of cases involving layoffs and job security.[20]

Healthcare employers also encounter problems with the FMLA because of the many different circumstances in which employees may request and use family leave. Many employers have difficulty in interpreting when and how the provisions are to be applied. Also, the need to arrange work coverage for employees on FMLA leaves can be particularly challenging for smaller employers. This difficulty is compounded because the law requires that workers on these leaves be offered similar jobs at similar levels of pay when they return to work. Many employers still find complying with the law to be difficult.

Family-Care Benefits

The growing emphasis on family issues is important in many healthcare organizations and for many workers. Many healthcare employers having a large female workforce, so adoption benefits, childcare programs, and elder programs are critical benefits for recruitment and retention purposes. Although studies indicate that males are becoming more involved in childcare responsibilities, a significant part of childcare responsibilities still rests on the shoulders of the female employees. If healthcare employers wish to be competitive for skilled female employees, they must include these programs in their benefits offerings.

Adoption Benefits   Many healthcare employers provide maternity and paternity benefits to employees who give birth to children. In comparison to those giving birth, a relatively small number of employees adopt children, but in the interest of fairness, a growing number of organizations provide benefits for employees who adopt children.

Child Care   Balancing work and family responsibilities is a major challenge for many healthcare workers. Whether single parents or dual-career couples, these employees often experience difficulty in obtaining high-quality, affordable child-care. Healthcare employers are addressing the child-care issue in several ways. From providing on-site day-care facilities to having referral services to aid parents in locating child-care providers.

Elder Care   Another family-related issue of growing importance is caring for elderly relatives. Various organizations have surveyed their employees and found that as many as 30% of them have had to miss work to care for an aging relative. The responsibilities associated with caring for elderly family members have resulted in reduced work performance, increased absenteeism, and more personal stress for the affected employees.

Benefits for Domestic Partners and Spousal Equivalents

As lifestyles change in the United States, employees who are not married but have close personal relationships with others are confronting healthcare employers with requests for benefits. The terminology often used to refer to individuals with such living arrangements is *domestic partners* and *spousal equivalents*.

The argument made by these employees is that if an employer provides benefits for the spouses of married employees, then benefits should be provided for employees without spouses but with alternative lifestyles and relationships. This view is reinforced by: (1) data showing that a significant percentage of heterosexual couples live together before or instead of formally marrying; and (2) the fact that more gays and lesbians are being open about their lifestyles.

The proportion of couples fitting the "traditional" definition of a family, including husband, wife, and children, is only 25% today. The number of Americans living in unmarried-partner households is growing much more rapidly than those living in married households. The latest census found about 600,000 same-sex couple homes, or about 0.5% of the total of the nation's households.[21] Several studies have show that employers who offer this coverage will experience enrollment in the 1% to 2% range. If coverage is offered to opposite-sex couples, enrollment rates will be closer to the 2%. About 22% of companies surveyed now offer such benefits, and two-thirds of the employers who offer the benefits cover both same- and opposite-sex couples who are not married.[22]

Decisions to extend benefits to domestic partners have come under attacks from certain religious leaders opposed to homosexual lifestyles. However, it must be noted that most employees using the domestic partner benefits are of the opposite sex and are involved in heterosexual relationships.

Time-Off Benefits

Healthcare employers give employees paid time off under a variety of circumstances. Paid lunch breaks and rest periods, holidays, and vacations are common. But leaves are given for a number of other purposes as well. Time-off benefits represent an estimated 5% to 13% of total compensation. Typical time-off benefits include *holiday pay, vacation pay,* and *leaves of absence.*

Medical and Sick Leave   Employers grant **leaves of absence,** taken as time off with or without pay, for a variety of reasons. Medical and sick leave and paid time off programs are closely related. Many employers allow employees to miss a limited number of days because of illness without losing pay. Some employers allow employees to accumulate unused sick leave, which may be used in case of catastrophic illnesses. Others pay employees for unused sick leave. Some organizations have shifted emphasis to reward people who do not use sick leave by giving them **well pay**—extra pay for not taking sick leave.

Paid Time-Off (PTO) and Extended Illness Banks (EIB)   Many healthcare employers have made use of the **paid time-off plan** and **extended illness banks**. PTO combines short-term sick/personal leave, vacations, and holidays or some combination, into a total number of hours or days that employees can take off with pay.[23] EIB programs allow employees to accrue time to be used for longer-term illness or health-related care that does not result in a disability, such as maternity care. One healthcare organization discovered that when it stopped designating a specific number of sick-leave days and a PTO plan was implemented, absenteeism dropped, time off was scheduled better, and employee acceptance of the leave policy improved. An example of PTO and EIB accrual is depicted in Figure 13-4.

Other Leaves   Other types of leaves are given for a variety of purposes. Some, such as *military leave, election leave,* and *jury leave,* are required by various state and

FIGURE 13-4   **Paid Time-Off and Extended Illness Bank Accrual**

	YEARS OF SERVICE	ANNUAL ACCRUAL FOR FULL-TIME EMPLOYEE # HOURS		
		PTO	EIB	TOTAL
Positions with 2 week (10 day) vacation allowances	1–5	176	56	232
Positions with 3 week (15 day) vacation allowances	5–12	216	56	272
Positions with 4 week (20 day) vacation allowances	20+	256	56	312

federal laws. Employers commonly pay the difference between the employee's regular pay and the military, election, or jury pay. Some firms grant employees military time off and give them regular pay while the employees also receive military pay. Federal law prohibits taking discriminatory action against military reservists by requiring them to take vacation time to attend summer camp or other training sessions. However, the leave request must be reasonable and truly required by the military.

Funeral or bereavement leave is another common leave offered to healthcare employees. A leave of up to three days for the death of immediate family members is usually given, as specified in many employers' policy manuals and employee handbooks. Some policies also give unpaid time off for the death of more distant relatives or friends.

BENEFITS ADMINISTRATION

Benefits Communication

Employees generally do not know much about the values and costs associated with the benefits they receive from employers. Yet benefits communication and benefits satisfaction are linked. Many employers have instituted special benefits communication systems to inform employees about the value of the benefits they provide.

Benefits Statements   Some healthcare employers also give each employee an annual *personal statement of benefits* that translates benefits into dollar amounts. Federal regulations under ERISA require that employees receive an annual pension-reporting statement, which also can be included in the personal statements. By having a personalized statement, each employee can see how much his or her own benefits are worth. Employers hope that by educating employees about benefit costs, they can manage expenditures better and can give employees a better appreciation for the employers' payments.

HRIS and Benefits Communication   The advent of HRIS options linked to intranets provides additional links to communicate benefits to employees. The use of employee self-service kiosks allows employees to obtain benefits information online. These kiosks and other information technology also allow employees to change their benefits choices, track their benefits balances, and submit questions to HR staff members and external benefits providers. HR professionals are utilizing information systems to communicate benefits information, conduct employee benefit surveys, and provide other benefits communications.[24]

Flexible Benefits

A **flexible benefits plan,** sometimes called a *flex* or *cafeteria* plan, allows employees to select the benefits they prefer from groups of benefits established by the employer. By making a variety of benefits selections available, the organization allows each employee to select an individual combination of benefits within some overall limits. As a result of the changing composition of the workforce, flexible benefits plans have grown in popularity.

Flexible Spending Accounts   Under current tax laws (Section 125 of the IRS Code), employees can divert some income before taxes into accounts to fund certain benefits. These **flexible spending accounts** allow employees to contribute pretax dollars to buy additional benefits.

Under tax laws at the time of this writing, the funds in the account can be used only to purchase any of the following: (1) additional health care (including offsetting deductibles), (2) life insurance, (3) disability insurance, and (4) dependent-care benefits. Flexible spending accounts have grown in popularity as more flexible benefits plans have been adopted by more healthcare employers.

Benefits in the Future

Employees' needs are changing. Those changes and the IRS code have made benefits increasingly more complex. As a result, benefit functions are among the most outsourced in HR. Pension plans, health plan administration, or COBRA tracking are all targets for benefit outsourcing, as are benefits administration, service, financial reporting and accounting, and compliance and reporting.

Many employees also have access to Internet-based benefits support systems. For instance, use of the Internet allows employees in a growing number of organizations to check their retirement fund balances and move funds among various financial options.

VARIABLE PAY: INCENTIVES FOR PERFORMANCE

Pay and benefits make up two components of compensation. The third component for many healthcare workers is variable pay. **Variable pay** which is compensation that is linked to individual, team, and organizational performance. Traditionally known as *incentives,* variable pay plans attempt to provide tangible rewards to employees for performance beyond normal expectations. Several types of variable pay can be used for individuals, groups, and organizations.

Types of Variable Pay

Individual incentives are given to reward the effort and performance of individuals. The most common means of providing healthcare employees variable pay are bonuses. Others include special recognition rewards, time-off and other things.

When an organization rewards an entire work group or *team* for its performance, cooperation among the members usually increases. However, competition among different teams for rewards can lead to decline in overall performance under certain circumstances. The most common team or group incentives are *gainsharing plans,* where employee teams that meet certain goals share in the gains measured against performance targets. Often, gainsharing programs focus on quality improvement, cost reduction, and other measurable results.

Organizational incentives reward people based on the performance results of the entire organization. This approach assumes that all employees working together can generate greater organizational results that lead to better financial performance. These programs often share some of the financial gains to the organization with employees through payments calculated as a percentage of each employee's base pay. Also, organizational incentives may be given as a lump-sum amount to all employees, or different amounts may be given to different levels of employees throughout the organization. For healthcare senior managers and executives, variable pay plans often are established to provide deferred compensation that minimizes the tax liabilities of the recipients. Figure 13-5 shows some of the programs under each type of incentive or variable pay plan.

Most healthcare employers adopt variable pay incentives in order to link individual performance to organizational goals and reward superior performance.[25] Other goals might include improving productivity or increasing employee retention. Variable pay plans can be considered successful if they meet the goals the organization had for them when they were initiated.

Effective Variable Pay Plans

Variable pay systems should be tied to desired performance. Employees must see a direct relationship between their efforts and their financial rewards. Indeed, higher-performing organizations give out far more incentive pay to their top performers than do lower-performing companies.[26]

FIGURE 13-5 Types of Variable Pay Plans In Healthcare

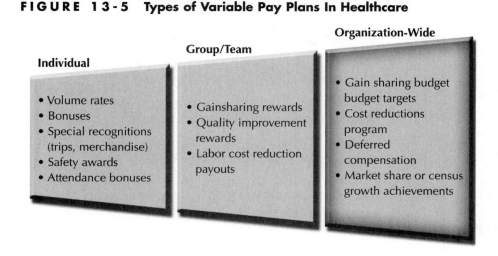

Individual
- Volume rates
- Bonuses
- Special recognitions (trips, merchandise)
- Safety awards
- Attendance bonuses

Group/Team
- Gainsharing rewards
- Quality improvement rewards
- Labor cost reduction payouts

Organization-Wide
- Gain sharing budget budget targets
- Cost reductions program
- Deferred compensation
- Market share or census growth achievements

Because people tend to produce what is measured and rewarded, healthcare organizations must make sure that what is being rewarded ties to meeting organizational objectives. Use of multiple measures helps assure that various performance dimensions are not omitted. For example, a hospital's patient scheduling department sets incentives for its employees to increase productivity by lowering their time spent per call. That reduction may occur, but customer service might drop as the schedulers rush callers to reduce talk time. Therefore, the department should consider both talk time and customer satisfaction survey results.

Indeed, linking pay to performance in a healthcare setting might not always be appropriate. For instance, if the output cannot be objectively measured, management may not be able to correctly reward the higher performers with more pay. Managers might not even be able to accurately identify the higher performers. Under those circumstances, individual variable pay is inappropriate.

Individual Incentives

As noted earlier, individual incentive systems try to relate individual effort to pay. Figure 13-6 depicts the popularity of individual incentive pay plans.

Bonuses   Individual employees may receive additional compensation payments in the form of a **bonus,** which is a one-time payment that does not become part of the employee's base pay. Generally, bonuses are less costly to the employer than other pay increases because they do not become part of employees' base wages, upon which future percentage increases are figured. Growing in popularity, individual bonuses often are used at the executive levels in organizations, but bonus usage also has spread to jobs at all levels in some firms. Bonuses can be used to reward employees for contributing new ideas, developing skills, or obtaining pro-

FIGURE 13-6   Popular Individual Incentive Pay Plans

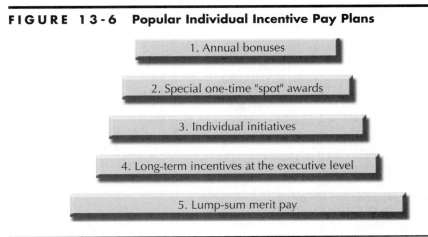

1. Annual bonuses

2. Special one-time "spot" awards

3. Individual initiatives

4. Long-term incentives at the executive level

5. Lump-sum merit pay

Adapted from: Incentive pay plans: "Which ones work . . . and why", *HR Focus,* April 2001, 3–4.

fessional certifications. When the skills or certification requirements are acquired by an employee, a pay increase or a one-time bonus may follow.

A bonus can recognize performance by an employee, a team, or the organization as a whole. When performance results are good, bonuses go up. When performance results are not met, bonuses go down. Most employers base part of the employee's bonus on individual performance and part on the organization, if appropriate.

Whatever method of determining bonuses is used, legal experts recommend that bonus plans be described in writing. A number of lawsuits have been filed by employees who leave organizations demanding payment of bonuses promised to them.

Special Incentive Programs   Numerous special incentive programs that provide awards to individuals have been used, ranging from one-time contests for meeting performance targets to rewards for performance over time. Although special programs can also be developed for groups and for entire organizations, these programs often focus on rewarding specific high-performing individuals. Some hospitals and medical centers have awarded bonuses to all employees after successful JCAHO reviews. Special incentives include special awards, recognition awards, and service awards.

Group/Team-Based Variable Pay

A group of employees is not necessarily a "team," but either one can be the basis for variable compensation. The use of work teams in organizations has implications for compensation of the teams and their members. Interestingly, although the use of teams has increased substantially in the past few years, the question of how to equitably compensate the individuals who compose the team remains a significant challenge. As Figure 13-7 notes, organizations establish group or team variable pay plans for a number of reasons.

FIGURE 13-7   Why Organizations Establish Team Variable Pay Plans

- Enhances productivity
- Ties earnings to team performance
- Improves quality
- Aids recruiting and retention of employees
- Improves employees morale

Team Variable Pay

Distributing Team Incentives   Several decisions about methods of distributing and allocating team rewards must be made. The two primary approaches for distributing team rewards are as follows:

1. *Same size reward for each team member*—In this approach, all team members receive the same payout, regardless of job levels, current pay, or seniority.
2. *Different size rewards for each team member*—Using this approach, employers vary individual rewards based on such factors as contribution to team results, current pay, years of experience, and skill levels of jobs performed.

Generally, more organizations use the first approach as an addition to different levels of individual pay. This method is used to reward team performance by making the team incentive equal, while still recognizing that individual pay differences exist and are important to many employees.[27]

Problems with Team-Based Incentives   The difference between rewarding team members *equally* or *equitably* triggers many of the problems associated with team-based incentives. Rewards distributed equally in amount to all team members may be perceived as "unfair" by employees who work harder, have more capabilities, or perform more difficult jobs. This problem is compounded when a poorly performing individual negatively influences the team results. Also, employees working in teams have shown a relatively low level of satisfaction with rewards that are the same for all, rather than having rewards based on performance, which often may be viewed more equitably.

Successful Team Incentives   The unique nature of the team and its members figures prominently in the success of establishing team-based rewards. The employer must consider the history of the group and its past performance. Use of incentives generally has proven to be more successful where groups have been used in the past and where those groups have performed well.

Another consideration for the success of team-based incentives is the size of the team. If a team becomes too large, employees may feel their individual efforts will have little or no effect on the total performance of the group and the resulting rewards. Team-based incentive plans may encourage teamwork in small groups where interdependence is high. Therefore, in those groups the use of team-based performance measures is recommended.

Group/team-based reward systems use various ways of compensating individuals. The components include individual wages and salaries in addition to team-based rewards. Most team-based organizations continue to pay individuals based either on the jobs performed or their competencies and capabilities. The two most frequently used types of group/team incentives situations are work team results and gainsharing.

Organizational Incentives

An organizational incentive system compensates all employees in the organization based on how well the organization as a whole performs during the year. The basic concept behind organizational incentive plans is that overall results depend on organizational cooperation. The purpose of these plans is to produce better results by rewarding cooperation throughout the organization. To be effective, an organizational incentive program should include everyone from non-exempt employees to managers and executives. As an example, a large dental clinic developed an organizational incentive plan based on patient satisfaction. It used aggregated information from its patient surveys to determine a base level of acceptable patient satisfaction scores and then set goals to increase patient satisfaction. Upon attainment of the goals, the clinic awarded *all* employees a significant year-end cash bonus.

CASE

Mercy Hospital, a 300-bed community hospital located in a suburban area of a large eastern city, was struggling with recruitment and retention issues. These issues were occurring in spite of area labor availability statistics that indicated that there was a sufficient supply of skilled healthcare workers to meet their needs, but apparently they were choosing to work elsewhere.

Mercy's HR Director undertook a comprehensive analysis of the recruitment and retention issues with the support of the Board and senior management of the hospital. The director utilized information from a recent employee satisfaction survey and exit interviews. From these sources she learned the following:

▶ Current employees believed that Mercy's benefits program was not competitive in comparison to other hospitals and companies in the area.
▶ Of the employees who voluntarily resigned from Mercy in the last twelve months, benefit issues were

critical. They reported receiving employment offers that included: lower healthcare insurance premiums; employer paid dental insurance; higher accruals on paid-time-off; and sign-on bonuses.
▶ Mercy's healthcare competitors were aware of Mercy's less-competitive benefits package and would aggressively recruit Mercy's employees, noting the differences when interviewing Mercy's employees.

Questions

1. Given the findings from the HR Director, what additional benefits plans should be considered by Mercy Hospital?
2. What would be the advantages and disadvantages to increasing the competitiveness of the benefits plans at Mercy Hospital?

END NOTES

1. Jerry Giesel, "Health Care Cost Increases Among Employers' Top Worries," *Business Insurance* (December 17, 2001).

2. Daniel Moskowita, "Care Package," *Human Resource Executive* (May 1, 2001), 1.

3. "Baby Boomers Need Attention Too," *Bulletin to Management* (July 13, 2000), 5–6.

4. Margaret M. Cole, "Employers Cater to Changing Benefit Needs, Survey Finds," *HR-News* (May 2001), 17; and Lore Lawrence, "Companies Still Offering Perks, but HR's Taking Another Look," *HR-News* (June 2001), 4.

5. Rodney K. Platt, "Value of Benefits Remains Constant," *Workspan* (June 2000), 34–39.

6. "50 Benefits and Perks That Make Employees Want to Stay Forever," *HR Focus* (July 2000), S2–S3.

7. Robert Schwab, "Employers Forces to Expand Benefits," *The Denver Post* (September 3, 2000), GL.

8. William Atkinson, "Is Worker's Comp Changing?" *HR Magazine* (July 2000), 50–61.

9. Atkinson, "Is Worker's Comp Changing" *HR Magazine* (July 2000), 50–61.

10. Anna M. Rappaport, Renee Maciacz and Ed Bancroft, "Exit Stage, Rightfully, Phased Retirement in the Spotlight," *World at Work Journal* (Fourth Quarter 2001), 30–36.

11. The Hay Group, *Social Security Summary 2000* (Philadelphia: Hay Group, 2000).

12. Julie Appleby, "Health Insurance Prices to Soar," *USA Today* (August 27, 2001), 1A–2A; and Steve Jordan, "Health Insurance Costs Set to Soar," *Omaha World-Herald* (November 4, 2001), 1D.

13. Mary S. Case, "A New Model for Controlling Health-Care Costs," *Workforce* (July 2000), 44.

14. Robert J. Chitadore, "Defined Contribution," *World at Work Journal* (Third Quarter 2001), 11–17.

15. Carolyn Hirschman, "More Choices, Less Cost?" (January 2002), 36–41.

16. Steve Jordon, "Wellness Is Insurer's 'Watchword,'" *Omaha World Herald* (January 21, 2001), 1B.

17. Alex M. (Kelly) Clarke, "The New HIPPA Regulations," *13th Annual Baird Holm Labor Law Forum 2001,* 57.

18. Miriam Basch Scott, "Disability Management," *Employee Benefits Plan Review* (March 2000), 16.

19. "Nine in 10 Employers Offer Educational Benefit Programs," *Bulletin to Management* (August 3, 2000), 244.

20. Sue Shellerbarger, "Work and Family," *The Wall Street Journal* (August 22, 2001), B1.

21. Genaro C. Aranas, "Gay Couples Lead 549,391 Households," *The Denver Post* (August 22, 2001), 7A.

22. Kim Mills, "Domestic Partner Benefits," *Workspan* (August 2000), 32–35; and "Benefits Policies," *Bulletin to Management* (December 21, 2000), 404.

23. Jackie Reinberg, "It's About Time: PTOs Gain Popularity," *Workspan* (February 2002), 53–55.

24. Susan J. Wells, "Communicating Benefits Information Online," *HR Magazine* (February 2001), 28–36.

25. "Short-Term Incentives Considered
    Ineffective, Survey Reveals," *HR News*
    (January 2000), 5.

26. "Towers Perrin Reveals How to
    Design the Most Effective Incentive
    Plans," *IOMA's Report on Salary Surveys*
    (March 2000), 14.

27. Todd Manas, and M. H. L. Vuitton,
    "Combining Reward Elements to
    Create the Right Team Chemistry,"
    Workspan (November 2000),
    46–52.

CHAPTER 14

Safety, Health, and Security in Healthcare Organizations

Learning Objectives

After you have read this chapter, you should be able to:

▶ Explain the nature of safety, health, and security in the healthcare workplace.

▶ Identify the various aspects of OSHA compliance.

▶ Define the components of an effective ergonomics program.

▶ Discuss health issues in the healthcare workplace.

▶ Understand the importance of dealing with workplace violence.

Safety, health, and security are important HR activities for healthcare organizations. Due to the nature of the healthcare work environment, it is especially important that healthcare organizations maintain effective programming in these areas.

SAFETY

The administrator of a small nursing home in the Midwest has worked hard to ensure that employees receive effective annual safety training. But after years of the same basic presentation format of classroom-style training that was receiving poor marks from the employees, she decided to radically change the presentation format. Her new approach was to present the training using a game-show format complete with an emcee, cheering audience, and prizes. The contestants (employees) were asked safety questions, and for giving correct answers they received T-shirts with the nursing home's logo on it.

The training received high ratings from the employees. In addition, the administrator is convinced that the employees' safety knowledge is much improved in comparison to previous years.

HEALTH

At Cincinnati's Children's Hospital, the safety/security and employee health departments report within the HR division. Some healthcare organizations have organized these functions differently (e.g., having the safety/security department report within the building and facilities division). Regardless of the reporting relationship, focusing organizational resources on safety and health management is critical for healthcare organizations. The rationale for this reporting relationship is that the combination of the safety/security and employee health functions supports an effective continuum of health and safety management for employees, patients, and visitors. These combined departments are responsible for safety, training, safety, and health awareness, security issue management, workers compensation and OSHA compliance. In addition, this structure allows for more efficient use of health and safety employees and the budgets dedicated to these activities.

SECURITY

A home health care agency hired a home health aide to provide home care, but failed to conduct a criminal-background check. Consequently, the agency failed to discover that its new employee had a criminal record, including six larceny-related convictions. The employee was later convicted of stabbing to death a patient in his care, along with the patient's grandmother. The patient's parents brought suit against the agency, winning compensatory and punitive damages of $26.5 million and sending the agency into bankruptcy.

In another case, Manor Park Nursing Home in Texas failed to do a criminal background check of an employee who later sexually assaulted a resident of the nursing home. The resident was awarded $1.1 million in a jury trial.[1] Healthcare providers have a special responsibility to employ healthcare workers who can be trusted to provide safe, competent care. Background checking is one example of how healthcare organizations can fulfill that responsibility.

As the opening examples illustrate, the healthcare workplace offers a unique set of safety, health, and security challenges. Not only are there the usual workplace safety, health, and security issues to contend with, but also there is the issue of protecting the patients, residents and clients that are cared for in the workplace. Protecting both healthcare workers and the individuals they provide care for is a critical responsibility for the leaders of healthcare organizations. Addressing health and safety, security issues is part of effective HR management.

NATURE OF SAFETY, HEALTH, AND SECURITY

The terms *safety, health,* and *security* are closely related. The broader and somewhat more nebulous term is **health,** which refers to a general state of physical, mental, and emotional well-being. A healthy person is one who is free of illness, injury, or mental and emotional problems that impair normal human activity. Health management practices in healthcare organizations strive to maintain the overall well-being of individuals.

Typically, **safety** refers to protecting the physical well-being of people. The main purpose of effective safety programs in organizations is to prevent work-related injuries and accidents. The purpose of **security** is protecting employees, patients/residents, clients and visitors, and organizational facilities. With the growth of workplace violence, security at work has become an even greater concern for healthcare employers and employees alike.

Safety, Health, and Security Responsibilities

The general goal of providing a safe, secure, and healthy workplace is attained by operating managers and HR staff members working together. The primary health, safety, and security responsibilities in an organization usually fall on supervisors and managers. An HR manager or safety specialist can help coordinate health and safety programs, investigate accidents, produce safety program materials, and conduct formal safety training. However, department supervisors and managers play key roles in maintaining safe working conditions and a healthy workforce. For example, a dental clinic supervisor has several health and safety responsibilities: reminding employees to wear the appropriate protective equipment and clothing; checking on the cleanliness of the work area; observing employees for any alcohol, drug, or emotional problems that may affect their work behavior; and conducting safety orientations and training in-services.

THE JOINT COMMISSION AND SAFETY, HEALTH AND SECURITY

The Joint Commission on the Accreditation of Healthcare Organizations (JCAHO) has several topic areas that contain standards specifically relating to safety, health and security. The two primary topic areas are environment of care and surveillance, prevention, and control of infection.

Environment of Care (EC)   Healthcare organizations must provide a safe, functional, and effective environment of care for patients, visitors, medical and nursing staffs, vendors, volunteers, students—anyone on the organization's campus. The standard requires the development of plans that address safety, security, hazardous materials and waste, emergency preparedness, life safety, medical equipment, and utility systems. These plans are designed to promote a safe, secure environment when effectively shared with staff. With education and ongoing supervision, staff members implement each phase of the plans. Figure 14-1 shows the components of an environment of care plan.

FIGURE 14-1   Components of the Environment of Care Plan

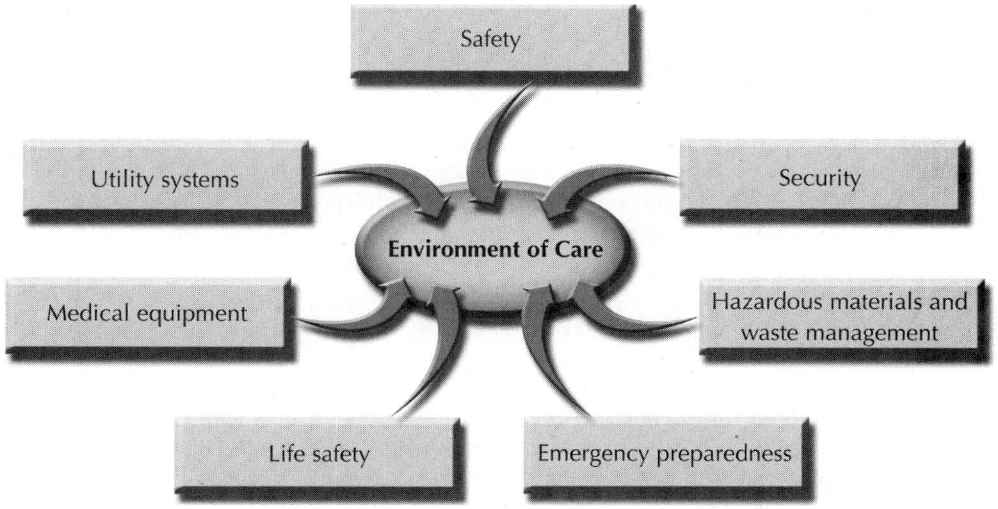

As depicted in Figure 14-1, an important component of the environment of care plans is emergency preparedness. The Joint Commission Feature on the next page discusses the HR management aspects of emergency preparedness.

Surveillance, Prevention, and Control of Infection (IC)

One significant element of concern not covered in the seven plan areas addressed in the Environment of Care standards is infection control. All staff in healthcare organizations have some infection control (IC) responsibilities and must competently perform their assigned role in the organization's safety management program. JCAHO has a set of standards that specifically addresses the protection of patients, staff and visitors, and focuses on identifying the organization's infection risks and taking the necessary risk-reduction steps. As an example, screening staff for tuberculosis, providing hepatitis B vaccinations, and implementing ongoing education regarding the importance of hand washing are risk-reduction activities.

LEGAL REQUIREMENTS FOR SAFETY AND HEALTH

Healthcare employers must comply with a variety of federal and state laws as part of their efforts when developing and maintaining healthy, safe, and secure workforces and working environments. A look at some major legal areas follows.

Workers' Compensation

Under state workers' compensation laws, employers contribute to an insurance fund to compensate employees for injuries received while on the job. Premiums paid reflect the accident rates at each employer; those employers with higher incident rates are assessed higher premiums. Also, these laws usually provide payments to injured workers for wage replacements, dependent on the amount of loss time and wage levels.[2] Workers' compensation payments also cover costs for medical bills and for retraining if a worker cannot go back to the current job.

Expanded Scope of Workers' Compensation   Workers' compensation coverage has been expanded in many states to include emotional impairment that may have resulted from physical injury, as well as job-related strain, stress, anxiety, and pressure.[3] Some cases of suicide also have been ruled to be job-related, with payments due under workers' compensation.

A new twist on workers' compensation coverage relates to the increasing use of telecommuting by employees. Healthcare organizations of all types and sizes frequently allow medical transcriptionists to work from home. An attempt by the U.S. Department of Labor to set regulations for employers with employees who work at home was widely disparaged by legislators and business representatives. Because of this negative reaction there have been limited federal regulations established in this area.

THE JOINT COMMISSION ON ACCREDITATION OF HEALTHCARE ORGANIZATIONS

The Joint Commission on Accreditation of Healthcare Organizations and Emergency Preparedness

The EC standards for the Joint Commission on Accreditation of Healthcare Organizations require member hospitals to conduct emergency preparedness drills regularly. The HR management implications of emergency preparedness are very significant. As proven by the events of September 11, 2001, the importance of having competent, well-trained healthcare workers that have the ability and skills to provide care in times of disaster has increased in importance.[4]

Healthcare HR professionals, along with healthcare managers and safety professionals, play key roles in preparing for disaster situations. Given the fact that healthcare organizations are both employers and care providers, disaster preparation is important for both the management of internal disasters, such as fires or hazardous chemical leaks or spills and dealing with the patient care needs or external disasters such as a plane or train accident may create. In both instances, healthcare workers are required to perform in extraordinary ways. Their personal safety maybe at risk or they may have to deal with the patient care needs of a high volume of critically injured or exposed patients.

The American Hospital Association, in a member advisory released after the terrorist attacks of September 11, suggested the use of the following checklist in preparing for a disaster:

▶ The hospital should focus efforts on a general "all hazards" plan that provides an adaptable framework for any crisis situation.
▶ The hospital should upgrade its disaster plan to include components for mass casualty terrorism, including chemical or biological incidents.
▶ The hospital's plan should be integrated with the emergency response agencies in the local community.
▶ The hospital should have a plan in place to support the families of staff members. In order for caregivers to remain at their jobs, they need assurance that their families and loved ones are being cared for.
▶ The hospital should ensure that its clinical and medical staff report unexpected illness patterns to the public health department and, if appropriate, the Centers for Disease Control and Prevention.[5]

It is not widely known that in most situations while working at home for an employer, individuals are covered under workers' compensation laws. Therefore, as an example, if a medical transcriptionist for a physician practice is injured while doing transcription work at home, the practice likely is liable for the injury.

FMLA and Workers' Compensation   The Family Medical Leave Act (FMLA) impacts workers' compensation as well. Injured employees may request additional leave time, even if it is unpaid. Some employers have policies that state that FMLA runs concurrently with any workers' compensation leave.[6]

Americans with Disabilities Act and Safety

The Americans with Disabilities Act (ADA) is another law affecting the health and safety policies and practices of healthcare employers. The ADA has created problems for some employers. For example, employers may try to return injured workers to "light-duty" work in order to reduce workers' compensation costs. Under the ADA, in making accommodations for injured employees through light-duty work, employers may be re-defining what really are the essential functions of a job. Making such accommodations for injured employees for a period of time may also require an employer to make accommodations for job applicants with disabilities.[7]

Safety and health record-keeping practices also have been affected by the following provision in the ADA:

> Information from all medical examinations and inquiries must be kept apart from general personnel files as a separate confidential medical record available only under limited conditions specified in the ADA.

As interpreted by attorneys and HR practitioners, this provision requires that all medical-related information be maintained separately from all other confidential files. In healthcare environments where managers are also clinicians (M.D.s, RNs, etc.) the confidentiality of employee medical information is especially difficult to manage. Managers/clinicians are used to viewing and commenting on medical information and often find it difficult to draw the line for their employee, as required by ADA. Also, specific access restrictions and security procedures must be adopted for medical records of all types, including employee medical benefit claims and treatment records.

OCCUPATIONAL SAFETY AND HEALTH ACT (OSHA)

The Occupational Safety and Health Act of 1970 was passed "to assure so far as possible every working man or woman in the Nation safe and healthful working conditions and to preserve our human resources." Every employer engaged in commerce who has one or more employees is covered by the act.[8] Employers in specific industries, such as coal mining, are covered under other health and safety acts. Federal, state, and local government employees also are covered by separate provisions or statutes.

The Occupational Health and Safety Act of 1970 established the Occupational Safety and Health Administration, known as OSHA, to administer its provisions. The act also established the National Institute of Occupational Safety and Health (NIOSH) as a supporting body to do research and develop standards. In addition, the Occupational Safety and Health Review Commission (OSHRC) has been established to review OSHA enforcement actions and address disputes between OSHA and employers who have been cited by OSHA inspectors.

OSHA Enforcement Standards

By making employers and employees more aware of safety and health considerations, OSHA has had a significant impact on organizations.[9] To implement OSHA, specific standards were established regulating equipment and working environments. But OSHA rules and standards often are complicated and technical. As an example, small, long-term care facilities and physician practices that do not have specialists on their staffs may find the standards difficult to read and understand. Conversely, organizations like the American Nurses Association and healthcare unions have accused OSHA of failing to vigorously address healthcare safety and health issues. These critics argue that OSHA inspectors do not have specific knowledge about problems in healthcare facilities. However, OSHA has focused a great deal of attention on healthcare with the establishment of the blood-borne pathogen standard, guidelines on the prevention of tuberculosis transmission, and training and consultation efforts in their targeting of the nursing home industry.[10]

A number of provisions have been recognized as key to OSHA compliance efforts by employers. Two of the most basic ones are important to all healthcare facilities:

1. *General duty*—The act requires that the employer has a "general duty" to provide safe and healthy working conditions, even in areas where OSHA standards have not been set. Healthcare employers who know or reasonably should know of unsafe or unhealthy conditions can be cited for violating the general duty clause. As an example, failing to remove snow or ice from an area that employees walk through could be a violation. The employer should know that the snow and ice could represent a slip hazard and should have the area rendered safe for employees.
2. *Notification and posters*—Employers are required to inform their employees of safety and health standards established by OSHA. Also, OSHA posters must be displayed in prominent locations in workplaces.

Personal Protective Equipment (PPE)   One goal of OSHA has been to develop standards for personal protective equipment (PPE) and clothing. These standards require healthcare employers to conduct an analyses of job hazards, provide adequate PPE to employees in those jobs, and train employees in the use

FIGURE 14-2 **Personal Protective Equipment Requirements**

POSITION	PPE
Dentist	Gowns, gloves, mask, protective eye wear
Operating Room Nurse	Gowns, gloves, mask, protective eye wear
Centrile Sterile Technician	Gowns, gloves, mask, protective eye wear
Autopsy Assistant	Mask, protective eye wear, impermeable (metal mesh) gloves and rubber aprons
Repair personnel	Safety glasses, hardhat, safety shoes
Cafeteria kitchen worker	Aprons, gloves, safety shoes

of PPE items. If the work environment presents hazards or if employees might have work contact with hazardous chemicals and substances, then employers are required to provide PPE to employees.[11] Common PPE items required for various healthcare positions are indicated on Figure 14-2.

Hazard Communication OSHA has enforcement responsibilities for the federal Hazard Communication Standard, which requires manufacturers, importers, distributors, and users of hazardous chemicals to evaluate, classify, and label these substances. This is an especially important standard for healthcare facilities, where chemicals of all types represents significant potential hazard to employees. Healthcare employers also must make available to employees, their representatives, and health professionals information about hazardous substances. This information is contained in *material safety data sheets* (MSDS), which must be kept readily accessible to those who work with chemicals and other substances. The MSDS also indicate antidotes or actions to be taken should someone come in contact with the substances. The standard also requires organizations to have a written hazard communication plan that details how requirements for labels, MSDS, and employee training are met in the employer's facility. Many organizations fail to adequately comply with this part of this standard. This has resulted in the hazard communication standard being the most frequently violated standard across all industry sectors.[12]

It should be noted that if there are numbers of workers for whom English is not their primary language, then the MSDS should be available in other languages. Workers must train annually on how to access, use and read the MSDS information. Further, as new chemicals are introduced into the workplace, employees should receive MSDS guidelines and orientation prior to the use or application of the new chemical.

As part of hazard communications, OSHA has established **lock-out/tag-out regulations.** To comply, locks and tags are provided to mechanics and trades persons for use when they make equipment inoperative for repair or adjustment to prevent accidental start-up of defective machinery. These safety locks and tags must be removed only by the person whose name is printed on the tag or engraved on the lock.

Blood-Borne Pathogens   The blood-borne pathogen standard resulted from a series of healthcare worker fatalities that were caused by workplace exposure to hepatitis B and HIV. The post-exposure assessment of the healthcare workplaces where the exposures occurred indicated that the workers were not provided with the necessary protective equipment or clothing, nor had they been given specific instruction on how to perform their jobs in a manner to protect them from exposure. As a result of these cases, OSHA issued a standard "to eliminate or minimize occupational exposure to hepatitis B virus (HBV), human immunodeficiency virus (HIV), and other bloodborne pathogens. This regulation is designed to protect employees who regularly are exposed to blood. Physicians and other healthcare workers such as laboratory workers, nurses, and medical technicians are at greatest risk. However, all employers covered by OSHA regulations must be prepared in workplaces where cuts and abrasions are common.

Ergonomics and OSHA

Ergonomics is the study and design of the work environment to address physiological and physical demands of individuals. In a work setting, ergonomic studies look at such factors as fatigue, lighting, tools, equipment layout, and placement of controls. Human factors engineering is a related field.

For a number of years, OSHA has been concerned about the large number of work-related injuries due to repetitive stress injuries, repetitive motion injuries, cumulative trauma disorders, carpal tunnel syndrome, and other ergonomic hazards in workplaces. **Cumulative trauma disorders (CTD)** occur when workers repetitively use the same muscles to perform tasks, resulting in muscular and skeletal injuries.

Carpal tunnel syndrome, one of the frequent cumulative trauma disorders, is an injury common to people who put their hands through repetitive motions. As an example, a pharmacist who must fill a significant number of liquid prescription medications may develop CTD from continually drawing back a syringe to measure out the appropriate volume for the prescription. The motion irritates the tendons in the "carpal tunnel" area of the wrist. As the tendons swell, they squeeze the medial nerve. The result is pain and numbness in the thumb, index finger, and middle finger. The hands of victims become clumsy and weak. Pain at night increases, and at advanced stages not even surgery can cure the problem. Sufferers of this trauma disorder eventually lose feeling in their hands if they do not receive timely treatment.

These problems are occurring in a variety of work settings. But healthcare office workers increasingly are experiencing CTD, primarily from extensive typing and data entry on computers and computer-related equipment. Most recently, attention has focused on the application of ergonomic principles to the design of workstations where computer operators work with personal computers (PCs) and video display terminals (VDTs) for extended periods of time.

OSHA Standards   To address such concerns, OSHA in 2000 developed some ergonomics standards to address *muscoloskeletal disorders.* Estimates are that 600,000 workers each year suffer such injuries.[13] Developments in this area can be monitored at the OSHA Web site, *http://www.osha.gov.*

Many employers have recognized that efforts to reduce CDT and other injuries are important. For example, at Enid Memorial Hospital in Enid, Oklahoma, the rate of workplace injuries was cut by 75% and lost workdays were reduced more than 85% over three years through an ergonomics program that stressed safe biomechanical lifting of patients.[14] Figure 14-3 on the next page depicts the components of an effective ergonomics program. With the rising incidence of ergonomic issues in healthcare it is important that healthcare employers of all sizes establish an ergonomic program.

Work Assignments and OSHA

The rights of employees regarding certain work assignments have been addressed as part of OSHA regulations. Two prominent areas where work assignments and concerns about safety and health meet are described next.

Work Assignments and Reproductive Health   Related to unsafe work is the issue of assigning employees to work in areas where their ability to have children may be affected by exposure to chemical hazards, biomedical waste, or radiation. Women who are able to bear children or who are pregnant have presented the primary concerns, but in some situations, the possibility that men might become sterile also has been a concern.

In a court case involving reproductive health, the Supreme Court held that Johnson Control's policy of keeping women of childbearing capacity out of jobs that might involve lead exposure violated the Civil Rights Act and the Pregnancy Discrimination Act.[15] The duties of many healthcare occupations may pose a threat to a healthcare worker's ability to conceive, maintain pregnancy, or deliver a healthy baby. Consistent with the Johnson's Control case, healthcare organizations cannot bar workers from these occupations to protect the health of the fetus, however healthcare employers need to protect themselves from liability from the effects of workplace exposure.

Although there is no *absolute* protection from liability for employers, the following actions are suggested:

▶ Maintain a safe workplace for all by seeking the safest methods.
▶ Comply with all state and federal safety laws.
▶ Inform employees of any known risks.
▶ Document employee acceptance of any risks.

Refusing Unsafe Work   Workers have refused to work when they considered the work unsafe. In many instances, that refusal has been found to be justified. Although such actions may be seen as insubordination by employers, in many

FIGURE 14-3   Components of an Effective Ergonomics Program

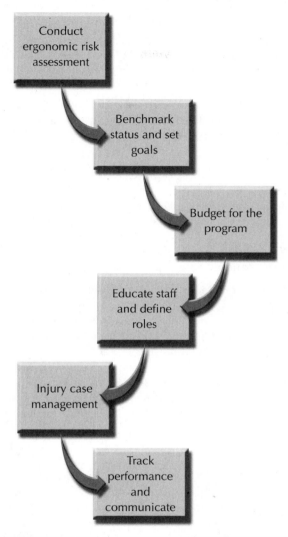

Source: Adapted from Bill Dwyre and Kevin Costello "Components of an Effective Ergonomics Program," *Professional Safety* (November 2000).

cases regulatory bodies and court decisions have supported that insubordination.[16] Based on several U.S. Supreme Court decisions, following are current legal conditions for refusing work because of safety concerns:

▶ The employee's fear is objectively reasonable.
▶ The employee has tried to have the dangerous condition corrected.
▶ Using normal procedures to solve the problem has not worked.

Record-Keeping Requirements

OSHA has established a standard national system for recording occupational injuries, accidents, and fatalities healthcare. Employers are generally required to maintain a detailed annual record of the various types of accidents for inspection by OSHA representatives and for submission to the agency. Employers that have had good safety records in previous years and that have fewer than ten employees are not required to keep detailed records. However, many organizations must complete OSHA form 300, including the following:

▶ Firms having frequent hospitalizations, injuries, or illnesses
▶ Firms having work-related deaths
▶ Firms included in OSHA's annual labor statistics survey

No one knows how many workplace accidents go unreported. It may be many more than anyone suspects, despite the fact that OSHA has increased its surveillance of accident-reporting records. OSHA guidelines state that facilities whose accident record is below the national average rarely need inspecting.

Reporting Injuries and Illnesses   Four types of injuries or illnesses have been defined by the Occupational Safety and Health Act of 1970:

1. *Injury- or Illness-Related Deaths*—These include death due to work-related injuries or illness.
2. *Lost-Time or Disability Injuries*—These include job-related injuries or disabling occurrences that cause an employee to miss his or her regularly scheduled work on the day following the accident.
3. *Medical-Care Injuries*—These injuries require treatment by a physician but do not cause an employee to miss a regularly scheduled work turn.
4. *Minor Injuries*—These injuries require first-aid treatment and do not cause an employee to miss the next regularly scheduled work turn.

OSHA Inspections

The Occupational Safety and Health Act provides for on-the-spot inspections by OSHA representatives, called compliance officers or inspectors. Under the original act, an employer could not refuse entry to an OSHA inspector, and it prohibited a compliance officer from notifying an organization before an inspection. Instead of allowing an employer to "tidy up," this no-knock provision permits inspection of normal operations. The U.S. Supreme Court ruled on the issue in the case of *Marshall v. Barlow's, Inc.* and rejected the government's arguments, holding that safety inspectors must produce a search warrant if an employer refuses to allow an inspector into the facility voluntarily. However, the Court ruled that an inspector does not have to show probable cause to obtain a search warrant. A warrant can easily be obtained if a search is part of a general enforcement plan.[17]

As a practical issue, most healthcare employers find that cooperating with a request for an OSHA inspection is appropriate. A senior-level manager, HR professional, or an internal health and safety specialist should accompany OSHA inspectors as they conduct an on-sight review of the health facility or organizational health and safety policies, procedures, and records.

Citations and Violations   Although OSHA inspectors can issue citations for violations of the provisions of the act, whether a citation is issued depends on the severity and extent of the problems, and on the employer's knowledge of them. In addition, depending on the nature and number of violations, penalties can be assessed against employers. The nature and extent of the penalties depend on the type and severity of the violations as determined by OSHA officials.

There are five types of violations, ranging from severe to minimal, including a special category for repeated violations:

1. *Imminent Danger*—When there is reasonable certainty that the condition will cause death or serious physical harm if it is not corrected immediately, an imminent-danger citation is issued and a notice posted by an inspector. Imminent-danger situations are handled on the highest-priority basis. If the condition is serious enough and the employer does not cooperate, a representative of OSHA may go to a federal judge and obtain an injunction to close the company until the condition is corrected. The absence of guard railings to prevent maintenance employees from falling off a roof into heavy machinery is one example.
2. *Serious*—When a condition could probably cause death or serious physical harm, and the employer should know of the condition, a serious-violation citation is issued. Examples are the absence of appropriate labeling on a container of hazardous chemical.
3. *Other Than Serious*—Other-than-serious violations could have an impact on employees' health or safety but probably would not cause death or serious harm. Having loose ropes in a work area might be classified as an other-than-serious violation.
4. *De Minimis*—A *de minimis* condition is one that is not directly and immediately related to employees' safety or health. No citation is issued, but the condition is mentioned to the employer. Lack of doors on toilet stalls is a common example of a *de minimis* violation.
5. *Willful and Repeated*—Citations for willful and repeated violations are issued to employers who have been previously cited for violations. If an employer knows about a safety violation or has been warned of a violation and does not correct the problem, a second citation is issued. The penalty for a willful and repeated violation can be very high. If death results from an accident that involves such a safety violation, a jail term of six months can be imposed on responsible executives or managers.

Critique of OSHA Inspection Efforts   OSHA has been criticized on several fronts. Because the agency has so many work sites to inspect, healthcare employers have only a relatively small chance of being inspected. Some suggest that many employers pay little attention to OSHA enforcement efforts for this reason.

Labor unions and others have criticized OSHA and Congress for not providing enough inspectors. For instance, it is common to find that many of the work sites at which workers suffered severe injuries or deaths had not been inspected in the previous five years. Employers, especially smaller ones, continue to complain about the complexity of complying with OSHA standards and the costs associated with penalties and with making changes required to remedy problem areas.

SAFETY MANAGEMENT

Effective safety management requires an organizational commitment to safe working conditions. But well-designed and managed safety programs can reduce accidents and the associated costs, such as workers' compensation and possible fines. Further, accidents and other safety concerns do decline as a result of an effective safety management program with a number of components.

Organizational Commitment and Safety Culture

At the heart of safety management is an organizational commitment to a comprehensive safety effort. This effort should be coordinated from the top level of management to include all members of the organization. It also should be reflected in managerial actions.[18] There are three different approaches that employers such as these use in managing safety. Figure 14-4 shows the organizational, engineering, and individual approaches and their components. Successful programs may use all three in dealing with safety issues.[19]

Safety and Engineering

Healthcare employers can prevent some accidents by designing processes, equipment, and work areas so that workers who perform potentially dangerous jobs cannot injure themselves and others. Providing safety equipment and guards on equipment, installing emergency switches, installing safety rails, keeping aisles clear, and installing adequate ventilation, lighting, heating, and air conditioning can all help make work environments safer.

Individual Considerations and Safety

Engineers approach safety from the perspective of redesigning the equipment, processes, or work area; industrial psychologists and human factors experts see safety differently. They are concerned with the proper match of individuals to jobs and emphasize employee training in safety methods, fatigue reduction, and health awareness. Experts have conducted numerous field studies with thousands of employees that looked at the "human factors" in accidents. The results show a definite relationship between emotional factors, such as stress, and accidents. Other studies point to the importance of individual differences, motivation, attitudes, and learning as key factors in controlling the human element in

FIGURE 14-4   **Approaches to Effective Safety Management**

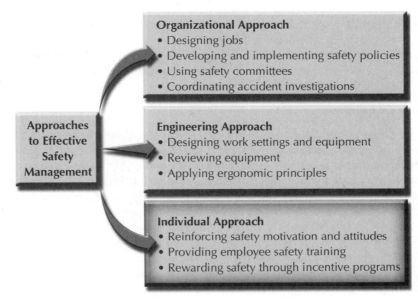

safety. The healthcare industry has been especially concerned about the fatigue factor for employees who work 10 and 12 hour shifts, or who may be required to work double shifts.

Attitudinal variables are among the individual factors that affect accident rates because more problems are caused by careless employees than by equipment or employer negligence. At one time, workers who were dissatisfied with their jobs were thought to have higher accident rates. However, this assumption has been questioned in recent years. Although employees' personalities, attitudes, and individual characteristics apparently have some influence on accidents, exact cause-and-effect relationships are difficult to establish.

Work schedules can be another cause for accidents. The relationship between work schedules and accidents can be explained as follows: Fatigue based on physical exertion sometimes exists in today's healthcare workplace. But boredom, which occurs when a person is required to do the same tasks for a long period of time, is rather common. As fatigue of this kind increases, motivation is reduced; along with decreased motivation, workers' attention wanders, and the likelihood of accidents increases. A particular area of concern in healthcare is *overtime* in work scheduling. Overtime work has been consistently related to accident or patient care incidents. Further, the more overtime worked, the more severe accidents appeared to be.

Another area of concern is the relationship of accident rates to different shifts, particularly late-night shifts. Because there tend to be fewer supervisors and managers working the 11 P.M. to 7 A.M. shift, workers tend to receive less training and supervision. Both of these factors lead to higher accident rates.

Safety Policies and Discipline

Designing safety policies and rules and disciplining violators are important components of safety efforts. Frequently reinforcing the need for safe behavior and supplying feedback on positive safety practices also are extremely effective in improving worker safety.[20] Such efforts must involve employees, supervisors, managers, safety specialists, and HR staff members.

Safety Committees

Employees frequently are involved in safety planning through safety committees, often composed of workers from a variety of levels and departments. A well-trained safety committee is a valuable tool to help organizations provide a safe workplace for employees and a broader base of support for safety initiatives.[21] A safety committee generally has regularly scheduled meetings, has specific responsibilities for conducting safety reviews, and makes recommendations for changes necessary to avoid future accidents. Usually, at least one member of the committee is from HR.

Care must be taken that managers do not compose a majority on a safety committee. Otherwise, the employer may be in violation of some provisions of the National Labor Relations Act. That act prohibits employers from dominating a labor organization. Some safety committees have been ruled to be labor organizations because they deal with working conditions.

In thirty-two states, all but the smallest employers may be required to establish safety committees. From time to time, legislation has been introduced at the federal level to require joint management/employee safety committees. But as yet, no federal provisions have been enacted.

Safety Training and Communications

One way to encourage employee safety is to involve all employees at various times in safety training. Convincing healthcare employees to keep safety standards continuously in mind while performing their jobs is difficult. Often, employees think that safety measures are bothersome and unnecessary until an injury occurs. For example, it might be necessary for employees to wear safety glasses in a laboratory most of the time. But if the glasses are awkward, employees may resist using them, even when they know they should have protection. Also, some employees who may have worked often without wearing the glasses might think this requirement is a nuisance. Because of such problems, safety training and communication efforts must address safety issues so that employees view safety as important and are motivated to follow safe work practices.

Employee Safety Motivation and Incentives

To encourage healthcare employees to work safely, many organizations have used safety contests and have given employees incentives for safe work behavior. Jewelry, clocks, watches, and even vacation time have been given as rewards for good safety records. Unfortunately, there is some evidence that incentives tend to reinforce underreporting and "creative" classifying of accidents. This concern about safety incentives was raised by OSHA. The concern is that in order to receive some incentives, employees and managers do not report accidents and injuries, so that they collect on the incentive rewards.[22]

Inspection, Accident Investigation, and Evaluation

It is not necessary to wait for an OSHA inspector to inspect the work area for safety hazards. Inspections may be done by a safety committee or by a safety coordinator. They should be done on a regular basis, because OSHA may inspect organizations with above-average lost workday rates more frequently. Additionally, given the parallel between JCAHO standards on the Environment of Care (EC) and OSHA standards, many healthcare organizations conduct mock surveys in advance of a JCAHO visit that are also useful for OSHA compliance.

When accidents occur, they should be investigated by the employer's safety committee or safety coordinator. In investigating the *scene* of an accident, it is important to determine the physical and environmental conditions that contributed to the accident. Poor lighting, poor ventilation, and wet floors are some possible contributors. Investigation at the scene should be done as soon as possible after an accident to ensure that the conditions under which the accident occurred have not changed significantly. One way to obtain an accurate view of the accident scene is with photographs or videotapes.

The second phase of the investigation is the *interview* of the injured employee, his or her supervisor, and witnesses to the accident. The interviewer attempts to determine what happened and how the accident was caused. These interviews may also generate some suggestions on how to prevent similar accidents in the future. In the third phase, based on observations of the scene and interviews, investigators complete an *accident investigation report*. This report form provides the data required by OSHA.

Finally, *recommendations* should be made on how the accident could have been prevented, and what changes are needed to avoid similar accidents. Identifying why an accident occurred is useful, but taking steps to prevent similar accidents from occurring also is important.

Closely related to accident investigation is *research* to determine ways of preventing accidents. Employing safety professionals or having outside experts evaluate the safety of working conditions is useful. If many similar accidents seem to occur in an organizational unit, a safety education training program may be necessary to emphasize safe working practices. As an example, a nursing home reported a greater-than-average number of back injuries among employees who assisted the residents. Safety training on the proper way to lift was initiated to reduce the number of back injuries.

Organizations should monitor and *evaluate* their safety efforts.[23] Just as organizational accounting records are audited, a firm's safety efforts should be audited periodically as well. Accident and injury statistics should be compared with previous accident patterns to identify any significant changes. This analysis should be designed to measure progress in safety management.

HEALTH

Employee health problems are varied—and somewhat inevitable. They can range from minor illnesses such as colds to serious illnesses related to the jobs performed. Some employees have emotional health problems; others have alcohol or drug problems. Some problems are chronic; others are transitory. But all can affect organizational operations and individual employee productivity.

Healthcare Workplace Health Issues

Healthcare employers face a variety of workplace issues. Previously in this chapter, cumulative trauma injuries, exposure to hazardous chemicals and blood-borne pathogens have been discussed, because OSHA has addressed these concerns through regulations or standards. But there are a number of other key health issues for healthcare workers, including substance abuse, emotional and mental problems, indoor air quality, latex allergies, inadvertent needle sticks, and slips and falls.

Substance Abuse   **Substance abuse** is defined as the use of illicit substances or the misuse of controlled substances, alcohol, or other drugs. There are millions of substance abusers in the general workforce, and they cost global employers billions of dollars annually. In the United States, chemical dependency affects an estimated 10% of the worker population. These workers are consistently late for work, are five times more likely to file a workers' compensation claim, are more likely to be absent for work, and have more on-the-job accidents.[24]

Healthcare workers are at an increased risk for developing chemical dependencies. Healthcare workers have easier access to controlled substances than do the general population, and healthcare workers experience unique stressors (e.g., regular exposure to death and individuals experiencing trauma or emotional suffering) that contribute to chemically-assisted coping. One study indicates that nurses are at risk, with 10% of nurses surveyed in the study indicating that they were addicted to at least one controlled substance. Figure 14-5 depicts the common signs of alcohol and drug abuse for nurses.

The Americans with Disabilities Act (ADA) affects how management can handle substance-abuse cases. Current illegal drug users are specifically excluded from the definition of *disabled* under the act. However, those addicted to legal substances (alcohol, for example) and prescription drugs are considered disabled under the ADA. Also, recovering alcoholics are considered disabled under the ADA.

Pre-employment alcohol and drug testing is used by many healthcare employers. Testing is also done following an accident or for reasonable cause, unless part of a random testing program instituted by employers.

FIGURE 14-5   Common Signs of Substance Abuse

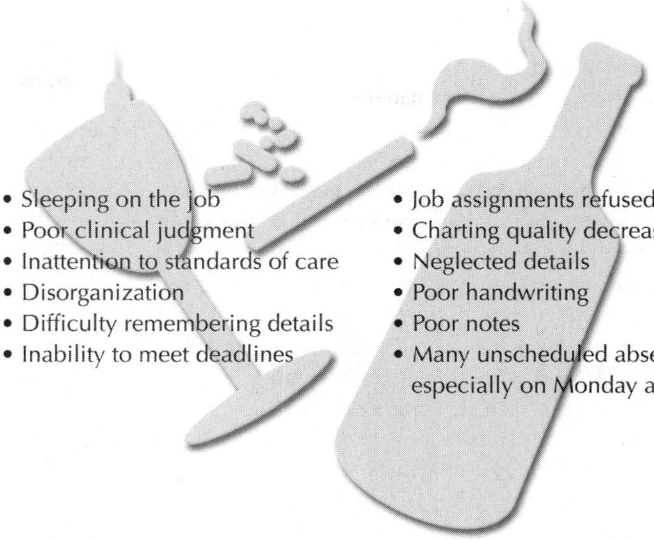

- Sleeping on the job
- Poor clinical judgment
- Inattention to standards of care
- Disorganization
- Difficulty remembering details
- Inability to meet deadlines

- Job assignments refused
- Charting quality decreased
- Neglected details
- Poor handwriting
- Poor notes
- Many unscheduled absences, especially on Monday and Friday

Source: Adapted from Susan Ponech, "Telltale Signs," *Nursing Management* (May, 2000).

To encourage employees to seek help for their substance-abuse problems, a **firm-choice option** is usually recommended and has been endorsed legally. In this procedure, the employee is privately confronted by a supervisor or manager about unsatisfactory work-related behaviors. Then, in keeping with the disciplinary system, he or she is offered a choice between help and discipline. Treatment options and consequences of further unsatisfactory performance are clearly discussed, including what the employer will do. Confidentiality and follow-up are critical when employers use the firm-choice option.

As a profession, nursing has been very aggressive in managing workplace substance abuse issues. According to the American Nurses Associations (ANA) Code of Ethics, impaired nurses may have difficulty remaining accountable to themselves and others for their own actions or in assessing self-competence. It is the responsibility of management and co-workers to respond to questionable practice as an advocate for the patient. The ANA suggests that an impaired nurse "receives assistance in regaining ability to function appropriately."[25]

Emotional/Mental Health Concerns   Many individuals today are facing work, family, and personal life pressures. These pressures are managed successfully by many people. But some individuals with medical histories have difficulties handling these demands. Also, specific events, such as death of a spouse, divorce, or medical problems, can affect individuals who otherwise have been coping successfully with those pressures. As noted earlier, a variety of emotional/mental health issues arise at work that must be addressed by employers. It is important to note that emotional/mental illnesses such as schizophrenia and depression are considered disabilities under the ADA. Therefore, employers should be cautious when using disciplinary policies if diagnosed employees have work-related problems.

Stress is one concern, whereby individuals cannot successfully handle the multiple demands they face. All people encounter stress, but it is when *stress overload* hits that work-related consequences can result. HR professionals, managers, and supervisors must be prepared to handle employee stress; otherwise, employees may burn out or exhibit various unhealthy behaviors, such as abusing alcohol, misusing prescription drugs, demonstrating outbursts of anger, or other symptoms. Healthcare employees are especially vulnerable to stress overload due to the nature and pace of their work. Beyond effects at communications and relieving some workload pressures, it is generally recommended that supervisors and managers contact the HR staff who may intervene and may recommend the affected employees to outside resources through employee assistance programs.[26]

Depression is another common emotional/mental health concern. Estimates are that 20% of individuals in workplaces suffer from depression. One indicator of the extent of clinical depression is that the sales of prescription drugs such as Prozac and Zoloft covered by employee benefits plans have risen significantly in the past several years.[27]

The effects of depression are seen at all levels, from the nursing units and business offices to executive suites. Carried to the extreme, depression can result in employee suicide. That guilt and sorrow felt by those who worked with the dead individuals must be dealt with by HR staff, often aided by crisis counselors. To deal with depression, it is recommended that HR professionals, managers, and supervisors be trained on recognizing the symptoms of depression and knowing what to do when symptoms are indicated in employees. Employees can be guided to employee assistance programs and aided with obtaining medical treatment.[28]

Workplace Air Quality   An increasing number of employees work in settings where air quality is a health issue.[29] One cause of poor air quality occurs in "sealed" buildings where windows cannot be opened when air flows are reduced to save energy and cut operating costs. Also, inadequate ventilation, as well as airborne contamination from carpets, molds, copy machines, adhesives, and fungi, can cause poor air quality and employee illnesses.[30]

Latex Allergy   For years, natural rubber latex allergies have been an employee concern where these rubber products, typically in the form of gloves, are used to protect employees form the spread of infection. Latex allergies were originally recognized in the 1970s but did not become a major concern until latex products began to gain wider use in response to the Center for Disease Control's 1987 recommendation that blood and body fluids should always be approached as if potentially infectious. In 1992, OSHA established the blood-borne pathogens standard requiring the use of barrier protection. The use of latex gloves by healthcare workers increased dramatically.[31]

OSHA estimates that 6% to 17% of exposed healthcare workers are allergic to natural rubber latex. The allergic employee experiences a simple irritation reaction. Although uncomfortable, usually it is not a serious problem in itself but can lead to more serious and detrimental allergic reactions, including serious health problems. Some argue that as more healthcare workers began to use latex gloves, the sheer increase in wearers statistically increased the number of people who might develop an allergy to latex.

Healthcare employers have attempted a number of actions to help allergic workers, including providing cotton glove liners for use with the latex glove, placing allergic workers in nonpatient-care positions, or by stocking latex-free carts on patient units. As an example, a major health system uses vinyl gloves as the standard examination glove.

Inadvertent Needle Sticks   Healthcare workers run the highest risk of disease transmission from injury by contaminated devises. Needles or syringes most frequently cause injury; about 20% of needle sticks fall into high-risk exposure to such blood-borne diseases as hepatitis B and C viruses and HIV.

Estimates of 600,000 to 800,000 needlestick injuries occur annually among healthcare workers in the United States. Nurses sustain the majority of these injuries, but other employees are also at risk, including physicians, nursing assistants, and environmental services personnel.[32]

To address this concern, the Needlestick Safety and Prevention Act (NSPA) was passed by Congress in November 2000. The NSPA mandated that OSHA revise the blood-borne pathogen standard to integrate the acts' requirements.

The new act focuses attention on safer medical devises, such as needleless medical devices for withdrawing fluids or administering medications and the incorporation of these devices in an organization's exposure control plan. The act also requires employers to solicit input from nonmanagerial healthcare workers regarding the identification, evaluation, and selection of safer medical devices.[33]

Slips and Falls   Slips and falls result in 15% of all accidental workplace deaths and 16% of accidents resulting in disability. Slips result in head or back injuries, lacerations, fractures, pulled muscles, and contusions, and cost employers billions of dollars annually.[34]

The healthcare workplace can offer its share of hazards, including wet floors, inclines, stairways, and cluttered passageways. Given the often-cluttered and busy nature of the healthcare workplace, protecting workers from slips and falls is a challenging task. Safety experts recommend the establishment of a comprehensive slip-prevention program focusing on risk assessment, good housekeeping, the use of slip-resistant flooring, and appropriate footwear. Employee awareness and safety training is also important.

Health Promotion

Healthcare employers who are concerned about maintaining a healthy workforce must move beyond simply providing healthy working conditions and emphasizes employee health and wellness in other ways. **Health promotion** is a supportive approach to facilitate, encourage, and help employees to enhance healthy actions and lifestyles. Going beyond just compliance with workplace safety and health regulations, organizations engage in health promotion by encouraging employees to make physiological, mental, and social choices that improve their health.[35]

Health promotion efforts can range from providing information and enhancing employee awareness of health issues to creating an organizational culture supportive of employee health enhancements, as Figure 14-6 indicates. The first level is useful and may have some impact on individuals, but much is left to individual initiatives to follow through and make changes in actions and behaviors. Employers provide information on such topics as weight control, stress management, nutrition, exercise, and smoking cessation. One indicator that many employers have limited their efforts to the first level is that 93% of surveyed employers have some type of health promotion program and 72% of them offer health education and training programs. However, only 27% of the firms conducted health risk screenings and appraisals.[36] Although such efforts may be beneficial for some employees,

FIGURE 14-6   Health Promotion Levels

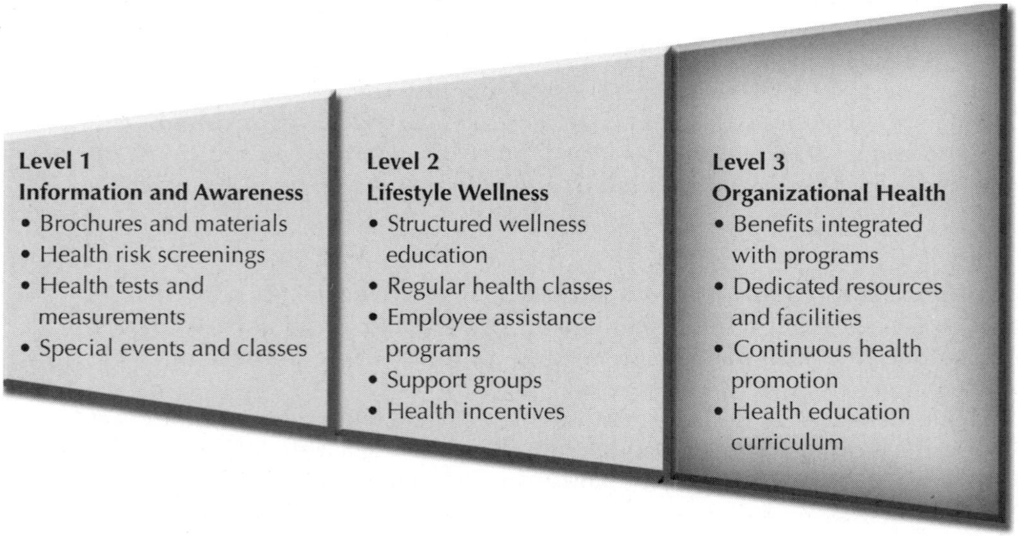

Level 1
Information and Awareness
- Brochures and materials
- Health risk screenings
- Health tests and
  measurements
- Special events and classes

Level 2
Lifestyle Wellness
- Structured wellness
  education
- Regular health classes
- Employee assistance
  programs
- Support groups
- Health incentives

Level 3
Organizational Health
- Benefits integrated
  with programs
- Dedicated resources
  and facilities
- Continuous health
  promotion
- Health education
  curriculum

Source: Developed by Kay G. Ryan, Ph.D., Methodist College of Health, and Robert L. Mathis, Ph.D., University of Nebraska at Omaha. May not be reproduced without permission.

employers who wish to impact employees' health must offer second level efforts through more comprehensive programs and efforts that focus on the lifestyle "wellness" of employees.

Wellness Programs   Employers' desires to improve productivity, decrease absenteeism, and control health-care costs have come together in the wellness movement. **Wellness programs** are designed to maintain or improve employee health before problems arise. Wellness programs encourage self-directed lifestyle changes.

There are a number of ways to assess the effectiveness of wellness programs. Participation rates by employees are one way. The participation rates vary by type of activity, but generally 20% to 40% of employees participate in the different activities in a wellness program. Although more participation would be beneficial, the programs have resulted in healthier lifestyles for more employees. Cost/benefit analyses tend to support the continuation of wellness programs as well.[37]

Employee Assistance Programs (EAPs)   One method that organizations are using as a broad-based response to health issues is the **employee assistance program (EAP),** which provides counseling and other help to employees having emotional, physical, or other personal problems. In such a program, an employer establishes a liaison with a social service counseling agency. Employees who have problems may then contact the agency, either voluntarily or by employer referral, for assistance with a broad range of problems. Counseling costs are paid for by the employer, either in total or up to a pre-established limit.

EAPs are attempts to help employees with a variety of problems. One survey of EAP counselors found that the most common employee issues dealt with were: (1) depression and anxiety, (2) marital and relationship problems, (3) legal difficulties, and (4) family and children concerns.[38] Other areas that also are commonly addressed as part of an EAP include substance abuse, financial counseling, and career advice. Critical to employee usage of an EAP is preserving confidentiality. That is why employers outsource EAPs to trained professionals, who usually report only the numbers of employees and services provided, rather than details on individuals using the EAP.

The effectiveness of EAPs depends upon how well they are integrated and supported in the workplace. One study of EAPs found that such support results in five times more supervisory referrals of employees to EAPs, and three times the numbers of employees with substance abuse problems who receive assistance.[39]

Organizational Health Culture   A number of employers, both large and small, have recognized that an organizational culture that emphasizes and supports health efforts is beneficial. Common to these employers is an integrative, broad-based effort supported both financially and managerially. Development of policies and procedures supporting health efforts, establishing on-site exercise facilities, and consistently promoting health programs all contribute to creating a health promotion environment throughout the organization.

SECURITY

Traditionally, when healthcare employers have addressed worker health, safety, and security, they have been concerned about reducing workplace accidents, improving workers' safety practices, and reducing health hazards at work. However, over the past decade providing security for employees' patients/residents/clients has grown in importance. Workplace violence has been an increasingly important topic for healthcare employers. Incidents of workplace violence occur regularly in hospitals, clinics, and nursing homes. The domestic problems of patients/residents/clients and their family members often erupt in verbal or physical assaults. Healthcare workers can easily get caught in the middle of these issues or are required to attempt to manage them.

Workplace Violence

Estimates by the National Institute for Occupational Safety and Health (NIOSH) are that 110 to 115 workplace homicides occur every week. Annually, NIOSH estimates that an additional million people are attacked at work.[40] About 70% of the workplace fatalities involved attacks against workers such as police officers, taxi drivers, and convenience store clerks. Often, these deaths occur during armed-robbery attempts. But what has shocked many employers in a variety of industries has been the number of disgruntled employees or former employees who have resorted to homicide in the workplace to deal with their anger and grievances. Research on individuals who have committed the most violent acts shows the relatively common profile that a profound humiliation or rejection, the end of a marriage, or the loss of a lawsuit or job may make a difficult employee take a distinct turn for the worse.

Domestic Causes of Workplace Violence   Violence that begins at home with family or friends can spill over to the workplace. Women are much more likely than men to experience violence committed as a result of a personal relationship. The same is true in the workplace. On the other hand, men are more likely to be attacked by a stranger. Close to one in five homicides of women at work are current or former husbands or boyfriends. Also, many abused women report frequently being harassed by abusing partners at work, by telephone, or in person.

As noted, many healthcare employers are unaware of domestic violence and its effects on employees. The worst reaction by employers is to ignore obvious signs of domestic violence. In fact, some employers have been sued and found liable for ignoring pleas for help from employees who later are victims of domestic violence in hospital parking lots or on employer premises.

Management of Workplace Violence   The increase in workplace violence has led many employers to develop workplace violence prevention and response policies and practices. As recommended by the American Society of Safety Engineers (ASSE), it is important for employers to conduct a *risk assessment* of the organization and its employees. Once such a study has been done, it is recommended that HR policies identify how workplace violence is to be dealt with in conjunction with disciplinary actions and referrals to employee assistance programs. An example of a workplace violence policy is on the book's website: *http://flynn.swlearning.com*

Often one step is to establish a **violence response team.** Composed of security personnel, key managers, HR staff members, and selected employees, these individuals function much like a safety committee, but with a different focus. At medical centers such as Cincinnati's Children's Hospital, these teams conduct such analyses, respond and investigate employee threats, and might even aid in calming angry, volatile employees.

However, employers must be careful, because they may face legal action for discrimination if they discharge employees for behaviors that often precede violent acts. For example, in several cases, employees who were terminated or suspended for making threats or even engaging in physical actions against co-workers have sued their employers, claiming they had mental disabilities under the Americans with Disabilities Act (ADA).

Post-violence response is another part of managing workplace violence. Whether the violence results in physical injuries or deaths, or just intense interpersonal conflicts, it is important that employers have plans to respond afterwards. Commonly employees may be fearful of returning to work or experience anxiety and sleeplessness, among other reactions. Providing referrals to EAP resources, allowing employees time to meet with HR staff, and providing trained counselors on site are all part of post-violence response efforts.[41]

Training on Workplace Violence   Managers, HR staff members, supervisors, and employees should be trained on how to recognize the signs of a potentially violent employee and what to do when violence occurs. For instance, this training may be important for the first contact with an organization, the receptionist, who may need to recognize warning signs of a potentially violent employee, former employee, or outsider.

During training at many organizations, participants learn the typical profile of potentially violent employees and are trained to notify the HR department and to refer employees to outside counseling professionals. Those services often are covered by employee assistance programs that are offered by employers.

Security Management

An overall approach to security management is needed to address a wide range of issues including workplace violence. Often, HR managers have responsibility for security programs, or they work closely with security mangers to address employee security issues.

Security Audit   Conducting a comprehensive review of organizational security is the purpose of a **security audit.** Sometimes called a *vulnerability analysis,* such an audit uses managers inside the organization—such as the HR manager and facilities manager—and outsiders, such as security consultants, police officers, fire officials, and computer security experts.

Typically, a security audit begins with a survey of the area around the facility. Such factors as lighting in parking lots, traffic flow, location of emergency response services, crime in the surrounding neighborhood, and the layout of the buildings and grounds are evaluated.[42] Also included is an audit of the security available within the firm, including the capabilities of guards and others involved with security. Another part of the security audit is a review of disaster plans, which addresses how to deal with disasters such as earthquakes, floods, tornados, hurricanes, fires, and civil disturbances.

Access Control   A key part of security is controlling access to the physical facilities of the organization. For instance, providing plexiglass partitions and requiring limited visitation have reduced violence in some emergency rooms.

Many healthcare organizations limit access to facilities and work areas by using electronic access or keycard systems. Although not foolproof, these systems can make it more difficult for an unauthorized person, such as an estranged husband or a gang member, to enter the premises. Access controls also can be used in elevators and stairwells to prevent unauthorized persons from entering certain areas within a facility. Many healthcare facilities that house patients or residents overnight do a complete lock-down overnight, with extremely tight controls on external access to the facility.

Computer Security   Yet another part of security is controlling access to computer systems. With so many transactions and records being handled by computers, it is crucial that adequate security provisions be in place to prevent unauthorized access to computer systems, including human resource information systems (HRIS). The growth of the Internet and e-mail systems has made computer security issues an even greater concern. This is particularly evident when individuals are terminated or leave an organization. HR staff must coordinate with information technology staff to change passwords, delete access codes, and otherwise protect company information systems.

Employee Screening and Selection

A key facet of providing security is to screen job applicants. As discussed in Chapter 6, there are legal limits on what can be done, particularly regarding the use of psychological tests and checking of references. However, firms that do not screen employees adequately may be subject to liability if an employee commits crimes later. For instance, an individual with a criminal record for assault was hired by a hospital to perform housekeeping. The employee assaulted and killed a pediatric patient, and the hospital was ruled liable. Of course, healthcare employers must be careful when selecting employees to use only job-related screening means and to avoid violating federal EEO laws and the Americans with Disabilities Act.

Security Personnel

Having sufficient security personnel who are adequately trained is a critical part of security management.[43] Many employers contract for this service with firms specializing in security. If employees are to be used, they must be selected and trained to handle a variety of workplace security problems, ranging from dealing with violent behavior by an employee to taking charge in natural disasters.

CASE

Crown Dental Services (CDS) is staffed by four dentists and twelve staff employees. It is a general dental practice that is extremely busy and productive. CDS's patients are very loyal, many of whom have used CDS for years.

Peggy, one of CDS's long-term dental assistants, has always been very popular with the patients and is frequently requested by the dentists to assist them with difficult procedures. Lately Peggy has been late for work, and one of the dentists observed that she is regularly absent on Mondays. During procedures, she has had attention lapses, and in one instance she bruised a patient's tongue with a suction device. When asked what happened, she blamed the event on the dentist she was assisting and threatened to walk out if the "harassment" over the incident persisted.

CDS's clinic manager was asked by the dentists to meet with them regarding Peggy's attendance, performance, and poor work attitude. During the meeting, drug or alcohol abuse was suggested, but the clinic manager quickly discarded that possibility as inconsistent with her knowledge of Peggy's past history with CDS.

The dentists concluded the meeting by requesting that the clinic manager develop a plan as to how to address Peggy's work-related problems.

Questions

1. What approaches should be used to identify the causes of Peggy's dysfunctional behavior?
2. If the clinic manager determines that drug or alcohol abuse is an issue, after all what steps should be taken to deal with her problem?

END NOTES

1. Carroll Lachnit, "Protecting People and Profits with Background Checks," *Workforce* (February 2002), 50–54.
2. Jim Bentley, "The Front Line," *Hospitals and Health Networks* (November 2001), 84.
3. "Disaster Readiness Advisory," *AHA Member Advisories* (September 21 2001), Available at *http://www.aha.org*.
4. Jon Grice, "The Cost of Comp," *Occupational Health & Safety* (February, 2001), 59–60.
5. William Atkinson, "Is Workers' Comp Changing?" *HR Magazine* (July 2000), 50–61.
6. Susan H. Abeln, "FMLA and Workers' Comp," *http://www.quinlan.com*.
7. Christopher G. Bell, "The ADA, FMLA, and Workers' Compensation,"

SHRM White Paper, (May 2001), *http://www.shrm.org.*

8. Occupational Safety and Health Organization, U.S. Department of Labor.

9. OSHA at 30: Three Decades of Progress in Occupational Safety and Health," *Job Safety & Health Quarterly* (Spring 2001), 23–32.

10. Kenneth L. Burgess and Berta H. Schweinberger, "OSHA as a Regulator of Assisted Living," *Nursing Homes* (August 2001), 50–51.

11. Bernard R. Blais, "Why Do a Visual Job Analysis?" *Occupational Health and Safety* (October 2001), 52–59.

12. Melissa Martin, "Hazard Communication," *Occupational Hazards* (May 2001), 28.

13. Susan Hall Fleming, "Ergonomics: Preventing Injury and Preserving Health," *Job Safety & Health Quarterly* (Winter 2000), 22–25.

14. "Ergonomics: Snapshots of Success," *Job Safety & Health Quarterly* (Winter 2000), 26.

15. *United Autoworkers v. Johnson Controls, Inc.,* 111 S. Ct. 1196 (1991).

16. Mark Harcourt and Sandra Harcourt, "When Can an Employee Refuse Unsafe Work and Expect to Be Protected from Discipline?" *Industrial & Labor Relations Review* 53 (2000), 684–704.

17. *Marshall v. Barlow's Inc.,* 98 S. Ct. 1816 (1978).

18. James G. Grant, "Involving the Total Organization," *Occupational Health & Safety* (September 2000), 64–65.

19. Melanie Herman, "Supervise, Supervise, Supervise," *Nonprofit World* (March/April 2002), 18–19.

20. Earl Blair and E. Scott Geller, "Behavior-Based Safety," *Occupational Health & Safety* (September 2000), 61–63.

21. Wayne Vanderhoof, "Training for the Safety Committee," *Occupational Hazards* (January 2002), 62–63.

22. Jeanie Casison, "Safety Dance: OSHA Weighs in Heavily on Incentive Programs," *Incentive* (May 2000), 9.

23. Robert A. Menard, *Occupational Health & Safety* (February 2001), 62–65.

24. Michael Prince, "Battling Workplace Drug Use," *Business Insurance* (January 29, 2001), 20.

25. Patricia Blair, "Report Impaired Practice—Stat," *Nursing Management* (January 2002), 24–25.

26. William Atkinson, "When Stress Won't Go Away," *HR Magazine* (December, 2000), 105–110.

27. Elyse Tanouye, "Mental Illness: A Rising Workplace Cost," *The Wall Street Journal* (June 13, 2001), B1+

28. Joseph Kline, Jr. and Lyle Sussman, "An Executive Guide to Workplace Depression," *Academy of Management Executive* (August 2000), 103–114.

29. Robert J. Grossman, "Out with the Bad Air," *HR Magazine* (October 2000), 37–45.

30. Michelle Conlin, "Is Your Office Killing You?" *Business Week* (June 5, 2000), 114–128.

31. Donna E. Corbin, "Latex Allergy and Dermatitis," *Occupational Health and Safety* (January 2002), 36–38.

32. Aruna Vadgama, "OSHA Bloodburne Pathogens Standard Revisited: Impact of the Needlestick Safety and Prevention Act," *Professional Safety* (February 2002), 42–48.

33. Gina Pugliese, "Set the Standard: Sharps with Protection," *Nursing Management* (June 2001), 50, 52.

34. Todd Nighswonger, "Get a Grip on Slips," *Occupational Hazards* (September 2000), 47–50.

35. Angela Downey, "Promoting Health on the Job," *CMA Management* (May 2001), 24–28.

36. "Employers Use Education, Incentives, Screenings to Reduce Health Care Costs," *Employee Benefit Plan Review* (August 2000), 18.

37. Bill Gillete, "Promoting Wellness Programs Results in a Healthier Bottom Line," *Managed Healthcare Executive* (February 2001), 45.

38. "Psychological Issues Most Often Addressed by EAPs" (July 5, 2000), *http://www.acaonline.org/newslinenews.*

39. Kenneth Collins, "HR Must Find New Ways to Battle Substance Abuse in the Workplace," *HR News* (April 2001), 11.

40. Marlene Piturro, "Workplace Violence," *Strategic Finance* (May 2001), 35–38.

41. (BW) "After the Shooting Stops," *Business Week* (March 12, 2001), 98–100.

42. Barbara A. Nadel, "Better Safe: Planning Secure Environments," *Area Development* (May 2001), 24–27.

43. Ronald J. Morris, "A Job Well Done," *Security Management* (April 2001), 58–62.

Glossary

A

Ability tests Tests that assess the skills that individuals have already learned.

Adversarial relationship Relationship between unions and management characterized by conflict and confrontation.

Alternative dispute resolutions Method of resolving differences between employees and their employers; these include arbitration, peer-review panels, and organizational ombudsmen.

Applicant pool All people who are actually evaluated for selection.

Applicant population A subset of the labor force population that is available for selection using a particular recruiting approach.

Aptitute tests Tests that measure general ability to learn or acquire a skill.

Arbitration Using a neutral third party to resolve a dispute.

Assessment center A series of evaluative exercises and tests used for selection and development.

B

Base pay Basic compensation that an employee receives, usually as a wage or salary.

Behavioral event interview An interview in which applicants are required to give specific examples of how they have handled a problem or situation in the past.

Behavior-based criteria Identification of behaviors that may lead to successful job performance.

Benchmark jobs Jobs that are found in other organizations and performed by several individuals who have similar duties that require similar KSAs.

Benefit An indirect reward given to an employee as a part of organizational membership, regardless of performance.

Benefits needs analysis A comprehensive look at all aspects of benefits in an organization.

Board of inquiry A board appointed by the FMCS Director to investigate, report, and recommend solutions to resolve contractual disputes.

Bona fide occupational qualification (BFOQ) A legitimate reason why an employer can exclude persons on otherwise illegal bases of consideration.

Broadbanding The practice of using fewer pay grades with much broader ranges than in traditional compensation systems.

C

Cash balance plans Pension plans that are a hybrid of defined-benefit and defined-contribution plans, based on a hypothetical account balance.

Central-tendency raters Managers who in the performance-review process, tend to rate all of their employees within a narrow range.

Certified Designation by the NLRB that a union has met the required conditions and received the necessary votes to become the bargaining representative of an employee group.

Chain-of-custody procedures Procedures that include keeping accurate records on how drug tests are conducted and tracked.

Checklist method Appraisal method that offers a list of words or statements that describes employees' performance.

Coaching Training and feedback given to employees by immediate supervisors.

Collaborative relationship The relationship between unions and management, characterized by an atmosphere in which there is shared responsibility to address the mutual interests and issues of both parties.

Compensation and benefits Rewards for performing organizational work, including wages or salary, incentive programs, and benefits.

Competencies Basic characteristics that can be linked to enhanced performance by individuals or teams.

Competency approach Method of job analysis that focuses on the competencies that individuals need in order to perform jobs, rather than on the tasks, duties, and responsibilities that compose a job.

Consolidated Omnibus Budget Reconciliation Act (COBRA) Law that requires that most employers offer extended healthcare coverage to designated groups of former employees or dependents of former employees.

Construct validity A method that shows a relationship between an abstract characteristic inferred from research and/or job performance.

Constructive discharge Situation when an employer creates impossible working conditions that force an employee to resign.

Contaminated criteria Measurement process that includes irrelevant criteria.

Content validity A logical non-statistical method used to identify the knowledge, skills, abilities, and other characteristics necessary to perform a job.

Contrast errors Situation in the performance-review process in which a manager compares employees to each other rather than to job-performance standards.

Contributory plan Pension plan in which the employee and employer both pay in money for benefits.

Co-payment Portion of a health insurance cost that employees are required to pay.

Core competency A unique capability in the organization that creates high value and differentiates the organization from its competition.

Cost-of-living adjustment (COLA) A standard raise based on an economic measure, such as the consumer price index.

Critical-incident narrative Appraisal method in which the manager documents incidents that are highly favorable or unfavorable representations of an employee's work performance.

Cumulative trauma disorders (CTD) Problems that occur when workers repetitively use the same muscles to perform tasks, resulting in muscular and skeletal injuries.

D

Decertified Designation by the NLRB that employees have met the required conditions to remove a union as their representative.

Deficient criteria Measurement process that omits significant criteria.

Defined-benefit plans Pension plans in which employees' contributions are based on actuarial calculations that focus on the benefits to be received by employees after retirement and the methods used to determine such benefits.

Defined-contribution plan Pension plan in which the employer makes an annual payment to an employee's account.

Delphi technique Forecasting method that uses input from a group of experts, whose opinions are sought through separate questionnaires on what forecasted situations will be.

Department A distinct grouping of organizational responsibilities.

Development An effort to improve employees' ability to handle a variety of assignments and to cultivate capabilities beyond those required by the current job.

Drug-Free Workplace Act of 1988 Law enacted to make workplaces free from the use of drugs or controlled substances.

Due process A method of questioning a disciplinary action.

Dues check-off process System in which union dues are automatically deducted from workers' paychecks.

Duty A work segment composed of several tasks that are performed by an individual.

E

Emotional intelligence Proficiencies in intra-personal and inter-personal skills in the areas of self-awareness, self-regulation, self-motivation, social awareness, and social skills.

Employee assistance program (EAP) A plan which provides counseling and other help to employees having emotional, mental, or other personal problems.

Employee development A process that focuses on individuals gaining new capabilities useful for both current and future jobs.

Employee handbook A publication containing an organization's HR policies.

Employee-relations philosophy A philosophy that outlines the rights of the employees and the rights of the employers.

Employment contract Formal agreement between an employer and an employee contractually defining the working relationship.

Employment Practices Liability Insurance Insurance that protects employers against lawsuits initiated by their employees.

Employment-at-will provisions Provisions in employment agreements and handbooks that state that employees may be terminated at any time for any reason.

Environment of care standards Joint Commission standards that address the factors that go into making a safe and secure environment.

Environmental scanning The process of studying the environment of the organization to pinpoint opportunities and threats.

Equal employment opportunity (EEO) A broad concept holding that individuals should have equal treatment in all employment-related actions.

Ergonomics The study and design of the work environment to address physiological and physical demands a position.

Essay Describes an employee's performance during a given evaluation period.

Essential functions Job activities that are required for the job to be done satisfactorily.

Estimates Forecasting method used to determine how many emplyees might be needed in the future.

Exception-based reviews Employee reviews that shorten the performance process and recognize behaviors that either exceed the job standards or identify behaviors that can be improved.

Exit interview An interview of those who are leaving the organization to determine the reasons for their departure.

Extended illness banks Program that allows employees to accrue time to be used for longer-term illness or health-related care that does not result in a disability, such as maternity care.

F

401(k) and 403(b) plans Retirement plans that allow employees to elect to reduce their current pay by a certain percentage, which is then used to fund a retirement plan.

Federal Mediation and Conciliation Services (FMCS) An agency charged with mediating labor negotiations when asked by negotiating parties or assigned by the FMCS Director.

Feedback systems Three components of performance appraisal: collecting data, evaluating data, and taking action based on the data.

Field-review A review of manager's comments about each employee's performance.

Firm-choice option An approach recommended to encourage employees to seek help for their substance-abuse problems or face discipline.

Flexible benefits plan A flex or cafeteria plan, that allows employees to select the benefits they prefer from groups of benefits established by the employer.

Flexible spending accounts A plan that allows employees to contribute pre-tax dollars to buy additional benefits.

For-cause testing Drug test used to test employees suspected of being under the influence of drugs while at work.

Forced distribution Appraisal method of ranking employees and using statistics to sort all employees along a bell curve.

Forecasting Using information from the past and present to identify expected future conditions.

Formal appraisal process Performance appraisal system that defines and evaluates an employee's job performance.

Funeral or bereavement leave Time off to attend to the arrangements and funeral after the death of an immediate family member.

G

Gainsharing plans Group incentive where employee teams that meet certain goals share in the gains measured against performance targets.

Gap analysis Process that identifies the distance between where an organization is with its employee capabilities and where it needs to be.

Glass ceiling Discriminatory practices that have prevented women and other protected-class members from advancing to executive-level jobs.

Graphic-rating scale A scale that allows the rater to mark an emplyee's performance on a continuum.

Green-circled employee An incumbent who is paid below the range set for the job.

Grievance procedure A formal process used to resolve issues between managers and workers.

H

Halo effect Situation in the performance-review process when a manager rates an employee high or low on all job standards based on one characteristic.

Health A general state of physical, mental, and emotional well-being.

Health Insurance Portability and Accountability Act (HIPAA) Law that allows employees to switch their health insurance coverage from one employer to another regardless of pre-existing conditions.

Health promotion A supportive approach to facilitate and encourage employees to enhance healthy actions and lifestyles.

HR development Focuses on individuals gaining new capabilities useful for both current and future jobs.

HR management Refers to the strategies, tactics, plans, and programs that organizations utilize to accomplish the work of the organization through its employees.

HR metrics Methods used to measure HR activities.

HR planning Phase in which managers attempt to anticipate forces that will influence the future supply of and demand for employees.

HR strategic planning The process of analyzing and identifying the need for and availability of human resources in order to accomplish organizational objectives.

Human Resource Information system (HRIS) An integrated system designed to provide information used in HR decision making.

I

Immediate confirmation Training concept that people learn best if reinforcement and feedback are given as soon as possible after training.

Immigration Reform and Control Act of 1986 (IRCA) A law that requires that within seventy-two hours of hiring, an employer must determine whether a job applicant is eligible to work in the U.S.

Impasse Situation in which negotiating parties cannot come to an agreement.

Implied contract Unwritten agreements between employers and employees, which suggest that an employee will be employed indefinitely or as long as the employee performs the job satisfactorily.

Independent contractors Workers who perform specific services on a contract basis.

Individual incentives Pay given to reward the effort and performance of individuals.

Individual retirement account (IRA) A special account in which an employee can set aside funds that will not be taxed until the employee accesses the funds at retirement.

Informal appraisal process Performance appraisal system conducted at the manager's discretion to praise employees or motivate better behavior.

Informal training Training that occurs through interactions and feedback among employees.

Integrated disability management programs Integrating disability programs with workers' compensation programs to reduce costs and coordinate claim processing.

Interest-based bargaining A style of negotiating contracts based on identifying and meeting the parties' mutual interests.

Internal recruiting Focusing on recruiting current employees and others with previous contact with an employing organization.

J

Job A grouping of common tasks, duties, and responsibilities.

Job analysis A systematic way to gather and analyze information about the content and human requirements of jobs and the context in which jobs are performed.

Job board A Web site on which employers can post jobs or search for candidates.

Job description Summary of multiple criteria that defines a job.

Job design Organizing tasks, duties, and responsibilities into a productive unit of work.

Job evaluation A systematic basis for determining the relative worth of jobs within an organization.

Job posting and bidding Method for recruiting employees, whereby the employer provides notices of job openings and employees respond by applying for specific openings.

Job rotation Shifting an employee from job to job.

Job satisfaction A positive emotional state resulting from job experiences.

Job-site development Development process that occurs on the job.

Joint Commission on Accreditation of Healthcare Organizations (JCAHO) A quality accreditation organization whose members subscribe to a standard-based review process.

L

Labor force population All individuals who are available for selection if all possible recruitment strategies are used.

Labor markets The external sources from which employers attract employees.

Labor-management committees Committees that are jointly sponsored by management and the union. Their purpose is to identify common problems, interpret contract language, and resolve the issues.

Landrum-Griffin Act Act that was designed to curtail corrupt union practices, including officials misusing pension funds and threatening workers in order to retain power.

Law of effect People tend to repeat responses that give them some type of positive reward and avoid actions associated with negative consequences.

Leaves of absence Time off with or without pay.

Leniency raters Managers who in the performance-review process give most of their employees high ratings.

Lock-out/tag-out regulations OSHA rules that require safety locks and tags on machinery and power sources to prevent accidental start-up of a machine when it is defective.

M

Managed care Approaches that monitor and reduce medical costs through restrictions and market-system alternatives.

Management by objectives Specifies the performance goals that an employee and manager agree to complete within a defined period.

Management rights clauses Clauses that vary from contract to contract and give management the exclusive right to manage, direct, and control its business.

Mandated benefits Benefits required by law.

Mediation A dispute process in which a trained mediator assists the parties in reaching a settlement.

Mental ability tests Tests that measure reasoning capabilities.

Mentoring A relationship in which experienced managers aid individuals in the earlier stages of their careers.

N

Narrative performance-appraisal method Method that provides comments using essays, documentation of critical incidents, or field reviews.

National Labor Relations Act (NLRA) Also known as the Wagner Act, a 1935 act passed to provide more specific guidelines to govern the relationship between unions, organizations, and employees.

National Labor Relations Board (NLRB) Board created by the National Labor Relations Act that enforces the provisions of the NLRA for both unions and organizations.

Nominal group technique Forecasting method that requires experts to meet face to face as independent ideas are generated.

Non-compete provisions Contract provisions that specify that employees will not compete with the organization if they leave.

Non-contributory plan Pension plan in which the employer provides all the funds for pension benefits.

Nurse Practice Act Law that sets professional practice standards for registered nurses.

O

Off-site development Process that gives individuals opportunities to get away from the job and concentrate solely on education or development.

Ombudsman A staff employee who administers a program designed to resolve disputes between employees and employers.

On-the-job training Planned training that uses a supervisor or manager to teach and show the employee what to do.

Organization chart A chart that depicts the relationships among jobs in an organization.

Organizational commitment The degree to which employees believe in and accept organizational goals and desire to remain with the organization.

Organizational culture A pattern of shared values and beliefs giving members of an organization meaning and providing them with rules for behavior.

Organizational incentives Compensation given to reward people based on the performance results of the organization.

Orientation The planned introduction of new employees to their jobs, co-workers, and the organization.

Outside rater An appraisal method in which an outside expert evaluates the employee's performance.

Outsourcing Using external training firms, consultants, or other entities to perform HR functions.

P

Paid time-off plan A time off program that combines short-term leave, vacation, and holiday pay into one bank.

Panel interview Several interviewers interview the candidate at the same time.

Pay adjustment matrix A salary guide chart in which adjustments are based in part on the person's pay, divided by the midpoint of the pay range.

Pay compression Shrinking the pay differences among individuals with different levels of experience and performance.

Pay grade A grouping of individual jobs having approximately the same job worth.

Pay survey A collection of data on compensation rates for workers performing similar jobs in other organizations.

Peer-review panel An internal committee of employees who review employee complaints and make decisions about them.

Pension plans Retirement benefits established and funded by employers and employees.

Performance appraisal The process of evaluating how well employees perform their jobs when compared to a set of standards, and then communicating that information to employees.

Performance consulting A process in which a trainer and the organizational client work together to boost workplace performance in support of organizational goals.

Performance-improvement plan Plan based on information managers receive about an employee's performance, implemented when the manager and employee meet to discuss job expectations.

Phased retirement A program that helps employees retire in stages.

Placement Fitting a person to the right job.

Portability Ability to move pension funds from one company to another.

Position A job performed by one person.

Predictors Identifiable indicators of the selection criteria.

Pre-employment drug test A test used to avoid hiring individuals who use illegal drugs or abuse legal drugs.

Preferred provider organization (PPO) A healthcare provider that contracts with an employer or an employer group to provide healthcare services to employees at a competitive rate.

Privacy Act of 1974 Law that issues regulations that affect human resource record-keeping systems, policies, and procedures.

Productivity A measure of the quantity and quality of work done, considering the cost of the resources it took to do the work.

Progressive discipline Five-step discipline process that gets more strict at each step.

Protected class People having certain designated characteristics such as minority race, women, individuals over age 40, individuals with disabilities, those with military experience, or certain religious beliefs.

Psychological contract The unwritten expectations that employees and employers have about the nature of their work relationships.

Psychology of selection Useful way to think about the way a selection decision should be approached and made.

Psychomotor tests Test that measures a person's dexterity, hand-eye coordination, arm-hand steadiness, and other factors.

Public-policy violation A provision under which an employee can sue an employer if the employee was discharged for reasons that violate some public policy.

R

Random testing Drug testing done in a random fashion.

Ranking Appraisal method that compares employees, against each other.

Rater bias Situation in the performance-review process when a manager has a bias against a certain employee or employee group based on the manager's own values or prejudices.

Realistic job preview (RJP) Part of a job selection process that is designed to inform job candidates of the organizational realities of the job so they can evaluate their own job expectations.

Reasonable care Employer practice of establishing sexual harassment policies, communicating with and training employees on harassment issues, and investigating and taking action when complaints are voiced.

Recruiting Identifying where to recruit, whom to recruit, and what the job requirements will be.

Red-circled employee An incumbent who is at the maximum of the range set for the job.

Reengineering Rethinking and redesigning work to improve cost, service, and speed.

Reinforcement Concept of training based on the law of effect.

Resource pools (float pools) Workers specifically hired to be available (float) to various units when the needs are higher than core staff can meet.

Results-based criteria Process that identifies behavior based on results that are easy to identify and evaluate.

Retention Keeping employees who have been recruited, selected, and trained.

Retention agreement A contract agreement that is designed to retain key employees during mergers, consolidations, or changes in the organizational leadership.

Review and rescission rights Rights and responsibilities of a prospective employee.

Right-to-sue letter A letter that notifies a complainant that he or she has ninety days in which to file a personal suit in federal court.

Rules of thumb Forecasting method that relies on general guidelines applied to specific situations within the organization.

S

Sabbatical leave Paid time off the job to develop and rejuvenate oneself.

Safety Protecting the physical well-being of people.

Salary Compensation based on a fixed amount, regardless of hours worked.

Security Protecting employees, patients/residents/clients, and visitors.

Security audit Conducting a comprehensive review of organizational security; sometimes called a vulnerability analysis.

Selection The process of choosing qualified individuals who have relevant qualifications to fill jobs in an organization.

Selection criterion a charactistic that a person must have to do the job successfully.

Self-rating Method of appraisal in which employees rate themselves.

Severance pay A security benefit voluntarily offered by employers to some employees who lose their jobs.

Shadowing programs Programs that provide an individual who is considering a position the opportunity to accompany a professional during a workday.

Sick-building syndrome A situation in which occupants experience acute health problems and discomfort that appear to be linked to time spent in a building.

Staffing Function of human resources designed to provide an adequate supply of qualified individuals to fill the jobs in an organization.

Statistical regression analysis Forecasting method that makes a statistical comparison of past relationships among various factors.

Statutory rights Existing laws, legislation, and evolving case law that protect employees' rights.

Step systems Pay system in which employees' wages are adjusted based on how long they have been with the organization.

Strategic HR management Use of employees to help an organization gain or keep a competitive advantage against its competitors.

Strategic training A process that focuses on efforts that develop individual worker competencies and produces ongoing value and competitive advantages for the organization.

Strict raters Managers who in the performance-review process, give all of their employees low ratings.

Strike contingency plans Plans that help assure communities that patients will receive continuous healthcare in the event of a strike.

Structured interview A set of standardized questions that are asked of all applicants so comparisons can be made among applicants.

Substance abuse The use of illicit substances or the misuse of controlled substances, alcohol, or other drugs.

Succession planning A process of identifying a longer-term plan for the orderly replacement of key employees.

T

360-degree appraisal Process of appraisal that involves getting performance evaluations from the full circle of individuals with whom the staff member has experience.

Taft-Hartley Act Act that equalized the effects of the NLRA by defining and prohibiting unfair labor practices by unions.

Task A distinct, identifiable work activity composed of motions.

Team or peer rating Performance-rating approach in which managers collect performance information by using teams and peers that the employee worked with during the evaluation period.

Temporary employees Workers who are hired on a rate-per-day or per-week basis as needed.

Ten-day strike notice Requirement that unions give healthcare organizations ten days' notice before striking against them.

Tentative agreement Situation in which union and management agree to move forward with a recommended contract.

Training A process whereby people acquire capabilities to aid in the achievement of organizational goals.

Training design Determining how the assessed needs are to be addressed, considering learning concepts, legal issues, and the types of training available.

Training needs assessment Considering employee and organizational performance issues to determine if training can be helpful.

Trait-based criteria Process that identifies subjective personal traits that may contribute to job success.

Transfer of training Process whereby trainees actually use on the job what was learned in training.

U

Unfair labor practices Actions defined by the National Labor Relations Act as illegal.

Union security clause Clause in union contracts that recognizes the exclusive right of a union to bargain on behalf of the employees.

Utilization review Review and audit of medical work, possibly including a second opinion, review of procedures used, or review of charges for procedures done.

V

Variable pay Compensation linked directly to individual, team, or organizational performance.

Vesting Assurance that employees have worked the minimum number of years to qualify for a pension plan.

Violence response team A group of security personnel, key managers, HR staff mem-

bers, and selected employees who analyze, respond to, and investigate workplace violence situations.

W

Wages Compensation based on hourly pay.

Wellness programs Programs designed to maintain or improve employee health before problems arise by encouraging personal lifestyle changes.

Whistleblowers Employees who report employer public-policy violations.

Whole learning (Gestalt learning) As applied to job training, a training concept in which instructions should be divided into smaller elements after employees have had the opportunity to see how the elements fit together.

Work analysis A study of the workflow, activities, context, and output of a job.

Workers' compensation Benefits provided to a person injured on the job.

Wrongful discharge Termination of employee for reasons that are illegal, that are improper, or that don't follow organizational policies.

Index